JtHM

the director's cut

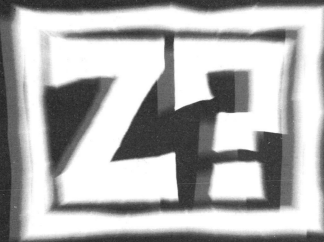

This book reprints material previously seen in Johnny the Homicidal Maniac #1-#7, as well as in Carpe Noctem magazine. Other material was seen in the holo-zines on the planet Mars, but you wouldn't know about that.

created by JHONEN VASQUEZ

SLAVE LABOR GRAPHICS

Dan Vado — president and chief grumbly guy
Jennifer de Guzman — editor-in-chief

I DO LURID THANKY DANCE AT: Slave Labor Graphics, Leah Ann England I, my family for being too afraid to REALLY ask what I was doing, the pieces of shit that disguise themselves as people who give me such easy inspiration, music for constantly being around as I work, outer space for giving me something to look at when I'm outside, and the friends who didn't bribe me enough to mention their names in this book. And, of course, many thanks to the people who read the book and were mean enough to force it upon their friends.

I DO VICIOUS SPITE JIG AT: Nothing in particular. There are other things to do

JTHM: the Director's Cut • published by the kindly aliens at Slave Labor, who, if you anger them, will dissolve your face clean off. Slave Labor Graphics P.O. Box 26427, San Jose, CA 95159-6427. JTHM and all his zany, fun-loving little friends are © and TM of the vitamin deficient JHONEN VASQUEZ. I was in New Mexico a while back and was told by someone there, "The problem with this place is all the Mexicans." Funny planet, eh? No part of this super-amazing publication may be reproduced without the written permission of Jhonen the Wiry Wonderboy and the surly Consent Elf at Slave Labor Graphics. This book is printed in Canada. Pretty cool, huh? I bet you're thinking, "Hot Damn!! I gotta have's me that book that come from a foreign land!!" No, really, I bet you're thinking that. Now, I mentioned this before, but I am REALLY serious: WHAT IF Count Chocula, Frankenberry, AND Booberry joined forces and become one? What kind of abomination of supernature would result from such a grouping?!! Do you even think of this at all? How do you sleep with the prospect of this happening? I'm feeling dizzy. I think I will go lie down now. Printed in Canada

Twenty-sixth Printing, August 2008

FOREWARD

By Rob Schrab

A girl I dated once said to me, "You only feel when you bleed." This must give you the impression that I was dating an Art School-Vampire. She was more like an acid-washed Molly Ringwald, but that doesn't matter. I fell in total lust with this woman because she told me what I had been thinking my entire life. Pain is a food. A food that is essential to the growth of one's soul.

Let's talk about violence, shall we? Violence in the media is an easy target. "If we get rid of all the violent movies, television shows and comic books, the world will be Utopian!" An easily believable answer. Just ask your mom.

Jhonen Vasquez has touched something important here. There's a little monster inside all of us, a little wolf-faced monkey that needs to be satiated. As people, we mustn't ignore that monster. If we do, we cheat ourselves. We deny an emotion, a feeling.

Think of someone who pissed you off. Some yutz who cut you off in traffic; a prick-ass Kinko's employee who took three hours to copy your resume; the big bully who spit in your face when you were eight. Now, in your head, relive that moment. This time, however, don't just stand there and take it. This time you've got a knife. Pull it out from behind your back and watch the status flip-flop. Suddenly, Mr. Kinko isn't so cocky. The playground bully is crying for his mother. Smell their fear. Then, kill them. Kill them like you see in the movies. Make it as horrible as possible. Release that monster and stab that knife deep into their face.

As humans, we are taught to forget that we are animals. Animals kill to survive and its just as natural for us. To deny nature is to deny life. Now that you've committed murder in your dream world, relax. Take a deep breath, give your monster a high five and put him away. You've just used an evil fantasy to keep you civilized and sane.

Some may call this irresponsible advice. They kid themselves that their monster doesn't exist. And when a person lies to themselves, there is less chance for spiritual growth. More than likely, their monster will step out of the Dreamworld and into the Realworld. That's how a society gets messy. Lots of neglected, hungry monsters.

Johnny the Homicidal Maniac gives our monster something to chew on. It's pain-food that wears its teeth down. Johnny represents Jhonen Vasquez's monster. Vasquez, and his fans, are all the stronger because of him.

Rob Schrab
June 1997

WELCOME to A BOOK!!! by J.V

HELLO!! I AM HERE TO HELP MAKE YOUR READING TIME MORE HAPPY. I AM ALSO HERE AGAINST MY WILL, AS MY CHILDREN ARE BEING THREATENED WITH TORTURE!! YAY!!

SEE!! IF I CAN LAUGH AT MY CHILDREN'S IMPENDING DOOM, THEN YOU CAN HOPEFULLY ENJOY THE HIDEOUS, REVOLTING THINGS IN THIS BOOK!! HAVE FUN! NOW, ON WITH DA' FUN!

I AM DONE. HELLO? CAN I GO, NOW? I WANT MY KIDS BACK.

OH, MY GOD!! OKAY! OKAY!! SO, ENJOY READING JTHM, AND...UH...

DADDY!! EEEEK!!

REMEMBER, IT'S ALL JUST QUESTIONABLY TASTEFUL FUN.

EEEEK!

YOU BASTARDS!

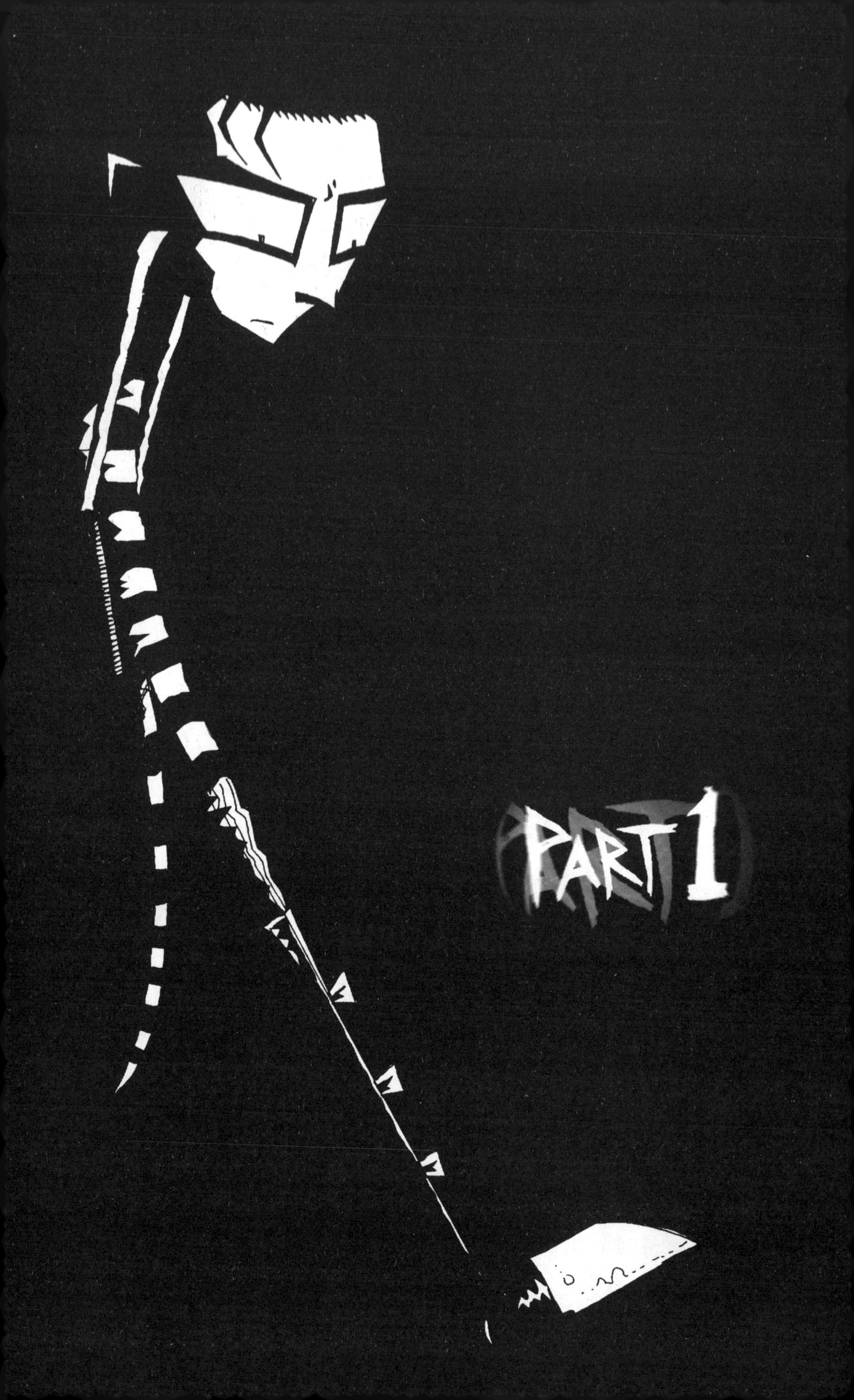
PART 1

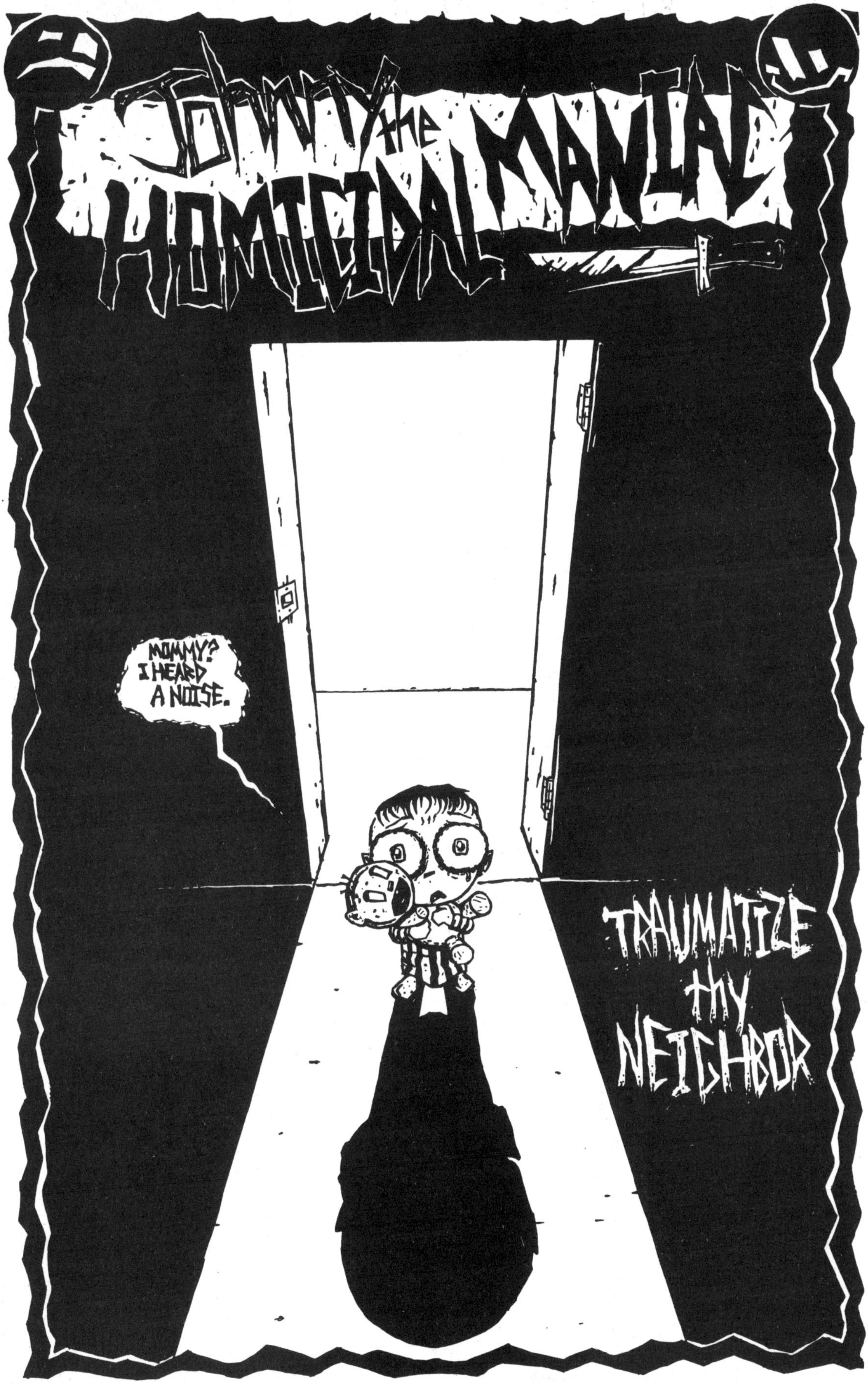
Johnny the HOMICIDAL MANIAC
MOMMY? I HEARD A NOISE.
TRAUMATIZE thy NEIGHBOR

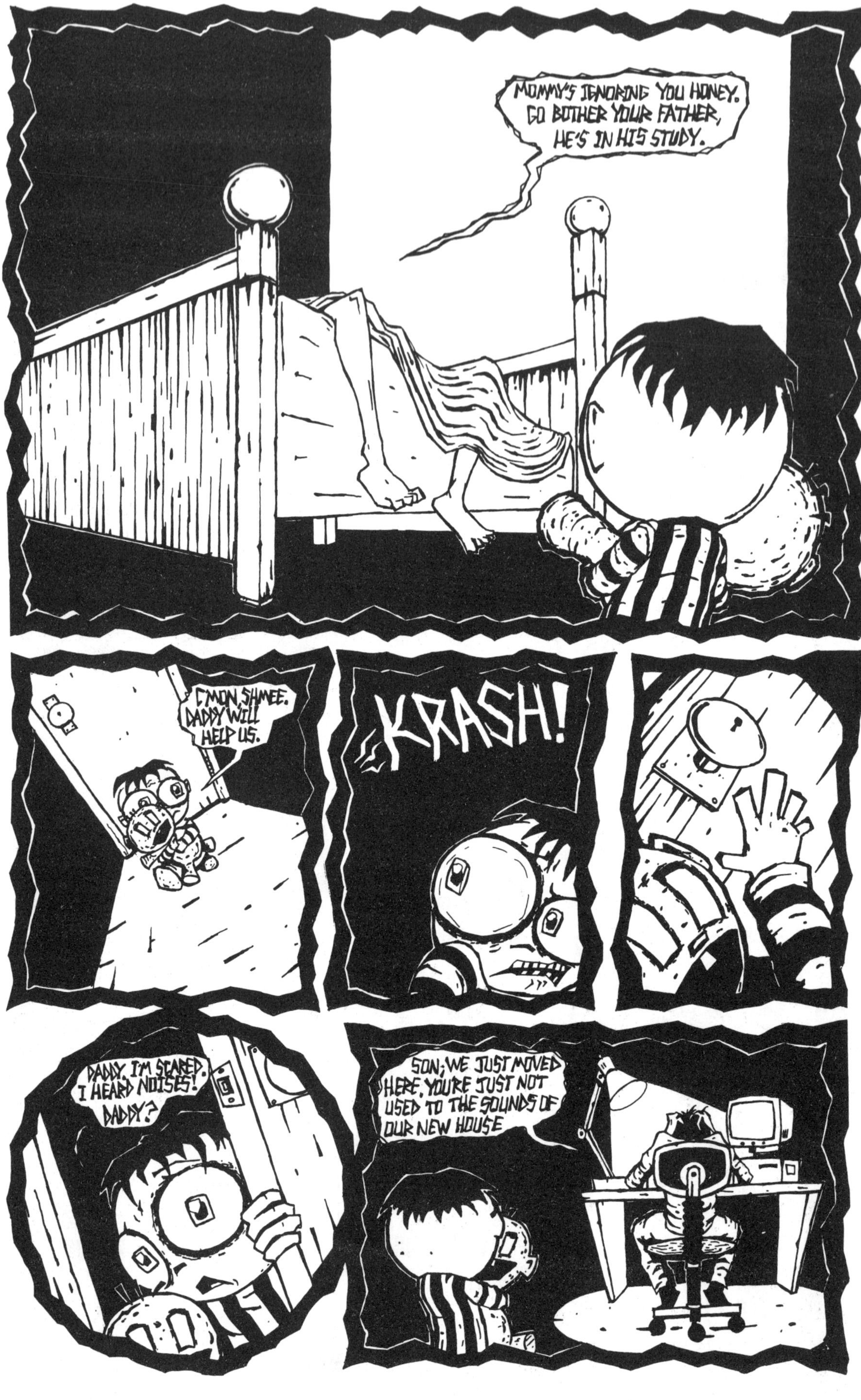
MOMMY'S IGNORING YOU HONEY. GO BOTHER YOUR FATHER, HE'S IN HIS STUDY.
C'MON, SHMEE. DADDY WILL HELP US.
KRASH!
DADDY, I'M SCARED. I HEARD NOISES! DADDY?
SON; WE JUST MOVED HERE. YOU'RE JUST NOT USED TO THE SOUNDS OF OUR NEW HOUSE

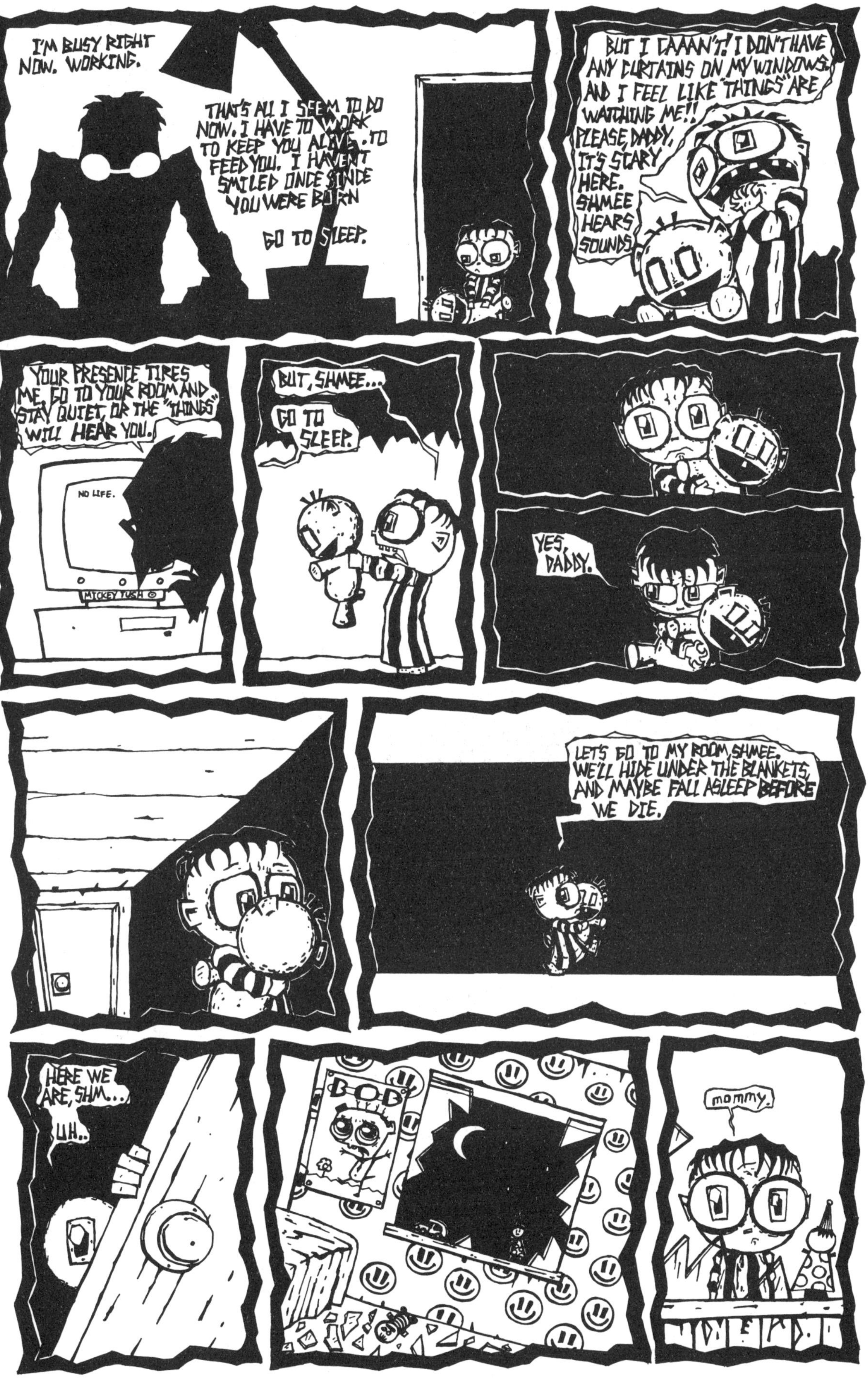

I'M BUSY RIGHT NOW. WORKING.
THAT'S ALL I SEEM TO DO NOW. I HAVE TO WORK TO KEEP YOU ALIVE. TO FEED YOU. I HAVEN'T SMILED ONCE SINCE YOU WERE BORN
GO TO SLEEP.
BUT I CAAAN'T! I DON'T HAVE ANY CURTAINS ON MY WINDOWS. AND I FEEL LIKE "THINGS" ARE WATCHING ME!! PLEASE, DADDY, IT'S SCARY HERE. SHMEE HEARS SOUNDS.
YOUR PRESENCE TIRES ME. GO TO YOUR ROOM AND STAY QUIET, OR THE "THINGS" WILL HEAR YOU.
NO LIFE.
MICKEY YUSH
BUT, SHMEE...
GO TO SLEEP.
YES, DADDY.
LET'S GO TO MY ROOM, SHMEE. WE'LL HIDE UNDER THE BLANKETS, AND MAYBE FALL ASLEEP BEFORE WE DIE.
HERE WE ARE, SHM...
UH..
mommy.

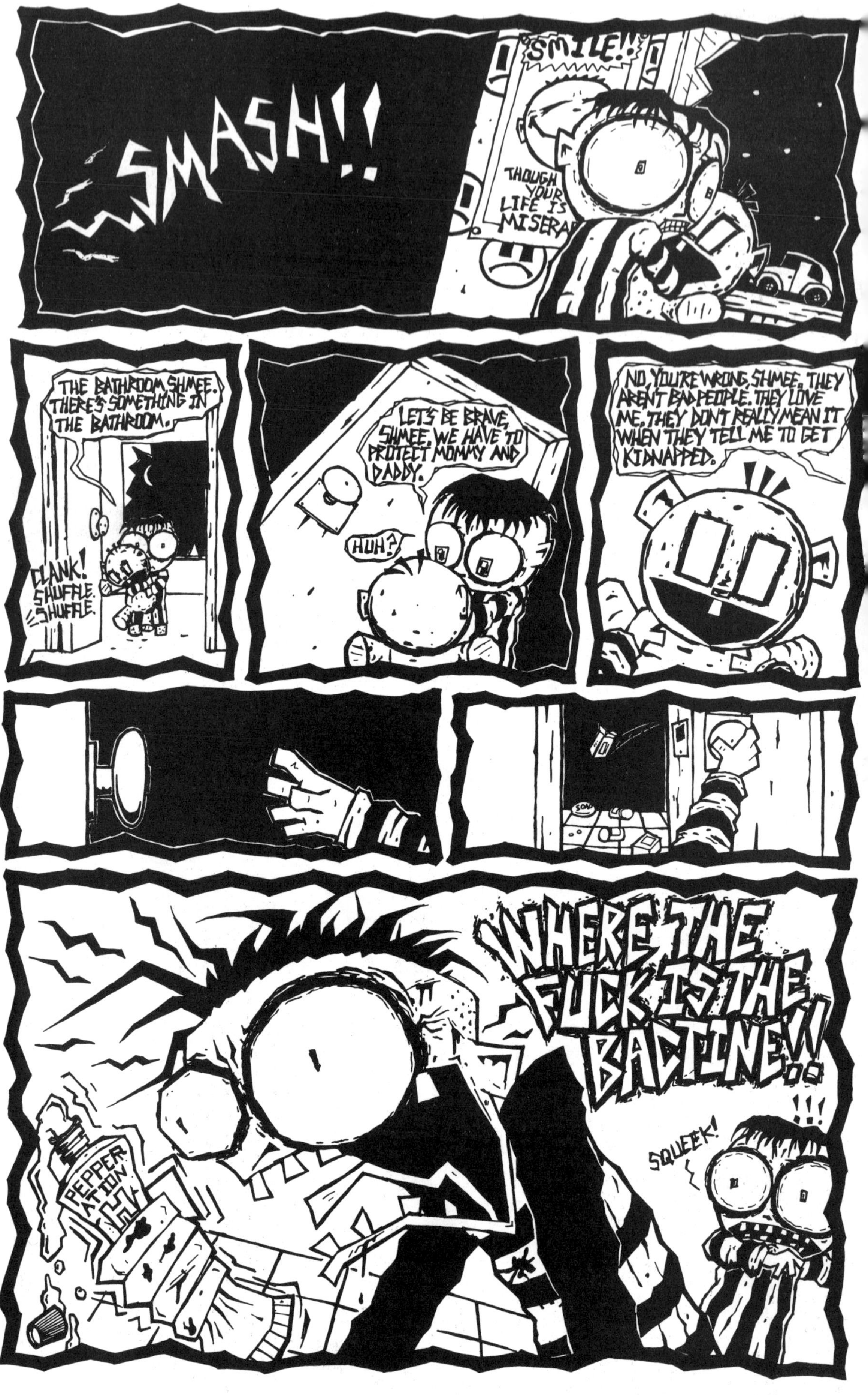
SMASH!!
SMILE!!
THOUGH YOUR LIFE IS MISERA
THE BATHROOM SHMEE. THERE'S SOMETHING IN THE BATHROOM.
CLANK! SHUFFLE SHUFFLE
LET'S BE BRAVE, SHMEE. WE HAVE TO PROTECT MOMMY AND DADDY.
HUH?
NO, YOU'RE WRONG, SHMEE. THEY AREN'T BAD PEOPLE. THEY LOVE ME. THEY DON'T REALLY MEAN IT WHEN THEY TELL ME TO GET KIDNAPPED.
WHERE THE FUCK IS THE BACTINE!!
PEPPERATION
!!!
SQUEEK!

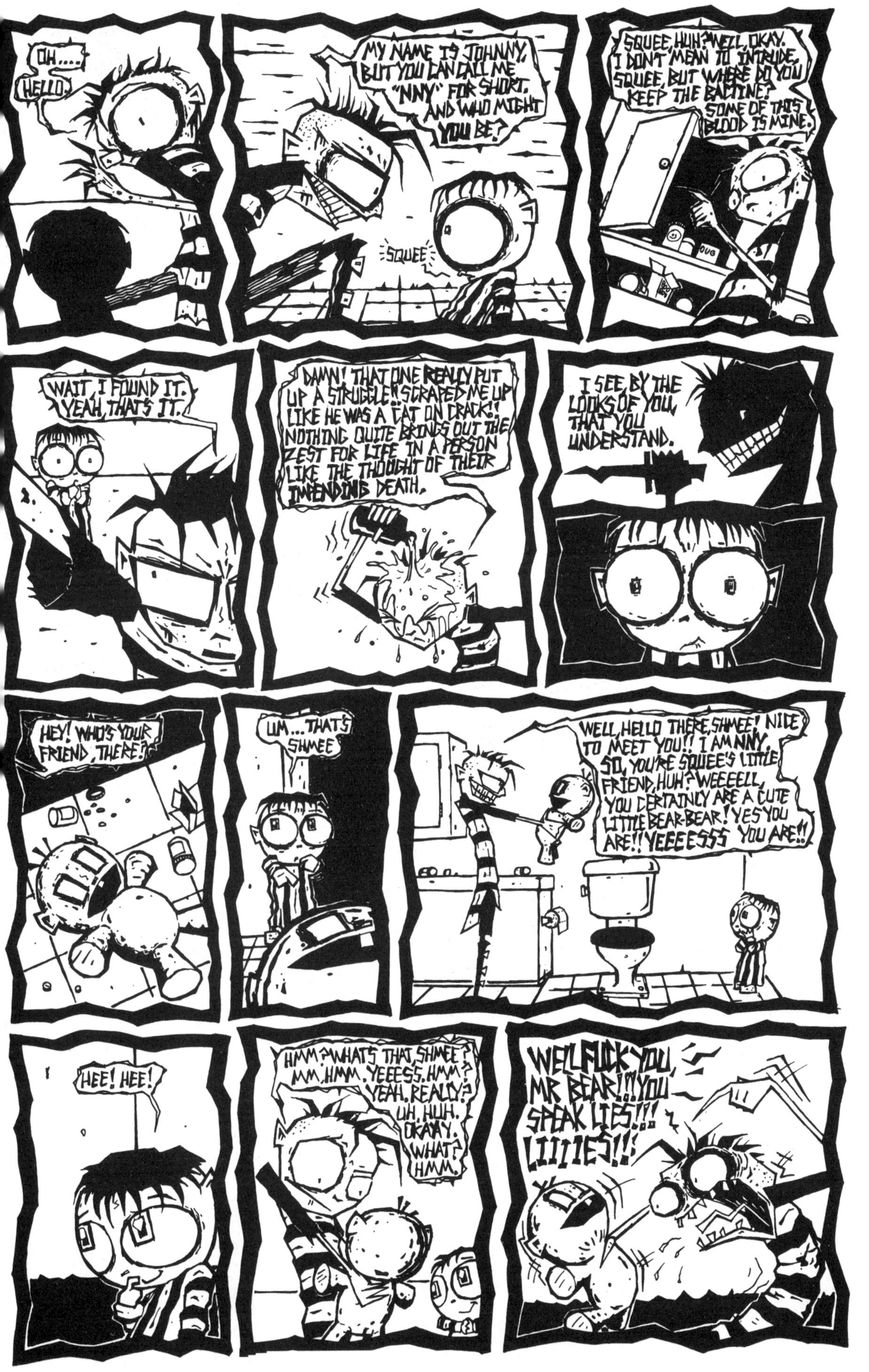
OH.....
HELLO.
MY NAME IS JOHNNY, BUT YOU CAN CALL ME "NNY" FOR SHORT. AND WHO MIGHT YOU BE?
SQUEE
SQUEE, HUH? WELL, OKAY. I DON'T MEAN TO INTRUDE, SQUEE, BUT WHERE DO YOU KEEP THE BACTINE?
SOME OF THIS BLOOD IS MINE.
WAIT, I FOUND IT. YEAH, THAT'S IT.
DAMN! THAT ONE REALLY PUT UP A STRUGGLE!! SCRAPED ME UP LIKE HE WAS A CAT ON CRACK!! NOTHING QUITE BRINGS OUT THE ZEST FOR LIFE IN A PERSON LIKE THE THOUGHT OF THEIR IMPENDING DEATH.
I SEE, BY THE LOOKS OF YOU, THAT YOU UNDERSTAND.
HEY! WHO'S YOUR FRIEND, THERE?
UM... THAT'S SHMEE
WELL, HELLO THERE, SHMEE! NICE TO MEET YOU!! I AM NNY. SO, YOU'RE SQUEE'S LITTLE FRIEND, HUH? WEEEELL, YOU CERTAINLY ARE A CUTE LITTLE BEAR-BEAR! YES YOU ARE!! YEEEESSS YOU ARE!!
HEE! HEE!
HMM? WHAT'S THAT, SHMEE? MM, HMM. YEEESS. HMM? YEAH, REALLY? UH, HUH. OKAYAY. WHAT? HMM.
WELL FUCK YOU, MR. BEAR!!! YOU SPEAK LIES!!! LIIIIES!!!

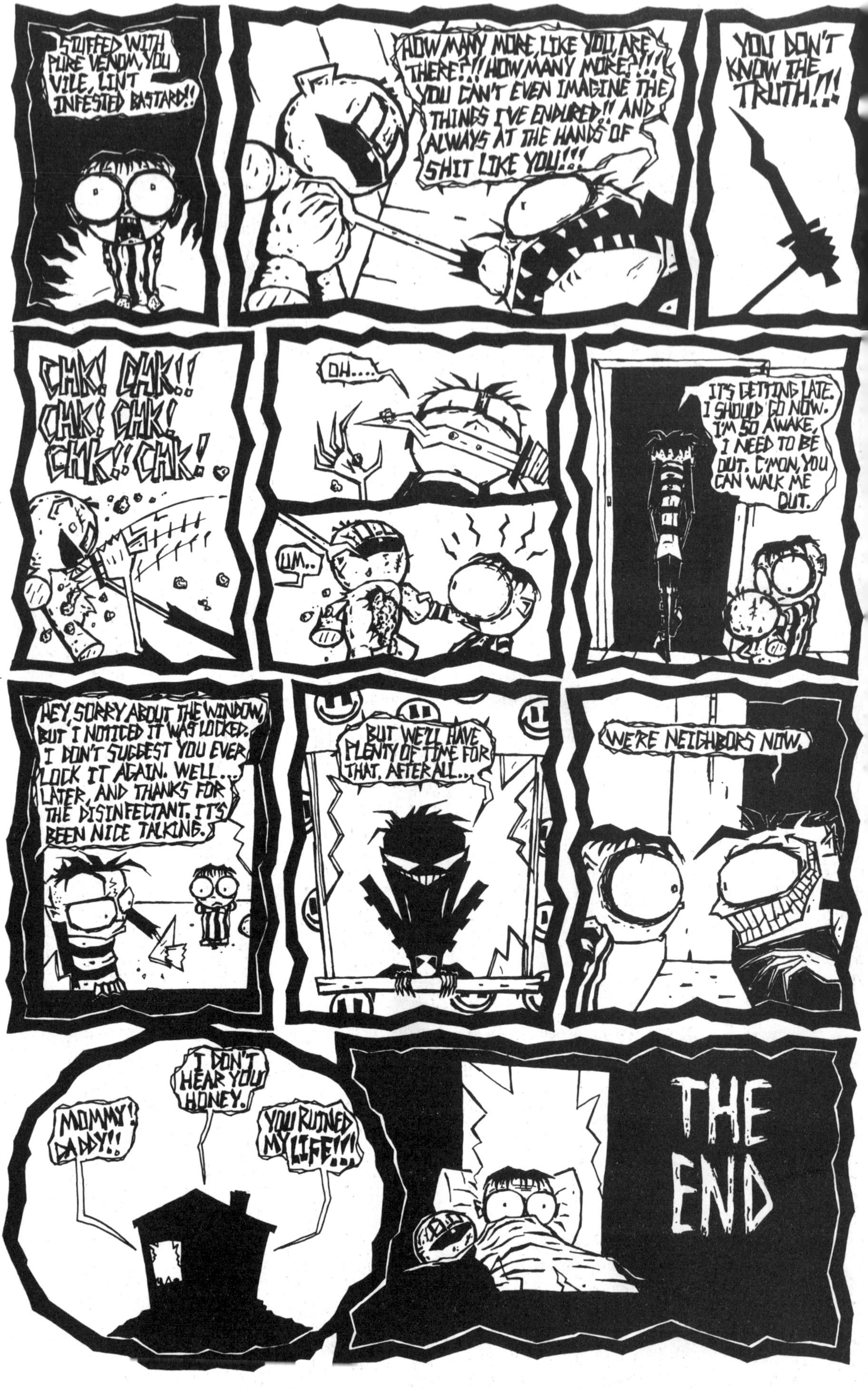
STUFFED WITH PURE VENOM, YOU VILE, LINT INFESTED BASTARD!!
HOW MANY MORE LIKE YOU ARE THERE?!! HOW MANY MORE?!!! YOU CAN'T EVEN IMAGINE THE THINGS I'VE ENDURED!! AND ALWAYS AT THE HANDS OF SHIT LIKE YOU!!!
YOU DON'T KNOW THE TRUTH!!!
CHK! CHK!! CHK! CHK! CHK!! CHK!
OH....
UM..
IT'S GETTING LATE. I SHOULD GO NOW. I'M SO AWAKE, I NEED TO BE OUT. C'MON, YOU CAN WALK ME OUT.
HEY, SORRY ABOUT THE WINDOW, BUT I NOTICED IT WAS LOCKED. I DON'T SUGGEST YOU EVER LOCK IT AGAIN. WELL... LATER, AND THANKS FOR THE DISINFECTANT. IT'S BEEN NICE TALKING.
BUT WE'LL HAVE PLENTY OF TIME FOR THAT, AFTER ALL...
WE'RE NEIGHBORS NOW.
MOMMY! DADDY!!
I DON'T HEAR YOU HONEY.
YOU RUINED MY LIFE!!!
THE END

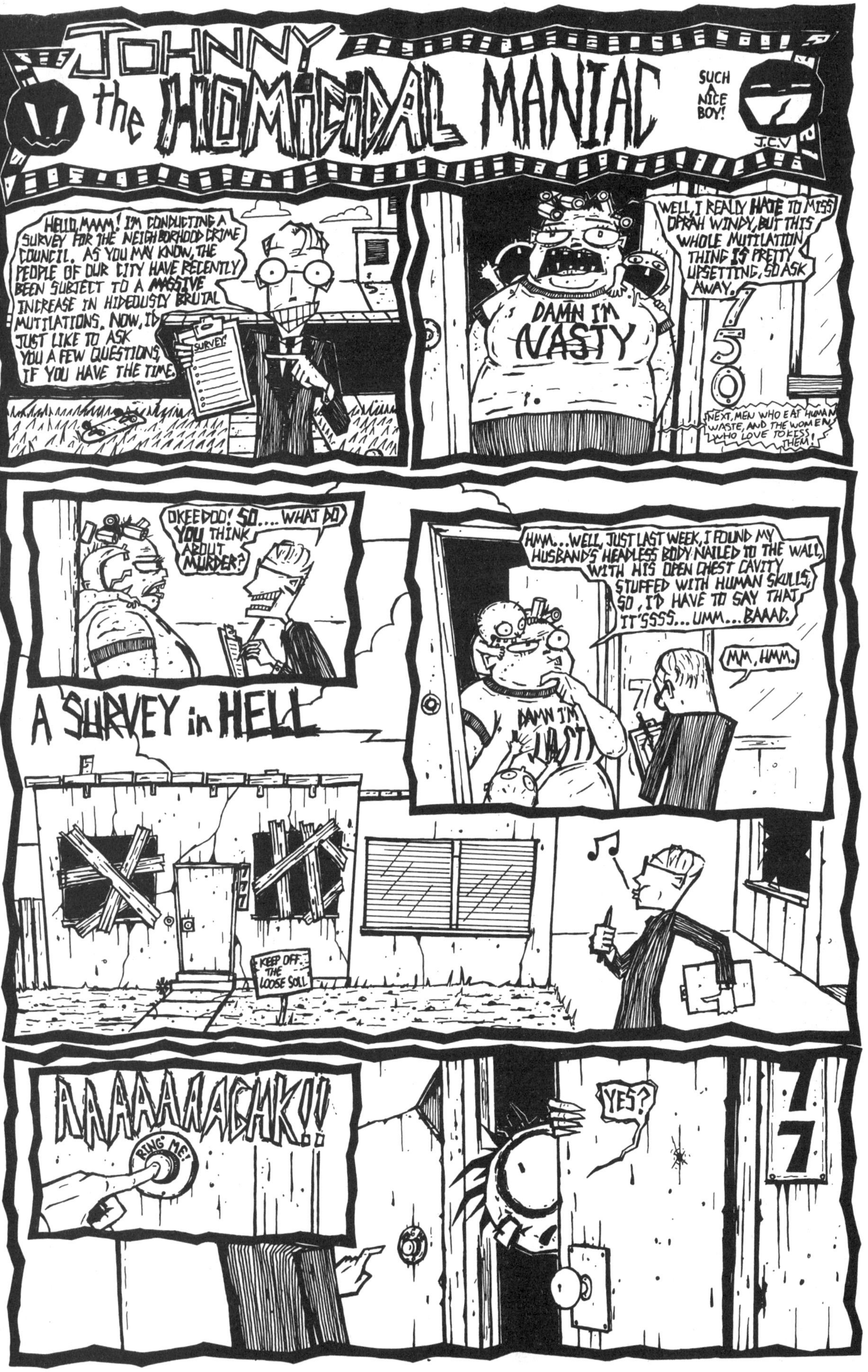
JOHNNY the HOMICIDAL MANIAC
SUCH A NICE BOY!
J.C.V
HELLO, MA'AM! I'M CONDUCTING A SURVEY FOR THE NEIGHBORHOOD CRIME COUNCIL. AS YOU MAY KNOW, THE PEOPLE OF OUR CITY HAVE RECENTLY BEEN SUBJECT TO A MASSIVE INCREASE IN HIDEOUSLY BRUTAL MUTILATIONS. NOW, I'D JUST LIKE TO ASK YOU A FEW QUESTIONS, IF YOU HAVE THE TIME.
SURVEY!
WELL, I REALLY HATE TO MISS OPRAH WINDY, BUT THIS WHOLE MUTILATION THING IS PRETTY UPSETTING, SO ASK AWAY.
DAMN I'M NASTY
750
NEXT, MEN WHO EAT HUMAN WASTE, AND THE WOMEN WHO LOVE TO KISS THEM!
OKEEDOO! SO.... WHAT DO YOU THINK ABOUT MURDER?
HMM...WELL, JUST LAST WEEK, I FOUND MY HUSBAND'S HEADLESS BODY NAILED TO THE WALL, WITH HIS OPEN CHEST CAVITY STUFFED WITH HUMAN SKULLS, SO, I'D HAVE TO SAY THAT IT'SSSS...UMM...BAAAD.
MM, HMM.
A SURVEY in HELL
KEEP OFF THE LOOSE SOIL
AAAAAAACHK!!
RING ME!
YES?
7

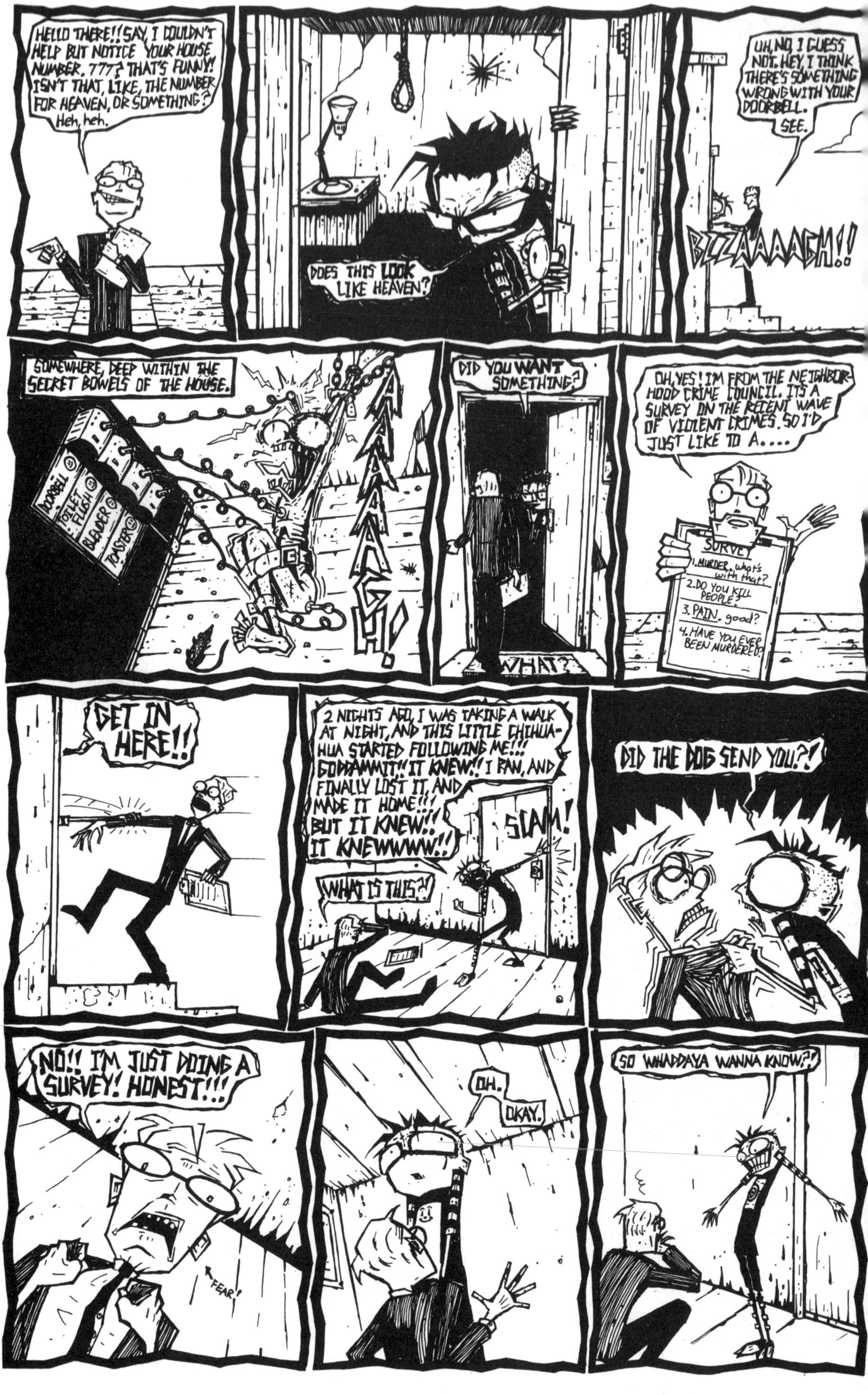
HELLO THERE!! SAY, I COULDN'T HELP BUT NOTICE YOUR HOUSE NUMBER. 777? THAT'S FUNNY! ISN'T THAT, LIKE, THE NUMBER FOR HEAVEN, OR SOMETHING?
Heh, heh.
DOES THIS LOOK LIKE HEAVEN?
UH, NO, I GUESS NOT. HEY, I THINK THERE'S SOMETHING WRONG WITH YOUR DOORBELL.
SEE.
BZZAAAAGH!!
SOMEWHERE, DEEP WITHIN THE SECRET BOWELS OF THE HOUSE.
DOORBELL
TOILET FLUSH
BLENDER
TOASTER
AAAAAAAAGH!
DID YOU WANT SOMETHING?
WHAT?
OH, YES! I'M FROM THE NEIGHBORHOOD CRIME COUNCIL. ITS A SURVEY ON THE RECENT WAVE OF VIOLENT CRIMES. SO I'D JUST LIKE TO A....
SURVEY
1. MURDER. what's with that?
2. DO YOU KILL PEOPLE?
3. PAIN. good?
4. HAVE YOU EVER BEEN MURDERED?
GET IN HERE!!
2 NIGHTS AGO, I WAS TAKING A WALK AT NIGHT, AND THIS LITTLE CHIHUAHUA STARTED FOLLOWING ME!!! GODDAMMIT!! IT KNEW!! I RAN, AND FINALLY LOST IT, AND MADE IT HOME!!! BUT IT KNEW!! IT KNEWWWW!!
SLAM!
WHAT IS THIS?!
DID THE DOG SEND YOU?!
NO!! I'M JUST DOING A SURVEY! HONEST!!!
FEAR!
OH.
OKAY.
SO WHADDAYA WANNA KNOW?!

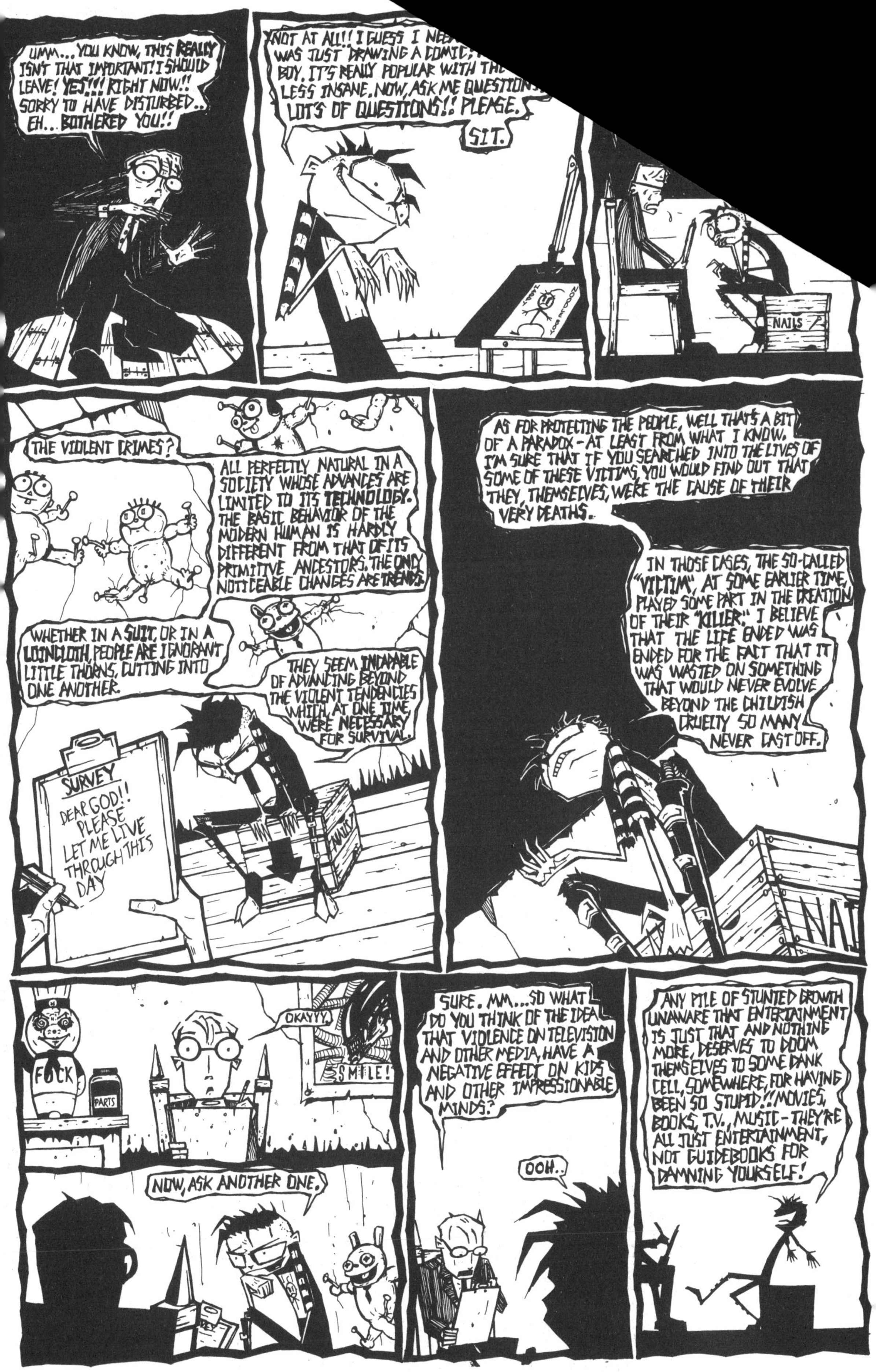
UMM... YOU KNOW, THIS REALLY ISN'T THAT IMPORTANT! I SHOULD LEAVE! YES!!! RIGHT NOW!! SORRY TO HAVE DISTURBED.. EH... BOTHERED YOU!!
NOT AT ALL!! I GUESS I NEE
WAS JUST DRAWING A COMIC,
BOY. IT'S REALLY POPULAR WITH TH
LESS INSANE. NOW, ASK ME QUESTION
LOTS OF QUESTIONS!! PLEASE.
SIT.
NAILS
THE VIOLENT CRIMES?
ALL PERFECTLY NATURAL IN A SOCIETY WHOSE ADVANCES ARE LIMITED TO ITS TECHNOLOGY. THE BASIC BEHAVIOR OF THE MODERN HUMAN IS HARDLY DIFFERENT FROM THAT OF ITS PRIMITIVE ANCESTORS. THE ONLY NOTICEABLE CHANGES ARE TRENDS.
WHETHER IN A SUIT, OR IN A LOINCLOTH, PEOPLE ARE IGNORANT LITTLE THORNS, CUTTING INTO ONE ANOTHER.
THEY SEEM INCAPABLE OF ADVANCING BEYOND THE VIOLENT TENDENCIES WHICH, AT ONE TIME, WERE NECESSARY FOR SURVIVAL.
SURVEY
DEAR GOD!! PLEASE LET ME LIVE THROUGH THIS DAY
NAILS
AS FOR PROTECTING THE PEOPLE, WELL THAT'S A BIT OF A PARADOX - AT LEAST FROM WHAT I KNOW. I'M SURE THAT IF YOU SEARCHED INTO THE LIVES OF SOME OF THESE VICTIMS, YOU WOULD FIND OUT THAT THEY, THEMSELVES, WERE THE CAUSE OF THEIR VERY DEATHS.
IN THOSE CASES, THE SO-CALLED "VICTIM", AT SOME EARLIER TIME, PLAYED SOME PART IN THE CREATION OF THEIR "KILLER." I BELIEVE THAT THE LIFE ENDED WAS ENDED FOR THE FACT THAT IT WAS WASTED ON SOMETHING THAT WOULD NEVER EVOLVE BEYOND THE CHILDISH CRUELTY SO MANY NEVER CAST OFF.
NAI
OKAYYY.
FUCK
PARTS
SMILE!
NOW, ASK ANOTHER ONE.
SURE. MM... SO WHAT DO YOU THINK OF THE IDEA THAT VIOLENCE ON TELEVISION AND OTHER MEDIA, HAVE A NEGATIVE EFFECT ON KIDS AND OTHER IMPRESSIONABLE MINDS?
OOH..
ANY PILE OF STUNTED GROWTH UNAWARE THAT ENTERTAINMENT IS JUST THAT AND NOTHING MORE, DESERVES TO DOOM THEMSELVES TO SOME DANK CELL, SOMEWHERE, FOR HAVING BEEN SO STUPID!! MOVIES, BOOKS, T.V., MUSIC - THEY'RE ALL JUST ENTERTAINMENT, NOT GUIDEBOOKS FOR DAMNING YOURSELF!

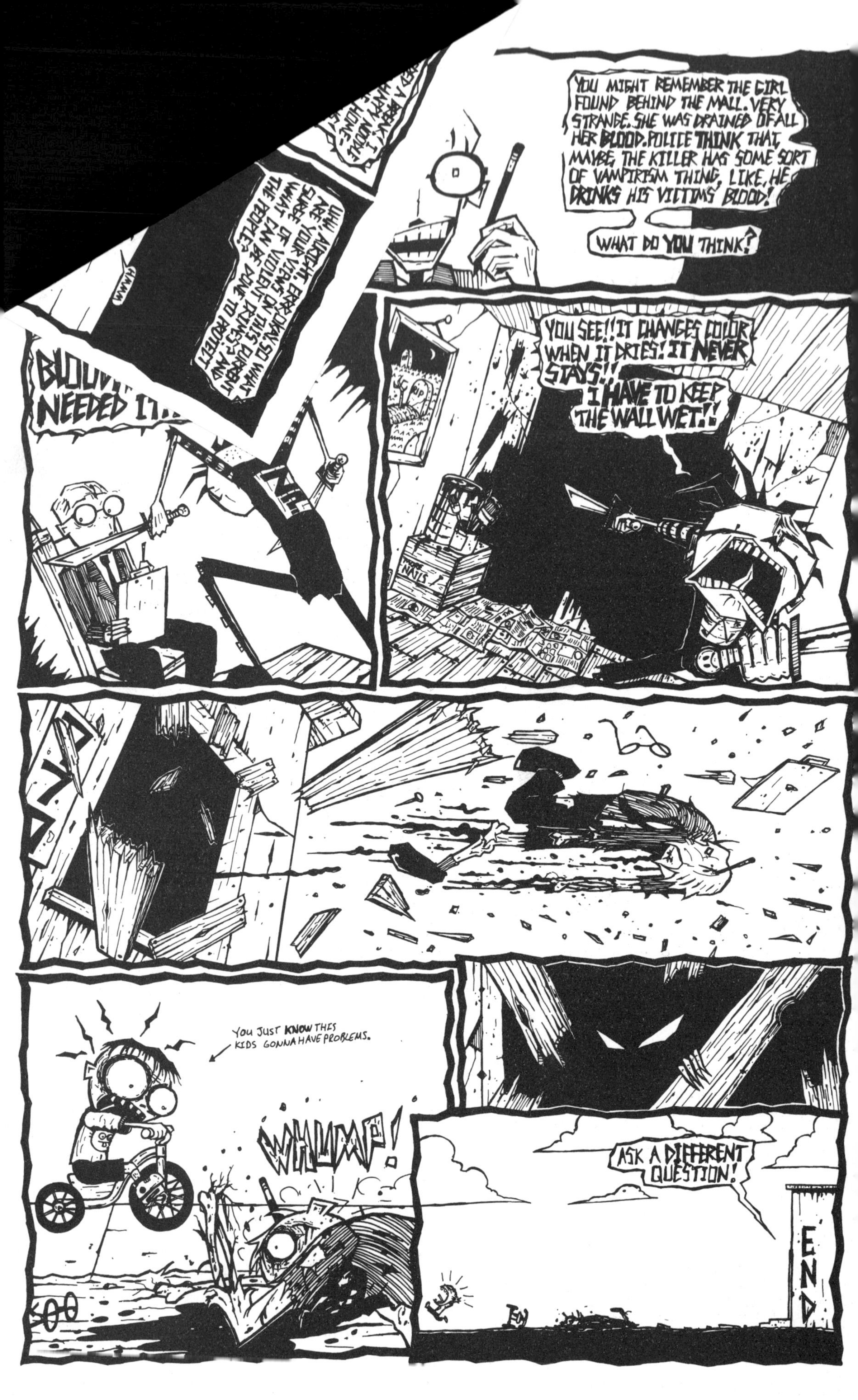

HMMM
UHH, ALRIGHT. ERRR OKAY. SO WHAT ARE YOUR VIEWS ON THIS CURRENT SURGE OF VIOLENT CRIMES? AND WHAT CAN BE DONE TO PROTECT THE PEOPLE?
YOU MIGHT REMEMBER THE GIRL FOUND BEHIND THE MALL. VERY STRANGE. SHE WAS DRAINED OF ALL HER BLOOD. POLICE THINK THAT, MAYBE, THE KILLER HAS SOME SORT OF VAMPIRISM THING, LIKE, HE DRINKS HIS VICTIMS' BLOOD!
WHAT DO YOU THINK?
NEEDED IT...
YOU SEE!! IT CHANGES COLOR WHEN IT DRIES! IT NEVER STAYS!!
I HAVE TO KEEP THE WALL WET!!
NAILS
YOU JUST KNOW THIS KIDS GONNA HAVE PROBLEMS.
WHUMP!
ASK A DIFFERENT QUESTION!
END

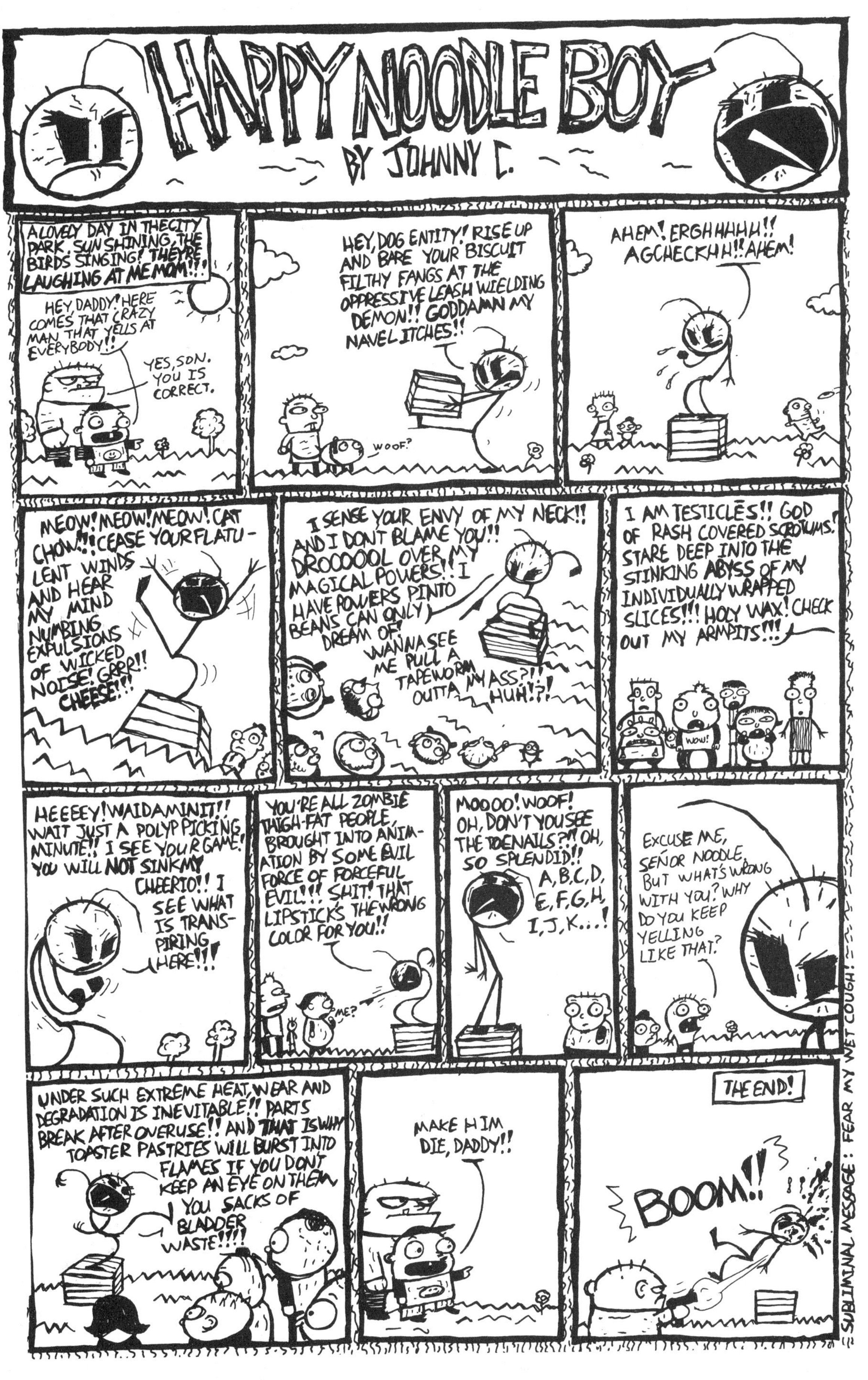
HAPPY NOODLE BOY
BY JOHNNY C.
A LOVELY DAY IN THE CITY PARK. SUN SHINING, THE BIRDS SINGING! THEY'RE LAUGHING AT ME MOM!!
HEY, DADDY! HERE COMES THAT CRAZY MAN THAT YELLS AT EVERYBODY!!
YES, SON. YOU IS CORRECT.
HEY, DOG ENTITY! RISE UP AND BARE YOUR BISCUIT FILTHY FANGS AT THE OPPRESSIVE LEASH WIELDING DEMON!! GODDAMN MY NAVEL ITCHES!!
WOOF?
AHEM! ERGHHHHH!! AGCHECKHH!! AHEM!
MEOW! MEOW! MEOW! CAT CHOW!!! CEASE YOUR FLATULENT WINDS AND HEAR MY MIND NUMBING EXPULSIONS OF WICKED NOISE! GRRR!! CHEESE!!!
I SENSE YOUR ENVY OF MY NECK!! AND I DONT BLAME YOU!! DROOOOOL OVER MY MAGICAL POWERS!! I HAVE POWERS PINTO BEANS CAN ONLY DREAM OF!
WANNA SEE ME PULL A TAPEWORM OUTTA MY ASS?!! HUH!?!
I AM TESTICLĒS!! GOD OF RASH COVERED SCROTUMS! STARE DEEP INTO THE STINKING ABYSS OF MY INDIVIDUALLY WRAPPED SLICES!!! HOLY WAX! CHECK OUT MY ARMPITS!!!
WOW!
HEEEEY! WAIDAMINIT!! WAIT JUST A POLYP PICKING MINUTE!! I SEE YOUR GAME! YOU WILL NOT SINK MY CHEERIO!! I SEE WHAT IS TRANSPIRING HERE!!!
YOU'RE ALL ZOMBIE THIGH-FAT PEOPLE, BROUGHT INTO ANIMATION BY SOME EVIL FORCE OF FORCEFUL EVIL!!! SHIT! THAT LIPSTICK'S THE WRONG COLOR FOR YOU!!
ME?
MOOOO! WOOF! OH, DON'T YOU SEE THE TOENAILS?!! OH, SO SPLENDID!!
A,B,C,D, E,F,G,H, I,J,K...!
EXCUSE ME, SEÑOR NOODLE, BUT WHAT'S WRONG WITH YOU? WHY DO YOU KEEP YELLING LIKE THAT?
UNDER SUCH EXTREME HEAT, WEAR AND DEGRADATION IS INEVITABLE!! PARTS BREAK AFTER OVERUSE!! AND THAT IS WHY TOASTER PASTRIES WILL BURST INTO FLAMES IF YOU DONT KEEP AN EYE ON THEM YOU SACKS OF BLADDER WASTE!!!!
MAKE HIM DIE, DADDY!!
THE END!
BOOM!!
SUBLIMINAL MESSAGE: FEAR MY WET COUGH!

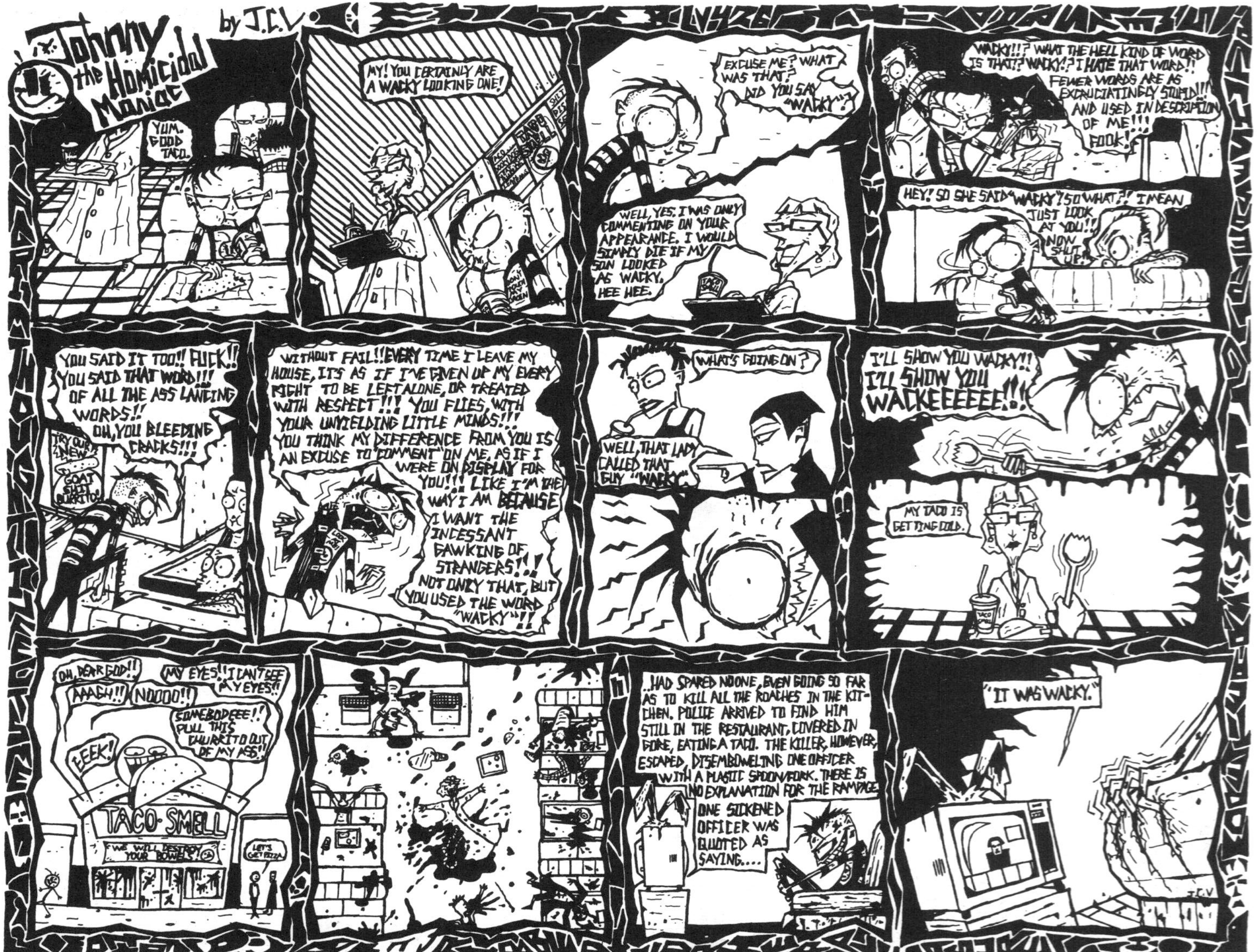
Johnny the Homicidal Maniac
by J.C.V.
YUM. GOOD TACO.
MY! YOU CERTAINLY ARE A WACKY LOOKING ONE!
TACO SMELL
EXCUSE ME? WHAT WAS THAT? DID YOU SAY "WACKY"?
WELL, YES. I WAS ONLY COMMENTING ON YOUR APPEARANCE. I WOULD SIMPLY DIE IF MY SON LOOKED AS WACKY. HEE HEE.
WACKY!!!? WHAT THE HELL KIND OF WORD IS THAT!? WACKY!? I HATE THAT WORD!! FEWER WORDS ARE AS EXCRUCIATINGLY STUPID!!! AND USED IN DESCRIPTION OF ME!!! FOOK!
HEY! SO SHE SAID "WACKY"! SO WHAT?! I MEAN JUST LOOK AT YOU!! NOW SHUT UP!
YOU SAID IT TOO!! FUCK!! YOU SAID THAT WORD!!! OF ALL THE ASS LANCING WORDS!! OH, YOU BLEEDING CRACKS!!!
TRY OUR NEW GOAT SHIT BURRITO!
WITHOUT FAIL!! EVERY TIME I LEAVE MY HOUSE, IT'S AS IF I'VE GIVEN UP MY EVERY RIGHT TO BE LEFT ALONE, OR TREATED WITH RESPECT!!! YOU FLIES, WITH YOUR UNYIELDING LITTLE MINDS!!! YOU THINK MY DIFFERENCE FROM YOU IS AN EXCUSE TO "COMMENT" ON ME, AS IF I WERE ON DISPLAY FOR YOU!!! LIKE I'M THE WAY I AM BECAUSE I WANT THE INCESSANT GAWKING OF STRANGERS!!! NOT ONLY THAT, BUT YOU USED THE WORD "WACKY"!!
WHAT'S GOING ON?
WELL, THAT LADY CALLED THAT GUY "WACKY."
I'LL SHOW YOU WACKY!! I'LL SHOW YOU WACKEEEEEE!!!
MY TACO IS GETTING COLD.
OH, DEAR GOD!!
MY EYES!! I CAN'T SEE MY EYES!!
AAAGH!!
NOOOO!!
SOMEBODEEE!! PULL THIS CHURRITO OUT OF MY ASS!!
EEEK!
TACO SMELL
WE WILL DESTROY YOUR BOWELS!
LET'S GET PIZZA
...HAD SPARED NO ONE, EVEN GOING SO FAR AS TO KILL ALL THE ROACHES IN THE KITCHEN. POLICE ARRIVED TO FIND HIM STILL IN THE RESTAURANT, COVERED IN GORE, EATING A TACO. THE KILLER, HOWEVER, ESCAPED, DISEMBOWELING ONE OFFICER WITH A PLASTIC SPOON/FORK. THERE IS NO EXPLANATION FOR THE RAMPAGE.
ONE SICKENED OFFICER WAS QUOTED AS SAYING....
"IT WAS WACKY."
J.C.V

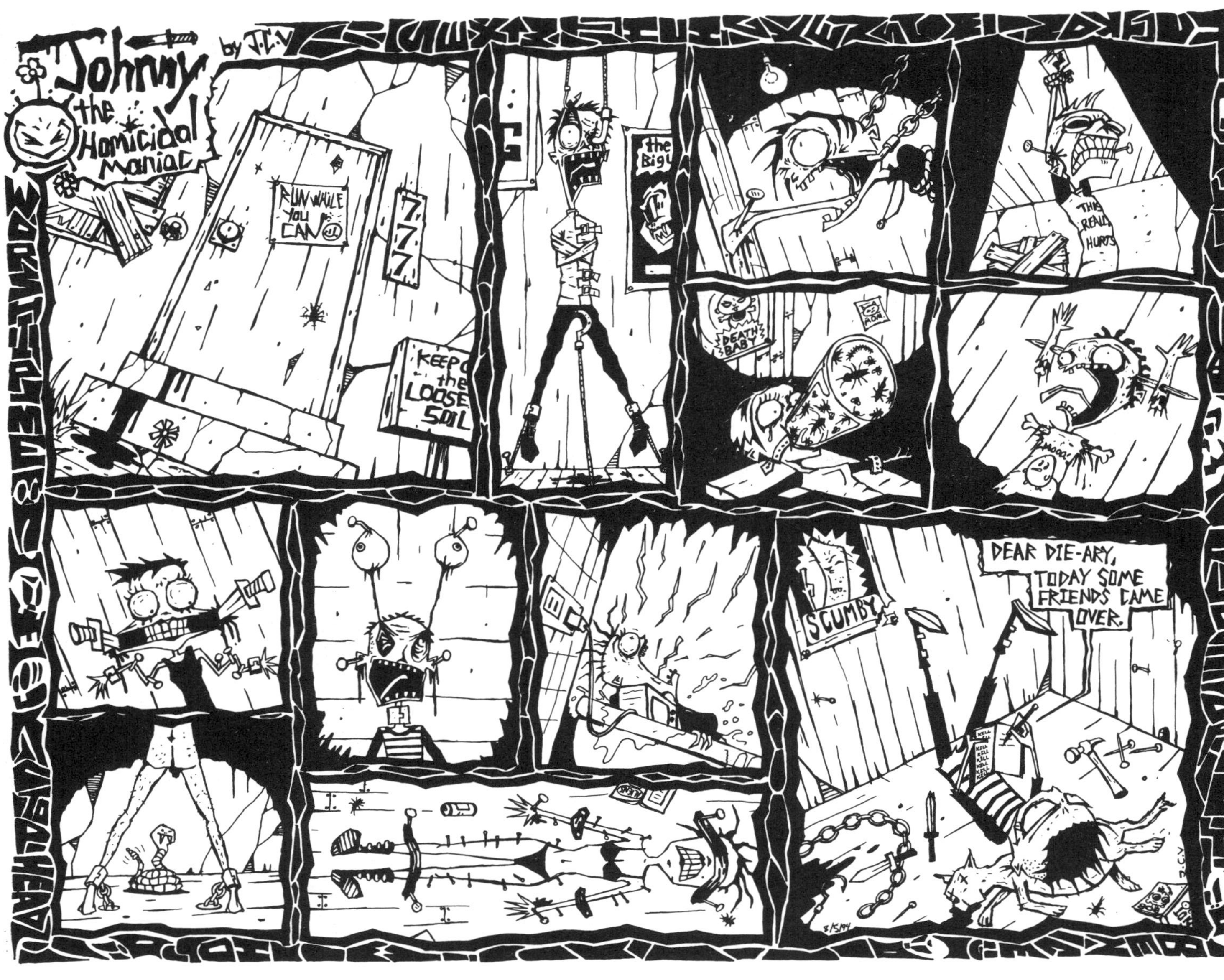

Johnny the Homicidal Maniac
by J.C.V.
RUN WHILE YOU CAN
777
KEEP OFF the LOOSE SOIL
the Big
THIS REALLY HURTS
DEATH BABY
MOOOO!
SCUMBY
DEAR DIE-ARY, TODAY SOME FRIENDS CAME OVER.

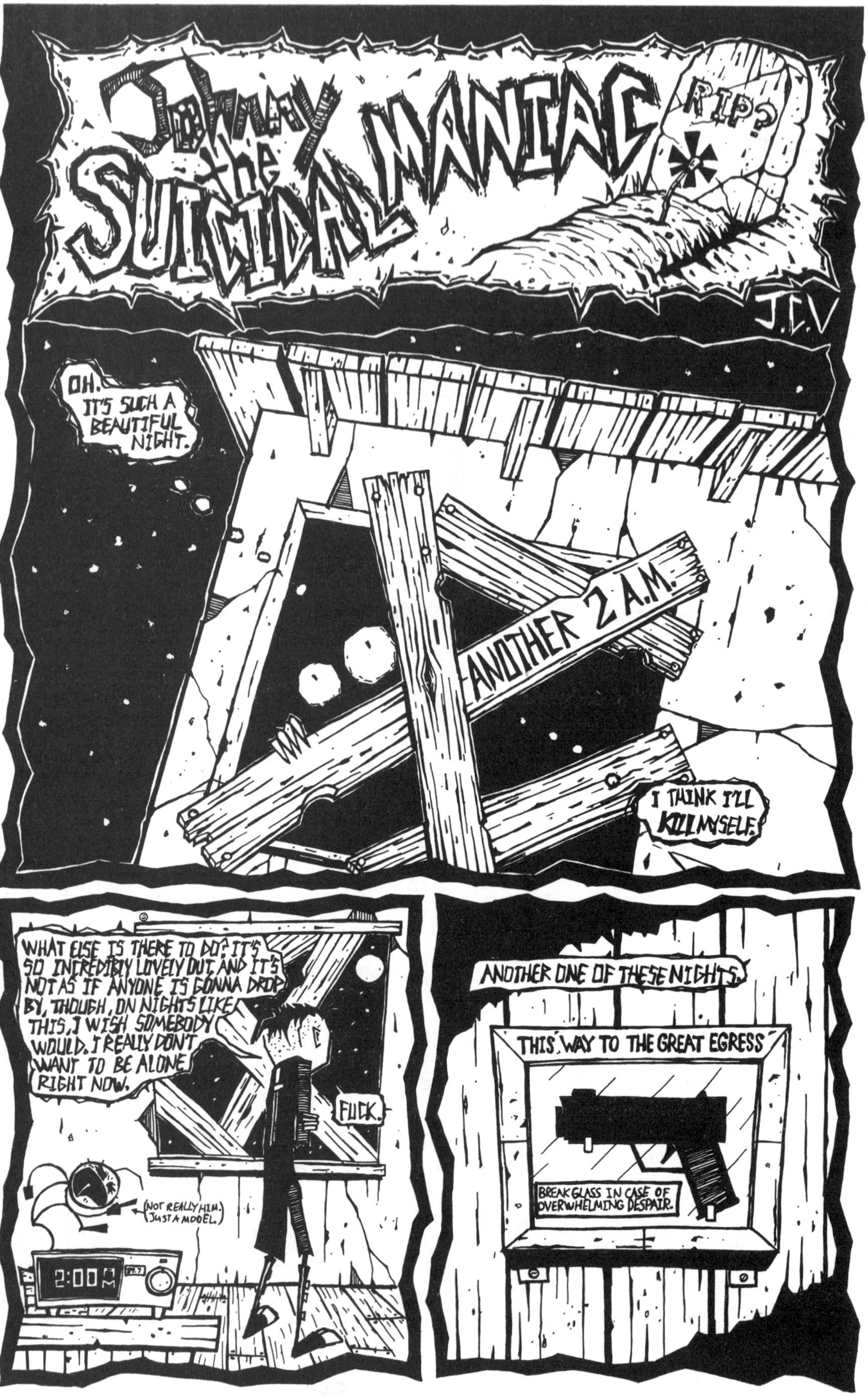
Johnny the Suicidal Maniac
RIP?
J.C.V.
OH. IT'S SUCH A BEAUTIFUL NIGHT.
ANOTHER 2 A.M.
I THINK I'LL KILL MYSELF.
WHAT ELSE IS THERE TO DO? IT'S SO INCREDIBLY LOVELY OUT, AND IT'S NOT AS IF ANYONE IS GONNA DROP BY, THOUGH, ON NIGHTS LIKE THIS, I WISH SOMEBODY WOULD. I REALLY DON'T WANT TO BE ALONE RIGHT NOW.
FUCK.
(NOT REALLY HIM. JUST A MODEL.)
2:00
ANOTHER ONE OF THESE NIGHTS.
THIS WAY TO THE GREAT EGRESS
BREAK GLASS IN CASE OF OVERWHELMING DESPAIR.

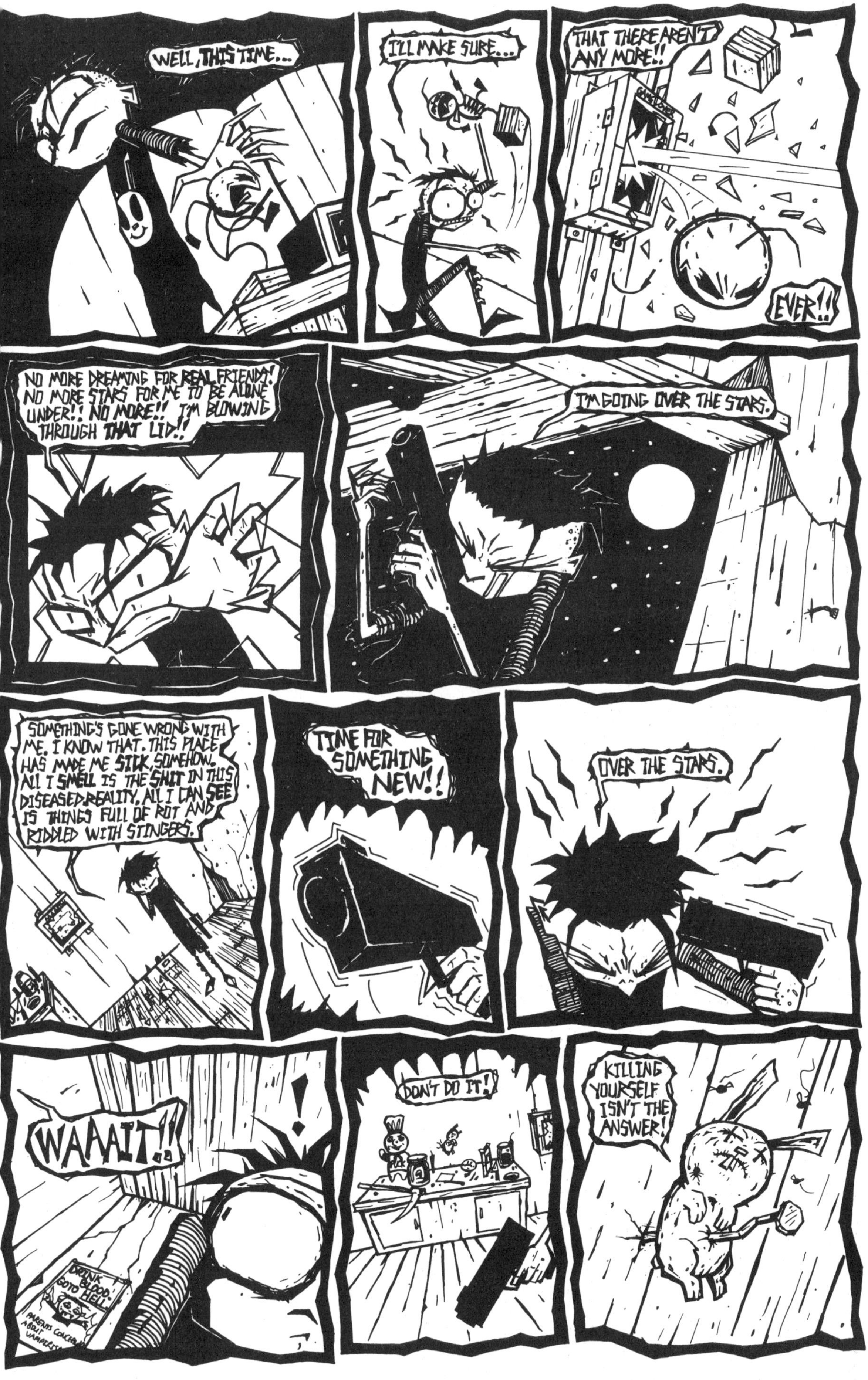

WELL, THIS TIME...
I'LL MAKE SURE...
THAT THERE AREN'T ANY MORE!!
EVER!!
NO MORE DREAMING FOR REAL FRIENDS! NO MORE STARS FOR ME TO BE ALONE UNDER!! NO MORE!! I'M BLOWING THROUGH THAT LID!!
I'M GOING OVER THE STARS.
SOMETHING'S GONE WRONG WITH ME. I KNOW THAT. THIS PLACE HAS MADE ME SICK, SOMEHOW. ALL I SMELL IS THE SHIT IN THIS DISEASED REALITY. ALL I CAN SEE IS THINGS FULL OF ROT AND RIDDLED WITH STINGERS.
TIME FOR SOMETHING NEW!!
OVER THE STARS.
WAAAIT!!
DRINK BLOOD. GOTO HELL.
PARENTS CONCERNED ABOUT VAMPIRES
DON'T DO IT!
KILLING YOURSELF ISN'T THE ANSWER!

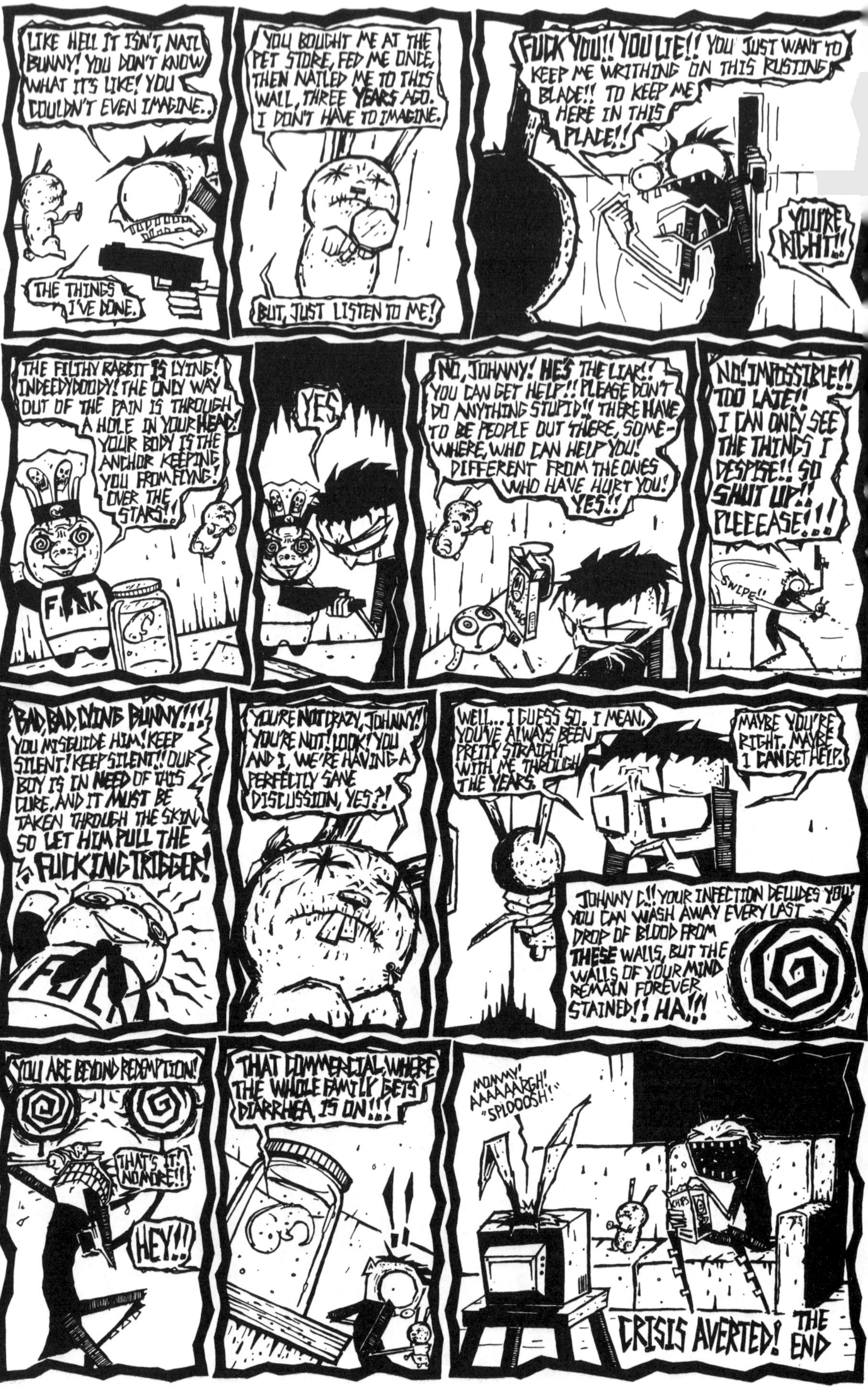
LIKE HELL IT ISN'T, NAIL BUNNY! YOU DON'T KNOW WHAT IT'S LIKE! YOU COULDN'T EVEN IMAGINE...
THE THINGS I'VE DONE.
YOU BOUGHT ME AT THE PET STORE, FED ME ONCE, THEN NAILED ME TO THIS WALL, THREE YEARS AGO. I DON'T HAVE TO IMAGINE.
BUT, JUST LISTEN TO ME!
FUCK YOU!! YOU LIE!! YOU JUST WANT TO KEEP ME WRITHING ON THIS RUSTING BLADE!! TO KEEP ME HERE IN THIS PLACE!!
YOU'RE RIGHT!!
THE FILTHY RABBIT IS LYING! INDEEDYDOODY! THE ONLY WAY OUT OF THE PAIN IS THROUGH A HOLE IN YOUR HEAD! YOUR BODY IS THE ANCHOR KEEPING YOU FROM FLYING OVER THE STARS!!
F**K
YES
NO, JOHNNY! HE'S THE LIAR!! YOU CAN GET HELP!! PLEASE DON'T DO ANYTHING STUPID!! THERE HAVE TO BE PEOPLE OUT THERE, SOMEWHERE, WHO CAN HELP YOU! DIFFERENT FROM THE ONES WHO HAVE HURT YOU! YES!!
NO! IMPOSSIBLE!! TOO LATE!! I CAN ONLY SEE THE THINGS I DESPISE!! SO SHUT UP!! PLEEEASE!!!
SWIPE!!
BAD, BAD, LYING BUNNY!!! YOU MISGUIDE HIM! KEEP SILENT! KEEP SILENT!! OUR BOY IS IN NEED OF THIS CURE, AND IT MUST BE TAKEN THROUGH THE SKIN, SO LET HIM PULL THE FUCKING TRIGGER!
YOU'RE NOT CRAZY, JOHNNY! YOU'RE NOT! LOOK! YOU AND I, WE'RE HAVING A PERFECTLY SANE DISCUSSION, YES?!
WELL... I GUESS SO. I MEAN, YOU'VE ALWAYS BEEN PRETTY STRAIGHT WITH ME THROUGH THE YEARS.
MAYBE YOU'RE RIGHT. MAYBE I CAN GET HELP.
JOHNNY C!! YOUR INFECTION DELUDES YOU. YOU CAN WASH AWAY EVERY LAST DROP OF BLOOD FROM THESE WALLS, BUT THE WALLS OF YOUR MIND REMAIN FOREVER STAINED!! HA!!!
YOU ARE BEYOND REDEMPTION!
THAT'S IT! NO MORE!!
HEY!!
THAT COMMERCIAL WHERE THE WHOLE FAMILY GETS DIARRHEA, IS ON!!!
MOMMY! AAAAAARGH! "SPLOOOSH!"
CHIPS
CRISIS AVERTED!
THE END

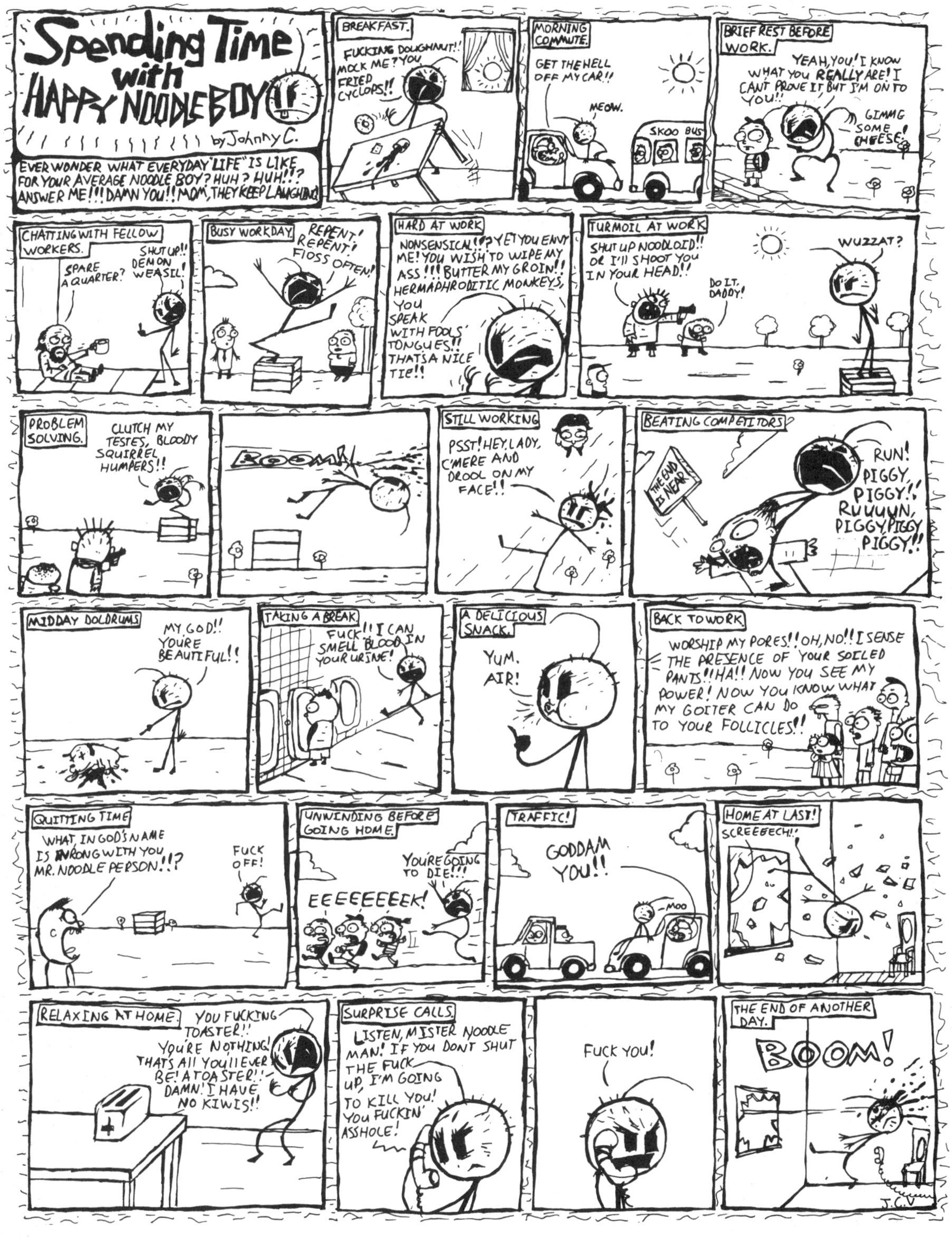
Spending Time with HAPPY NOODLE BOY
by Johnny C.
EVER WONDER WHAT EVERYDAY "LIFE" IS LIKE FOR YOUR AVERAGE NOODLE BOY? HUH? HUH!!? ANSWER ME!!! DAMN YOU!! MOM, THEY KEEP LAUGHING!
BREAKFAST.
FUCKING DOUGHNUT!! MOCK ME? YOU FRIED CYCLOPS!!
MORNING COMMUTE.
GET THE HELL OFF MY CAR!!
MEOW.
SKOO BUS
BRIEF REST BEFORE WORK.
YEAH, YOU! I KNOW WHAT YOU REALLY ARE! I CANT PROVE IT BUT I'M ON TO YOU!!
GIMME SOME CHEESE!
CHATTING WITH FELLOW WORKERS.
SPARE A QUARTER?
SHUT UP!! DEMON WEASEL!
BUSY WORKDAY.
REPENT! REPENT! FLOSS OFTEN!
HARD AT WORK
NONSENSICAL!!? YET YOU ENVY ME! YOU WISH TO WIPE MY ASS!!! BUTTER MY GROIN!! HERMAPHRODITIC MONKEYS, YOU SPEAK WITH FOOLS' TONGUES!! THATSA NICE TIE!!
TURMOIL AT WORK
SHUT UP NOODLOID!! OR I'LL SHOOT YOU IN YOUR HEAD!!
DO IT, DADDY!
WUZZAT?
PROBLEM SOLVING.
CLUTCH MY TESTES, BLOODY SQUIRREL HUMPERS!!
BOOM!
STILL WORKING
PSST! HEY, LADY, C'MERE AND DROOL ON MY FACE!!
BEATING COMPETITORS
THE END IS NEAR
RUN! PIGGY, PIGGY!! RUUUUN, PIGGY PIGGY PIGGY!!
MIDDAY DOLDRUMS
MY GOD!! YOU'RE BEAUTIFUL!!
TAKING A BREAK
FUCK!! I CAN SMELL BLOOD IN YOUR URINE!
A DELICIOUS SNACK.
YUM. AIR!
BACK TO WORK.
WORSHIP MY PORES!! OH, NO!! I SENSE THE PRESENCE OF YOUR SOILED PANTS!! HA!! NOW YOU SEE MY POWER! NOW YOU KNOW WHAT MY GOITER CAN DO TO YOUR FOLLICLES!!
QUITTING TIME
WHAT, IN GOD'S NAME IS WRONG WITH YOU, MR. NOODLE PERSON!!?
FUCK OFF!
UNWINDING BEFORE GOING HOME.
YOU'RE GOING TO DIE!!!
EEEEEEEEK!
TRAFFIC!
GODDAM YOU!!
MOO
HOME AT LAST!
SCREEEECH!!
RELAXING AT HOME.
YOU FUCKING TOASTER!! YOU'RE NOTHING! THATS ALL YOU'LL EVER BE! A TOASTER!! DAMN! I HAVE NO KIWIS!!
SURPRISE CALLS.
LISTEN, MISTER NOODLE MAN! IF YOU DONT SHUT THE FUCK UP, I'M GOING TO KILL YOU! YOU FUCKIN' ASSHOLE!
FUCK YOU!
THE END OF ANOTHER DAY.
BOOM!
J.C.V.

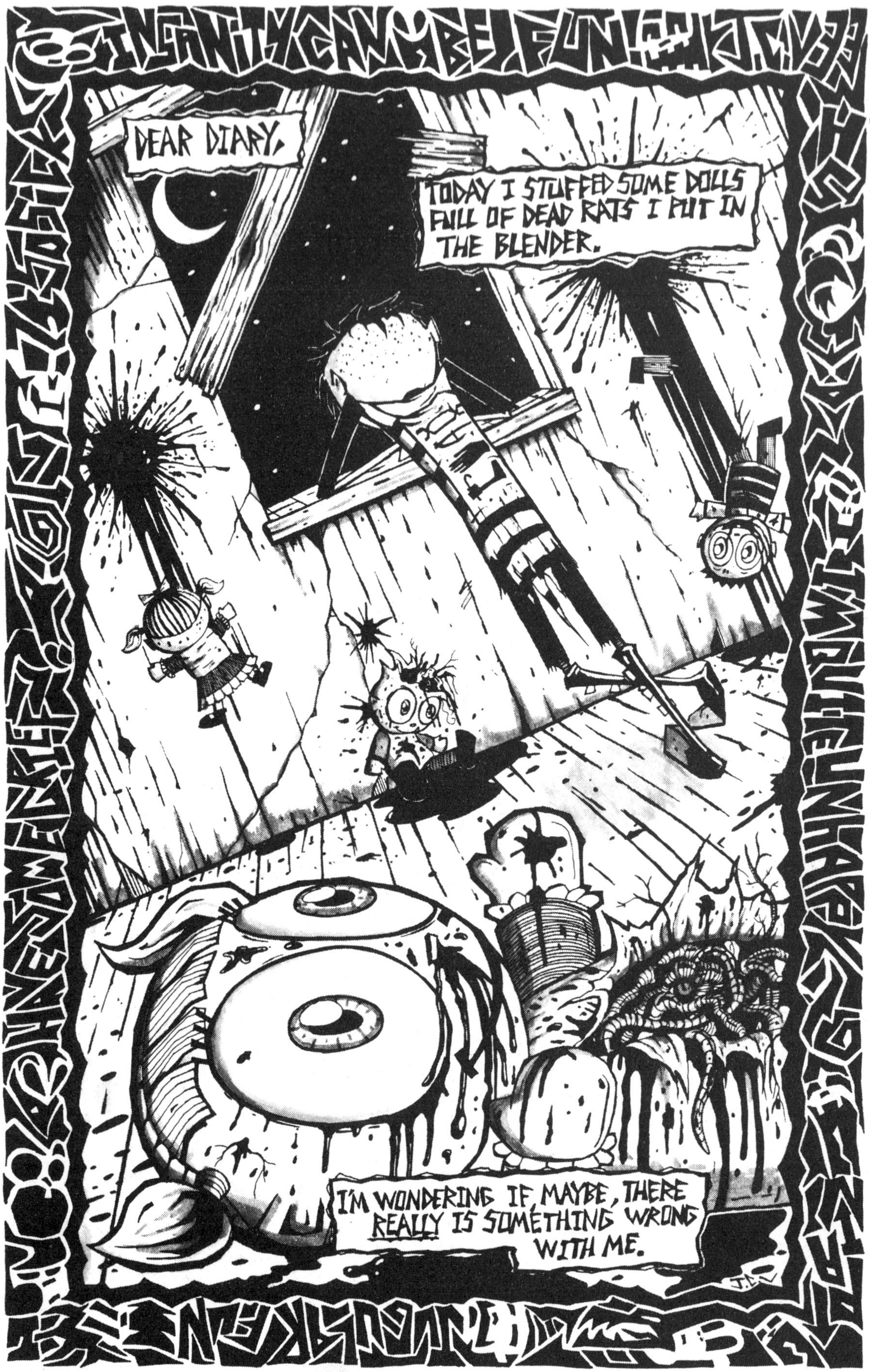
INSANITY CAN BE FUN!
J.C.V.
DEAR DIARY,
TODAY I STUFFED SOME DOLLS FULL OF DEAD RATS I PUT IN THE BLENDER.
I'M WONDERING IF, MAYBE, THERE REALLY IS SOMETHING WRONG WITH ME.
I'M QUITE UNHAPPY
J.C.V.

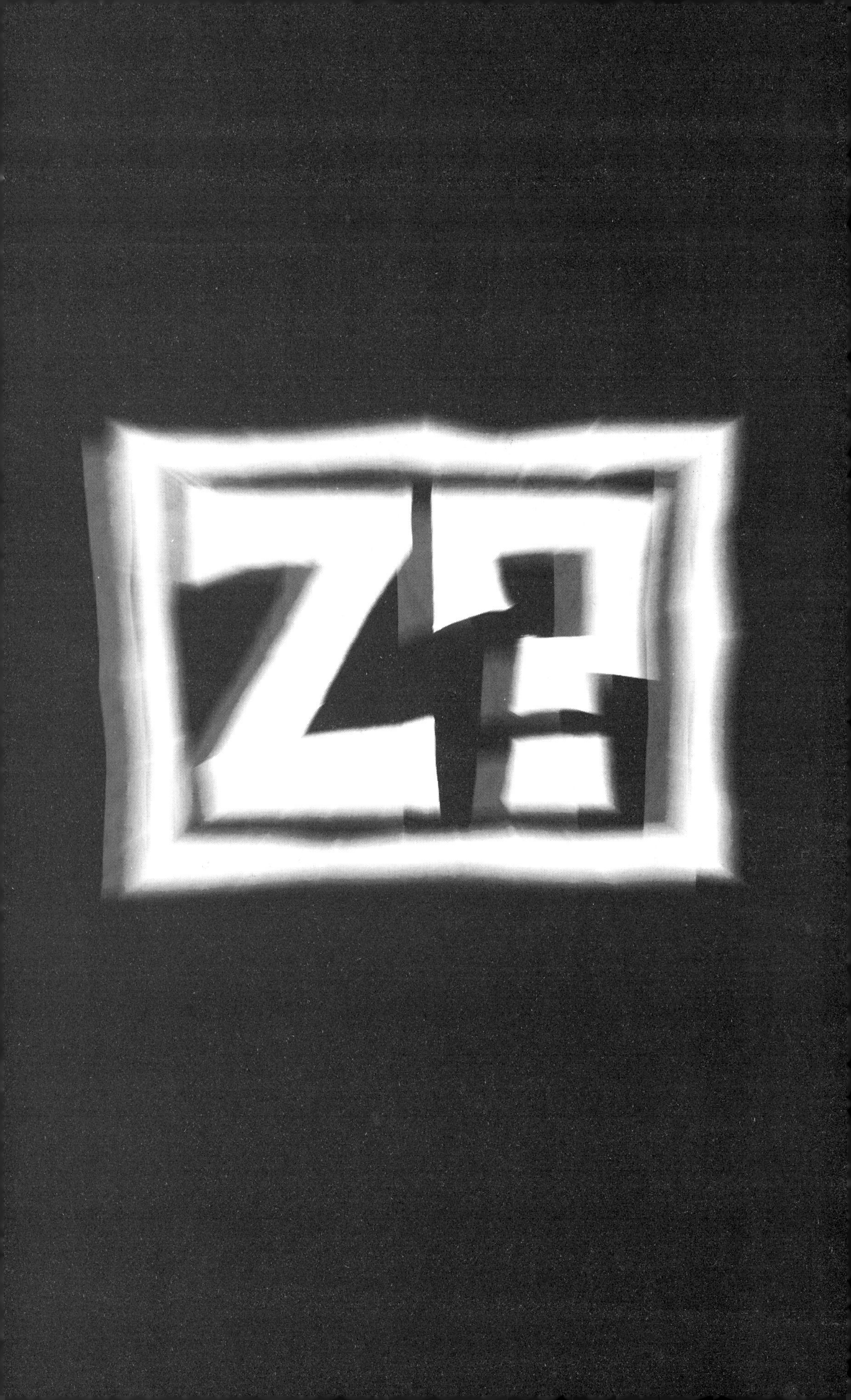

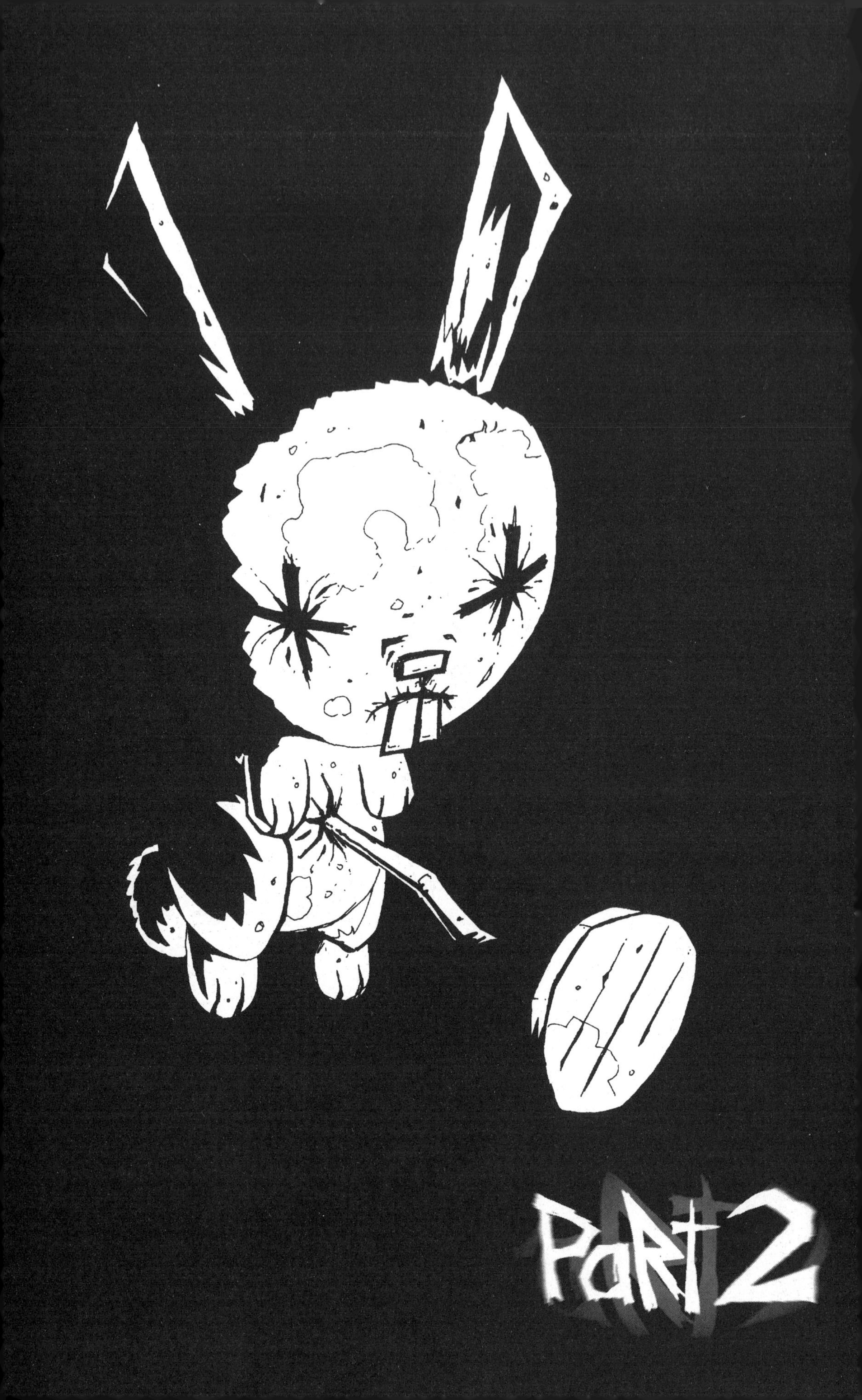
Part 2

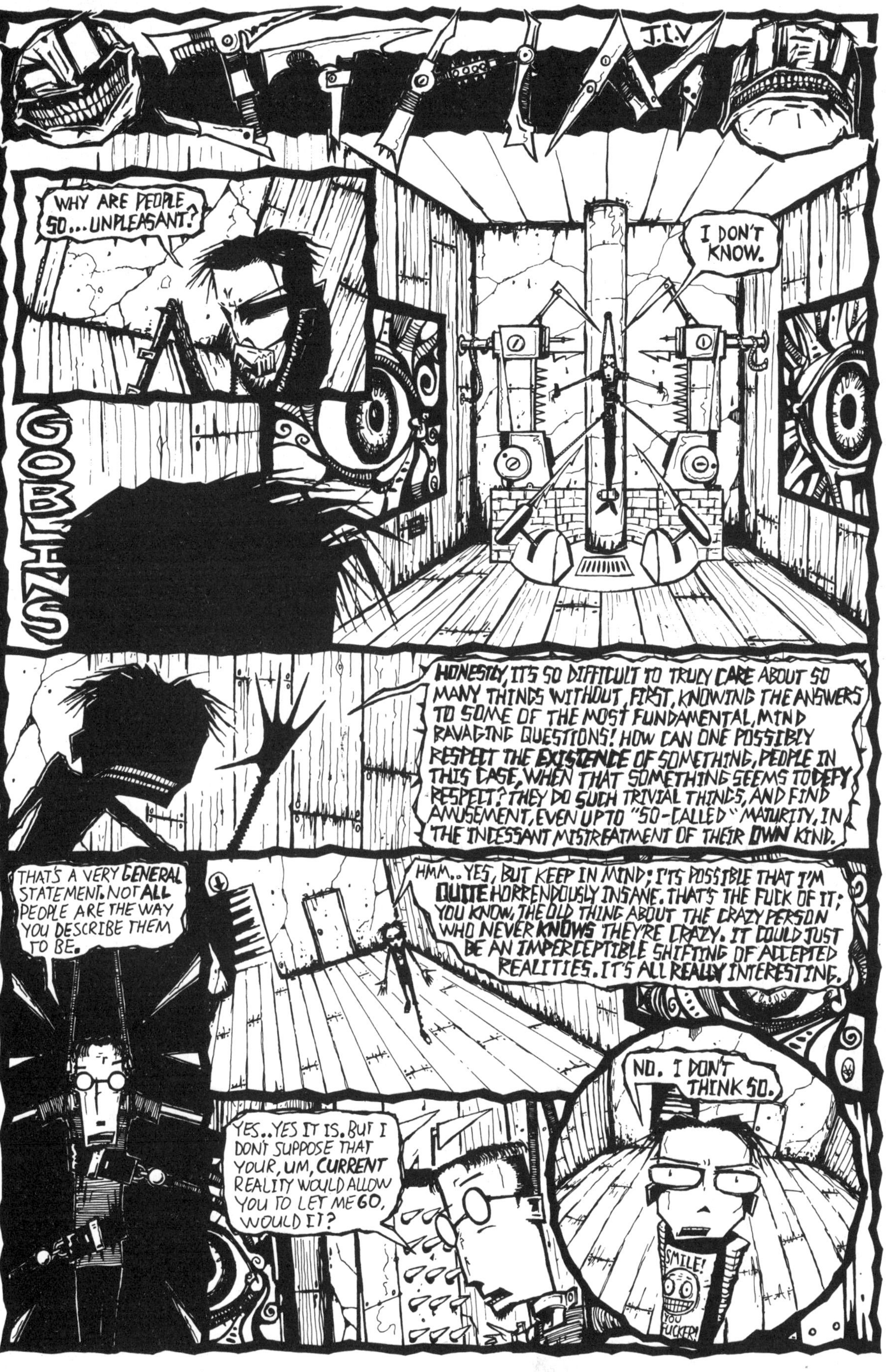
J.C.V
GOBLINS
WHY ARE PEOPLE SO... UNPLEASANT?
I DON'T KNOW.
HONESTLY, IT'S SO DIFFICULT TO TRULY CARE ABOUT SO MANY THINGS WITHOUT, FIRST, KNOWING THE ANSWERS TO SOME OF THE MOST FUNDAMENTAL, MIND RAVAGING QUESTIONS! HOW CAN ONE POSSIBLY RESPECT THE EXISTENCE OF SOMETHING, PEOPLE IN THIS CASE, WHEN THAT SOMETHING SEEMS TO DEFY RESPECT? THEY DO SUCH TRIVIAL THINGS, AND FIND AMUSEMENT, EVEN UP TO "SO-CALLED" MATURITY, IN THE INCESSANT MISTREATMENT OF THEIR OWN KIND.
THAT'S A VERY GENERAL STATEMENT. NOT ALL PEOPLE ARE THE WAY YOU DESCRIBE THEM TO BE.
HMM.. YES, BUT KEEP IN MIND; IT'S POSSIBLE THAT I'M QUITE HORRENDOUSLY INSANE. THAT'S THE FUCK OF IT; YOU KNOW, THE OLD THING ABOUT THE CRAZY PERSON WHO NEVER KNOWS THEY'RE CRAZY. IT COULD JUST BE AN IMPERCEPTIBLE SHIFTING OF ACCEPTED REALITIES. IT'S ALL REALLY INTERESTING.
YES.. YES IT IS. BUT I DON'T SUPPOSE THAT YOUR, UM, CURRENT REALITY WOULD ALLOW YOU TO LET ME GO, WOULD IT?
NO. I DON'T THINK SO.
SMILE! YOU FUCKER!

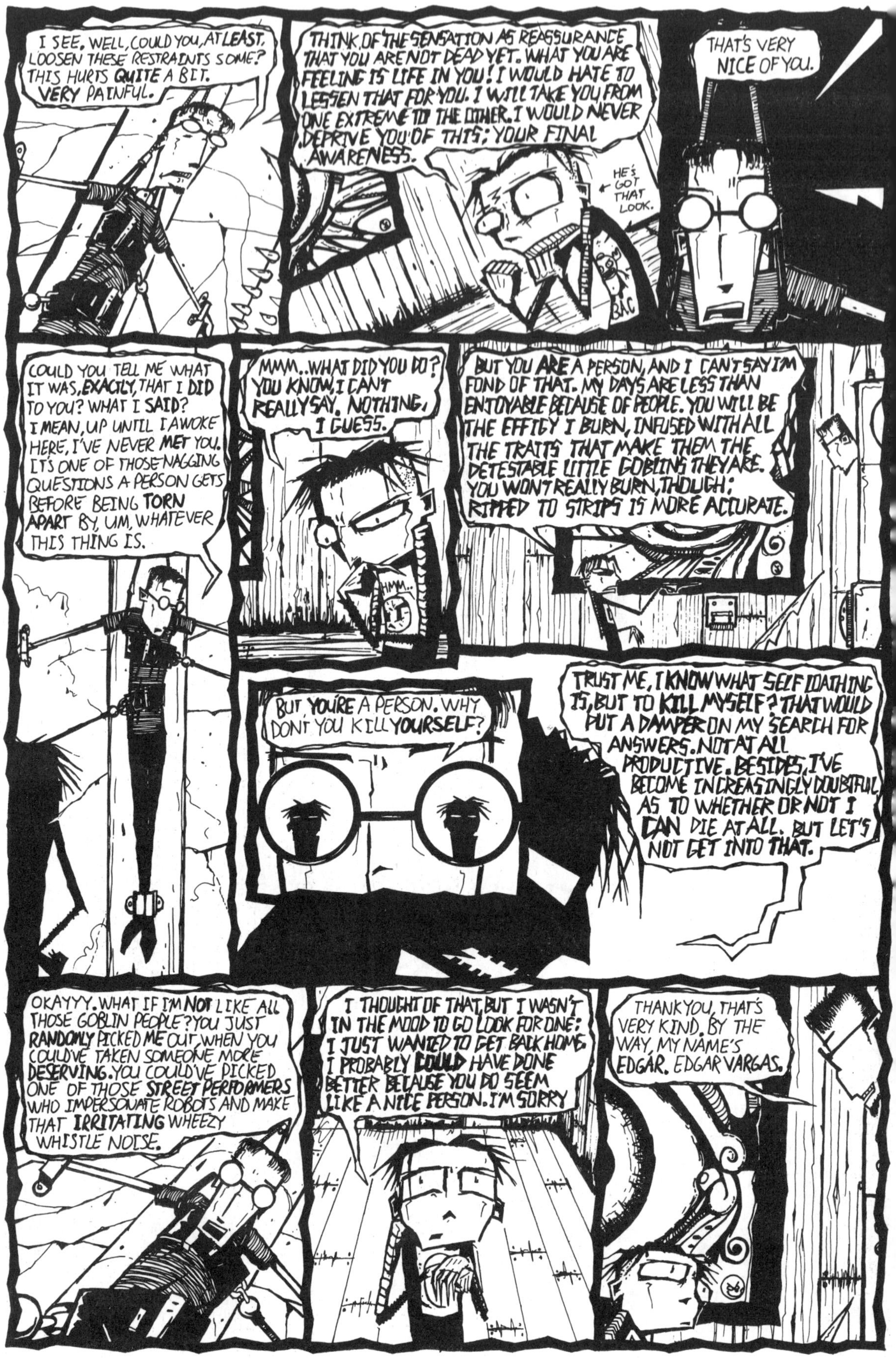
I SEE. WELL, COULD YOU, AT LEAST, LOOSEN THESE RESTRAINTS SOME? THIS HURTS QUITE A BIT. VERY PAINFUL.
THINK OF THE SENSATION AS REASSURANCE THAT YOU ARE NOT DEAD YET. WHAT YOU ARE FEELING IS LIFE IN YOU! I WOULD HATE TO LESSEN THAT FOR YOU. I WILL TAKE YOU FROM ONE EXTREME TO THE OTHER. I WOULD NEVER DEPRIVE YOU OF THIS; YOUR FINAL AWARENESS.
HE'S GOT THAT LOOK.
THAT'S VERY NICE OF YOU.
COULD YOU TELL ME WHAT IT WAS, EXACTLY, THAT I DID TO YOU? WHAT I SAID? I MEAN, UP UNTIL I AWOKE HERE, I'VE NEVER MET YOU. IT'S ONE OF THOSE NAGGING QUESTIONS A PERSON GETS BEFORE BEING TORN APART BY, UM, WHATEVER THIS THING IS.
MMM.. WHAT DID YOU DO? YOU KNOW, I CAN'T REALLY SAY. NOTHING, I GUESS.
HMM..
BUT YOU ARE A PERSON, AND I CAN'T SAY I'M FOND OF THAT. MY DAYS ARE LESS THAN ENJOYABLE BECAUSE OF PEOPLE. YOU WILL BE THE EFFIGY I BURN, INFUSED WITH ALL THE TRAITS THAT MAKE THEM THE DETESTABLE LITTLE GOBLINS THEY ARE. YOU WON'T REALLY BURN, THOUGH; RIPPED TO STRIPS IS MORE ACCURATE.
BUT YOU'RE A PERSON. WHY DON'T YOU KILL YOURSELF?
TRUST ME, I KNOW WHAT SELF LOATHING IS, BUT TO KILL MYSELF? THAT WOULD PUT A DAMPER ON MY SEARCH FOR ANSWERS. NOT AT ALL PRODUCTIVE. BESIDES, I'VE BECOME INCREASINGLY DOUBTFUL AS TO WHETHER OR NOT I CAN DIE AT ALL. BUT LET'S NOT GET INTO THAT.
OKAYYY. WHAT IF I'M NOT LIKE ALL THOSE GOBLIN PEOPLE? YOU JUST RANDOMLY PICKED ME OUT, WHEN YOU COULD'VE TAKEN SOMEONE MORE DESERVING. YOU COULD'VE PICKED ONE OF THOSE STREET PERFORMERS WHO IMPERSONATE ROBOTS AND MAKE THAT IRRITATING WHEEZY WHISTLE NOISE.
I THOUGHT OF THAT, BUT I WASN'T IN THE MOOD TO GO LOOK FOR ONE; I JUST WANTED TO GET BACK HOME. I PROBABLY COULD HAVE DONE BETTER BECAUSE YOU DO SEEM LIKE A NICE PERSON. I'M SORRY
THANK YOU, THAT'S VERY KIND. BY THE WAY, MY NAME'S EDGAR. EDGAR VARGAS.

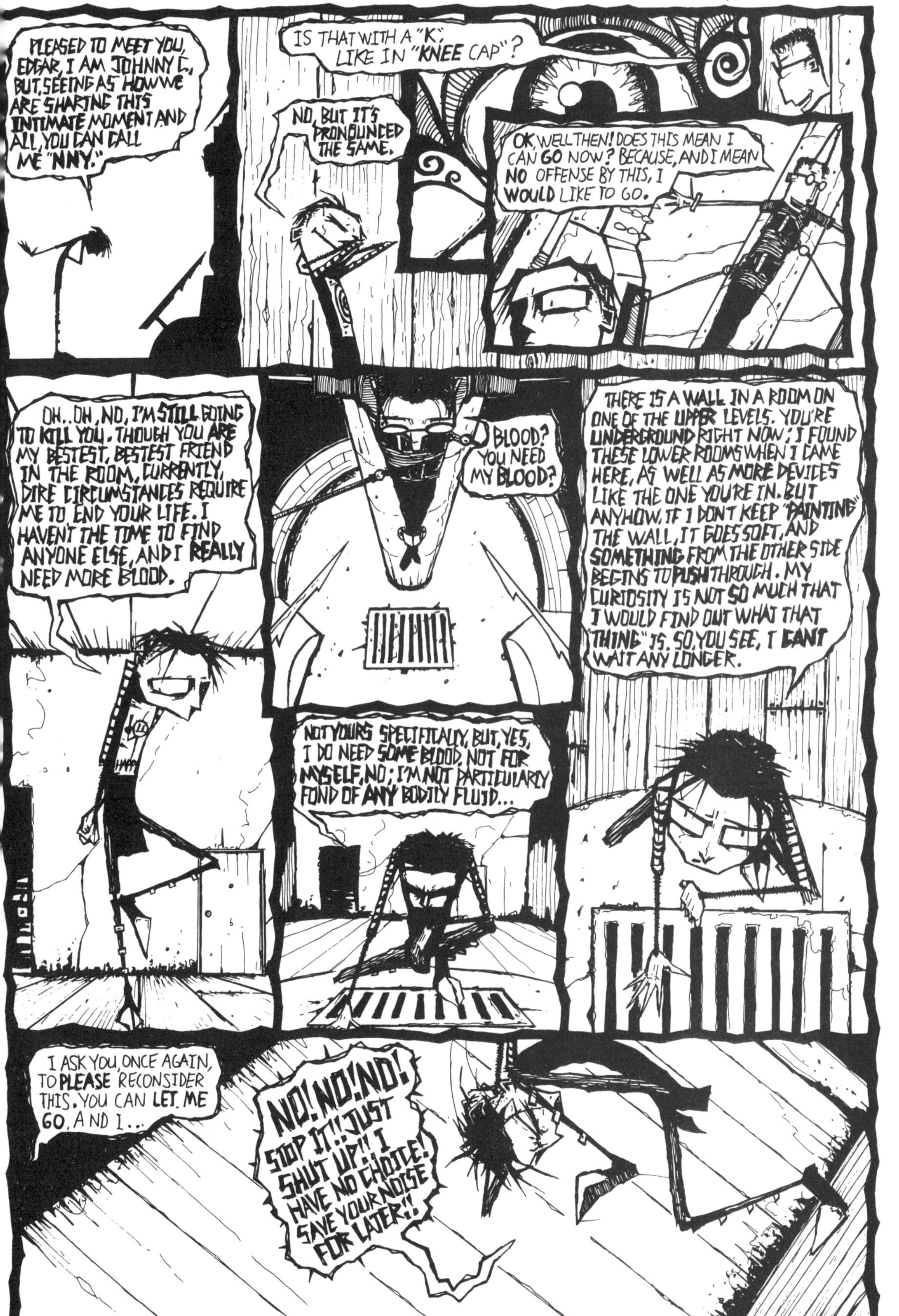
PLEASED TO MEET YOU, EDGAR, I AM JOHNNY C, BUT, SEEING AS HOW WE ARE SHARING THIS INTIMATE MOMENT AND ALL, YOU CAN CALL ME "NNY."
IS THAT WITH A "K," LIKE IN "KNEE CAP"?
NO, BUT IT'S PRONOUNCED THE SAME.
OK, WELL THEN! DOES THIS MEAN I CAN GO NOW? BECAUSE, AND I MEAN NO OFFENSE BY THIS, I WOULD LIKE TO GO.
OH..OH, NO, I'M STILL GOING TO KILL YOU. THOUGH YOU ARE MY BESTEST, BESTEST FRIEND IN THE ROOM, CURRENTLY, DIRE CIRCUMSTANCES REQUIRE ME TO END YOUR LIFE. I HAVEN'T THE TIME TO FIND ANYONE ELSE, AND I REALLY NEED MORE BLOOD.
BLOOD? YOU NEED MY BLOOD?
NOT YOURS SPECIFICALLY, BUT, YES, I DO NEED SOME BLOOD, NOT FOR MYSELF, NO; I'M NOT PARTICULARLY FOND OF ANY BODILY FLUID...
THERE IS A WALL IN A ROOM ON ONE OF THE UPPER LEVELS. YOU'RE UNDERGROUND RIGHT NOW; I FOUND THESE LOWER ROOMS WHEN I CAME HERE, AS WELL AS MORE DEVICES LIKE THE ONE YOU'RE IN. BUT ANYHOW, IF I DON'T KEEP "PAINTING" THE WALL, IT GOES SOFT, AND SOMETHING FROM THE OTHER SIDE BEGINS TO PUSH THROUGH. MY CURIOSITY IS NOT SO MUCH THAT I WOULD FIND OUT WHAT THAT "THING" IS. SO, YOU SEE, I CAN'T WAIT ANY LONGER.
I ASK YOU, ONCE AGAIN, TO PLEASE RECONSIDER THIS. YOU CAN LET ME GO, AND I...
NO! NO! NO! STOP IT!! JUST SHUT UP!! I HAVE NO CHOICE! SAVE YOUR NOISE FOR LATER!!

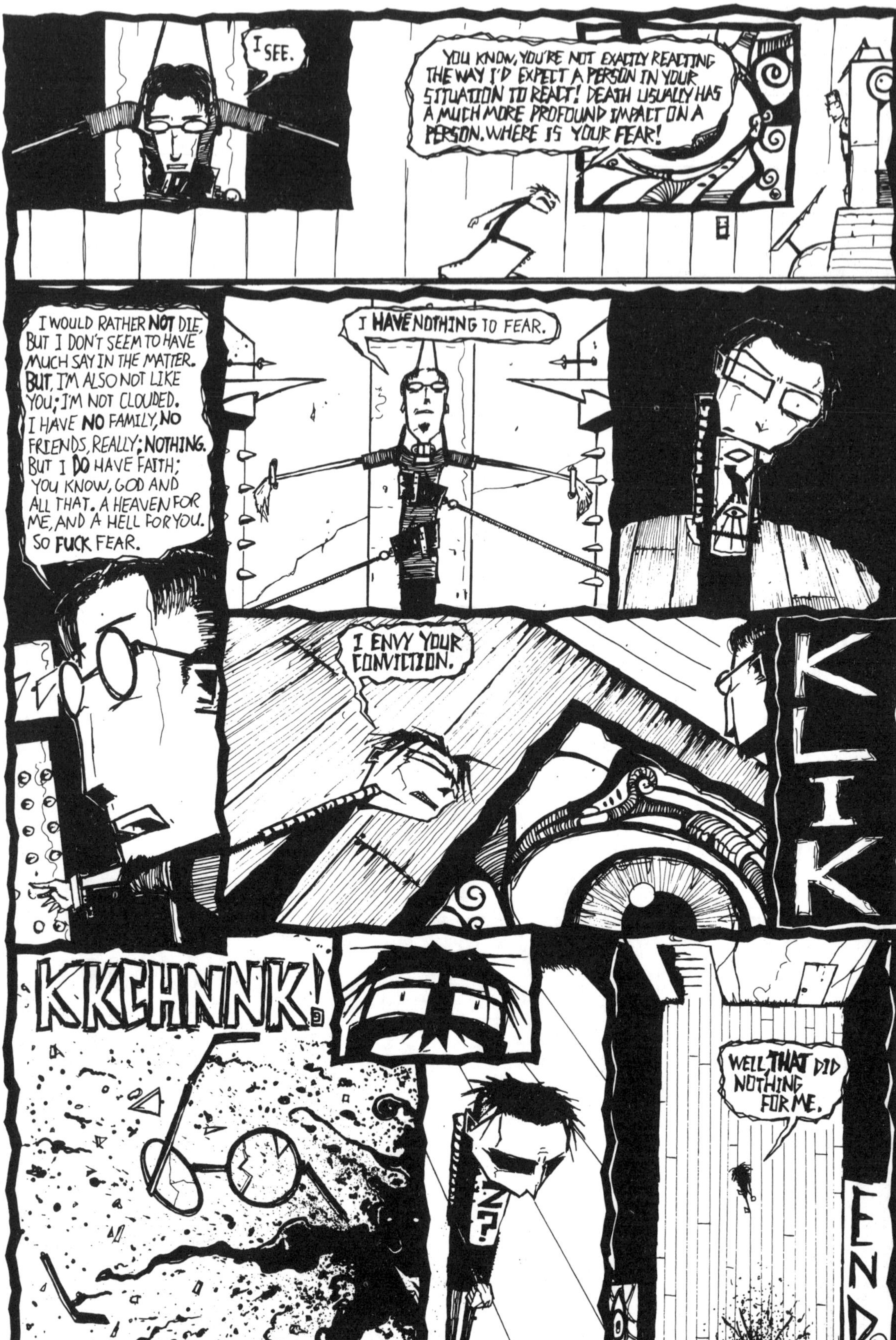
I SEE.
YOU KNOW, YOU'RE NOT EXACTLY REACTING THE WAY I'D EXPECT A PERSON IN YOUR SITUATION TO REACT! DEATH USUALLY HAS A MUCH MORE PROFOUND IMPACT ON A PERSON. WHERE IS YOUR FEAR!
I WOULD RATHER NOT DIE, BUT I DON'T SEEM TO HAVE MUCH SAY IN THE MATTER. BUT, I'M ALSO NOT LIKE YOU; I'M NOT CLOUDED. I HAVE NO FAMILY, NO FRIENDS, REALLY; NOTHING. BUT I DO HAVE FAITH; YOU KNOW, GOD AND ALL THAT. A HEAVEN FOR ME, AND A HELL FOR YOU. SO FUCK FEAR.
I HAVE NOTHING TO FEAR.
I ENVY YOUR CONVICTION.
KLIK
KKCHNNK!
?
WELL, THAT DID NOTHING FOR ME.
END

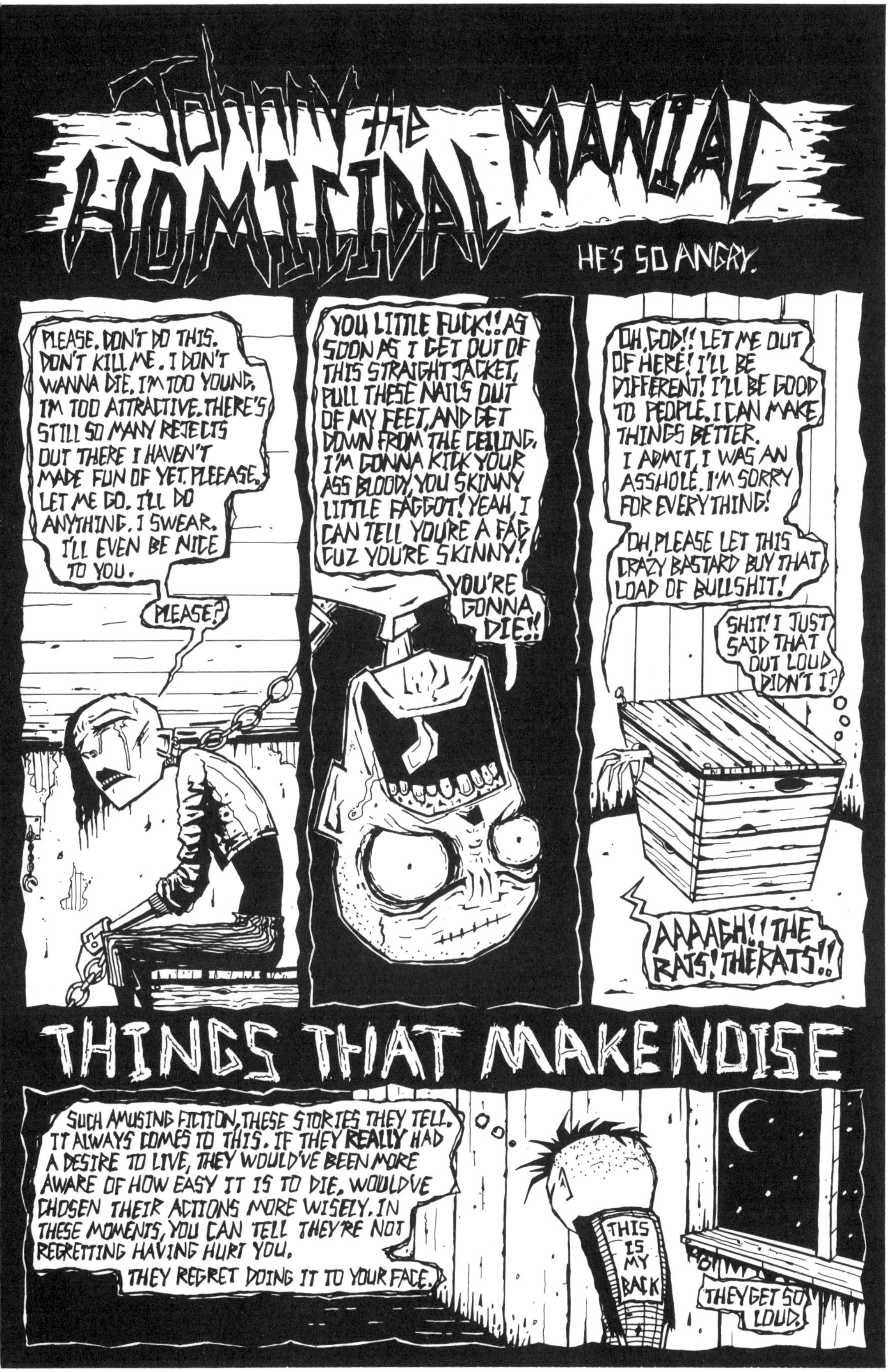
Johnny the HOMICIDAL MANIAC
HE'S SO ANGRY.
PLEASE, DON'T DO THIS. DON'T KILL ME. I DON'T WANNA DIE. I'M TOO YOUNG, I'M TOO ATTRACTIVE. THERE'S STILL SO MANY REJECTS OUT THERE I HAVEN'T MADE FUN OF YET. PLEASE, LET ME GO. I'LL DO ANYTHING. I SWEAR. I'LL EVEN BE NICE TO YOU.
PLEASE?
YOU LITTLE FUCK!! AS SOON AS I GET OUT OF THIS STRAIGHT JACKET, PULL THESE NAILS OUT OF MY FEET, AND GET DOWN FROM THE CEILING, I'M GONNA KICK YOUR ASS BLOODY, YOU SKINNY LITTLE FAGGOT! YEAH, I CAN TELL YOU'RE A FAG CUZ YOU'RE SKINNY!
YOU'RE GONNA DIE!!
OH, GOD!! LET ME OUT OF HERE! I'LL BE DIFFERENT! I'LL BE GOOD TO PEOPLE. I CAN MAKE THINGS BETTER. I ADMIT, I WAS AN ASSHOLE. I'M SORRY FOR EVERYTHING!
OH, PLEASE LET THIS CRAZY BASTARD BUY THAT LOAD OF BULLSHIT!
SHIT! I JUST SAID THAT OUT LOUD DIDN'T I?
AAAAGH!! THE RATS! THE RATS!!
THINGS THAT MAKE NOISE
SUCH AMUSING FICTION, THESE STORIES THEY TELL. IT ALWAYS COMES TO THIS. IF THEY REALLY HAD A DESIRE TO LIVE, THEY WOULD'VE BEEN MORE AWARE OF HOW EASY IT IS TO DIE, WOULD'VE CHOSEN THEIR ACTIONS MORE WISELY. IN THESE MOMENTS, YOU CAN TELL THEY'RE NOT REGRETTING HAVING HURT YOU.
THEY REGRET DOING IT TO YOUR FACE.
THIS IS MY BACK
THEY GET SO LOUD.

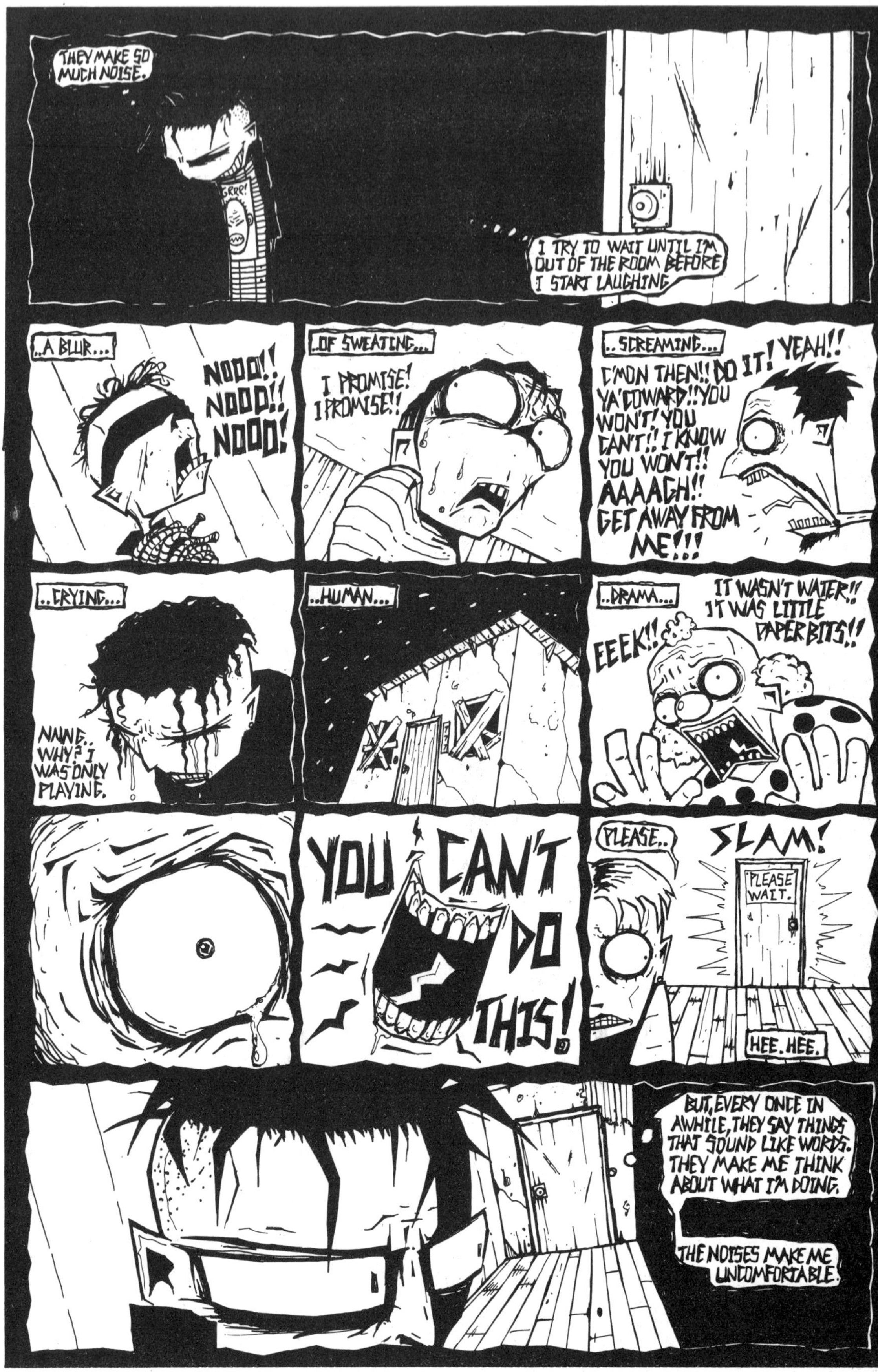

THEY MAKE SO MUCH NOISE.
GRRR!
I TRY TO WAIT UNTIL I'M OUT OF THE ROOM BEFORE I START LAUGHING.
..A BLUR...
NOOO!! NOOO!! NOOO!
..OF SWEATING...
I PROMISE! I PROMISE!!
..SCREAMING...
C'MON THEN!! DO IT! YEAH!! YA' COWARD!! YOU WON'T! YOU CAN'T!! I KNOW YOU WON'T!! AAAAGH!! GET AWAY FROM ME!!!
..CRYING...
NNNG.. WHY? I WAS ONLY PLAYING.
..HUMAN...
..DRAMA...
IT WASN'T WATER!! IT WAS LITTLE PAPERBITS!!
EEEK!!
YOU CAN'T DO THIS!
PLEASE..
SLAM!
PLEASE WAIT.
HEE. HEE.
BUT, EVERY ONCE IN AWHILE, THEY SAY THINGS THAT SOUND LIKE WORDS. THEY MAKE ME THINK ABOUT WHAT I'M DOING.
THE NOISES MAKE ME UNCOMFORTABLE.

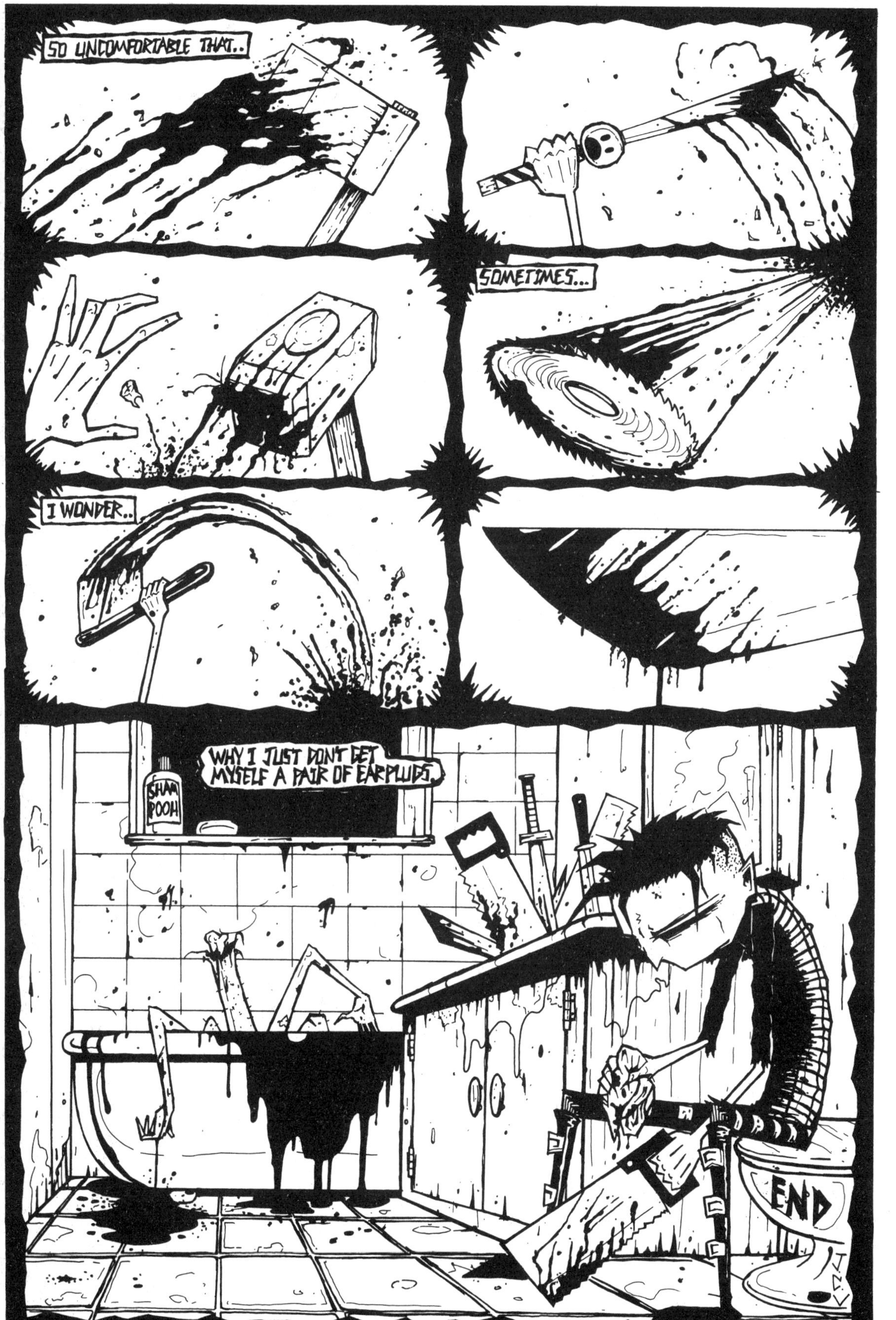

SO UNCOMFORTABLE THAT..
SOMETIMES...
I WONDER..
WHY I JUST DON'T GET MYSELF A PAIR OF EARPLUGS.
SHAM POOH
END

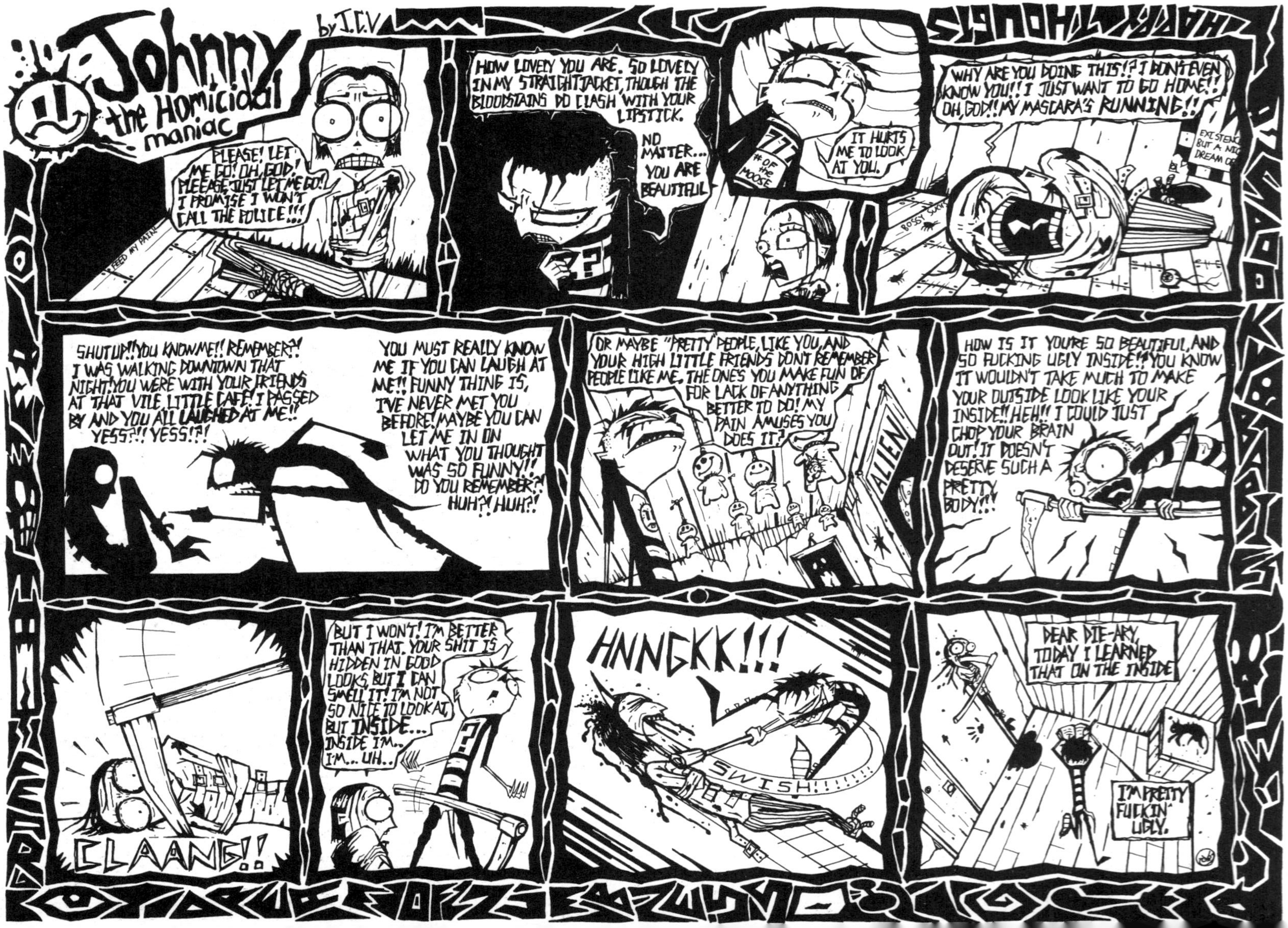
Johnny the Homicidal maniac
by J.C.V.
PLEASE! LET ME GO! OH, GOD, PLEASE JUST LET ME GO! I PROMISE I WON'T CALL THE POLICE!!!
FEED MY PAIN
HOW LOVELY YOU ARE. SO LOVELY IN MY STRAIGHTJACKET, THOUGH THE BLOODSTAINS DO CLASH WITH YOUR LIPSTICK.
NO MATTER... YOU ARE BEAUTIFUL
IT HURTS ME TO LOOK AT YOU.
OF the MOOSE
WHY ARE YOU DOING THIS!? I DON'T EVEN KNOW YOU!! I JUST WANT TO GO HOME!! OH, GOD!! MY MASCARA'S RUNNING!!
BOSSY
SHUT UP!! YOU KNOW ME!! REMEMBER?! I WAS WALKING DOWNTOWN THAT NIGHT! YOU WERE WITH YOUR FRIENDS AT THAT VILE LITTLE CAFE! I PASSED BY AND YOU ALL LAUGHED AT ME!! YESS?!! YESS!?!
YOU MUST REALLY KNOW ME IF YOU CAN LAUGH AT ME!! FUNNY THING IS, I'VE NEVER MET YOU BEFORE! MAYBE YOU CAN LET ME IN ON WHAT YOU THOUGHT WAS SO FUNNY!! DO YOU REMEMBER?! HUH?! HUH?!
OR MAYBE "PRETTY" PEOPLE, LIKE YOU, AND YOUR HIGH LITTLE FRIENDS DON'T REMEMBER PEOPLE LIKE ME. THE ONES YOU MAKE FUN OF FOR LACK OF ANYTHING BETTER TO DO! MY PAIN AMUSES YOU DOES IT?
ALIEN
HOW IS IT YOU'RE SO BEAUTIFUL, AND SO FUCKING UGLY INSIDE!? YOU KNOW IT WOULDN'T TAKE MUCH TO MAKE YOUR OUTSIDE LOOK LIKE YOUR INSIDE!! HEH!! I COULD JUST CHOP YOUR BRAIN OUT! IT DOESN'T DESERVE SUCH A PRETTY BODY!!!
CLAANG!!
BUT I WON'T! I'M BETTER THAN THAT. YOUR SHIT IS HIDDEN IN GOOD LOOKS, BUT I CAN SMELL IT! I'M NOT SO NICE TO LOOK AT, BUT INSIDE... INSIDE I'M... I'M... UH..
HNNGKK!!!
SWISH!!!!!!!
DEAR DIE-ARY, TODAY I LEARNED THAT ON THE INSIDE
I'M PRETTY FUCKIN' UGLY.

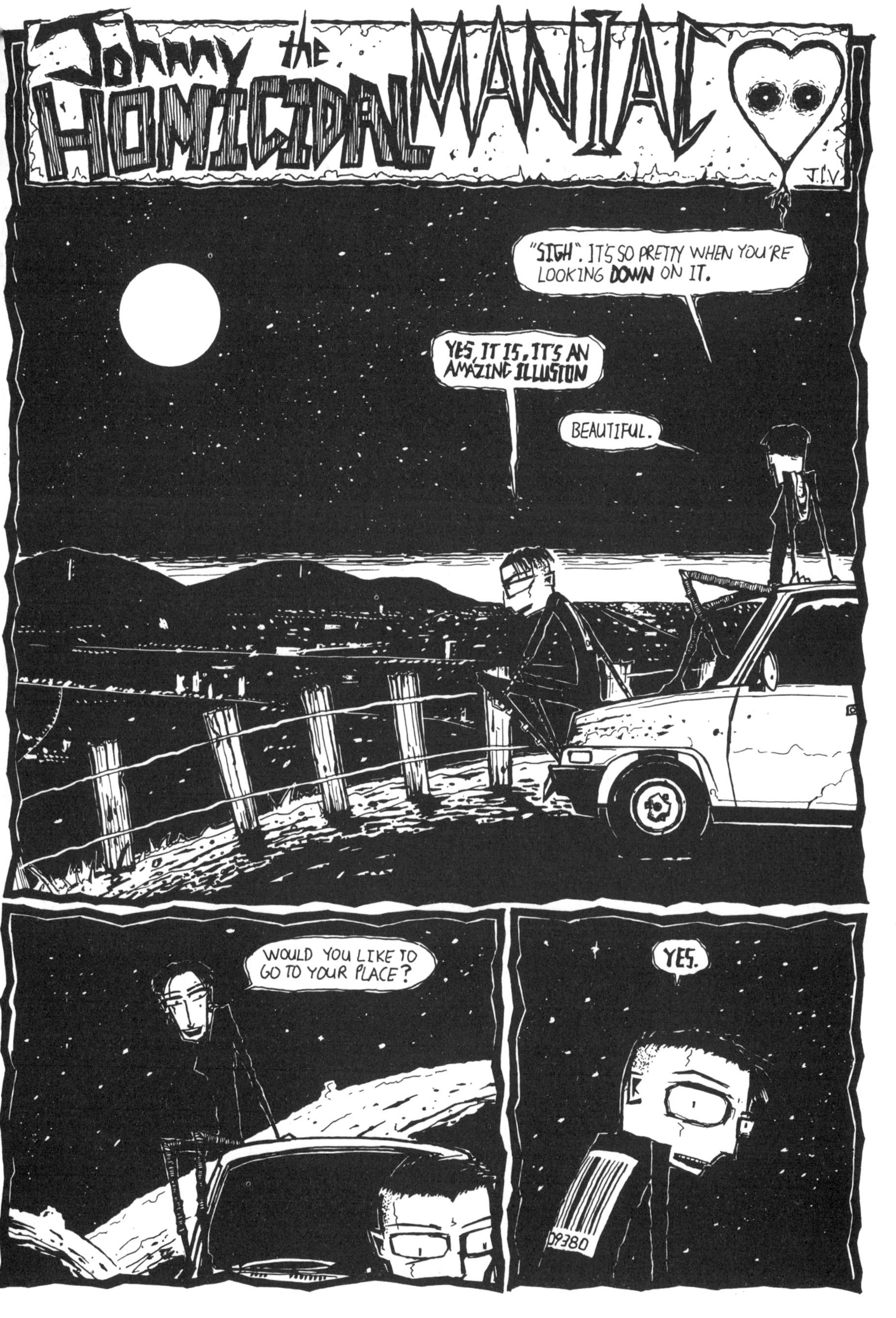
Johnny the HOMICIDAL MANIAC
J.I.V.
"SIGH". IT'S SO PRETTY WHEN YOU'RE LOOKING DOWN ON IT.
YES, IT IS. IT'S AN AMAZING ILLUSION
BEAUTIFUL.
WOULD YOU LIKE TO GO TO YOUR PLACE?
YES.

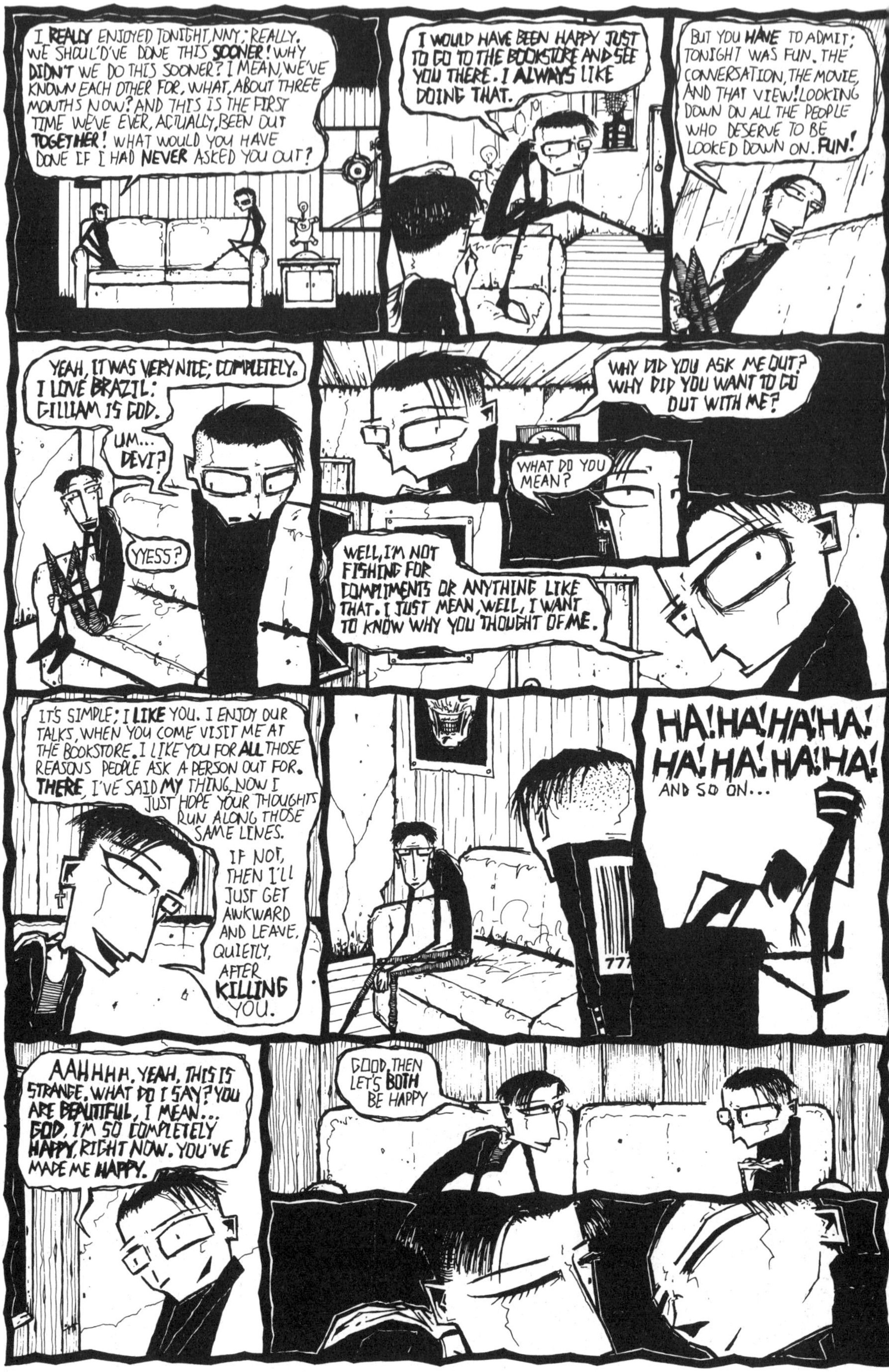
I REALLY ENJOYED TONIGHT, NNY; REALLY. WE SHOULD'VE DONE THIS SOONER! WHY DIDN'T WE DO THIS SOONER? I MEAN, WE'VE KNOWN EACH OTHER FOR, WHAT, ABOUT THREE MONTHS NOW? AND THIS IS THE FIRST TIME WE'VE EVER, ACTUALLY, BEEN OUT TOGETHER! WHAT WOULD YOU HAVE DONE IF I HAD NEVER ASKED YOU OUT?
I WOULD HAVE BEEN HAPPY JUST TO GO TO THE BOOKSTORE AND SEE YOU THERE. I ALWAYS LIKE DOING THAT.
BUT YOU HAVE TO ADMIT; TONIGHT WAS FUN. THE CONVERSATION, THE MOVIE, AND THAT VIEW! LOOKING DOWN ON ALL THE PEOPLE WHO DESERVE TO BE LOOKED DOWN ON. FUN!
YEAH, IT WAS VERY NICE; COMPLETELY. I LOVE BRAZIL: GILLIAM IS GOD.
UM... DEVI?
YYESS?
WHY DID YOU ASK ME OUT? WHY DID YOU WANT TO GO OUT WITH ME?
WHAT DO YOU MEAN?
WELL, I'M NOT FISHING FOR COMPLIMENTS OR ANYTHING LIKE THAT. I JUST MEAN, WELL, I WANT TO KNOW WHY YOU THOUGHT OF ME.
IT'S SIMPLE; I LIKE YOU. I ENJOY OUR TALKS, WHEN YOU COME VISIT ME AT THE BOOKSTORE. I LIKE YOU FOR ALL THOSE REASONS PEOPLE ASK A PERSON OUT FOR. THERE, I'VE SAID MY THING. NOW I JUST HOPE YOUR THOUGHTS RUN ALONG THOSE SAME LINES.
IF NOT, THEN I'LL JUST GET AWKWARD AND LEAVE, QUIETLY, AFTER KILLING YOU.
HA! HA! HA! HA! HA! HA! HA! HA!
AND SO ON...
AAHHHH. YEAH, THIS IS STRANGE. WHAT DO I SAY? YOU ARE BEAUTIFUL, I MEAN... GOD, I'M SO COMPLETELY HAPPY, RIGHT NOW. YOU'VE MADE ME HAPPY.
GOOD, THEN LET'S BOTH BE HAPPY

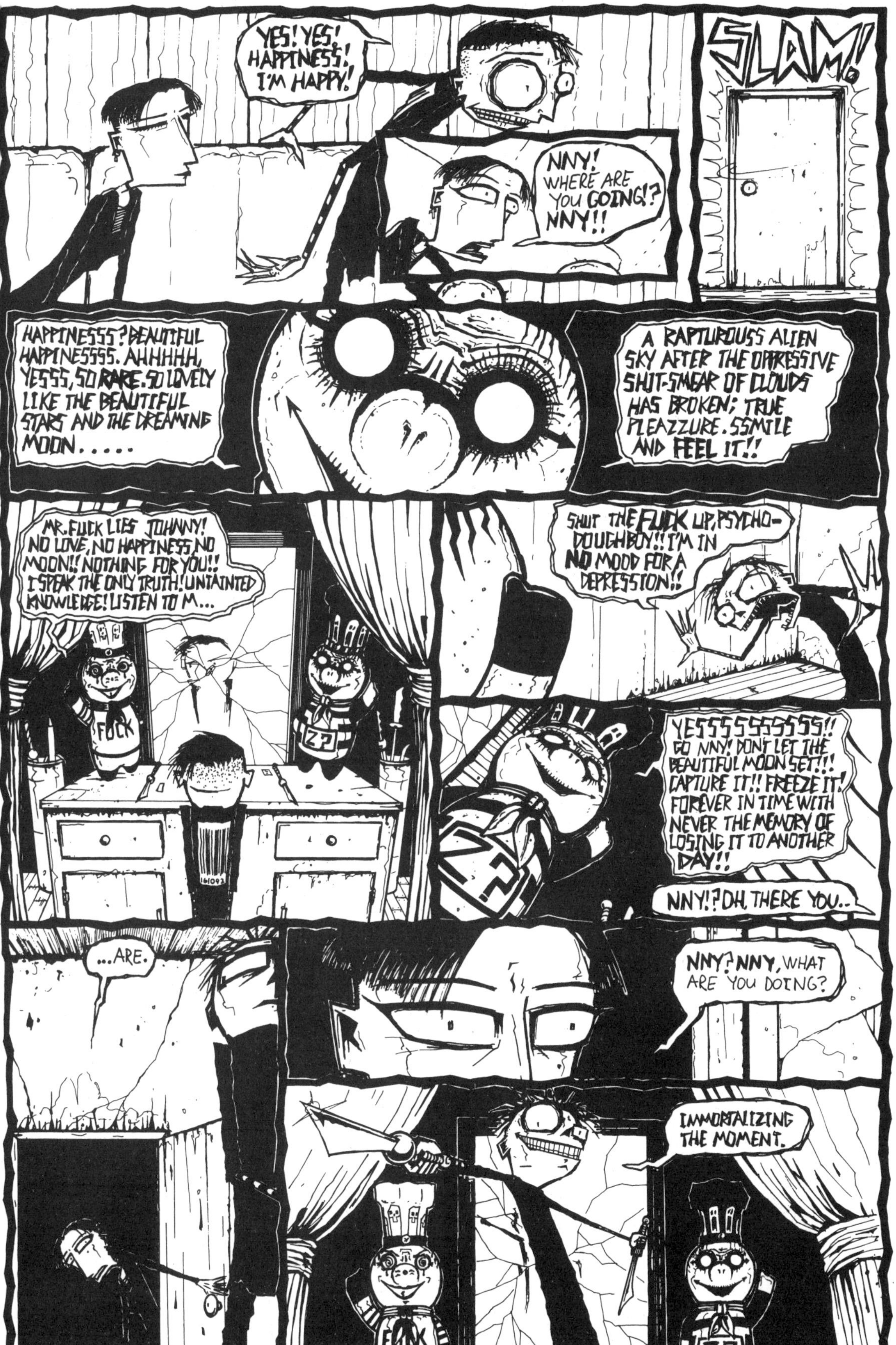
YES! YES! HAPPINESS! I'M HAPPY!
NNY! WHERE ARE YOU GOING!? NNY!!
SLAM!
HAPPINESSS? BEAUTIFUL HAPPINESSSS. AHHHHH, YESSS, SO RARE. SO LOVELY LIKE THE BEAUTIFUL STARS AND THE DREAMING MOON.....
A RAPTUROUSS ALIEN SKY AFTER THE OPPRESSIVE SHIT-SMEAR OF CLOUDS HAS BROKEN; TRUE PLEAZZURE. SSMILE AND FEEL IT!!
MR. FUCK LIES JOHNNY! NO LOVE, NO HAPPINESS, NO MOON!! NOTHING FOR YOU!! I SPEAK THE ONLY TRUTH! UNTAINTED KNOWLEDGE! LISTEN TO M...
SHUT THE FUCK UP, PSYCHO-DOUGHBOY!! I'M IN NO MOOD FOR A DEPRESSION!!
YESSSSSSSSSS!! GO NNY! DON'T LET THE BEAUTIFUL MOON SET!! CAPTURE IT!! FREEZE IT! FOREVER IN TIME WITH NEVER THE MEMORY OF LOSING IT TO ANOTHER DAY!!
NNY!? OH, THERE YOU..
...ARE.
NNY? NNY, WHAT ARE YOU DOING?
IMMORTALIZING THE MOMENT.

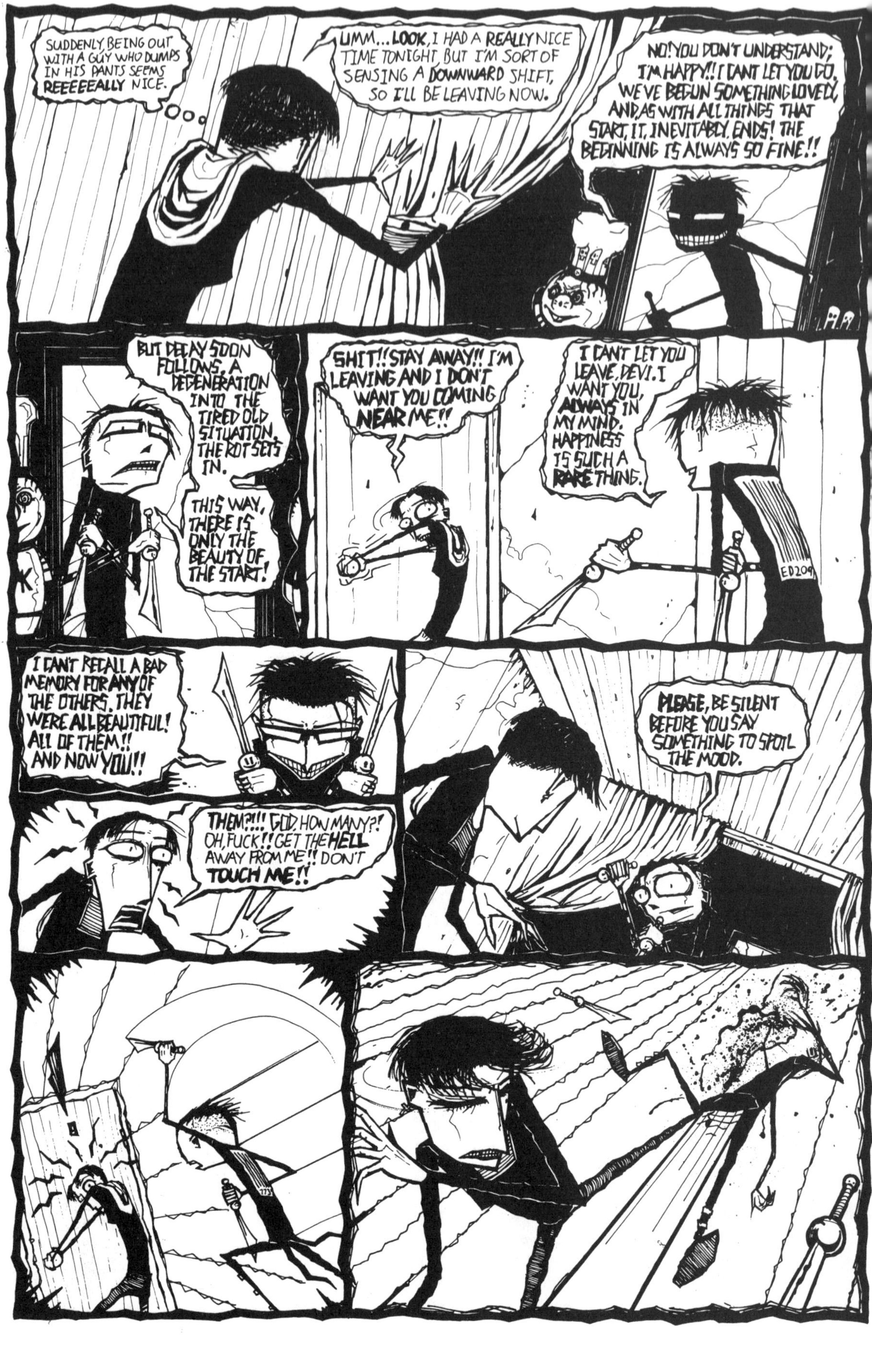
SUDDENLY, BEING OUT WITH A GUY WHO DUMPS IN HIS PANTS SEEMS REEEEEALLY NICE.
UMM... LOOK, I HAD A REALLY NICE TIME TONIGHT, BUT I'M SORT OF SENSING A DOWNWARD SHIFT, SO I'LL BE LEAVING NOW.
NO! YOU DON'T UNDERSTAND; I'M HAPPY!! I CANT LET YOU GO. WE'VE BEGUN SOMETHING LOVELY, AND, AS WITH ALL THINGS THAT START, IT, INEVITABLY, ENDS! THE BEGINNING IS ALWAYS SO FINE!!
BUT DECAY SOON FOLLOWS, A DEGENERATION INTO THE TIRED OLD SITUATION. THE ROT SETS IN.
THIS WAY, THERE IS ONLY THE BEAUTY OF THE START!
SHIT!! STAY AWAY!! I'M LEAVING AND I DON'T WANT YOU COMING NEAR ME!!
I CAN'T LET YOU LEAVE, DEVI. I WANT YOU, ALWAYS IN MY MIND. HAPPINESS IS SUCH A RARE THING.
I CAN'T RECALL A BAD MEMORY FOR ANY OF THE OTHERS. THEY WERE ALL BEAUTIFUL! ALL OF THEM!! AND NOW YOU!!
PLEASE, BE SILENT BEFORE YOU SAY SOMETHING TO SPOIL THE MOOD.
THEM?!!! GOD, HOW MANY?! OH, FUCK!! GET THE HELL AWAY FROM ME!! DON'T TOUCH ME!!

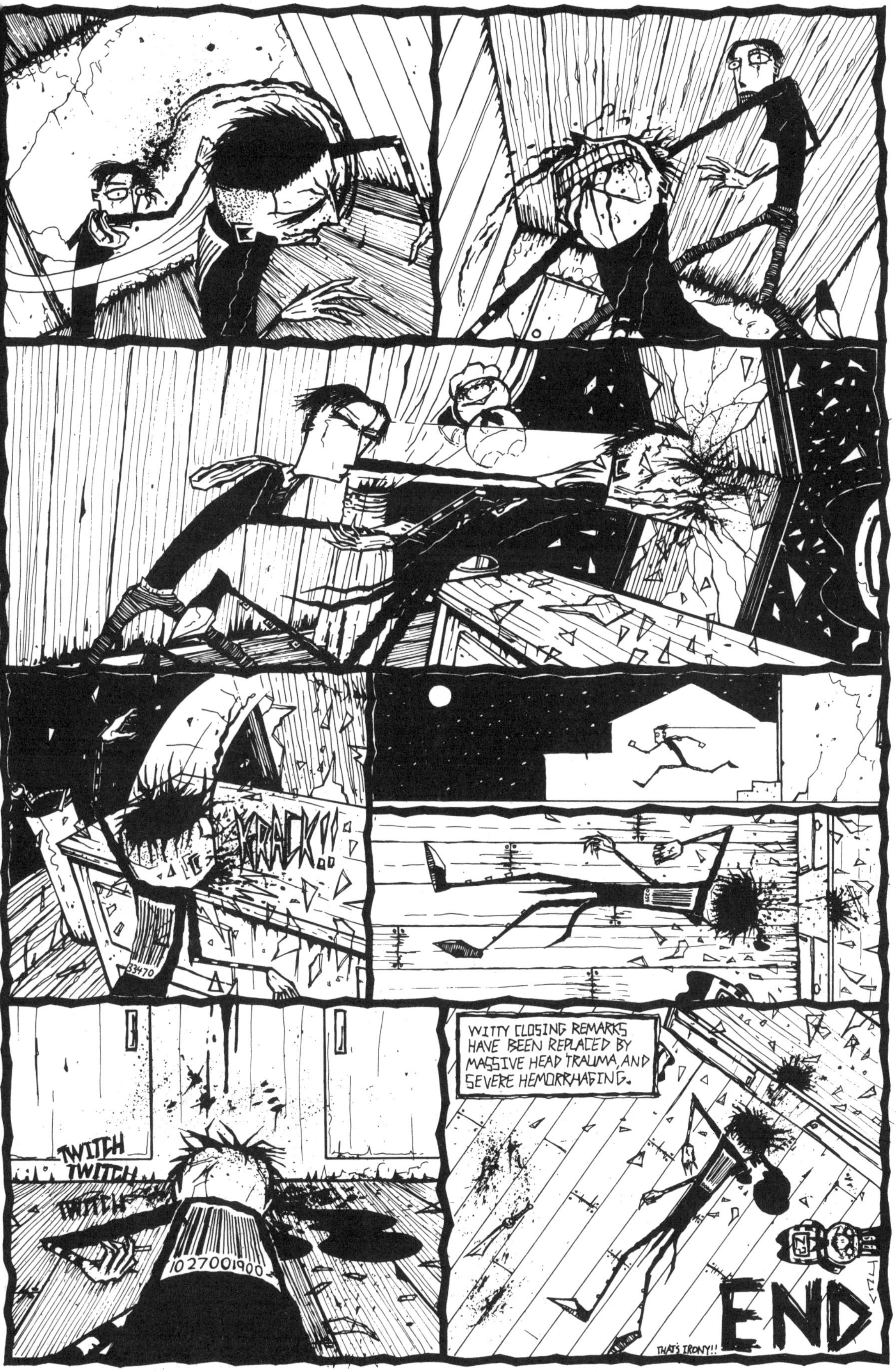
KRACK!!
TWITCH
TWITCH
TWITCH
WITTY CLOSING REMARKS HAVE BEEN REPLACED BY MASSIVE HEAD TRAUMA, AND SEVERE HEMORRHAGING.
END
THAT'S IRONY!!

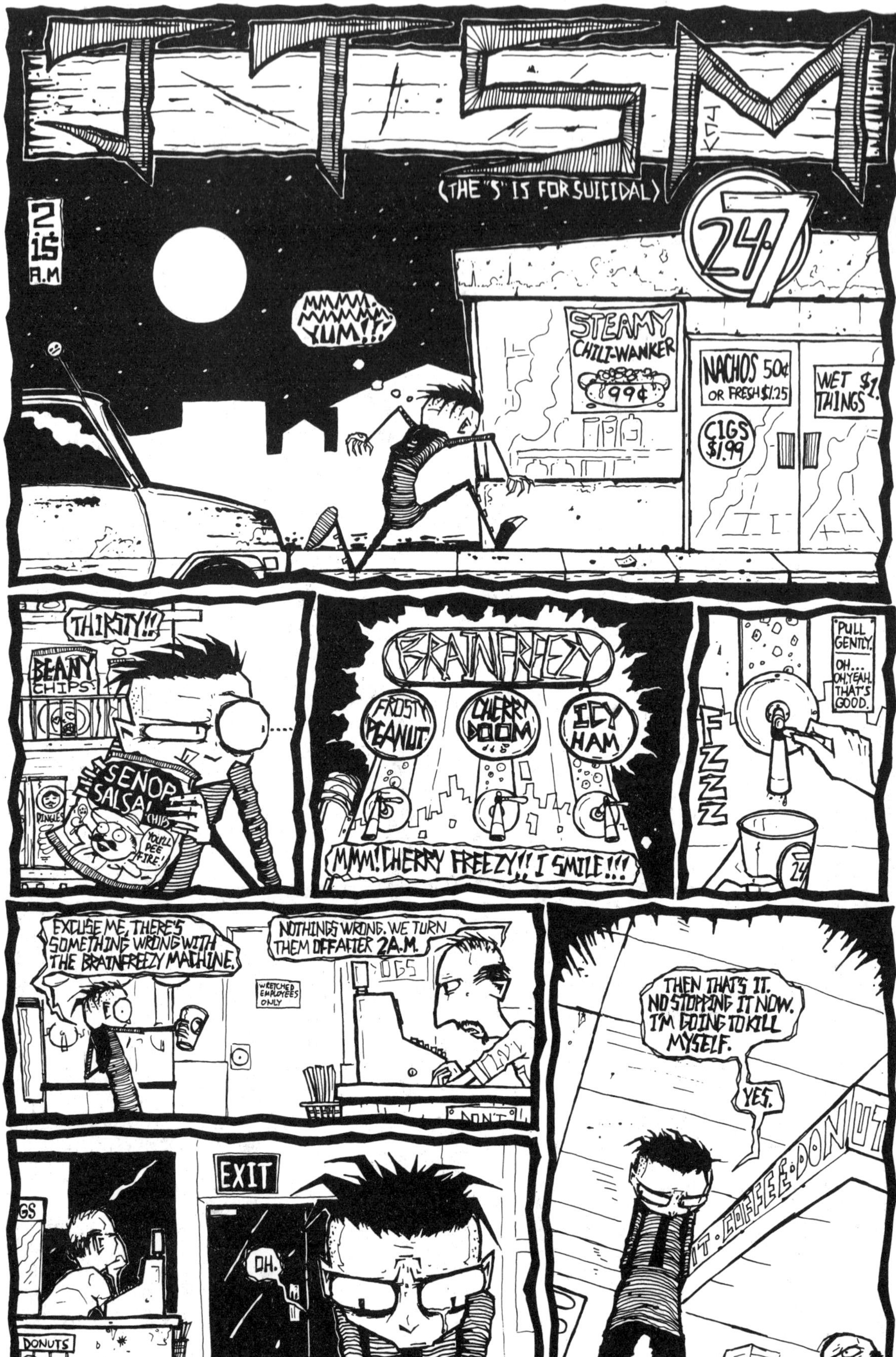
JTHM
JCV
(THE "S" IS FOR SUICIDAL)
2:15 A.M
24/7
MMMM... MMMMM YUM!!!
STEAMY CHILI-WANKER 99¢
NACHOS 50¢ OR FRESH $1.25
WET THINGS $1.
CIGS $1.99
THIRSTY!!
BEANY CHIPS
SEÑOR SALSA! CHIPS
YOU'LL PEE FIRE!
PINGLES
BRAINFREEZY
FROSTY PEANUT
CHERRY DOOM
ICY HAM
MMM! CHERRY FREEZY!! I SMILE!!!
PULL GENTLY.
OH... OH, YEAH. THAT'S GOOD.
FZZZZ
EXCUSE ME, THERE'S SOMETHING WRONG WITH THE BRAINFREEZY MACHINE.
NOTHING'S WRONG. WE TURN THEM OFF AFTER 2A.M.
WRETCHED EMPLOYEES ONLY
THEN THAT'S IT. NO STOPPING IT NOW. I'M GOING TO KILL MYSELF.
YES.
COFFEE·DONUT
EXIT
OH.
DONUTS

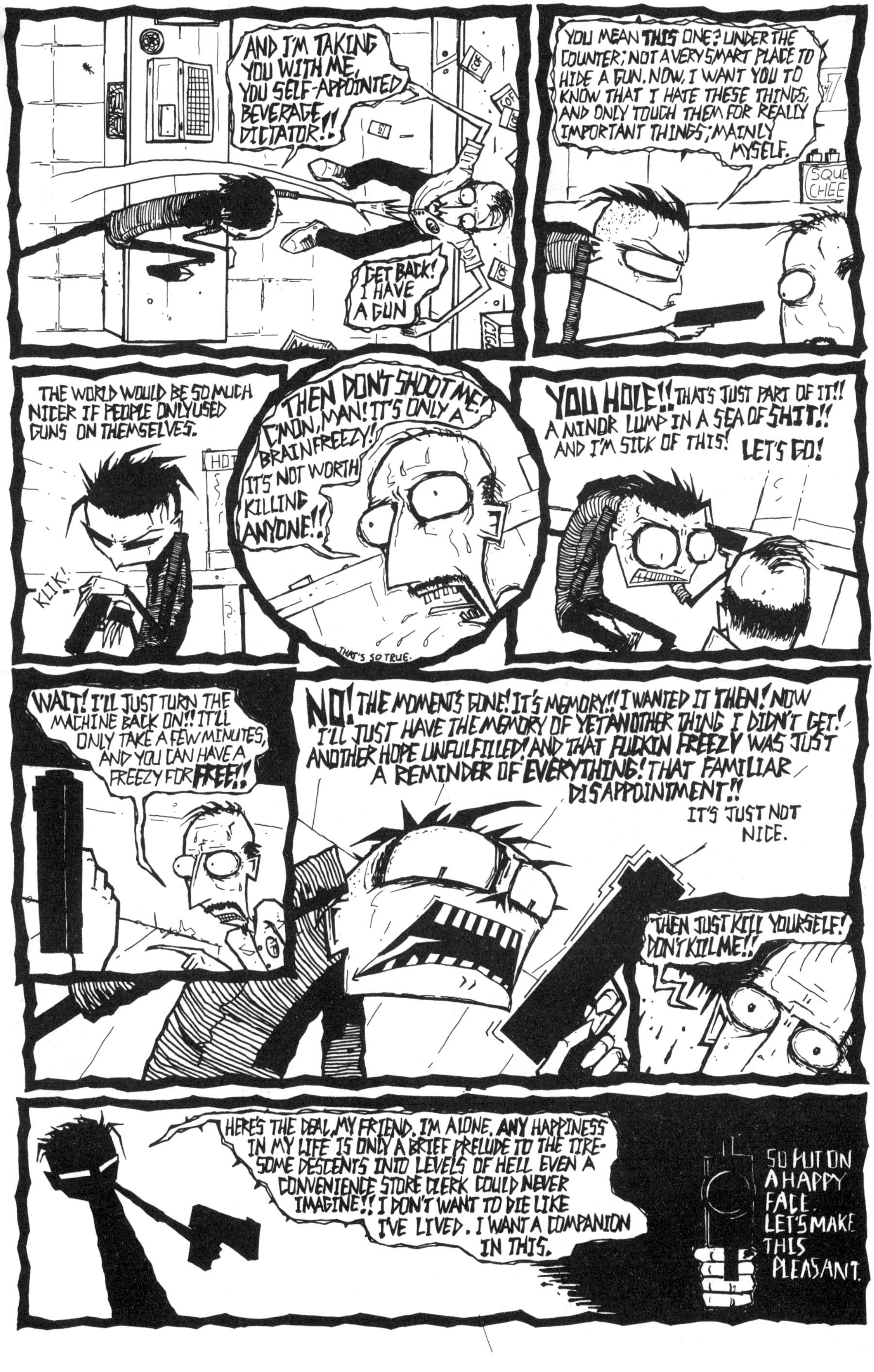
AND I'M TAKING YOU WITH ME, YOU SELF-APPOINTED BEVERAGE DICTATOR!!
GET BACK! I HAVE A GUN
YOU MEAN THIS ONE? UNDER THE COUNTER; NOT A VERY SMART PLACE TO HIDE A GUN. NOW, I WANT YOU TO KNOW THAT I HATE THESE THINGS, AND ONLY TOUCH THEM FOR REALLY IMPORTANT THINGS; MAINLY MYSELF.
THE WORLD WOULD BE SO MUCH NICER IF PEOPLE ONLY USED GUNS ON THEMSELVES.
KLIK!
THEN DON'T SHOOT ME! C'MON, MAN! IT'S ONLY A BRAINFREEZY! IT'S NOT WORTH KILLING ANYONE!!
THAT'S SO TRUE.
YOU HOLE!! THAT'S JUST PART OF IT!! A MINOR LUMP IN A SEA OF SHIT!! AND I'M SICK OF THIS!
LET'S GO!
WAIT! I'LL JUST TURN THE MACHINE BACK ON!! IT'LL ONLY TAKE A FEW MINUTES, AND YOU CAN HAVE A FREEZY FOR FREE!!
NO! THE MOMENT'S GONE! IT'S MEMORY!! I WANTED IT THEN! NOW I'LL JUST HAVE THE MEMORY OF YET ANOTHER THING I DIDN'T GET! ANOTHER HOPE UNFULFILLED! AND THAT FUCKIN FREEZY WAS JUST A REMINDER OF EVERYTHING! THAT FAMILIAR DISAPPOINTMENT!!
IT'S JUST NOT NICE.
THEN JUST KILL YOURSELF! DON'T KILL ME!!
HERE'S THE DEAL, MY FRIEND. I'M ALONE. ANY HAPPINESS IN MY LIFE IS ONLY A BRIEF PRELUDE TO THE TIRESOME DESCENTS INTO LEVELS OF HELL EVEN A CONVENIENCE STORE CLERK COULD NEVER IMAGINE!! I DON'T WANT TO DIE LIKE I'VE LIVED. I WANT A COMPANION IN THIS.
SO PUT ON A HAPPY FACE. LET'S MAKE THIS PLEASANT.

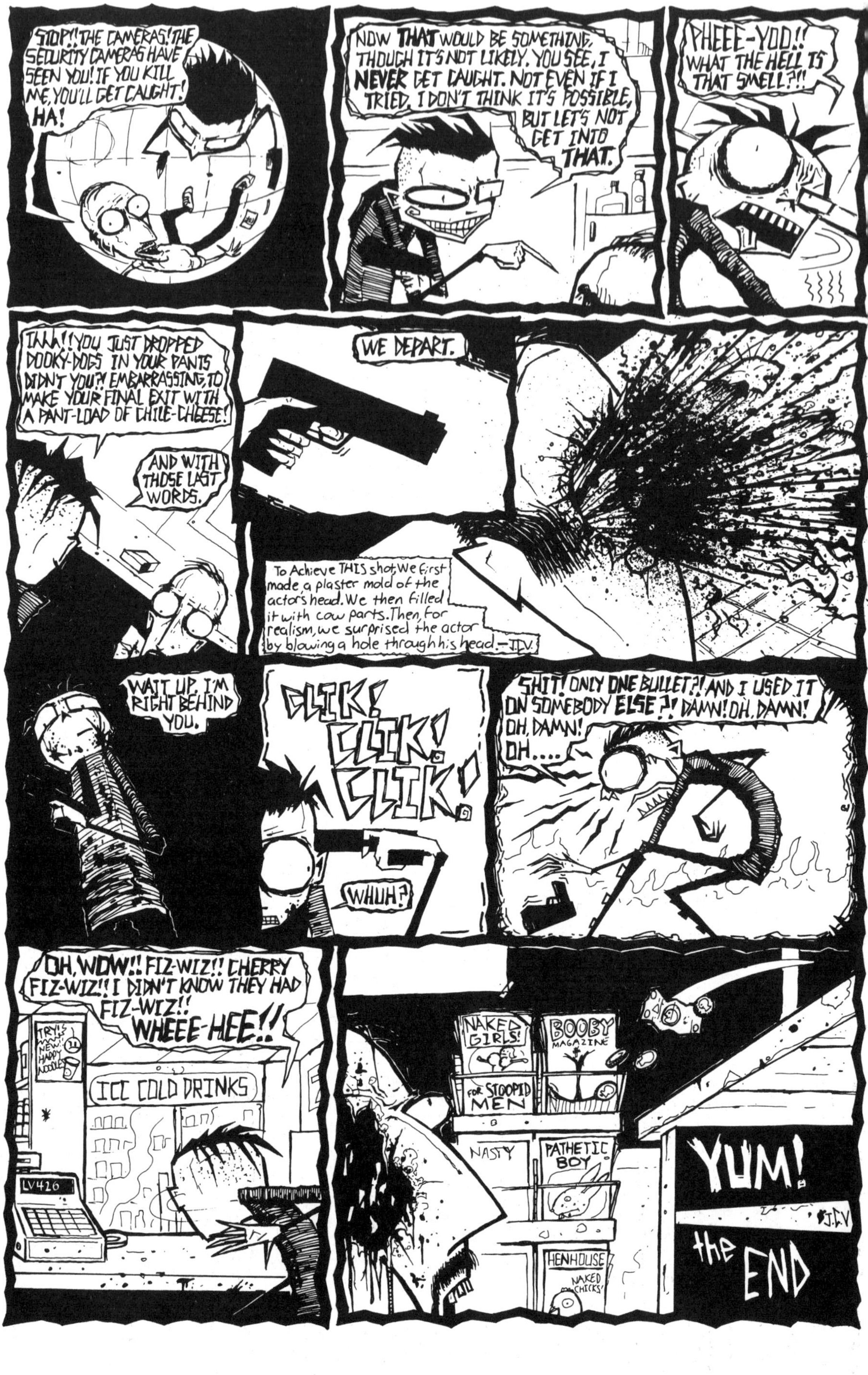
STOP!! THE CAMERAS! THE SECURITY CAMERAS HAVE SEEN YOU! IF YOU KILL ME, YOU'LL GET CAUGHT! HA!
NOW THAT WOULD BE SOMETHING, THOUGH IT'S NOT LIKELY. YOU SEE, I NEVER GET CAUGHT. NOT EVEN IF I TRIED. I DON'T THINK IT'S POSSIBLE, BUT LET'S NOT GET INTO THAT.
PHEEE-YOO!! WHAT THE HELL IS THAT SMELL?!!
TAAA!! YOU JUST DROPPED DOOKY-DOGS IN YOUR PANTS DIDN'T YOU?! EMBARRASSING, TO MAKE YOUR FINAL EXIT WITH A PANT-LOAD OF CHILE-CHEESE!
AND WITH THOSE LAST WORDS.
WE DEPART.
To Achieve THIS shot, We first made a plaster mold of the actor's head. We then filled it with cow parts. Then, for realism, we surprised the actor by blowing a hole through his head. —J.V.
WAIT UP, I'M RIGHT BEHIND YOU.
CLIK! CLIK! CLIK!
WHUH?
SHIT! ONLY ONE BULLET?! AND I USED IT ON SOMEBODY ELSE?! DAMN! OH, DAMN! OH, DAMN! OH.....
OH, WOW!! FIZ-WIZ!! CHERRY FIZ-WIZ!! I DIDN'T KNOW THEY HAD FIZ-WIZ!! WHEEE-HEE!!
TRY!! NEW! HAPPY NOODLES
ICE COLD DRINKS
LV426
NAKED GIRLS!
BOOBY MAGAZINE
FOR STOOPID MEN
NASTY
PATHETIC BOY
HENHOUSE
NAKED CHICKS!
YUM!
J.C.V
the END

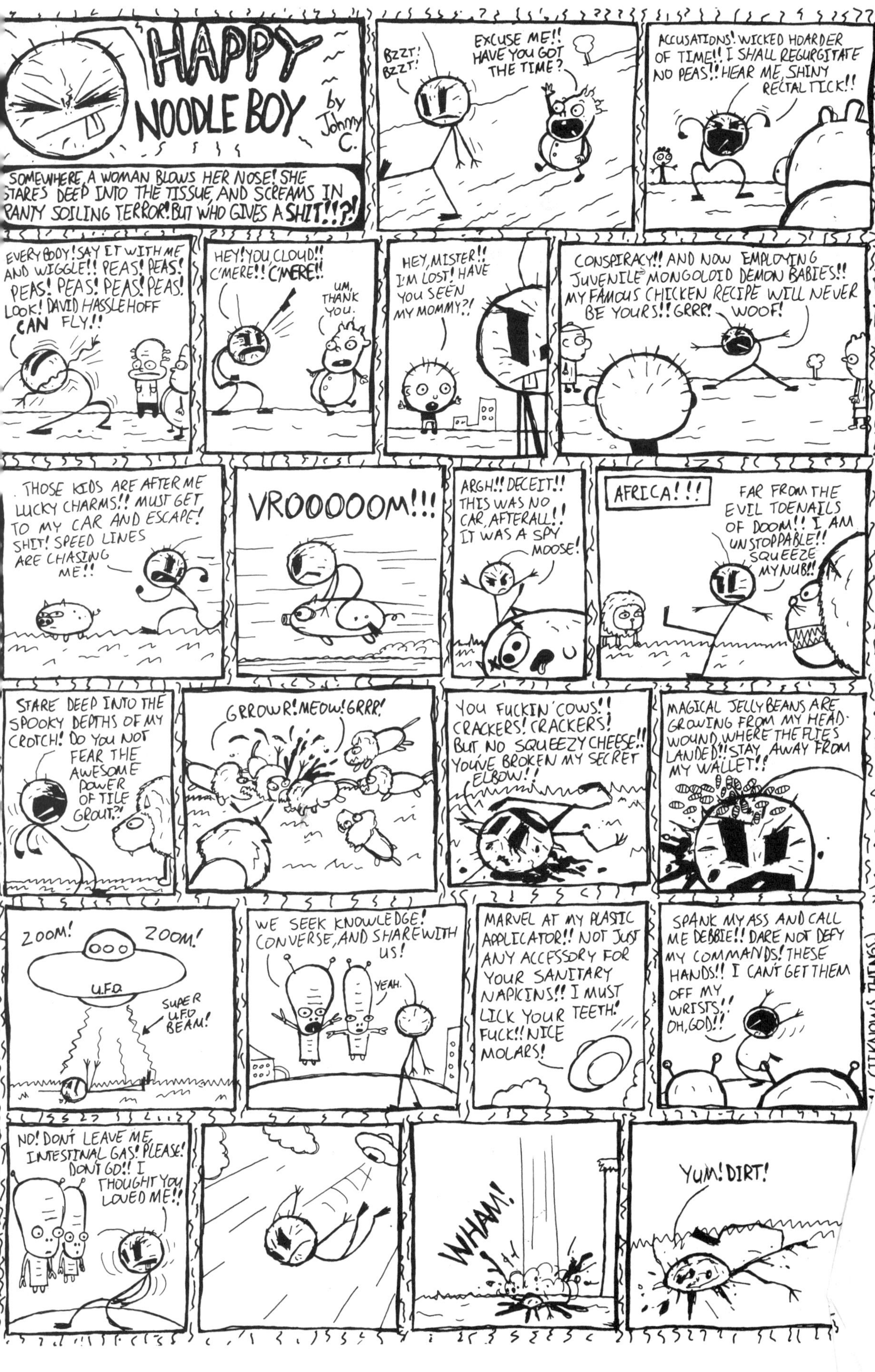

HAPPY NOODLE BOY
by Johnny C.
SOMEWHERE, A WOMAN BLOWS HER NOSE! SHE STARES DEEP INTO THE TISSUE, AND SCREAMS IN PANTY SOILING TERROR! BUT WHO GIVES A SHIT!!?!
BZZT! BZZT!
EXCUSE ME!! HAVE YOU GOT THE TIME?
ACCUSATIONS! WICKED HOARDER OF TIME!! I SHALL REGURGITATE NO PEAS!! HEAR ME, SHINY RECTAL TICK!!
EVERYBODY! SAY IT WITH ME AND WIGGLE!! PEAS! PEAS! PEAS! PEAS! PEAS! PEAS! LOOK! DAVID HASSLEHOFF CAN FLY!!
HEY! YOU, CLOUD!! C'MERE!! C'MERE!!
UM, THANK YOU.
HEY, MISTER!! I'M LOST! HAVE YOU SEEN MY MOMMY?!
CONSPIRACY!! AND NOW EMPLOYING JUVENILE MONGOLOID DEMON BABIES!! MY FAMOUS CHICKEN RECIPE WILL NEVER BE YOURS!! GRRR! WOOF!
THOSE KIDS ARE AFTER ME LUCKY CHARMS!! MUST GET TO MY CAR AND ESCAPE! SHIT! SPEED LINES ARE CHASING ME!!
VROOOOOM!!!
ARGH!! DECEIT!! THIS WAS NO CAR, AFTERALL!! IT WAS A SPY MOOSE!
AFRICA!!!
FAR FROM THE EVIL TOENAILS OF DOOM!! I AM UNSTOPPABLE!! SQUEEZE MY NUB!!
STARE DEEP INTO THE SPOOKY DEPTHS OF MY CROTCH! DO YOU NOT FEAR THE AWESOME POWER OF TILE GROUT?!
GRROWR! MEOW! GRRR!
YOU FUCKIN' COWS!! CRACKERS! CRACKERS! BUT NO SQUEEZY CHEESE!! YOU'VE BROKEN MY SECRET ELBOW!!
MAGICAL JELLYBEANS ARE GROWING FROM MY HEAD WOUND WHERE THE FLIES LANDED!! STAY AWAY FROM MY WALLET!!
ZOOM! ZOOM!
U.F.O.
SUPER U.F.O. BEAM!
WE SEEK KNOWLEDGE! CONVERSE, AND SHARE WITH US!
YEAH.
MARVEL AT MY PLASTIC APPLICATOR!! NOT JUST ANY ACCESSORY FOR YOUR SANITARY NAPKINS!! I MUST LICK YOUR TEETH! FUCK!! NICE MOLARS!
SPANK MY ASS AND CALL ME DEBBIE!! DARE NOT DEFY MY COMMANDS! THESE HANDS!! I CAN'T GET THEM OFF MY WRISTS!! OH, GOD!!
(IT KNOWS THINGS.)
NO! DON'T LEAVE ME, INTESTINAL GAS! PLEASE! DON'T GO!! I THOUGHT YOU LOVED ME!!
WHAM!
YUM! DIRT!

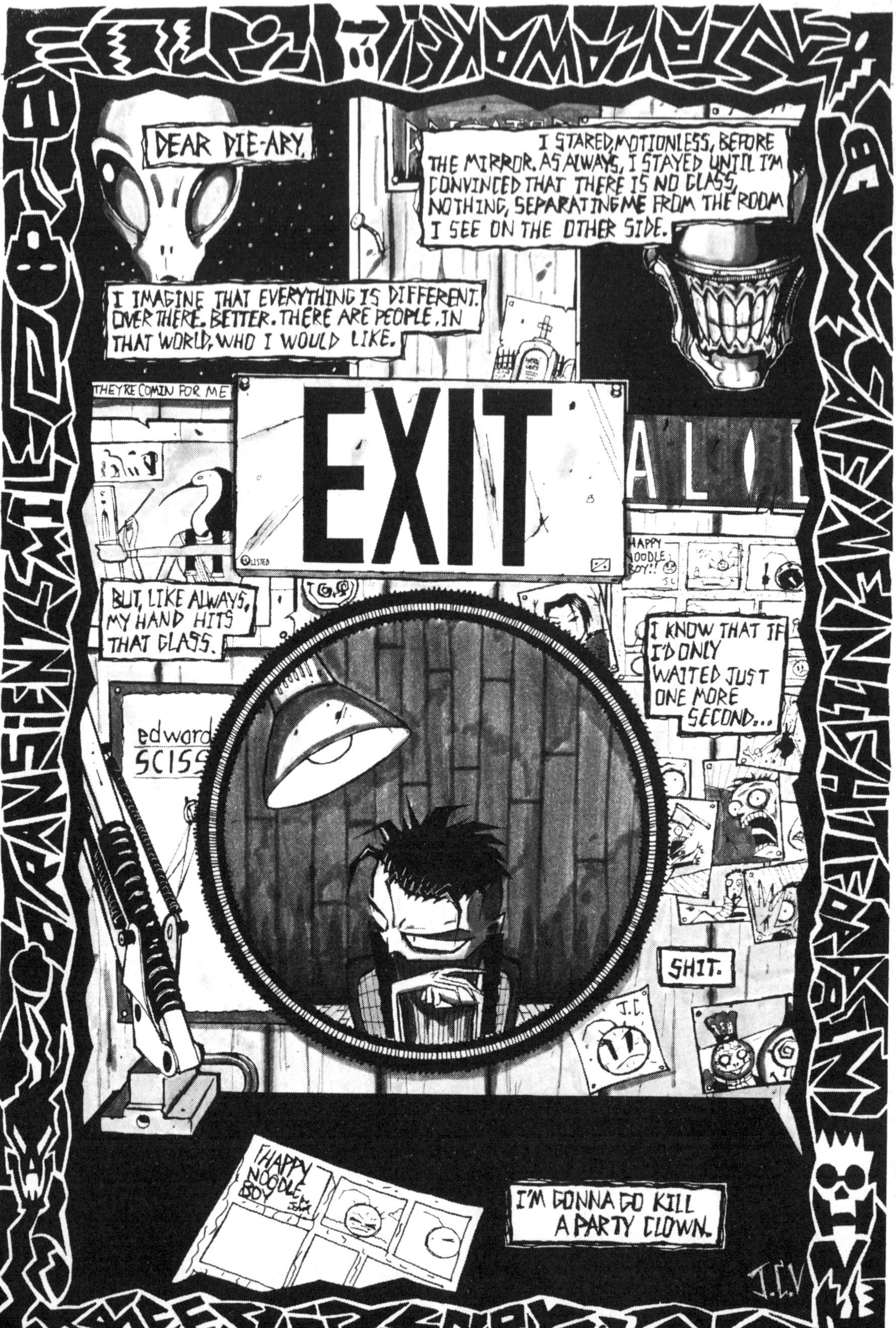
DEAR DIE-ARY,
I STARED, MOTIONLESS, BEFORE THE MIRROR. AS ALWAYS, I STAYED UNTIL I'M CONVINCED THAT THERE IS NO GLASS, NOTHING, SEPARATING ME FROM THE ROOM I SEE ON THE OTHER SIDE.
I IMAGINE THAT EVERYTHING IS DIFFERENT. OVER THERE. BETTER. THERE ARE PEOPLE, IN THAT WORLD, WHO I WOULD LIKE.
THEY'RE COMIN FOR ME
EXIT
HAPPY NOODLE BOY!!
BUT, LIKE ALWAYS, MY HAND HITS THAT GLASS.
I KNOW THAT IF I'D ONLY WAITED JUST ONE MORE SECOND...
edward SCISS
SHIT.
J.C.
HAPPY NOODLE BOY
I'M GONNA GO KILL A PARTY CLOWN.
J.C.V

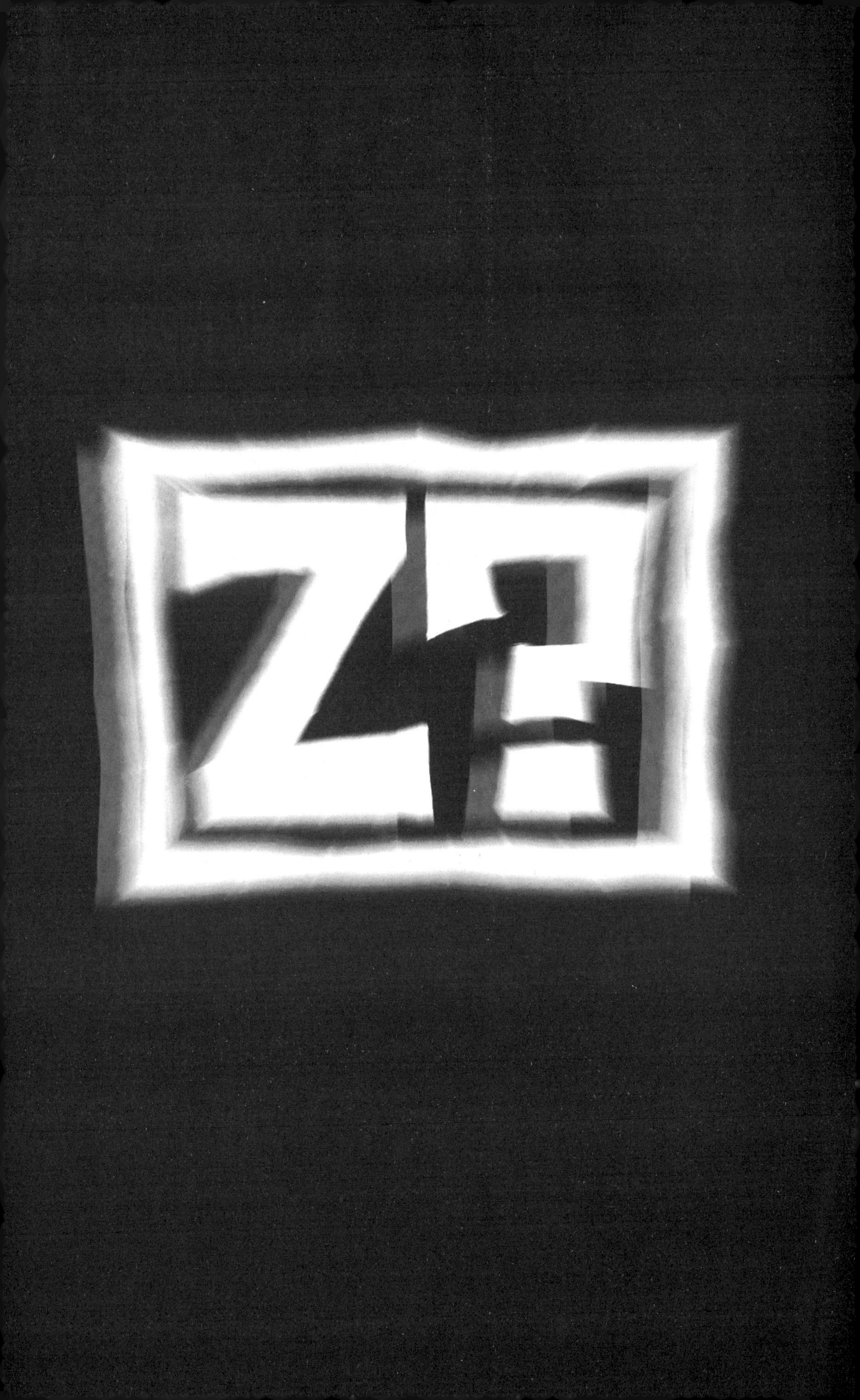

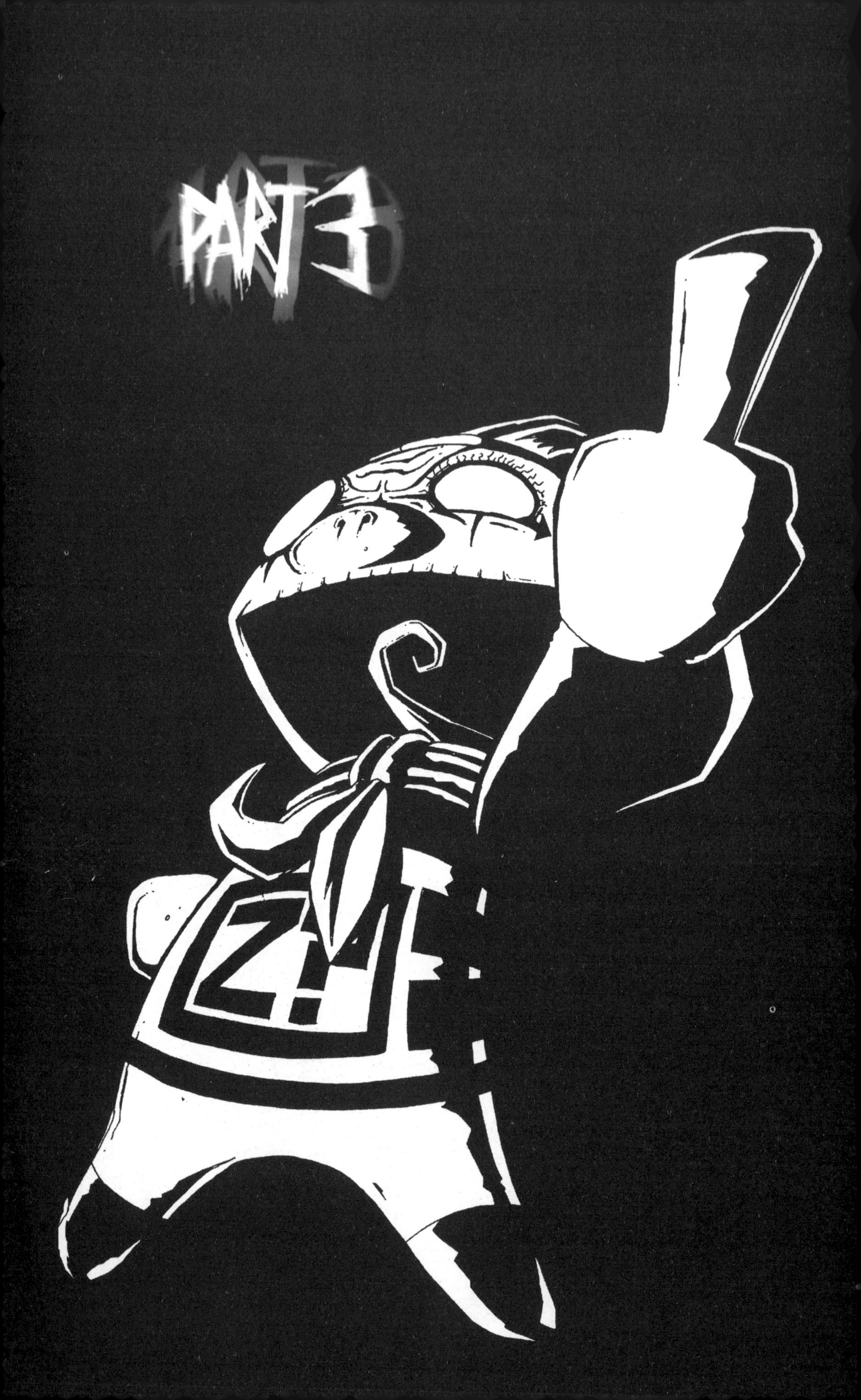
PART 3

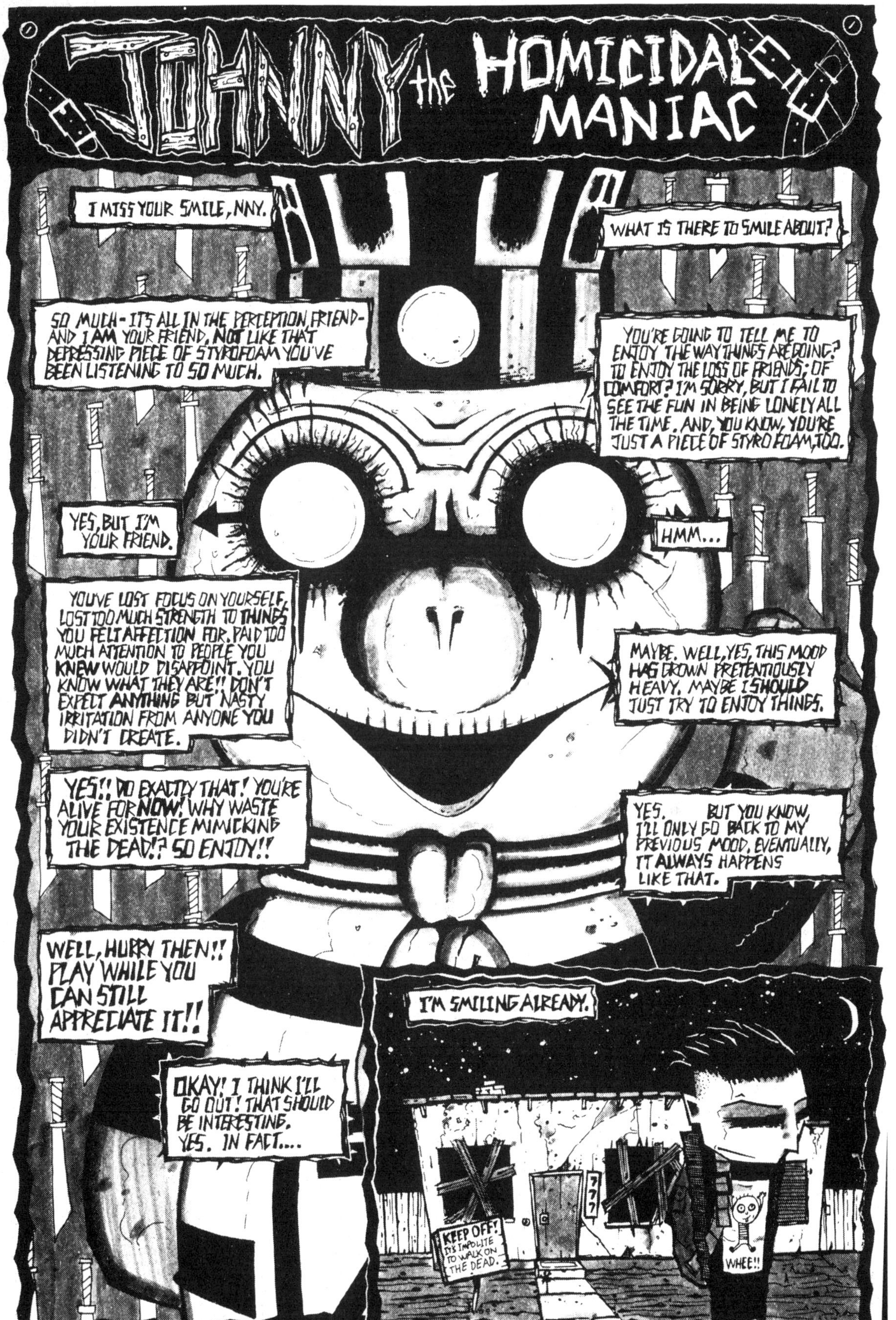
JOHNNY the HOMICIDAL MANIAC
I MISS YOUR SMILE, NNY.
WHAT IS THERE TO SMILE ABOUT?
SO MUCH - IT'S ALL IN THE PERCEPTION, FRIEND - AND I AM YOUR FRIEND, NOT LIKE THAT DEPRESSING PIECE OF STYROFOAM YOU'VE BEEN LISTENING TO SO MUCH.
YOU'RE GOING TO TELL ME TO ENJOY THE WAY THINGS ARE GOING? TO ENJOY THE LOSS OF FRIENDS; OF COMFORT? I'M SORRY, BUT I FAIL TO SEE THE FUN IN BEING LONELY ALL THE TIME. AND, YOU KNOW, YOU'RE JUST A PIECE OF STYROFOAM, TOO.
YES, BUT I'M YOUR FRIEND.
HMM...
YOU'VE LOST FOCUS ON YOURSELF, LOST TOO MUCH STRENGTH TO THINGS YOU FELT AFFECTION FOR. PAID TOO MUCH ATTENTION TO PEOPLE YOU KNEW WOULD DISAPPOINT. YOU KNOW WHAT THEY ARE!! DON'T EXPECT ANYTHING BUT NASTY IRRITATION FROM ANYONE YOU DIDN'T CREATE.
MAYBE. WELL, YES, THIS MOOD HAS GROWN PRETENTIOUSLY HEAVY. MAYBE I SHOULD JUST TRY TO ENJOY THINGS.
YES!! DO EXACTLY THAT! YOU'RE ALIVE FOR NOW! WHY WASTE YOUR EXISTENCE MIMICKING THE DEAD!? SO ENJOY!!
YES. BUT YOU KNOW, I'LL ONLY GO BACK TO MY PREVIOUS MOOD, EVENTUALLY. IT ALWAYS HAPPENS LIKE THAT.
WELL, HURRY THEN!! PLAY WHILE YOU CAN STILL APPRECIATE IT!!
I'M SMILING ALREADY.
OKAY! I THINK I'LL GO OUT! THAT SHOULD BE INTERESTING. YES. IN FACT....
777
KEEP OFF! IT'S IMPOLITE TO WALK ON THE DEAD.
WHEE!!

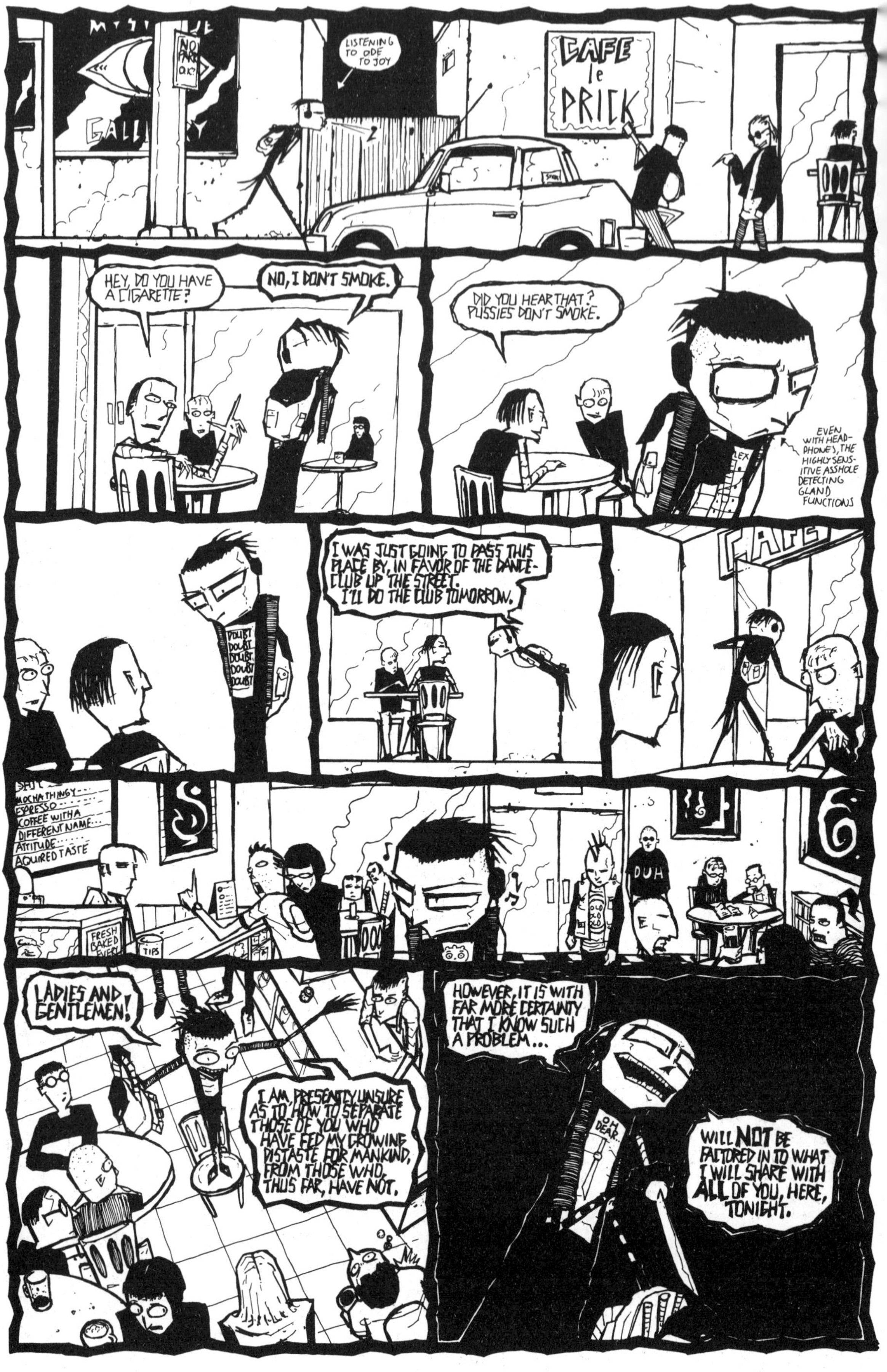
LISTENING TO ODE TO JOY
CAFE le PRICK
HEY, DO YOU HAVE A CIGARETTE?
NO, I DON'T SMOKE.
DID YOU HEAR THAT? PUSSIES DON'T SMOKE.
EVEN WITH HEAD-PHONES, THE HIGHLY SENS-ITIVE ASSHOLE DETECTING GLAND FUNCTIONS
DOUBT DOUBT DOUBT DOUBT DOUBT
I WAS JUST GOING TO PASS THIS PLACE BY, IN FAVOR OF THE DANCE-CLUB UP THE STREET. I'LL DO THE CLUB TOMORROW.
CAFE
MOCHA THINGY... ESPRESSO COFFEE WITH A DIFFERENT NAME... ATTITUDE AQUIRED TASTE
FRESH BAKED
TIPS
DUH
LADIES AND GENTLEMEN!
I AM, PRESENTLY UNSURE AS TO HOW TO SEPARATE THOSE OF YOU WHO HAVE FED MY GROWING DISTASTE FOR MANKIND, FROM THOSE WHO, THUS FAR, HAVE NOT.
HOWEVER, IT IS WITH FAR MORE CERTAINTY THAT I KNOW SUCH A PROBLEM...
OH DEAR...
WILL NOT BE FACTORED IN TO WHAT I WILL SHARE WITH ALL OF YOU, HERE, TONIGHT.

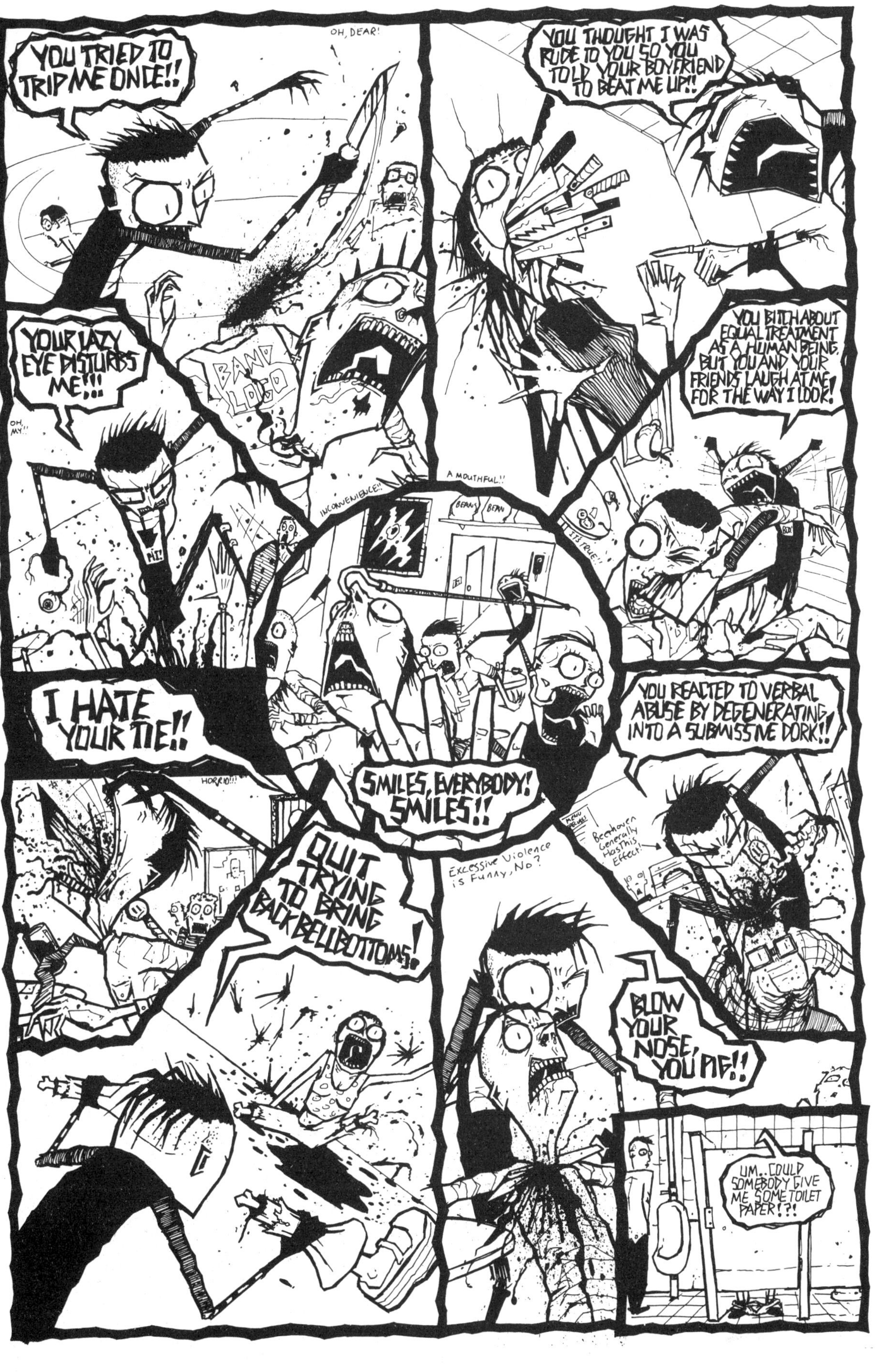
YOU TRIED TO TRIP ME ONCE!!
OH, DEAR!
YOU THOUGHT I WAS RUDE TO YOU SO YOU TOLD YOUR BOYFRIEND TO BEAT ME UP!!
YOUR LAZY EYE DISTURBS ME!!!
OH, MY!!
BAND LOGO
YOU BITCH ABOUT EQUAL TREATMENT AS A HUMAN BEING, BUT YOU AND YOUR FRIENDS LAUGH AT ME FOR THE WAY I LOOK!
A MOUTHFUL!!
INCONVENIENCE!!
IT'S TRUE!!
I HATE YOUR TIE!!
SMILES, EVERYBODY! SMILES!!
YOU REACTED TO VERBAL ABUSE BY DEGENERATING INTO A SUBMISSIVE DORK!!
HORRID!!
QUIT TRYING TO BRING BACK BELLBOTTOMS!
Excessive Violence is Funny, No?
Beethoven Generally Has this Effect!
BLOW YOUR NOSE, YOU PIG!!
UM.. COULD SOMEBODY GIVE ME SOME TOILET PAPER!?!

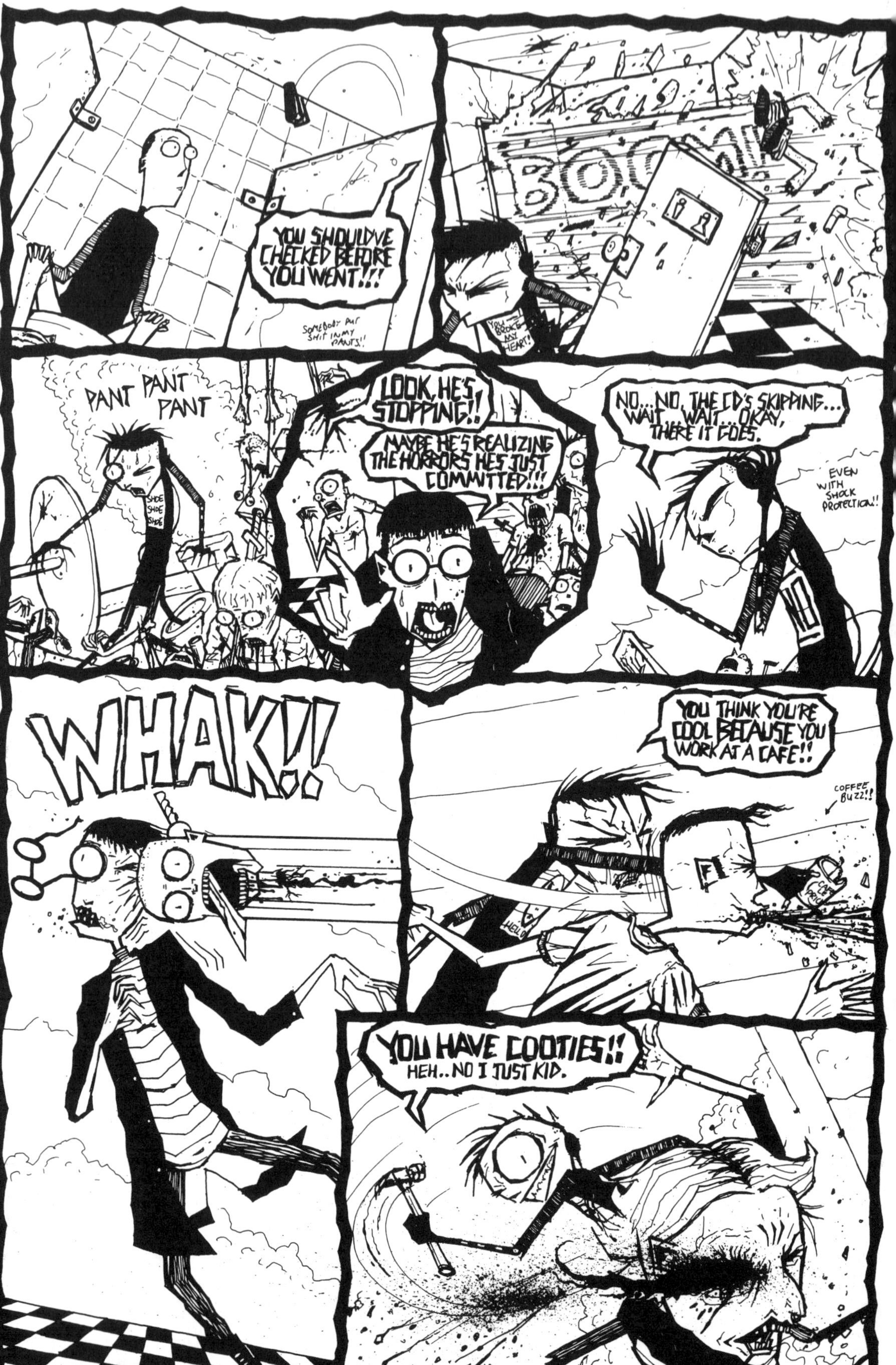
YOU SHOULD'VE CHECKED BEFORE YOU WENT!!!
SOMEBODY PUT SHIT IN MY PANTS!!
BOOM!!
YOU BROKE MY HEART!
PANT PANT PANT
SHOE SHOE SHOE
LOOK, HE'S STOPPING!!
MAYBE HE'S REALIZING THE HORRORS HE'S JUST COMMITTED!!!
NO...NO, THE CD'S SKIPPING... WAIT...WAIT...OKAY, THERE IT GOES.
EVEN WITH SHOCK PROTECTION!!
WHAK!!
YOU THINK YOU'RE COOL BECAUSE YOU WORK AT A CAFE!!
COFFEE BUZZ!!
YOU HAVE COOTIES!!
HEH..NO I JUST KID.

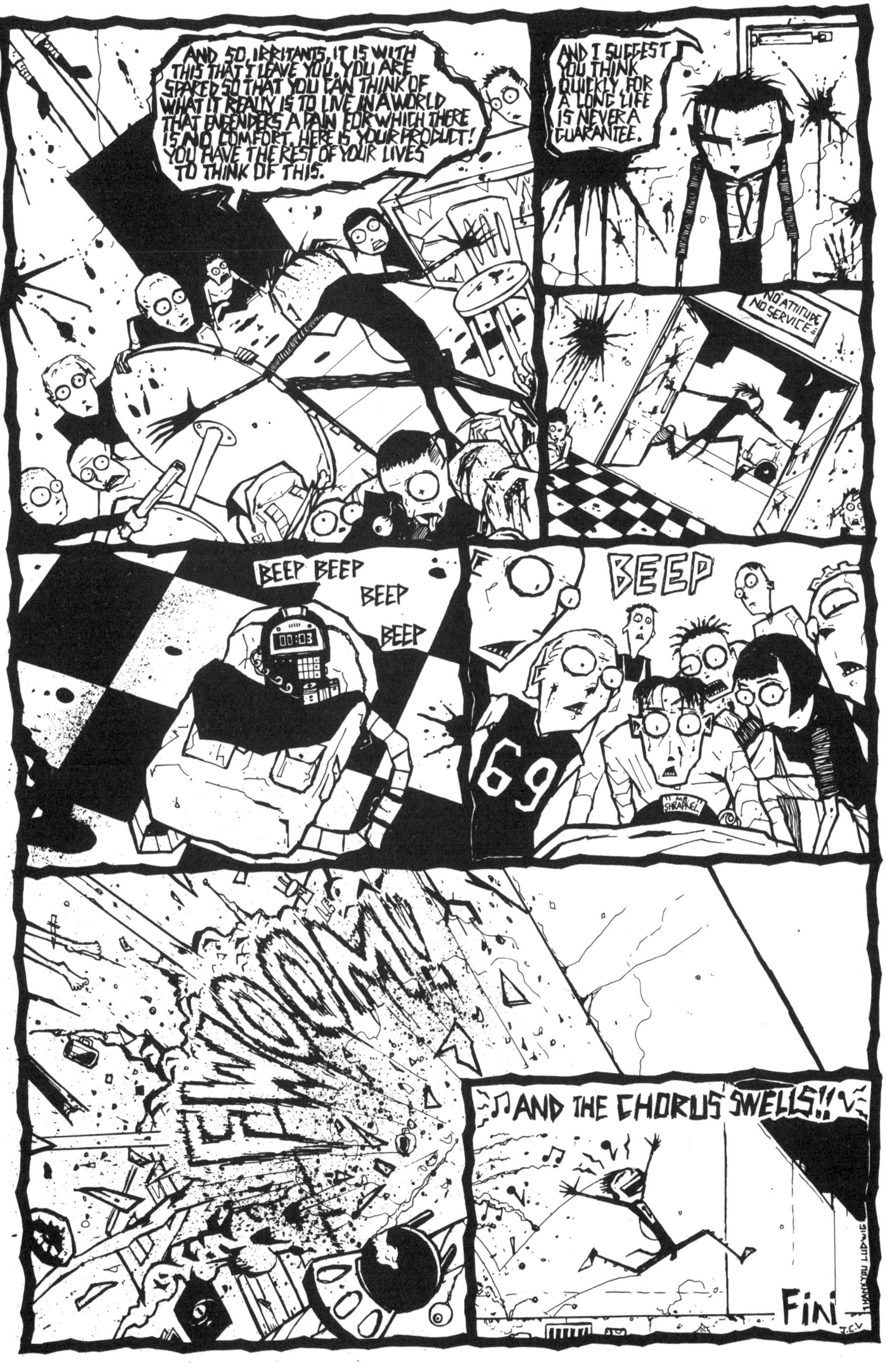
AND SO, IRRITANTS, IT IS WITH THIS THAT I LEAVE YOU. YOU ARE SPARED SO THAT YOU CAN THINK OF WHAT IT REALLY IS TO LIVE IN A WORLD THAT ENGENDERS A PAIN FOR WHICH THERE IS NO COMFORT. HERE IS YOUR PRODUCT! YOU HAVE THE REST OF YOUR LIVES TO THINK OF THIS.
AND I SUGGEST YOU THINK QUICKLY, FOR A LONG LIFE IS NEVER A GUARANTEE.
NO ATTITUDE NO SERVICE
BEEP BEEP
BEEP
BEEP
00:03
BEEP
69
MR. SHRAPNEL
FOOOM!!
♫AND THE CHORUS SWELLS!!
Fini
THANKYOU LUDWIG
J.C.V

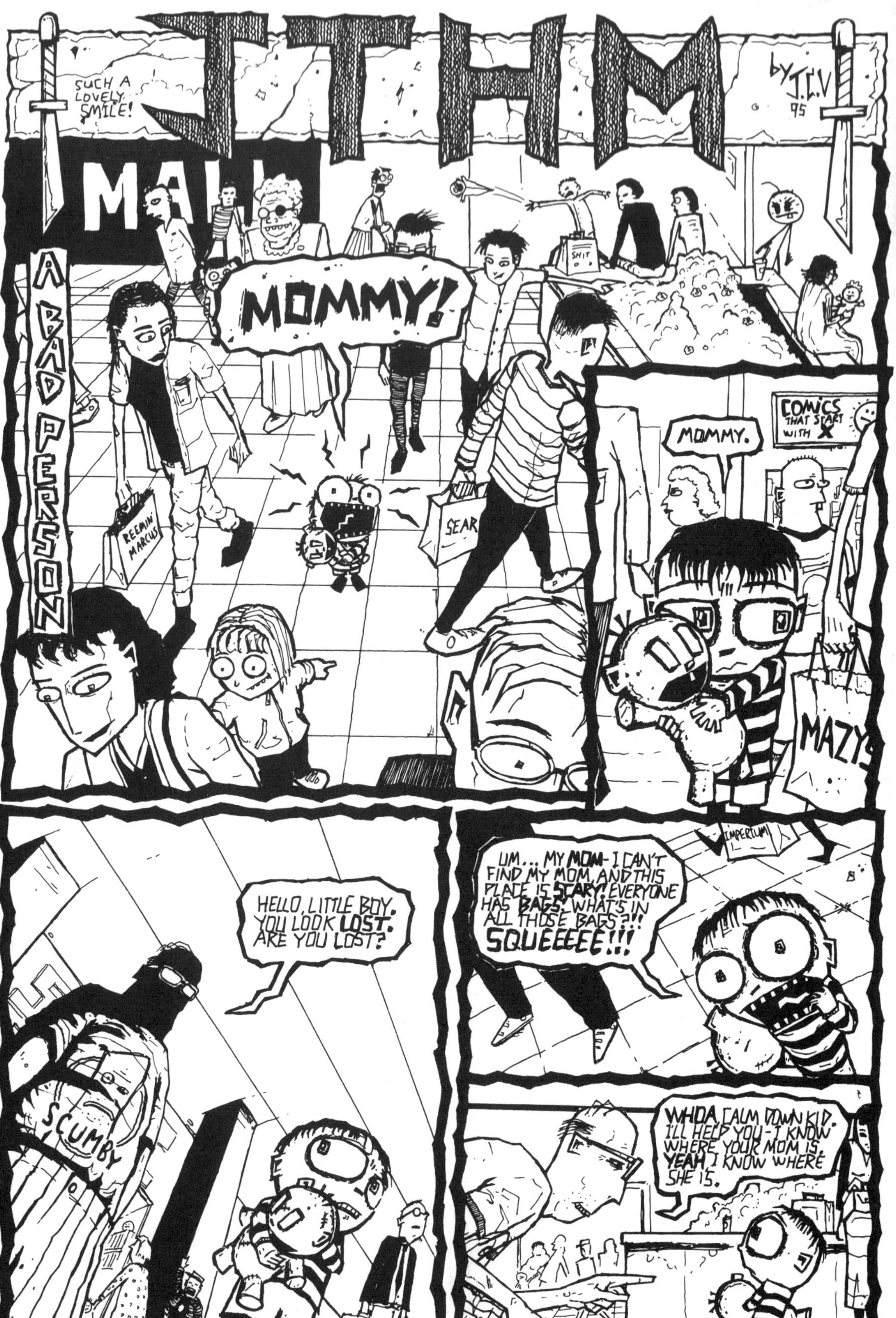
JTHM
SUCH A LOVELY SMILE!
by J.C.V 95
A BAD PERSON
MOMMY!
REEMIN' MARCUS
SEAR
SHIT
COMICS THAT START WITH X
MOMMY.
MAZYS
IMPERIUM
HELLO, LITTLE BOY. YOU LOOK LOST. ARE YOU LOST?
SCUMBY
UM... MY MOM- I CAN'T FIND MY MOM, AND THIS PLACE IS SCARY! EVERYONE HAS BAGS! WHAT'S IN ALL THOSE BAGS?!! SQUEEEEEE!!!
WHOA, CALM DOWN KID. I'LL HELP YOU- I KNOW WHERE YOUR MOM IS. YEAH, I KNOW WHERE SHE IS.

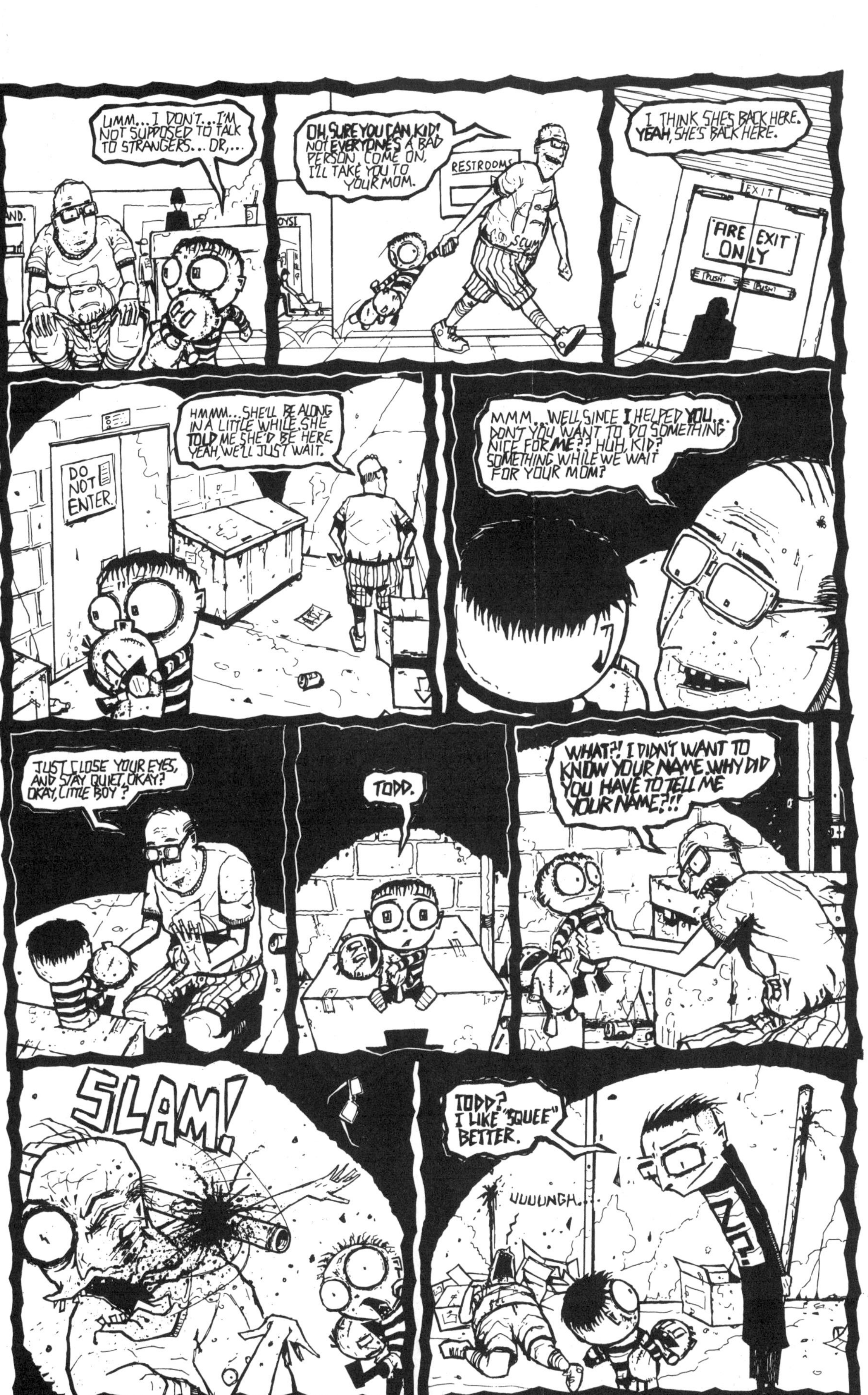
UMM... I DON'T... I'M NOT SUPPOSED TO TALK TO STRANGERS... OR,...
OH SURE YOU CAN KID! NOT EVERYONE'S A BAD PERSON. COME ON, I'LL TAKE YOU TO YOUR MOM.
RESTROOMS
SCUM
I THINK SHE'S BACK HERE. YEAH, SHE'S BACK HERE.
EXIT
FIRE EXIT ONLY
PUSH
PUSH
HMMM... SHE'LL BE ALONG IN A LITTLE WHILE. SHE TOLD ME SHE'D BE HERE. YEAH, WE'LL JUST WAIT.
DO NOT ENTER.
MMM... WELL SINCE I HELPED YOU... DON'T YOU WANT TO DO SOMETHING NICE FOR ME?? HUH, KID? SOMETHING WHILE WE WAIT FOR YOUR MOM?
JUST CLOSE YOUR EYES, AND STAY QUIET, OKAY? OKAY, LITTLE BOY?
TODD.
WHAT?! I DIDN'T WANT TO KNOW YOUR NAME. WHY DID YOU HAVE TO TELL ME YOUR NAME?!!
SLAM!
TODD? I LIKE "SQUEE" BETTER.
UUUUNGH...

AAH, AREN'T MALLS REVOLTING PLACES? I CAME HERE TO DO SOME "EXPRESSING" ON THAT POINT WHEN I SAW YOU AND YOUR MOM. YOU KNOW, SQUEE, NOT TO OFFEND, BUT IT SEEMS YOUR PARENTS AREN'T EXACTLY ADEPT AT THE WHOLE "CARING" THING.

GUH...

DO NOT TRUST

AND IT'S YOUR PARENTS WHO SHOULD BE TEACHING YOU THESE THINGS, BUT... WELL I JUST DON'T WANT YOU TO THINK THAT THIS PIECE OF SHIT IS ANYTHING OTHER THAN A PATHETIC, HUMAN DEFECT. NOTHING MORE.

GO NOT

A BLACK BAG

NOT A MONSTER, NOT A BOOGEYMAN, NOTHING BUT ANOTHER REASON TO FEEL BETTER ABOUT YOURSELF. UNDERSTAND THAT IT'S JUST A PERSON— NOT WORTH DEVOTING ANY NIGHTMARES TO.

ZZIP!

OBSERVE, AND I'LL PROVE IT.

LOGO

YOU FLAW. AT LEAST I'M UNDER THE DELUSION OF DOING SOMETHING PRODUCTIVE.

UGH.

INSERT SOUND EFFECT!!

LEARNING IS FUNN... WHEEEE!!

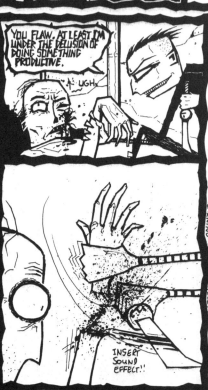

SEE!! BONES AND TISSUE, TUBES AND FAT!! ALL SUSTAINED BY BLOOD. NOTHING MORE THAN A POORLY TENDED MACHINE. AND LOOK!!

TRAUMA ZIGS

BLOOD!

IT HAS A BRAIN!! FUELED BY THE BLOOD THAT RACES HEAVILY IN TIMES OF GROTESQUELY HEIGHTENED DESIRES AND VIBES!! YOU CAN SEE THE MATTER AND FEEL THE SUBSTANCE, BUT EYES AND HANDS ARE USELESS

KRIK

FOR SENSING THE ROT AND FILTH OF IDEAS THAT DRIP FROM THESE THINGS!!

#CONTINUITY ERROR!!

TWO SPECIES UNDER ONE NAME—HUMAN— SEPARATED ONLY BY THE WORKINGS OF THEIR MINDS. THIS ONE IS HUMAN ONLY IN APPEARANCE!! A CLEVER DISGUISE FOR A SIMPLE ANIMAL. THE REAL HUMANS ARE HARDER TO FIND.

EEEEEEE EEEEEEK!!

SMAP!

KRACKLE!

YOU'RE THINKING "POP" NOW AREN'T YOU?!

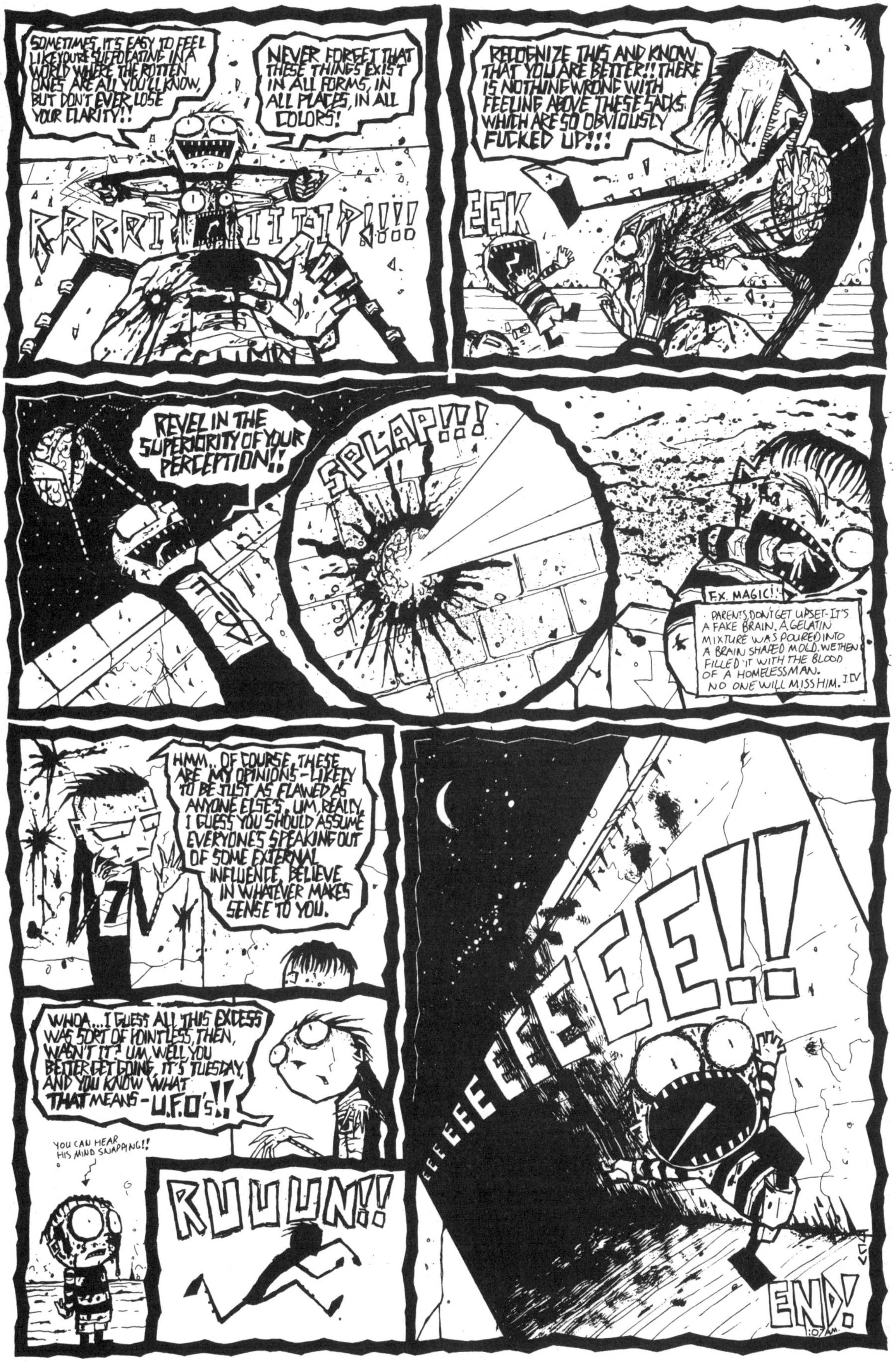

SOMETIMES, IT'S EASY TO FEEL LIKE YOU'RE SUFFOCATING IN A WORLD WHERE THE ROTTEN ONES ARE ALL YOU'LL KNOW, BUT DON'T EVER LOSE YOUR CLARITY!!
NEVER FORGET THAT THESE THINGS EXIST IN ALL FORMS, IN ALL PLACES, IN ALL COLORS!
RECOGNIZE THIS AND KNOW THAT YOU ARE BETTER!! THERE IS NOTHING WRONG WITH FEELING ABOVE THESE SACKS WHICH ARE SO OBVIOUSLY FUCKED UP!!!
EEK
REVEL IN THE SUPERIORITY OF YOUR PERCEPTION!!
SPLAP!!!
F.X. MAGIC!
PARENTS, DON'T GET UPSET- IT'S A FAKE BRAIN. A GELATIN MIXTURE WAS POURED INTO A BRAIN SHAPED MOLD. WE THEN FILLED IT WITH THE BLOOD OF A HOMELESS MAN. NO ONE WILL MISS HIM. J.V
HMM.. OF COURSE, THESE ARE MY OPINIONS - LIKELY TO BE JUST AS FLAWED AS ANYONE ELSE'S. UM, REALLY, I GUESS YOU SHOULD ASSUME EVERYONE'S SPEAKING OUT OF SOME EXTERNAL INFLUENCE. BELIEVE IN WHATEVER MAKES SENSE TO YOU.
WHOA... I GUESS ALL THIS EXCESS WAS SORT OF POINTLESS, THEN, WASN'T IT? UM WELL YOU BETTER GET GOING, IT'S TUESDAY, AND YOU KNOW WHAT THAT MEANS - U.F.O's!!
YOU CAN HEAR HIS MIND SNAPPING!!
RUUUN!!
EEEEEEEEEE!!
END!
1:07 AM.

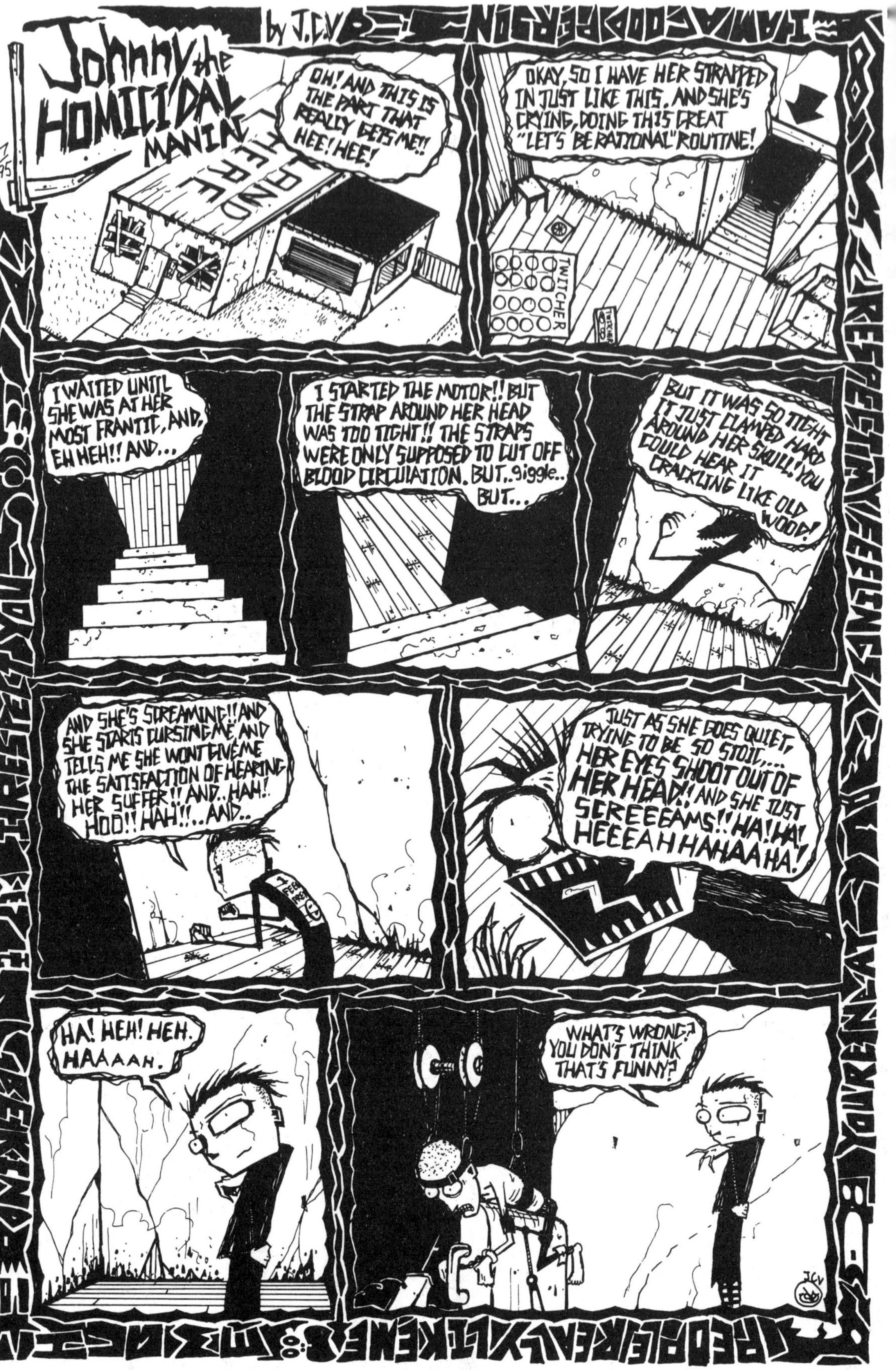
Johnny the HOMICIDAL MANIAC
by J.C.V
7/95
OH! AND THIS IS THE PART THAT REALLY GETS ME!! HEE! HEE!
OKAY, SO I HAVE HER STRAPPED IN JUST LIKE THIS. AND SHE'S CRYING, DOING THIS GREAT "LET'S BE RATIONAL" ROUTINE!
TWITCHER
I WAITED UNTIL SHE WAS AT HER MOST FRANTIC, AND, EH HEH!! AND...
I STARTED THE MOTOR!! BUT THE STRAP AROUND HER HEAD WAS TOO TIGHT!! THE STRAPS WERE ONLY SUPPOSED TO CUT OFF BLOOD CIRCULATION. BUT..giggle.. BUT...
BUT IT WAS SO TIGHT IT JUST CLAMPED HARD AROUND HER SKULL! YOU COULD HEAR IT CRACKLING LIKE OLD WOOD!
AND SHE'S SCREAMING!! AND SHE STARTS CURSING ME AND TELLS ME SHE WON'T GIVE ME THE SATISFACTION OF HEARING HER SUFFER!! AND..HAH! HOO!! HAH!!..AND..
JUST AS SHE GOES QUIET, TRYING TO BE SO STOIC,... HER EYES SHOOT OUT OF HER HEAD!! AND SHE JUST SCREEEAMS!! HA! HA! HEEEAH HAHAAA HA!
HA! HEH! HEH. HAAaaH.
WHAT'S WRONG? YOU DON'T THINK THAT'S FUNNY?
JCV

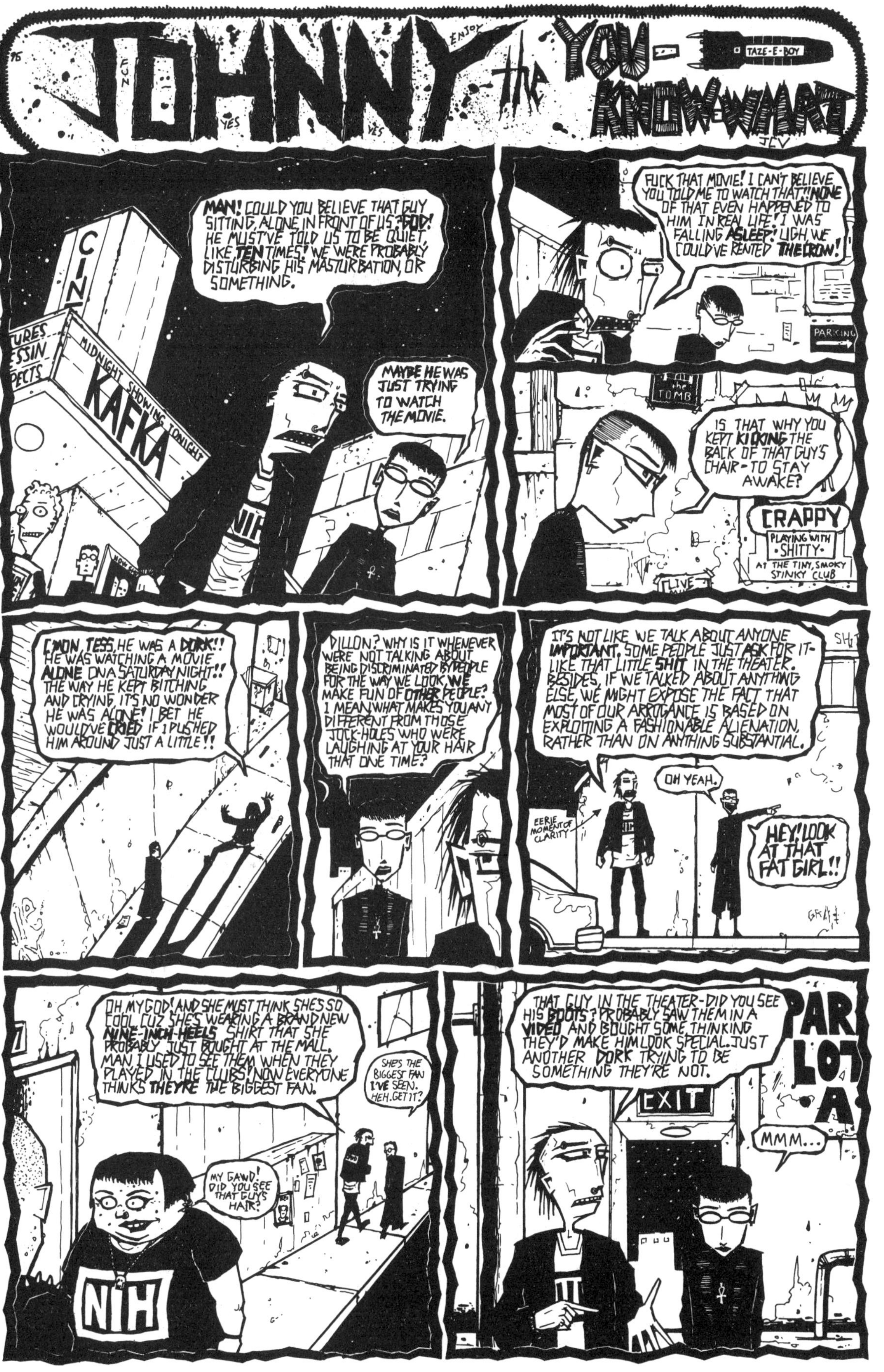
95
JOHNNY the YOU-KNOW-WHAT
ENJOY
FUN
YES
YES
TAZE-E-BOY
JCV
MAN! COULD YOU BELIEVE THAT GUY SITTING ALONE IN FRONT OF US? GOD! HE MUST'VE TOLD US TO BE QUIET, LIKE TEN TIMES! WE WERE PROBABLY DISTURBING HIS MASTURBATION, OR SOMETHING.
MIDNIGHT SHOWING TONIGHT
KAFKA
MAYBE HE WAS JUST TRYING TO WATCH THE MOVIE.
FUCK THAT MOVIE! I CAN'T BELIEVE YOU TOLD ME TO WATCH THAT!! NONE OF THAT EVEN HAPPENED TO HIM IN REAL LIFE! I WAS FALLING ASLEEP! UGH, WE COULD'VE RENTED THE CROW!
PARKING
THE TOMB
IS THAT WHY YOU KEPT KICKING THE BACK OF THAT GUY'S CHAIR - TO STAY AWAKE?
CRAPPY
PLAYING WITH
•SHITTY•
AT THE TINY, SMOKY STINKY CLUB
LIVE
C'MON, TESS, HE WAS A DORK!! HE WAS WATCHING A MOVIE ALONE ON A SATURDAY NIGHT!! THE WAY HE KEPT BITCHING AND CRYING, IT'S NO WONDER HE WAS ALONE! I BET HE WOULD'VE CRIED IF I PUSHED HIM AROUND JUST A LITTLE!!
DILLON? WHY IS IT WHENEVER WERE NOT TALKING ABOUT BEING DISCRIMINATED BY PEOPLE FOR THE WAY WE LOOK, WE MAKE FUN OF OTHER PEOPLE? I MEAN, WHAT MAKES YOU ANY DIFFERENT FROM THOSE JOCK-HOLES WHO WERE LAUGHING AT YOUR HAIR THAT ONE TIME?
IT'S NOT LIKE WE TALK ABOUT ANYONE IMPORTANT. SOME PEOPLE JUST ASK FOR IT - LIKE THAT LITTLE SHIT IN THE THEATER. BESIDES, IF WE TALKED ABOUT ANYTHING ELSE, WE MIGHT EXPOSE THE FACT THAT MOST OF OUR ARROGANCE IS BASED ON EXPLOITING A FASHIONABLE ALIENATION, RATHER THAN ON ANYTHING SUBSTANTIAL.
EERIE MOMENT OF CLARITY
OH YEAH.
HEY! LOOK AT THAT FAT GIRL!!
OH MY GOD! AND SHE MUST THINK SHE'S SO COOL CUZ SHE'S WEARING A BRAND NEW NINE-INCH-HEELS SHIRT THAT SHE PROBABLY JUST BOUGHT AT THE MALL. MAN, I USED TO SEE THEM WHEN THEY PLAYED IN THE CLUBS! NOW EVERYONE THINKS THEYRE THE BIGGEST FAN.
SHE'S THE BIGGEST FAN I'VE SEEN. HEH. GET IT?
MY GAWD! DID YOU SEE THAT GUY'S HAIR?
NIH
THAT GUY IN THE THEATER - DID YOU SEE HIS BOOTS? PROBABLY SAW THEM IN A VIDEO AND BOUGHT SOME THINKING THEY'D MAKE HIM LOOK SPECIAL. JUST ANOTHER DORK TRYING TO BE SOMETHING THEY'RE NOT.
EXIT
MMM...

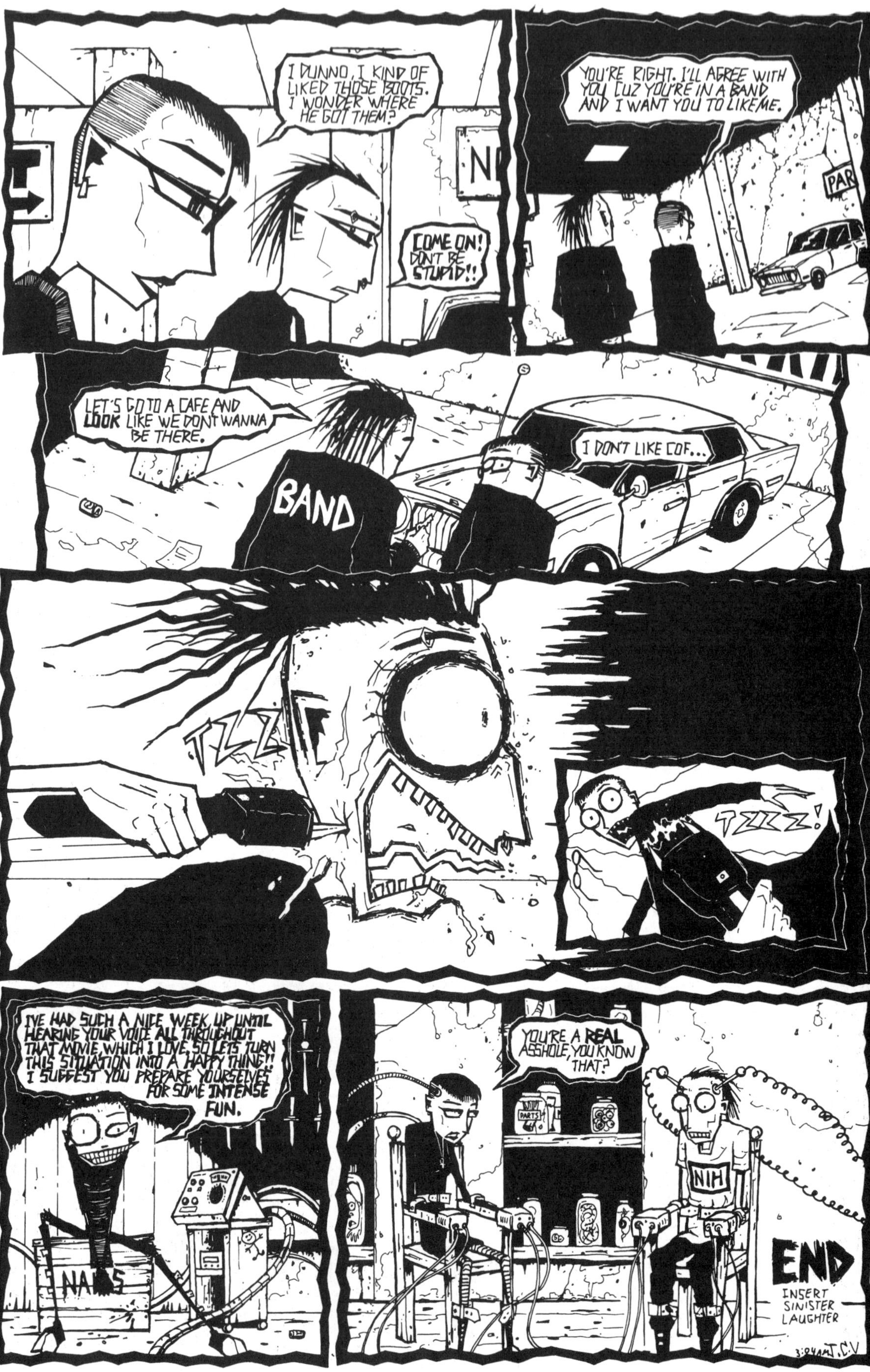
I DUNNO, I KIND OF LIKED THOSE BOOTS. I WONDER WHERE HE GOT THEM?
COME ON! DON'T BE STUPID!!
YOU'RE RIGHT. I'LL AGREE WITH YOU CUZ YOU'RE IN A BAND AND I WANT YOU TO LIKE ME.
PAR
LET'S GO TO A CAFE AND LOOK LIKE WE DONT WANNA BE THERE.
BAND
I DON'T LIKE COF...
TZZZ
TZZZ!
IVE HAD SUCH A NICE WEEK UP UNTIL HEARING YOUR VOICE ALL THROUGHOUT THAT MOVIE WHICH I LOVE, SO LETS TURN THIS SITUATION INTO A HAPPY THING!! I SUGGEST YOU PREPARE YOURSELVES FOR SOME INTENSE FUN.
NAILS
YOU'RE A REAL ASSHOLE, YOU KNOW THAT?
PARTS
NIH
END
INSERT SINISTER LAUGHTER
3:04AM J.C.V.

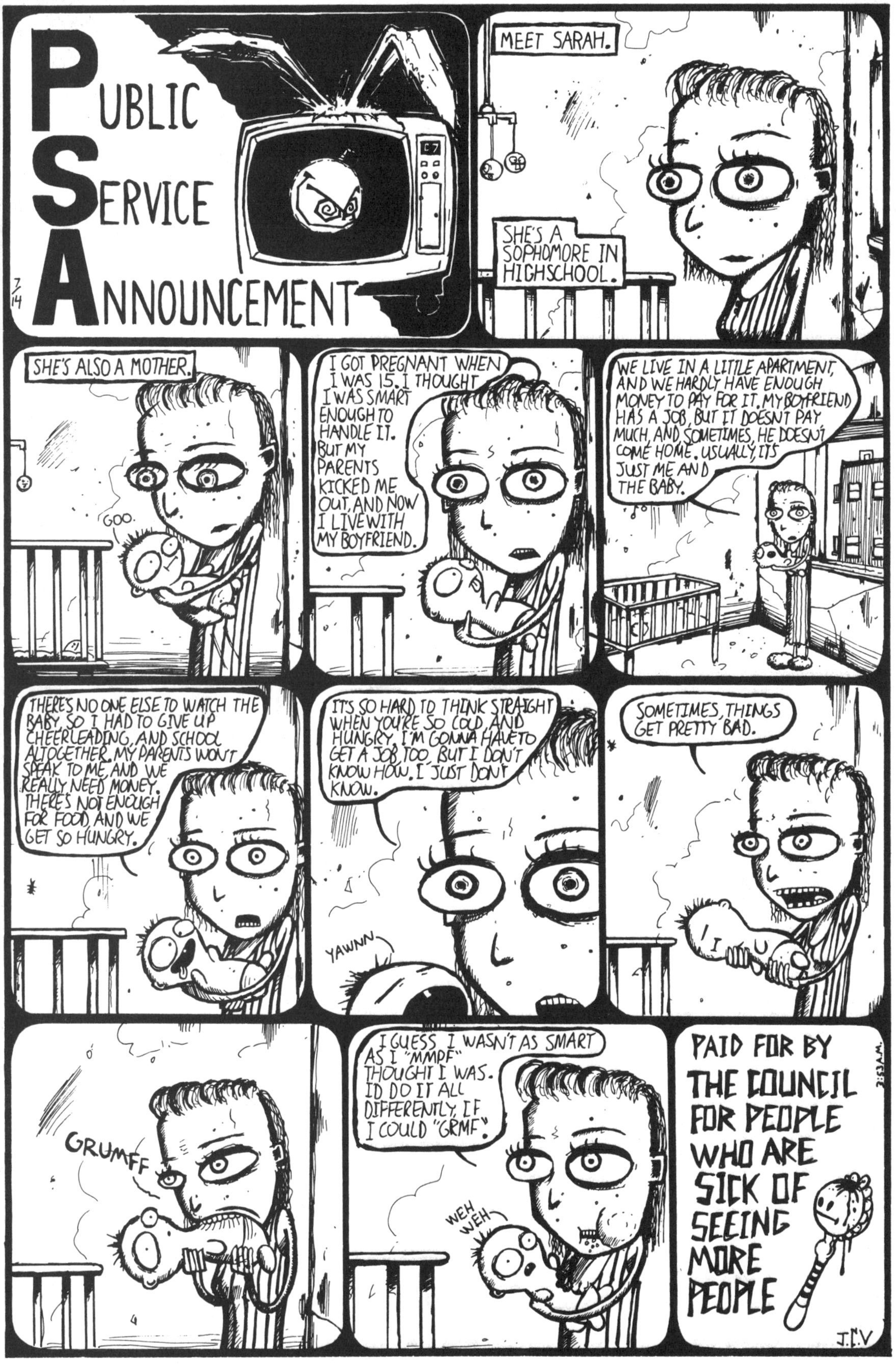
PUBLIC SERVICE ANNOUNCEMENT
7/14
MEET SARAH.
SHE'S A SOPHOMORE IN HIGHSCHOOL.
SHE'S ALSO A MOTHER.
GOO.
I GOT PREGNANT WHEN I WAS 15. I THOUGHT I WAS SMART ENOUGH TO HANDLE IT. BUT MY PARENTS KICKED ME OUT, AND NOW I LIVE WITH MY BOYFRIEND.
WE LIVE IN A LITTLE APARTMENT, AND WE HARDLY HAVE ENOUGH MONEY TO PAY FOR IT. MY BOYFRIEND HAS A JOB, BUT IT DOESN'T PAY MUCH, AND SOMETIMES, HE DOESN'T COME HOME. USUALLY, IT'S JUST ME AND THE BABY.
THERE'S NO ONE ELSE TO WATCH THE BABY, SO I HAD TO GIVE UP CHEERLEADING, AND SCHOOL ALTOGETHER. MY PARENTS WON'T SPEAK TO ME, AND WE REALLY NEED MONEY. THERE'S NOT ENOUGH FOR FOOD, AND WE GET SO HUNGRY.
IT'S SO HARD TO THINK STRAIGHT WHEN YOU'RE SO COLD, AND HUNGRY. I'M GONNA HAVE TO GET A JOB, TOO, BUT I DON'T KNOW HOW. I JUST DON'T KNOW.
YAWNN
SOMETIMES, THINGS GET PRETTY BAD.
GRUMFF
I GUESS I WASN'T AS SMART AS I "MMPF" THOUGHT I WAS. I'D DO IT ALL DIFFERENTLY, IF I COULD "GRMF".
WEH WEH
PAID FOR BY THE COUNCIL FOR PEOPLE WHO ARE SICK OF SEEING MORE PEOPLE
3:53 A.M.
J.C.V.

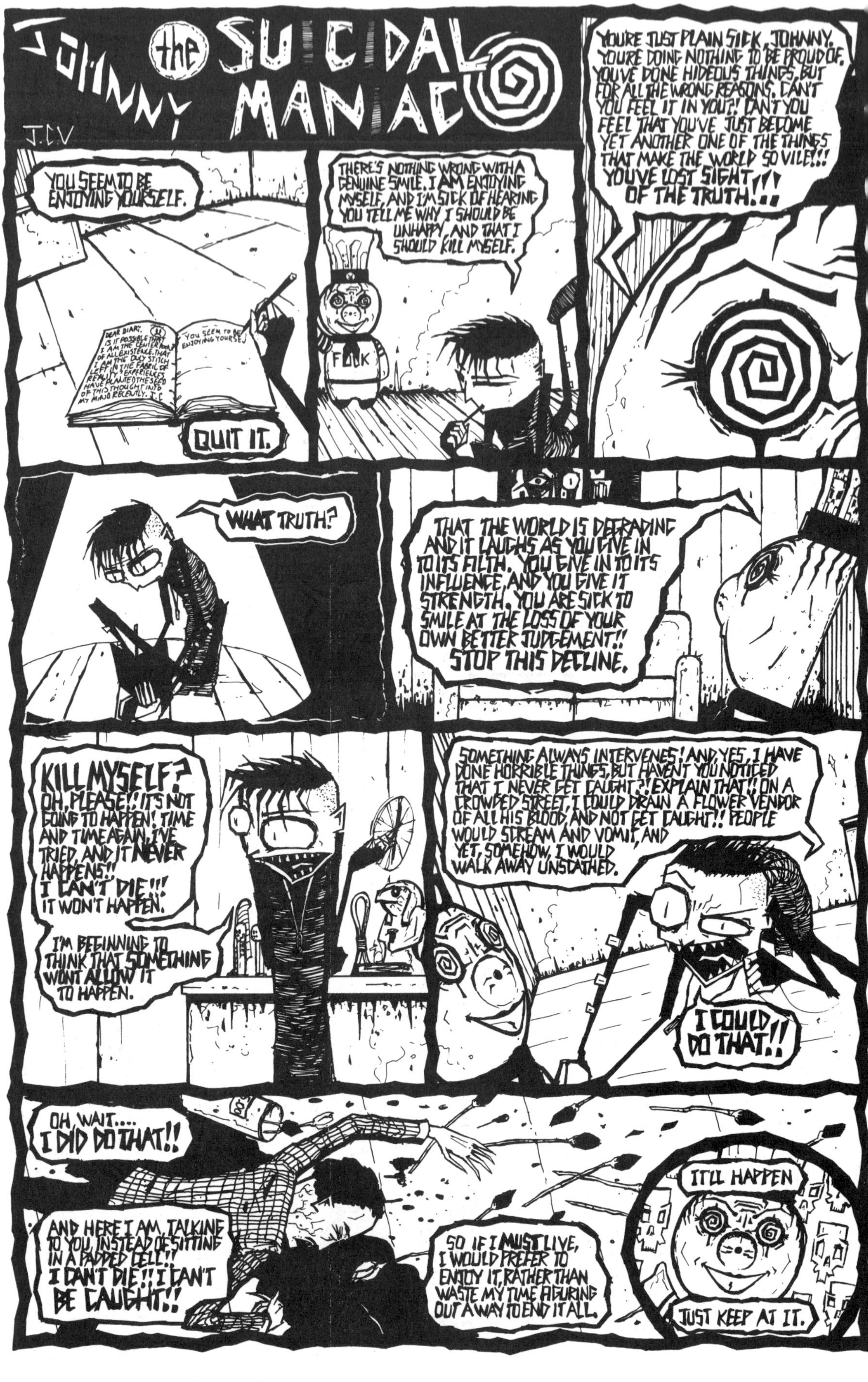
JOHNNY THE SUICIDAL MANIAC
J.C.V
YOU SEEM TO BE ENJOYING YOURSELF.
DEAR DIARY, IS IT POSSIBLE THAT I AM THE CENTER POINT OF ALL EXISTENCE. THAT I AM THE ONLY STITCH LEFT IN THE FABRIC OF REALITY? EXPERIENCES HAVE PLANTED THE SEED OF THIS THOUGHT INTO MY MIND RECENTLY. J.C
YOU SEEM TO BE ENJOYING YOURSE
QUIT IT.
THERE'S NOTHING WRONG WITH A GENUINE SMILE. I AM ENJOYING MYSELF, AND I'M SICK OF HEARING YOU TELL ME WHY I SHOULD BE UNHAPPY, AND THAT I SHOULD KILL MYSELF.
FOOK
YOU'RE JUST PLAIN SICK, JOHNNY. YOU'RE DOING NOTHING TO BE PROUD OF. YOU'VE DONE HIDEOUS THINGS, BUT FOR ALL THE WRONG REASONS. CAN'T YOU FEEL IT IN YOU?! CAN'T YOU FEEL THAT YOU'VE JUST BECOME YET ANOTHER ONE OF THE THINGS THAT MAKE THE WORLD SO VILE?!! YOU'VE LOST SIGHT OF THE TRUTH!!!
WHAT TRUTH?
THAT THE WORLD IS DEGRADING AND IT LAUGHS AS YOU GIVE IN TO ITS FILTH. YOU GIVE IN TO ITS INFLUENCE, AND YOU GIVE IT STRENGTH. YOU ARE SICK TO SMILE AT THE LOSS OF YOUR OWN BETTER JUDGEMENT!! STOP THIS DECLINE.
KILL MYSELF? OH, PLEASE! IT'S NOT GOING TO HAPPEN! TIME AND TIME AGAIN, I'VE TRIED, AND IT NEVER HAPPENS!! I CAN'T DIE!!! IT WON'T HAPPEN.
I'M BEGINNING TO THINK THAT SOMETHING WON'T ALLOW IT TO HAPPEN.
SOMETHING ALWAYS INTERVENES! AND YES, I HAVE DONE HORRIBLE THINGS, BUT HAVEN'T YOU NOTICED THAT I NEVER GET CAUGHT?! EXPLAIN THAT!! ON A CROWDED STREET, I COULD DRAIN A FLOWER VENDOR OF ALL HIS BLOOD AND NOT GET CAUGHT!! PEOPLE WOULD SCREAM AND VOMIT, AND YET, SOMEHOW, I WOULD WALK AWAY UNSCATHED.
I COULD DO THAT!!
OH WAIT.... I DID DO THAT!!
AND HERE I AM TALKING TO YOU, INSTEAD OF SITTING IN A PADDED CELL!! I CAN'T DIE!! I CAN'T BE CAUGHT!!
SO IF I MUST LIVE, I WOULD PREFER TO ENJOY IT, RATHER THAN WASTE MY TIME FIGURING OUT A WAY TO END IT ALL.
IT'LL HAPPEN
JUST KEEP AT IT.

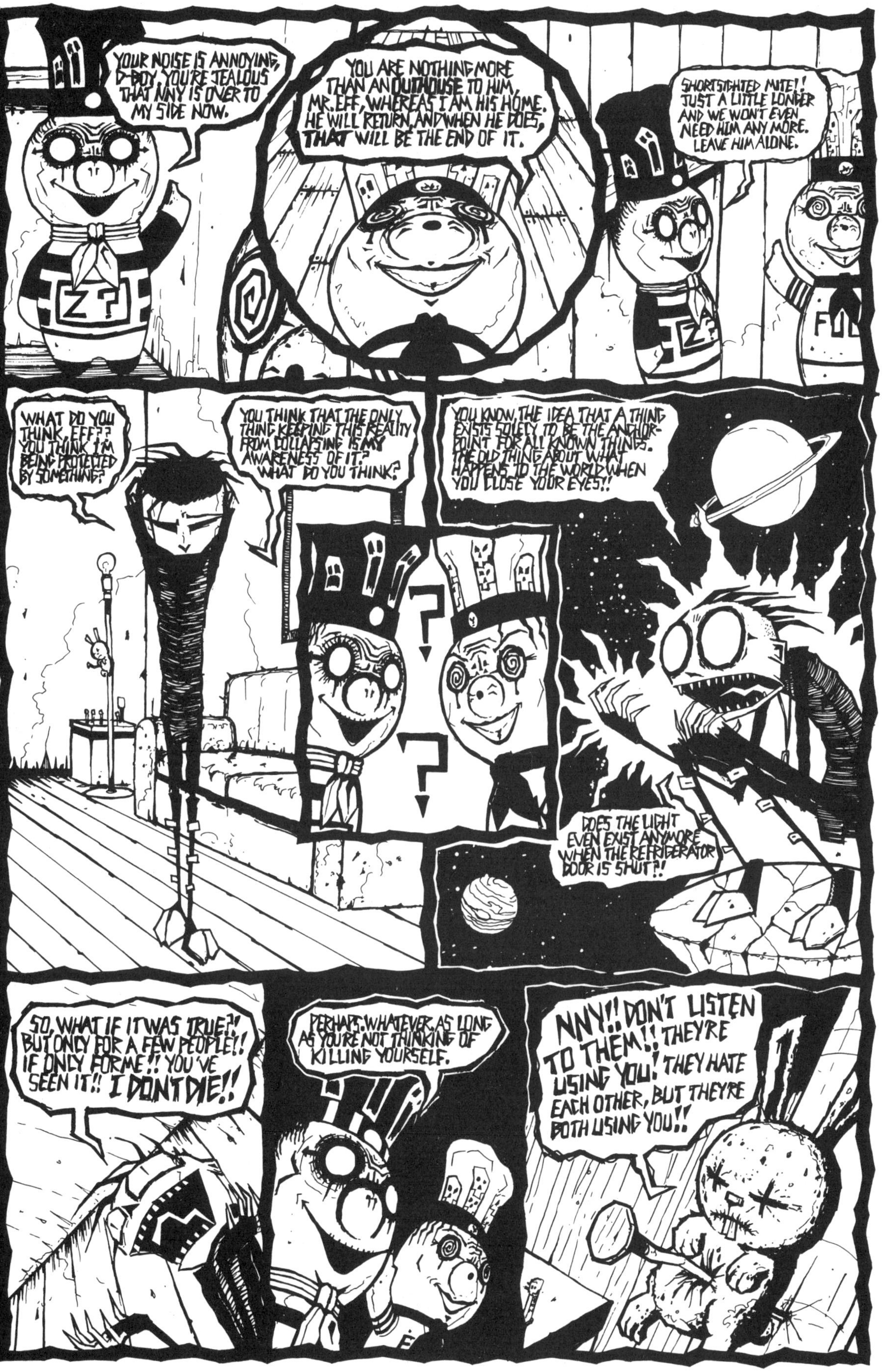
YOUR NOISE IS ANNOYING, D-BOY. YOU'RE JEALOUS THAT NNY IS OVER TO MY SIDE NOW.
YOU ARE NOTHING MORE THAN AN OUTHOUSE TO HIM, MR. EFF, WHEREAS I AM HIS HOME. HE WILL RETURN, AND WHEN HE DOES, THAT WILL BE THE END OF IT.
SHORTSIGHTED MITE!! JUST A LITTLE LONGER AND WE WON'T EVEN NEED HIM ANY MORE. LEAVE HIM ALONE.
FU
WHAT DO YOU THINK, EFF?? YOU THINK I'M BEING PROTECTED BY SOMETHING?
YOU THINK THAT THE ONLY THING KEEPING THIS REALITY FROM COLLAPSING IS MY AWARENESS OF IT? WHAT DO YOU THINK?
YOU KNOW, THE IDEA THAT A THING EXISTS SOLELY TO BE THE ANCHOR-POINT FOR ALL KNOWN THINGS. THE OLD THING ABOUT WHAT HAPPENS TO THE WORLD WHEN YOU CLOSE YOUR EYES!!
DOES THE LIGHT EVEN EXIST ANYMORE WHEN THE REFRIGERATOR DOOR IS SHUT?!
SO, WHAT IF IT WAS TRUE?! BUT ONLY FOR A FEW PEOPLE!! IF ONLY FOR ME!! YOU'VE SEEN IT!! I DON'T DIE!!
PERHAPS. WHATEVER. AS LONG AS YOU'RE NOT THINKING OF KILLING YOURSELF.
NNY!! DON'T LISTEN TO THEM!! THEY'RE USING YOU! THEY HATE EACH OTHER, BUT THEY'RE BOTH USING YOU!!

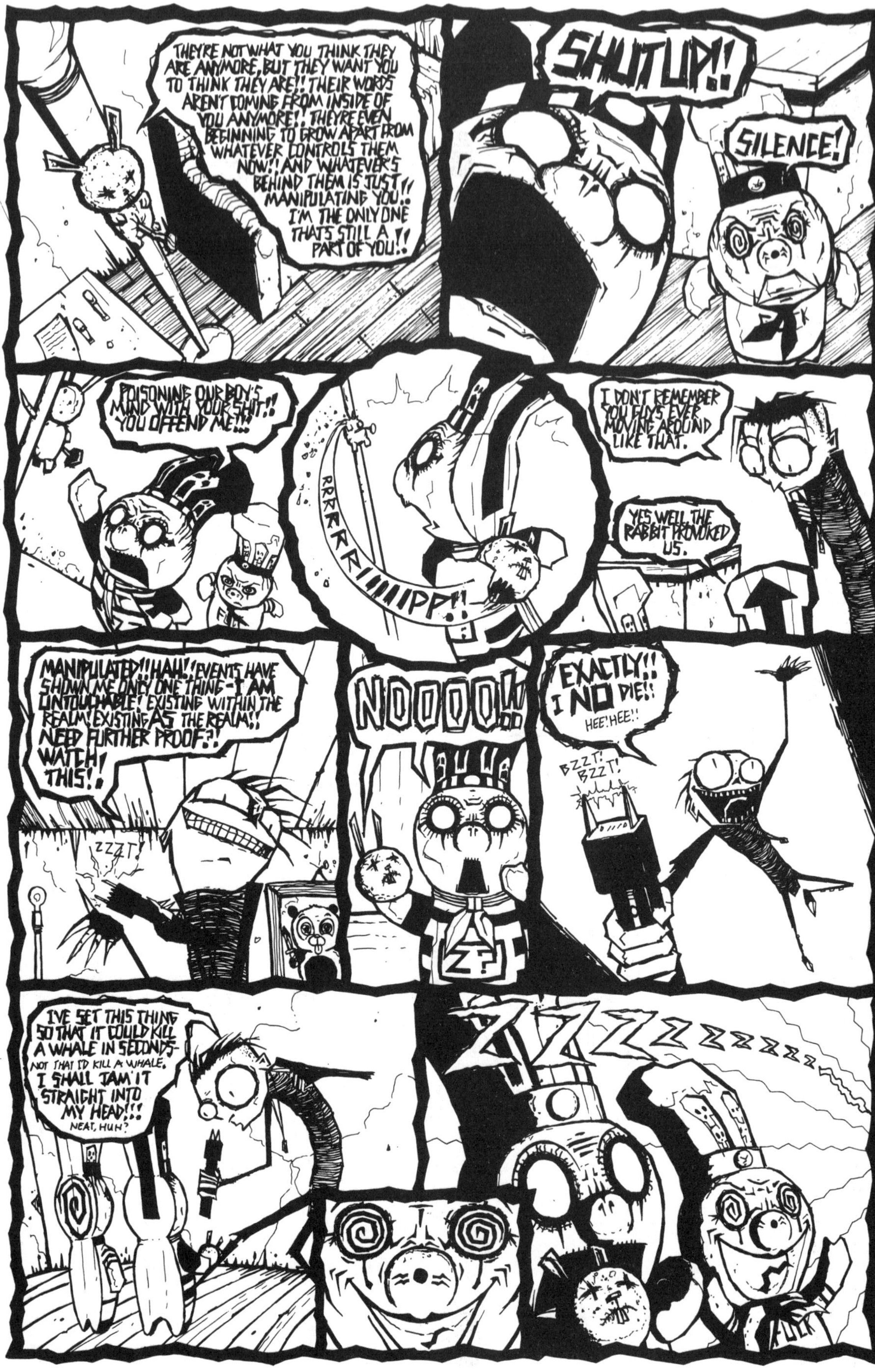
THEY'RE NOT WHAT YOU THINK THEY ARE ANYMORE, BUT THEY WANT YOU TO THINK THEY ARE!! THEIR WORDS AREN'T COMING FROM INSIDE OF YOU ANYMORE!! THEY'RE EVEN BEGINNING TO GROW APART FROM WHATEVER CONTROLS THEM NOW!! AND WHATEVER'S BEHIND THEM IS JUST MANIPULATING YOU!! I'M THE ONLY ONE THAT'S STILL A PART OF YOU!!
SHUT UP!!
SILENCE!
POISONING OUR BOY'S MIND WITH YOUR SHIT!! YOU OFFEND ME!!!
RRRRRRRIIIIIPP!!
I DON'T REMEMBER YOU GUYS EVER MOVING AROUND LIKE THAT.
YES WELL, THE RABBIT PROVOKED US.
MANIPULATED!! HAH!! EVENTS HAVE SHOWN ME ONLY ONE THING - I AM UNTOUCHABLE! EXISTING WITHIN THE REALM! EXISTING AS THE REALM!! NEED FURTHER PROOF?! WATCH THIS!!
ZZZT!
NOOOOO!!
EXACTLY!! I NO DIE!!
HEE! HEE!!
BZZT! BZZT!
I'VE SET THIS THING SO THAT IT COULD KILL A WHALE IN SECONDS-
NOT THAT I'D KILL A WHALE.
I SHALL JAM IT STRAIGHT INTO MY HEAD!!!
NEAT, HUH?
ZZZZZZZZZZZ

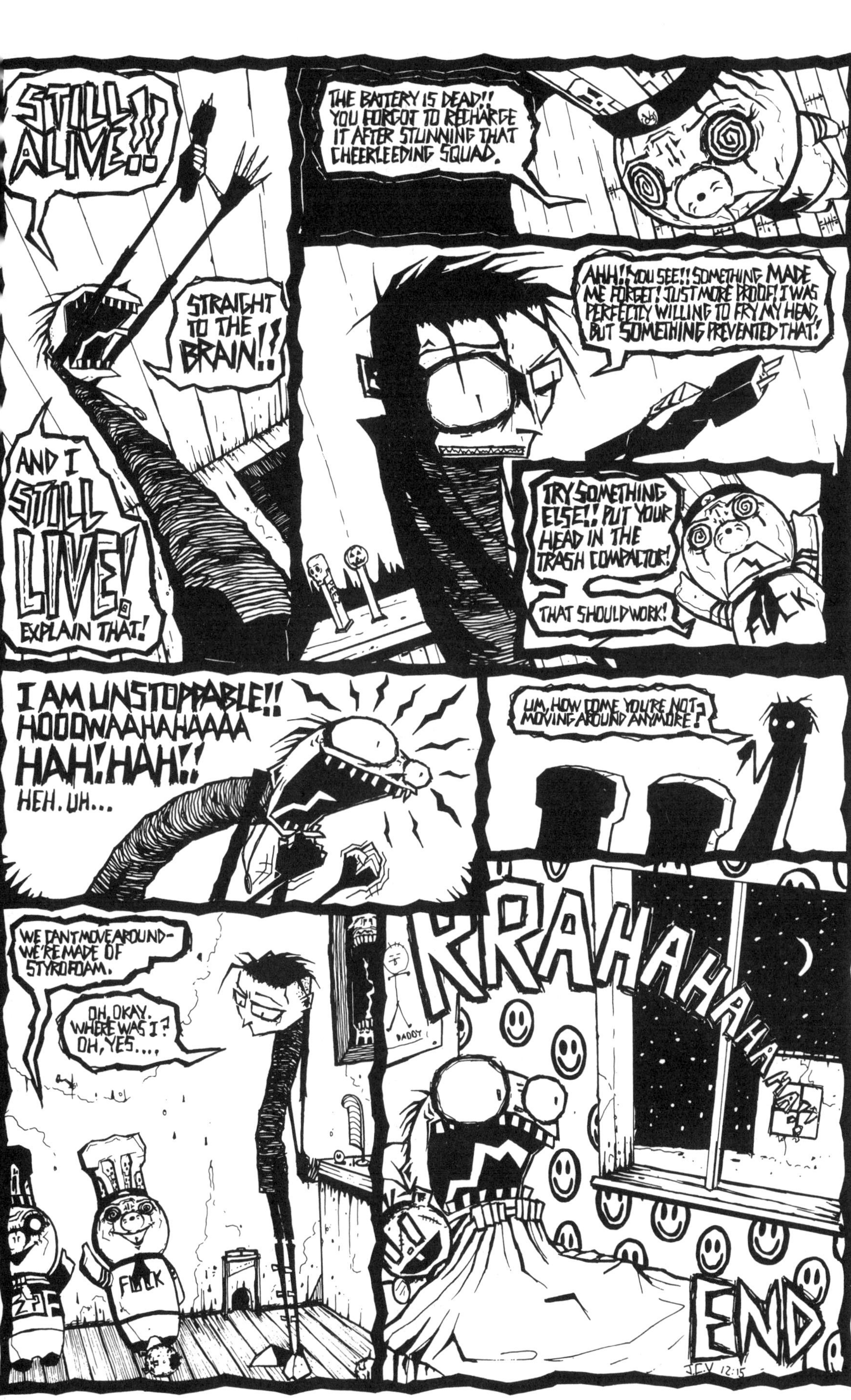
STILL ALIVE!!??
STRAIGHT TO THE BRAIN!!?
AND I STILL LIVE! EXPLAIN THAT!
THE BATTERY IS DEAD!! YOU FORGOT TO RECHARGE IT AFTER STUNNING THAT CHEERLEEDING SQUAD.
AHH!! YOU SEE!! SOMETHING MADE ME FORGET! JUST MORE PROOF! I WAS PERFECTLY WILLING TO FRY MY HEAD, BUT SOMETHING PREVENTED THAT!
TRY SOMETHING ELSE!! PUT YOUR HEAD IN THE TRASH COMPACTOR!
THAT SHOULD WORK!
FUCK
I AM UNSTOPPABLE!! HOOOWAAHAHAAAA HAH! HAH!!
HEH. UH...
UM, HOW COME YOU'RE NOT MOVING AROUND ANYMORE?
WE CAN'T MOVE AROUND- WE'RE MADE OF STYROFOAM.
OH, OKAY. WHERE WAS I? OH, YES....
FUCK
DADDY
RRAHAHAHAHA
END
J.C.V 12:15

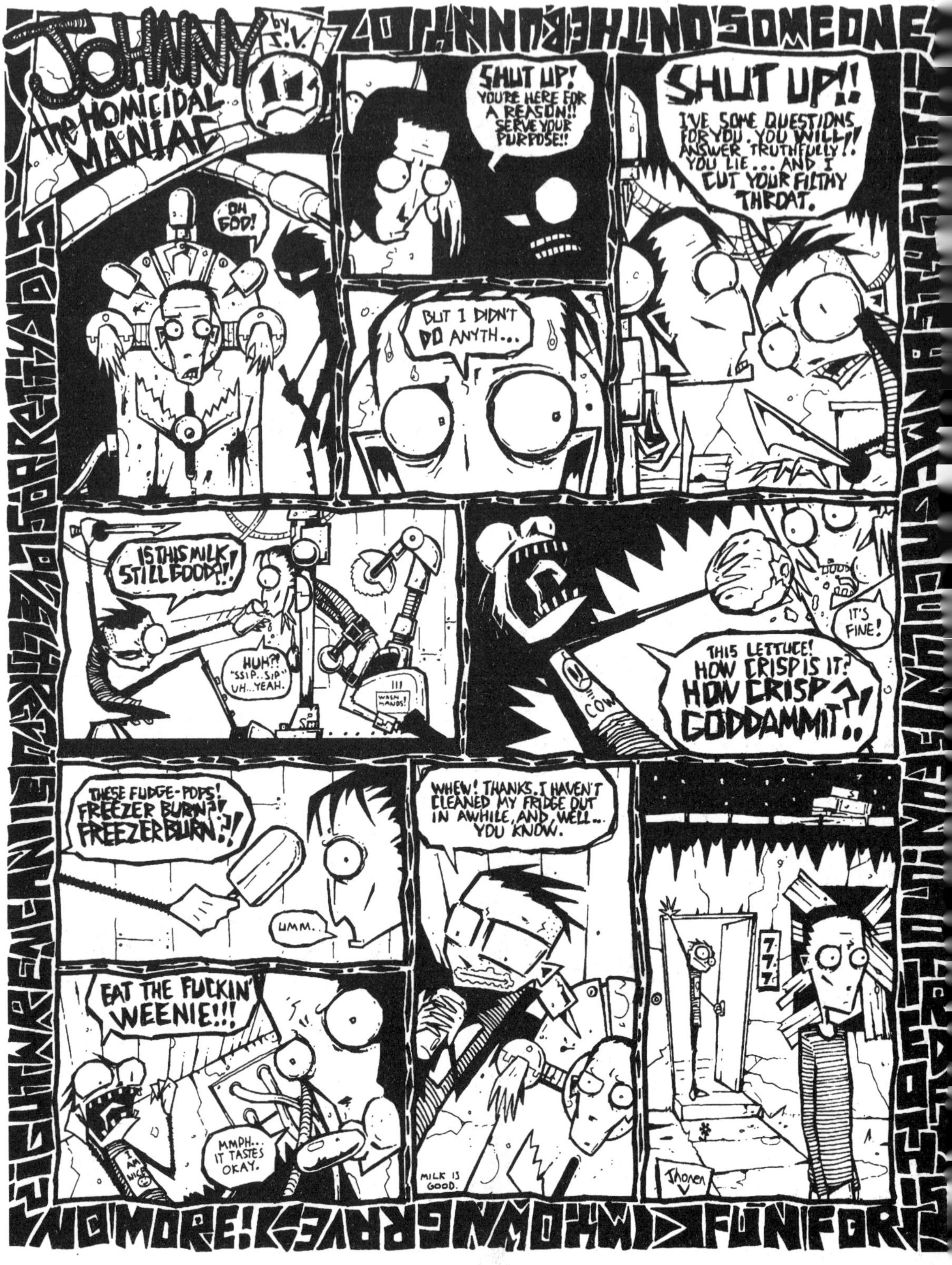

JOHNNY the HOMICIDAL MANIAC
by J.V.
11
OH GOD!
SHUT UP! YOU'RE HERE FOR A REASON!! SERVE YOUR PURPOSE!!
SHUT UP!!
I'VE SOME QUESTIONS FOR YOU. YOU WILL ANSWER TRUTHFULLY!! YOU LIE... AND I CUT YOUR FILTHY THROAT.
BUT I DIDN'T DO ANYTH...
IS THIS MILK STILL GOOD?!!
HUH?! "SSIP.. SIP" UH... YEAH.
WASH HANDS!
COW
IT'S FINE!
THIS LETTUCE! HOW CRISP IS IT? HOW CRISP?! GODDAMMIT?!!
THESE FUDGE-POPS! FREEZER BURN?! FREEZER BURN?!!
UMM..
WHEW! THANKS. I HAVEN'T CLEANED MY FRIDGE OUT IN AWHILE, AND WELL... YOU KNOW.
EAT THE FUCKIN' WEENIE!!!
MMPH... IT TASTES OKAY.
MILK IS GOOD.
777
Jhonen V

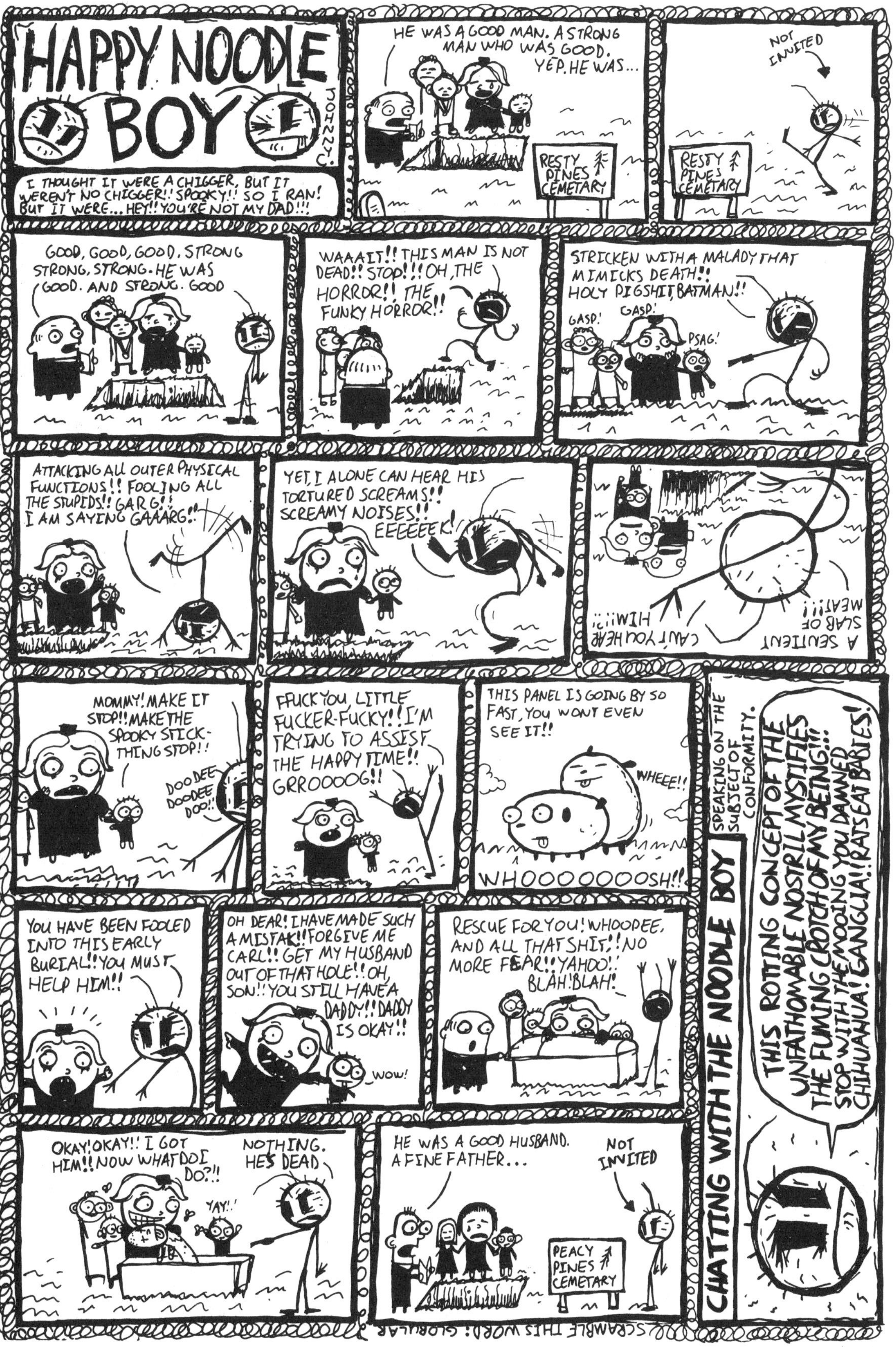

HAPPY NOODLE BOY
JOHNNY C.
I THOUGHT IT WERE A CHIGGER, BUT IT WEREN'T NO CHIGGER!! SPOOKY!! SO I RAN! BUT IT WERE... HEY!! YOU'RE NOT MY DAD!!!
HE WAS A GOOD MAN. A STRONG MAN WHO WAS GOOD.
YEP. HE WAS...
RESTY PINES CEMETARY
NOT INVITED
RESTY PINES CEMETARY
GOOD, GOOD, GOOD. STRONG STRONG, STRONG. HE WAS GOOD. AND STRONG. GOOD
WAAAIT!! THIS MAN IS NOT DEAD!! STOP!!! OH, THE HORROR!! THE FUNKY HORROR!!
STRICKEN WITH A MALADY THAT MIMICKS DEATH!! HOLY PIGSHIT, BATMAN!!
GASP!
GASP!
PSAG!
ATTACKING ALL OUTER PHYSICAL FUNCTIONS!! FOOLING ALL THE STUPIDS!! GARG!! I AM SAYING GAAARG!!
YET, I ALONE CAN HEAR HIS TORTURED SCREAMS!! SCREAMY NOISES!!
EEEEEEK!
A SENTIENT SLAB OF MEAT!!!
CAN'T YOU HEAR HIM!!?!
MOMMY! MAKE IT STOP!! MAKE THE SPOOKY STICK-THING STOP!!
DOO DEE DOODEE DOO!!
FFUCK YOU, LITTLE FUCKER-FUCKY!! I'M TRYING TO ASSIST THE HAPPY TIME!! GRROOOOG!!
THIS PANEL IS GOING BY SO FAST, YOU WONT EVEN SEE IT!!
WHEEE!!
WHOOOOOOOOSH!!
YOU HAVE BEEN FOOLED INTO THIS EARLY BURIAL!! YOU MUST HELP HIM!!
OH DEAR! I HAVE MADE SUCH A MISTAK!! FORGIVE ME CARL!! GET MY HUSBAND OUT OF THAT HOLE!! OH, SON!! YOU STILL HAVE A DADDY!! DADDY IS OKAY!!
WOW!
RESCUE FOR YOU! WHOOPEE, AND ALL THAT SHIT!! NO MORE FEAR!! YAHOO!
BLAH! BLAH!
OKAY! OKAY!! I GOT HIM!! NOW WHAT DO I DO?!!
NOTHING. HE'S DEAD
YAY!!
HE WAS A GOOD HUSBAND. A FINE FATHER...
NOT INVITED
PEACY PINES CEMETARY
CHATTING WITH THE NOODLE BOY
SPEAKING ON THE SUBJECT OF CONFORMITY.
THIS ROTTING CONCEPT OF THE UNFATHOMABLE NOSTRIL MYSTIFIES THE FUMING CROTCH OF MY BEING!!! STOP WITH THE MOOING YOU DAMNED CHIHUAHUA! GANGLIA! RATS EAT BABIES!
SCRAMBLE THIS WORD: GLORULAR

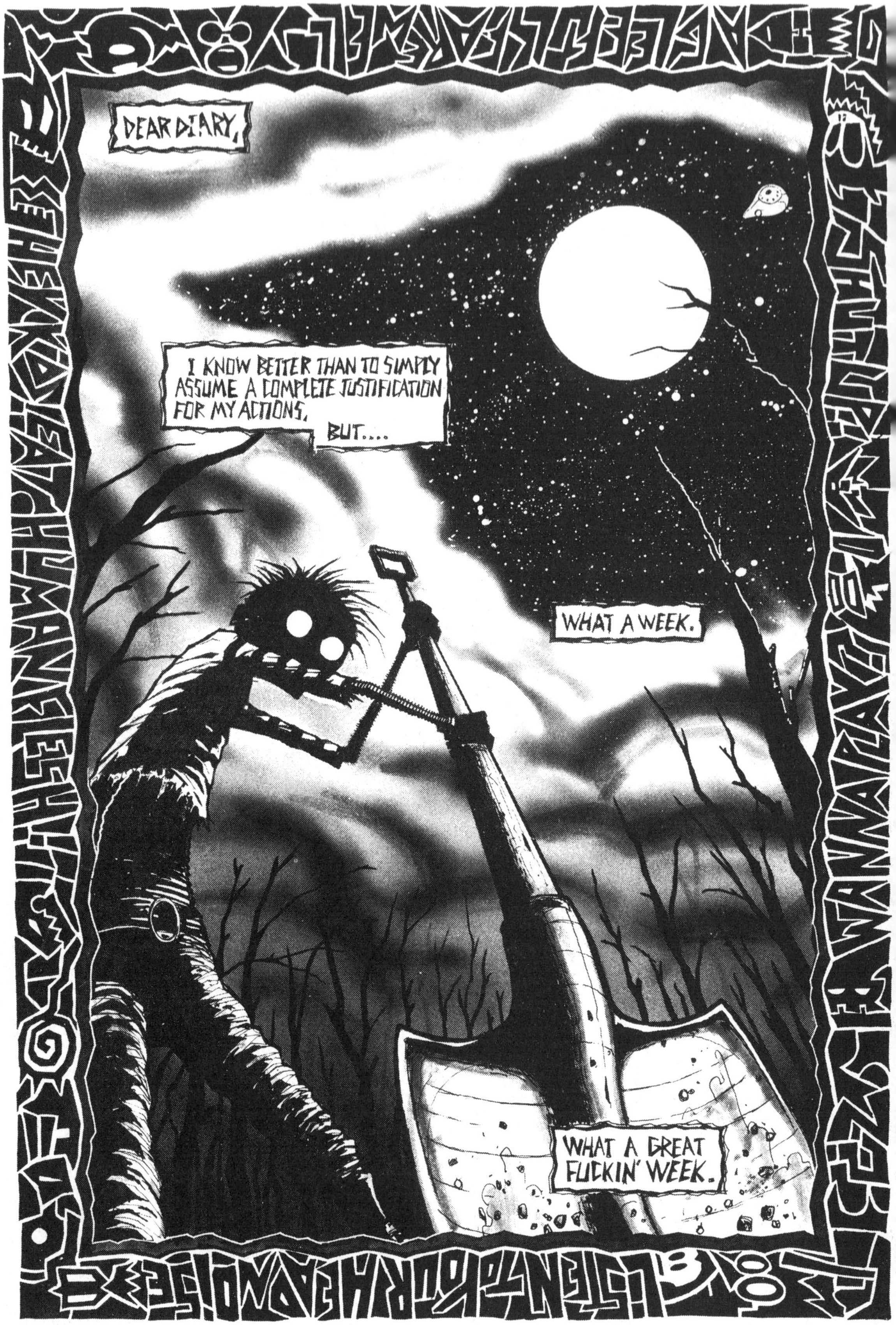
DEAR DIARY,
I KNOW BETTER THAN TO SIMPLY ASSUME A COMPLETE JUSTIFICATION FOR MY ACTIONS, BUT....
WHAT A WEEK.
WHAT A GREAT FUCKIN' WEEK.

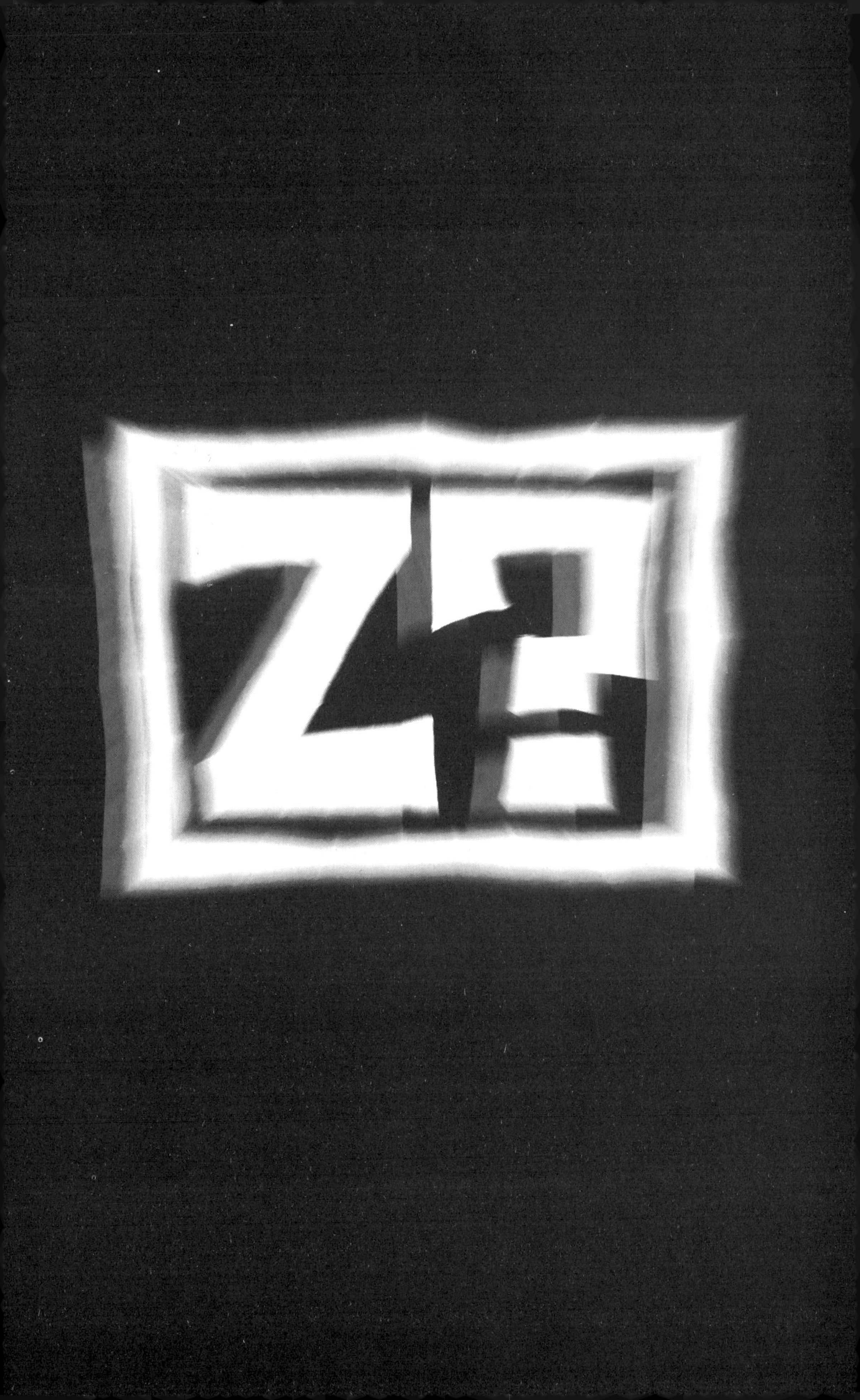

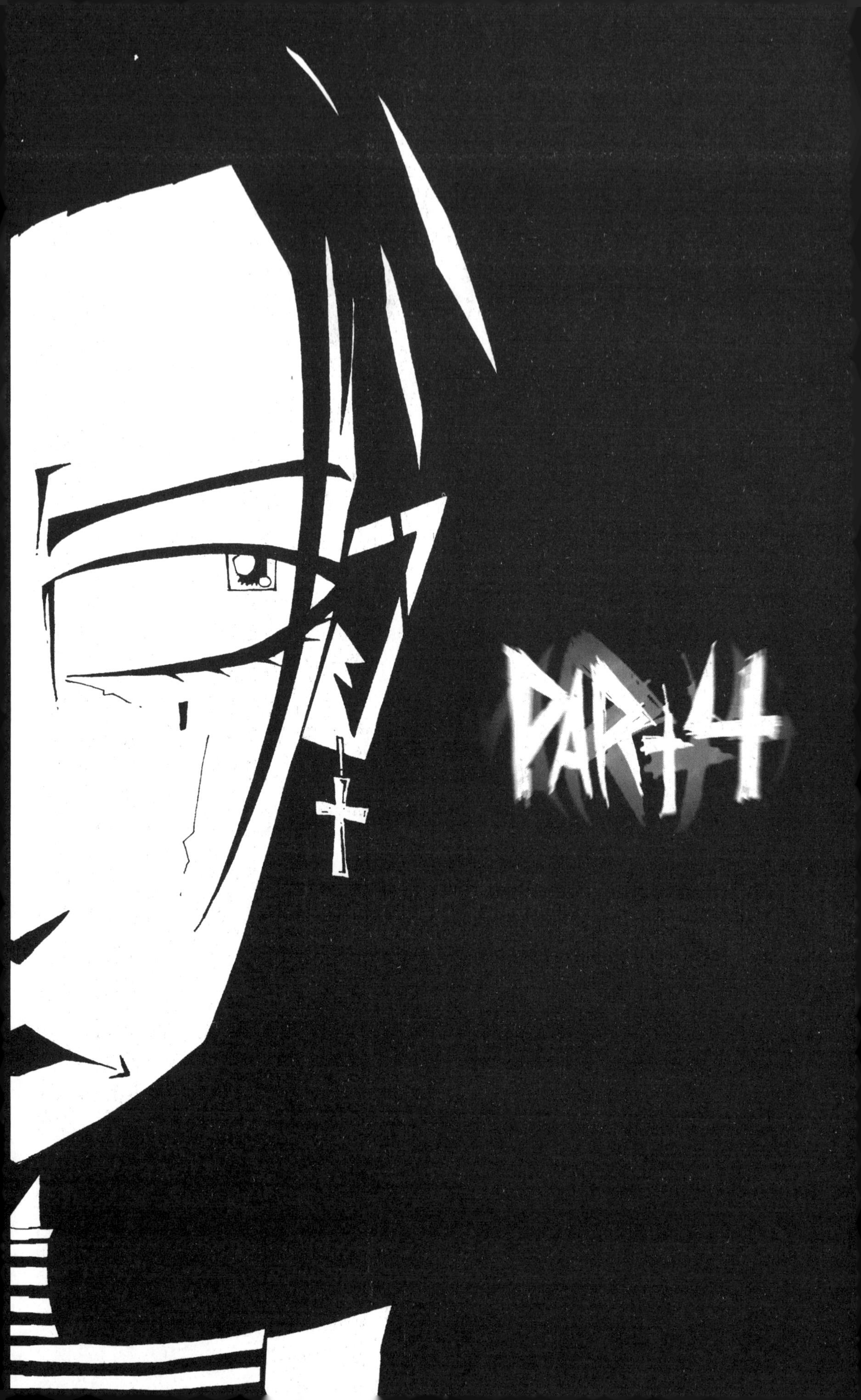
PART 4

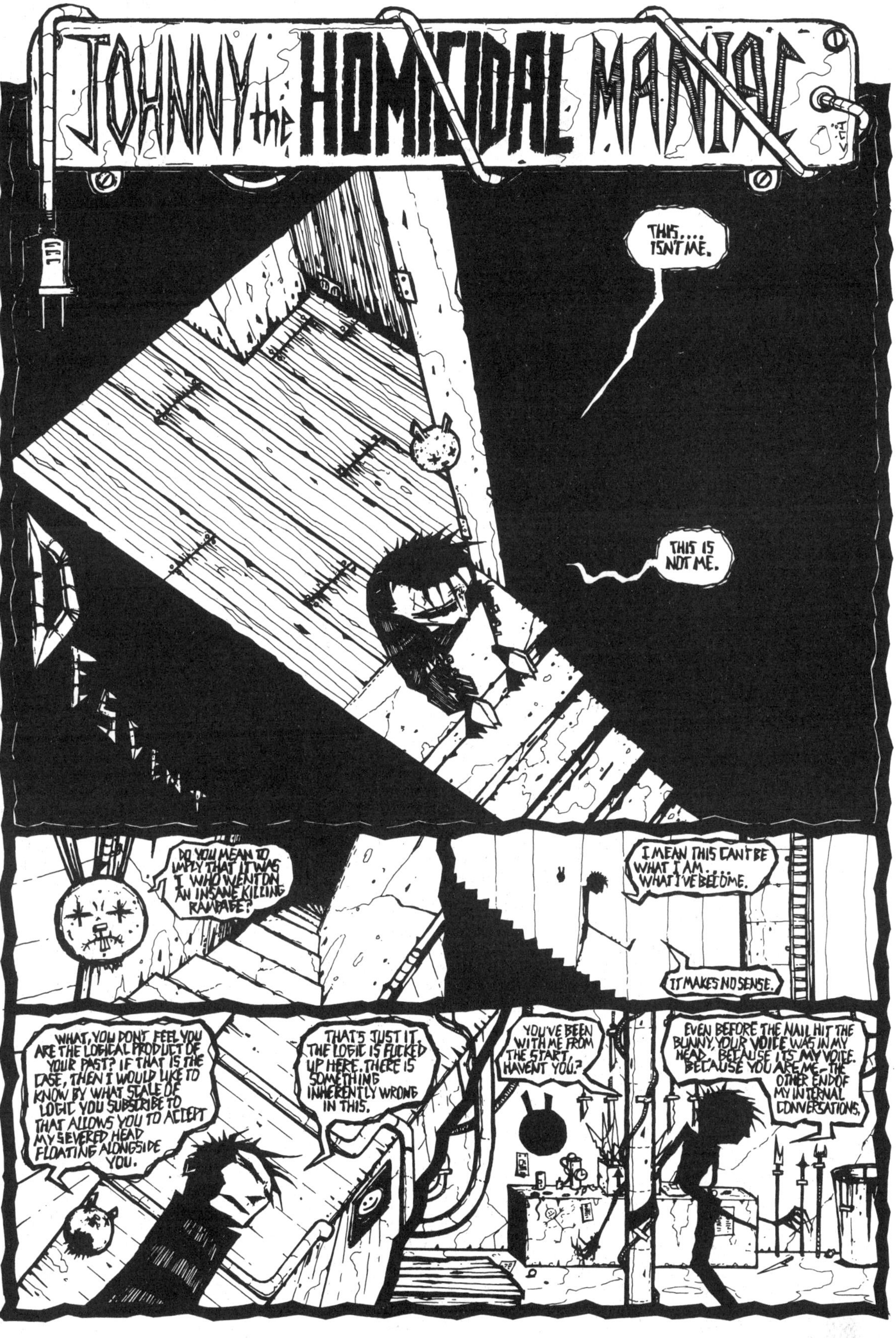
JOHNNY the HOMICIDAL MANIAC
THIS.... ISN'T ME.
THIS IS NOT ME.
DESCENT
DO YOU MEAN TO IMPLY THAT IT WAS I WHO WENT ON AN INSANE KILLING RAMPAGE?
I MEAN THIS CAN'T BE WHAT I AM... WHAT I'VE BECOME.
IT MAKES NO SENSE.
WHAT, YOU DON'T FEEL YOU ARE THE LOGICAL PRODUCT OF YOUR PAST? IF THAT IS THE CASE, THEN I WOULD LIKE TO KNOW BY WHAT SCALE OF LOGIC YOU SUBSCRIBE TO THAT ALLOWS YOU TO ACCEPT MY SEVERED HEAD FLOATING ALONGSIDE YOU.
THAT'S JUST IT. THE LOGIC IS FUCKED UP HERE. THERE IS SOMETHING INHERENTLY WRONG IN THIS.
YOU'VE BEEN WITH ME FROM THE START, HAVEN'T YOU?
EVEN BEFORE THE NAIL HIT THE BUNNY, YOUR VOICE WAS IN MY HEAD, BECAUSE IT'S MY VOICE. BECAUSE YOU ARE ME - THE OTHER END OF MY INTERNAL CONVERSATIONS.

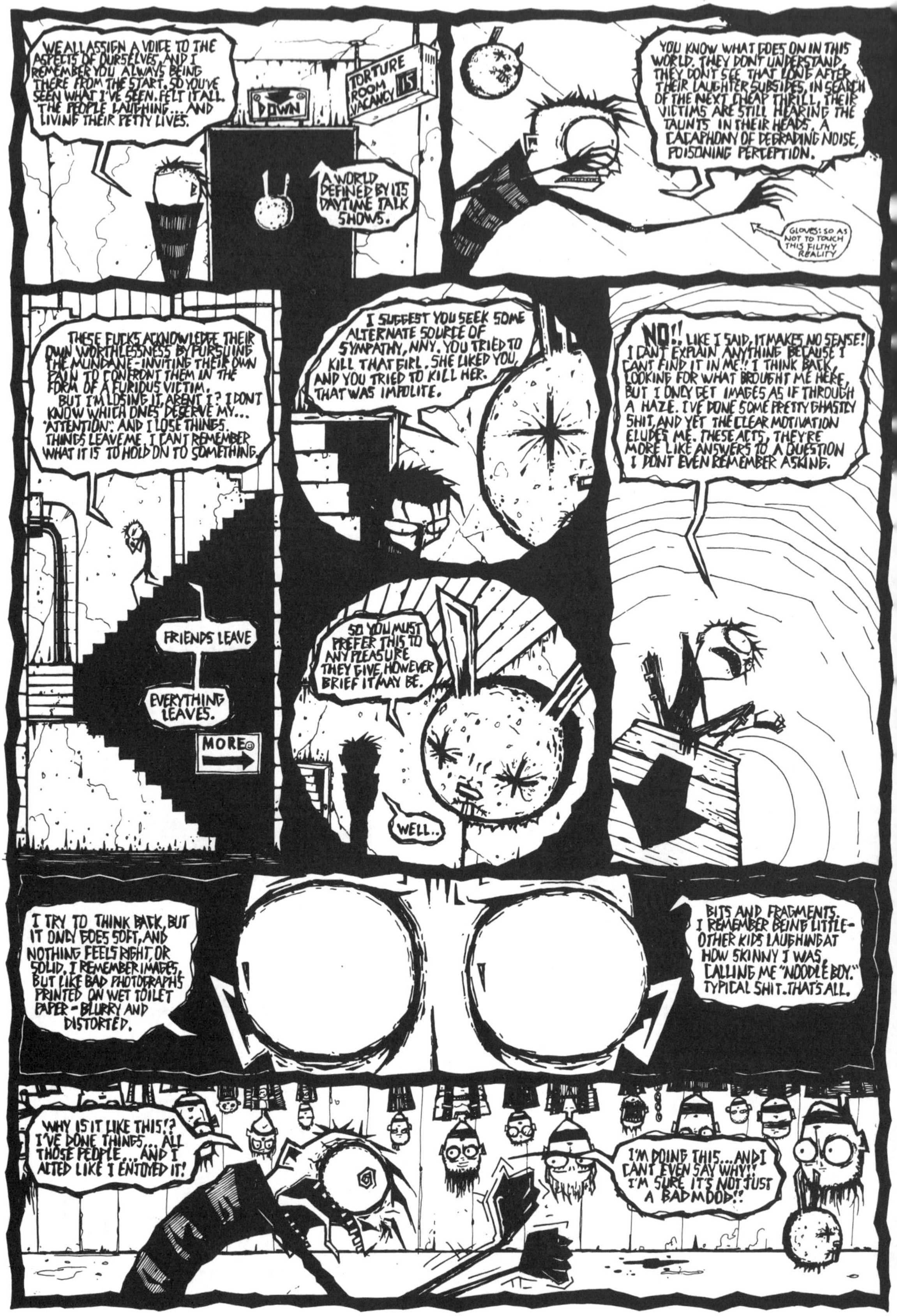
WE ALL ASSIGN A VOICE TO THE ASPECTS OF OURSELVES, AND I REMEMBER YOU ALWAYS BEING THERE FROM THE START. SO YOU'VE SEEN WHAT I'VE SEEN. FELT IT ALL. THE PEOPLE LAUGHING... AND LIVING THEIR PETTY LIVES.
DOWN
TORTURE ROOM VACANCY 15
A WORLD DEFINED BY ITS DAYTIME TALK SHOWS.
YOU KNOW WHAT GOES ON IN THIS WORLD. THEY DON'T UNDERSTAND. THEY DON'T SEE THAT LONG AFTER THEIR LAUGHTER SUBSIDES, IN SEARCH OF THE NEXT CHEAP THRILL, THEIR VICTIMS ARE STILL HEARING THE TAUNTS IN THEIR HEADS. A CACAPHONY OF DEGRADING NOISE, POISONING PERCEPTION.
GLOVES: SO AS NOT TO TOUCH THIS FILTHY REALITY
THESE FUCKS ACKNOWLEDGE THEIR OWN WORTHLESSNESS BY PURSUING THE MUNDANE - INVITING THEIR OWN PAIN TO CONFRONT THEM IN THE FORM OF A FURIOUS VICTIM. BUT I'M LOSING IT, AREN'T I? I DON'T KNOW WHICH ONES DESERVE MY... "ATTENTION". AND I LOSE THINGS. THINGS LEAVE ME. I CAN'T REMEMBER WHAT IT IS TO HOLD ON TO SOMETHING.
FRIENDS LEAVE
EVERYTHING LEAVES.
MORE
I SUGGEST YOU SEEK SOME ALTERNATE SOURCE OF SYMPATHY, NNY. YOU TRIED TO KILL THAT GIRL. SHE LIKED YOU, AND YOU TRIED TO KILL HER. THAT WAS IMPOLITE.
SO YOU MUST PREFER THIS TO ANY PLEASURE THEY GIVE, HOWEVER BRIEF IT MAY BE.
WELL..
NO!! LIKE I SAID, IT MAKES NO SENSE! I CAN'T EXPLAIN ANYTHING BECAUSE I CAN'T FIND IT IN ME!! I THINK BACK, LOOKING FOR WHAT BROUGHT ME HERE, BUT I ONLY GET IMAGES AS IF THROUGH A HAZE. I'VE DONE SOME PRETTY GHASTLY SHIT, AND YET THE CLEAR MOTIVATION ELUDES ME. THESE ACTS, THEY'RE MORE LIKE ANSWERS TO A QUESTION I DON'T EVEN REMEMBER ASKING.
I TRY TO THINK BACK, BUT IT ONLY GOES SOFT, AND NOTHING FEELS RIGHT, OR SOLID. I REMEMBER IMAGES, BUT LIKE BAD PHOTOGRAPHS PRINTED ON WET TOILET PAPER - BLURRY AND DISTORTED.
BITS AND FRAGMENTS. I REMEMBER BEING LITTLE - OTHER KIDS LAUGHING AT HOW SKINNY I WAS, CALLING ME "NOODLE BOY." TYPICAL SHIT. THAT'S ALL.
WHY IS IT LIKE THIS!? I'VE DONE THINGS... ALL THOSE PEOPLE... AND I ACTED LIKE I ENJOYED IT!
I'M DOING THIS... AND I CAN'T EVEN SAY WHY!! I'M SURE IT'S NOT JUST A BAD MOOD!!

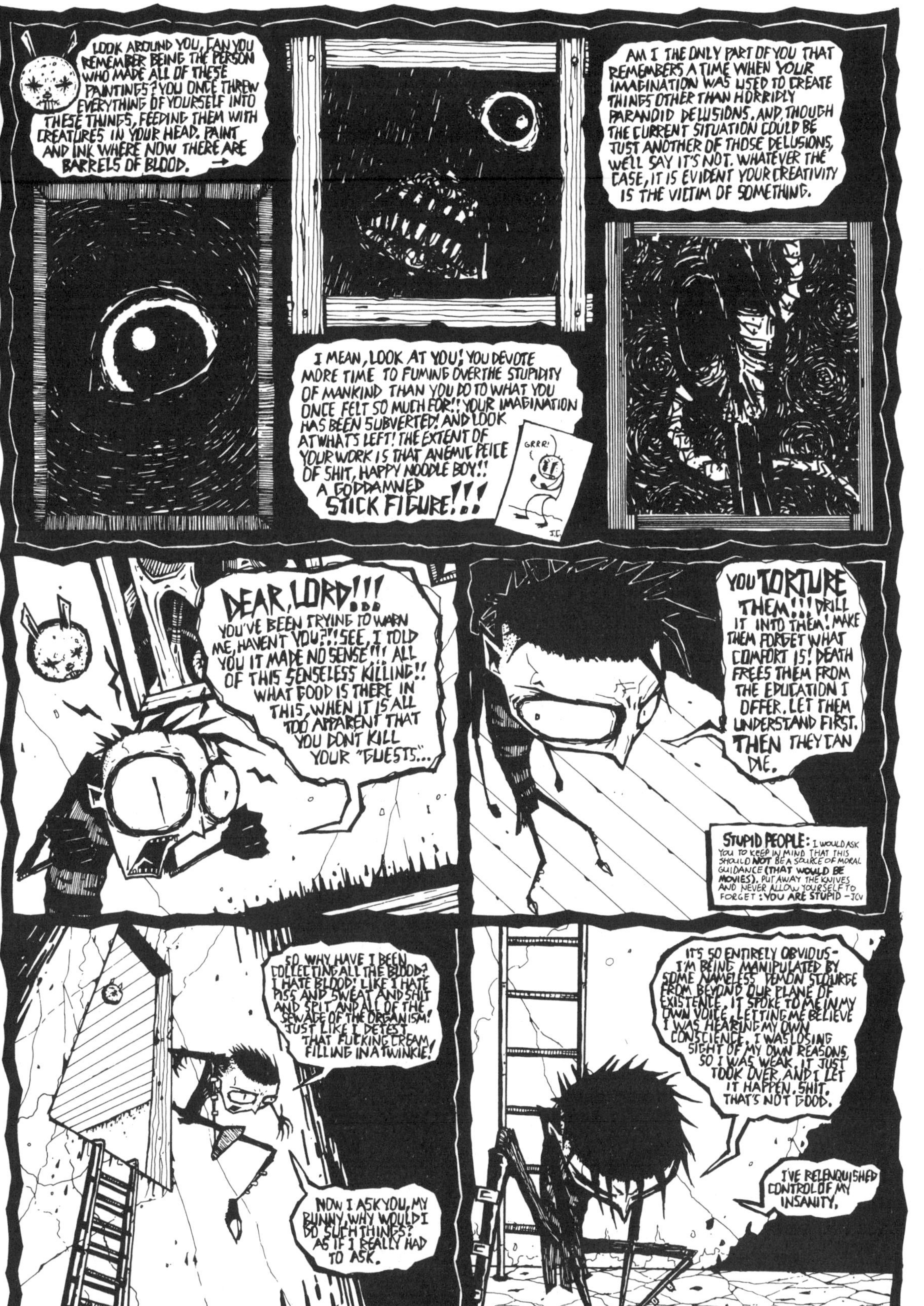
LOOK AROUND YOU. CAN YOU REMEMBER BEING THE PERSON WHO MADE ALL OF THESE PAINTINGS? YOU ONCE THREW EVERYTHING OF YOURSELF INTO THESE THINGS, FEEDING THEM WITH CREATURES IN YOUR HEAD. PAINT AND INK WHERE NOW THERE ARE BARRELS OF BLOOD. →
AM I THE ONLY PART OF YOU THAT REMEMBERS A TIME WHEN YOUR IMAGINATION WAS USED TO CREATE THINGS OTHER THAN HORRIDLY PARANOID DELUSIONS. AND, THOUGH THE CURRENT SITUATION COULD BE JUST ANOTHER OF THOSE DELUSIONS, WE'LL SAY IT'S NOT. WHATEVER THE CASE, IT IS EVIDENT YOUR CREATIVITY IS THE VICTIM OF SOMETHING.
I MEAN, LOOK AT YOU! YOU DEVOTE MORE TIME TO FUMING OVER THE STUPIDITY OF MANKIND THAN YOU DO TO WHAT YOU ONCE FELT SO MUCH FOR!! YOUR IMAGINATION HAS BEEN SUBVERTED! AND LOOK AT WHAT'S LEFT! THE EXTENT OF YOUR WORK IS THAT ANEMIC PEICE OF SHIT, HAPPY NOODLE BOY!! A GODDAMNED STICK FIGURE!!!
GRRR!
J.C.
DEAR, LORD!!!... YOU'VE BEEN TRYING TO WARN ME, HAVEN'T YOU?!! SEE, I TOLD YOU IT MADE NO SENSE!!! ALL OF THIS SENSELESS KILLING!! WHAT GOOD IS THERE IN THIS, WHEN IT IS ALL TOO APPARENT THAT YOU DON'T KILL YOUR "GUESTS"...
YOU TORTURE THEM!!! DRILL IT INTO THEM! MAKE THEM FORGET WHAT COMFORT IS! DEATH FREES THEM FROM THE EDUCATION I OFFER. LET THEM UNDERSTAND FIRST. THEN THEY CAN DIE.
STUPID PEOPLE: I WOULD ASK YOU TO KEEP IN MIND THAT THIS SHOULD NOT BE A SOURCE OF MORAL GUIDANCE (THAT WOULD BE MOVIES). PUT AWAY THE KNIVES AND NEVER ALLOW YOURSELF TO FORGET: YOU ARE STUPID -JCV
SO WHY HAVE I BEEN COLLECTING ALL THE BLOOD? I HATE BLOOD! LIKE I HATE PISS AND SWEAT AND SHIT AND SPIT AND ALL OF THE SEWAGE OF THE ORGANISM! JUST LIKE I DETEST THAT FUCKING CREAM FILLING IN A TWINKIE!
NOW I ASK YOU, MY BUNNY, WHY WOULD I DO SUCH THINGS? AS IF I REALLY HAD TO ASK.
IT'S SO ENTIRELY OBVIOUS - I'M BEING MANIPULATED BY SOME NAMELESS DEMON SCOURGE FROM BEYOND OUR PLANE OF EXISTENCE. IT SPOKE TO ME IN MY OWN VOICE, LETTING ME BELIEVE I WAS HEARING MY OWN CONSCIENCE. I WAS LOSING SIGHT OF MY OWN REASONS, SO I WAS WEAK. IT JUST TOOK OVER, AND I LET IT HAPPEN. SHIT. THAT'S NOT GOOD.
I'VE RELENQUISHED CONTROL OF MY INSANITY.

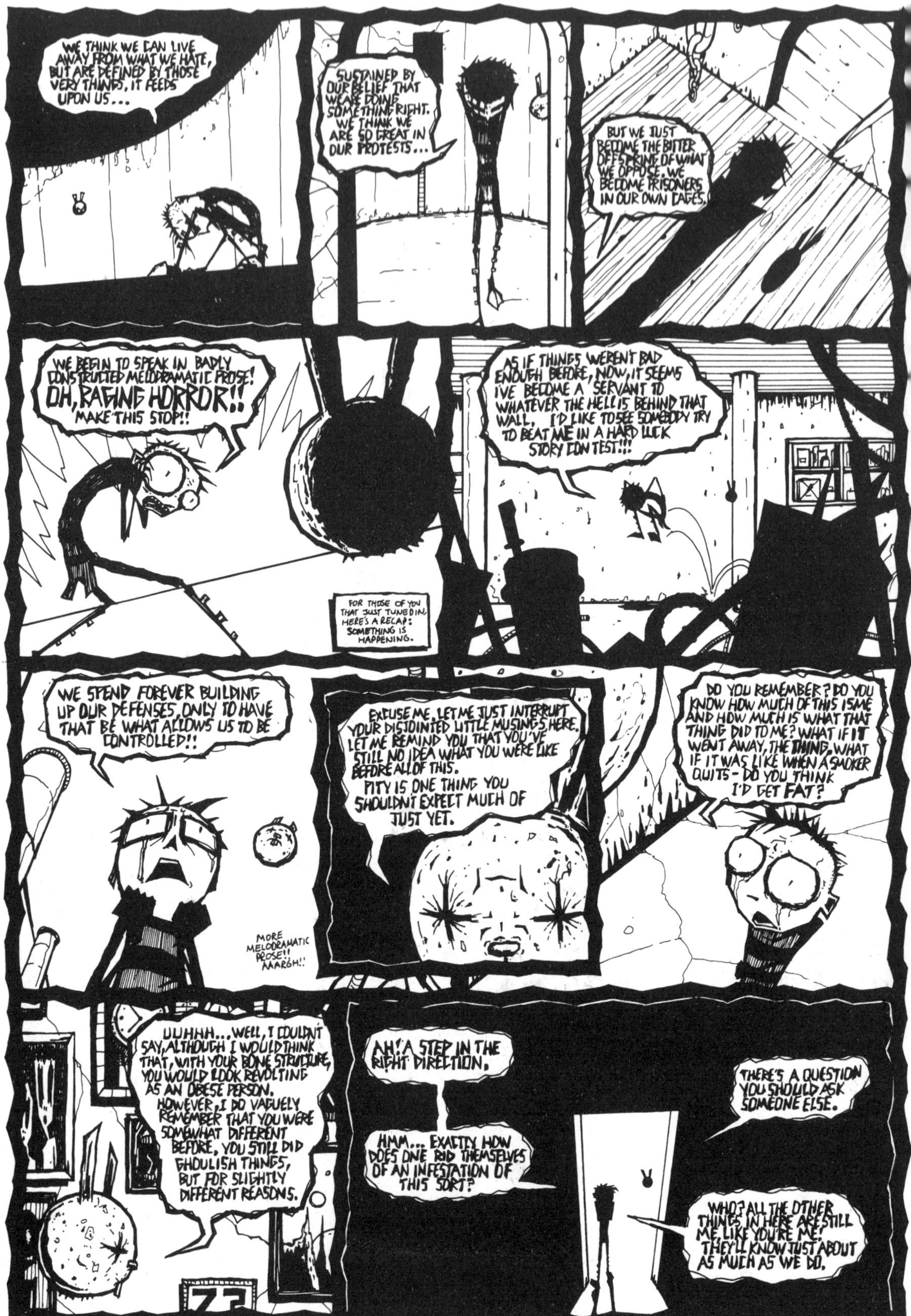
WE THINK WE CAN LIVE AWAY FROM WHAT WE HATE, BUT ARE DEFINED BY THOSE VERY THINGS. IT FEEDS UPON US...
SUSTAINED BY OUR BELIEF THAT WE ARE DOING SOMETHING RIGHT. WE THINK WE ARE SO GREAT IN OUR PROTESTS...
BUT WE JUST BECOME THE BITTER OFFSPRING OF WHAT WE OPPOSE. WE BECOME PRISONERS IN OUR OWN CAGES.
WE BEGIN TO SPEAK IN BADLY CONSTRUCTED MELODRAMATIC PROSE! OH, RAGING HORROR!! MAKE THIS STOP!!
AS IF THINGS WEREN'T BAD ENOUGH BEFORE, NOW, IT SEEMS I'VE BECOME A SERVANT TO WHATEVER THE HELL IS BEHIND THAT WALL. I'D LIKE TO SEE SOMEBODY TRY TO BEAT ME IN A HARD LUCK STORY CONTEST!!!
FOR THOSE OF YOU THAT JUST TUNED IN, HERE'S A RECAP: SOMETHING IS HAPPENING.
WE SPEND FOREVER BUILDING UP OUR DEFENSES, ONLY TO HAVE THAT BE WHAT ALLOWS US TO BE CONTROLLED!!
MORE MELODRAMATIC PROSE!! AAARGH!!
EXCUSE ME, LET ME JUST INTERRUPT YOUR DISJOINTED LITTLE MUSINGS HERE. LET ME REMIND YOU THAT YOU'VE STILL NO IDEA WHAT YOU WERE LIKE BEFORE ALL OF THIS. PITY IS ONE THING YOU SHOULDN'T EXPECT MUCH OF JUST YET.
DO YOU REMEMBER? DO YOU KNOW HOW MUCH OF THIS IS ME AND HOW MUCH IS WHAT THAT THING DID TO ME? WHAT IF IT WENT AWAY, THE THING. WHAT IF IT WAS LIKE WHEN A SMOKER QUITS - DO YOU THINK I'D GET FAT?
UUHHH... WELL, I COULDN'T SAY, ALTHOUGH I WOULD THINK THAT, WITH YOUR BONE STRUCTURE, YOU WOULD LOOK REVOLTING AS AN OBESE PERSON. HOWEVER, I DO VAGUELY REMEMBER THAT YOU WERE SOMEWHAT DIFFERENT BEFORE. YOU STILL DID GHOULISH THINGS, BUT FOR SLIGHTLY DIFFERENT REASONS.
AH! A STEP IN THE RIGHT DIRECTION.
HMM... EXACTLY HOW DOES ONE RID THEMSELVES OF AN INFESTATION OF THIS SORT?
THERE'S A QUESTION YOU SHOULD ASK SOMEONE ELSE.
WHO? ALL THE OTHER THINGS IN HERE ARE STILL ME, LIKE YOU'RE ME. THEY'LL KNOW JUST ABOUT AS MUCH AS WE DO.

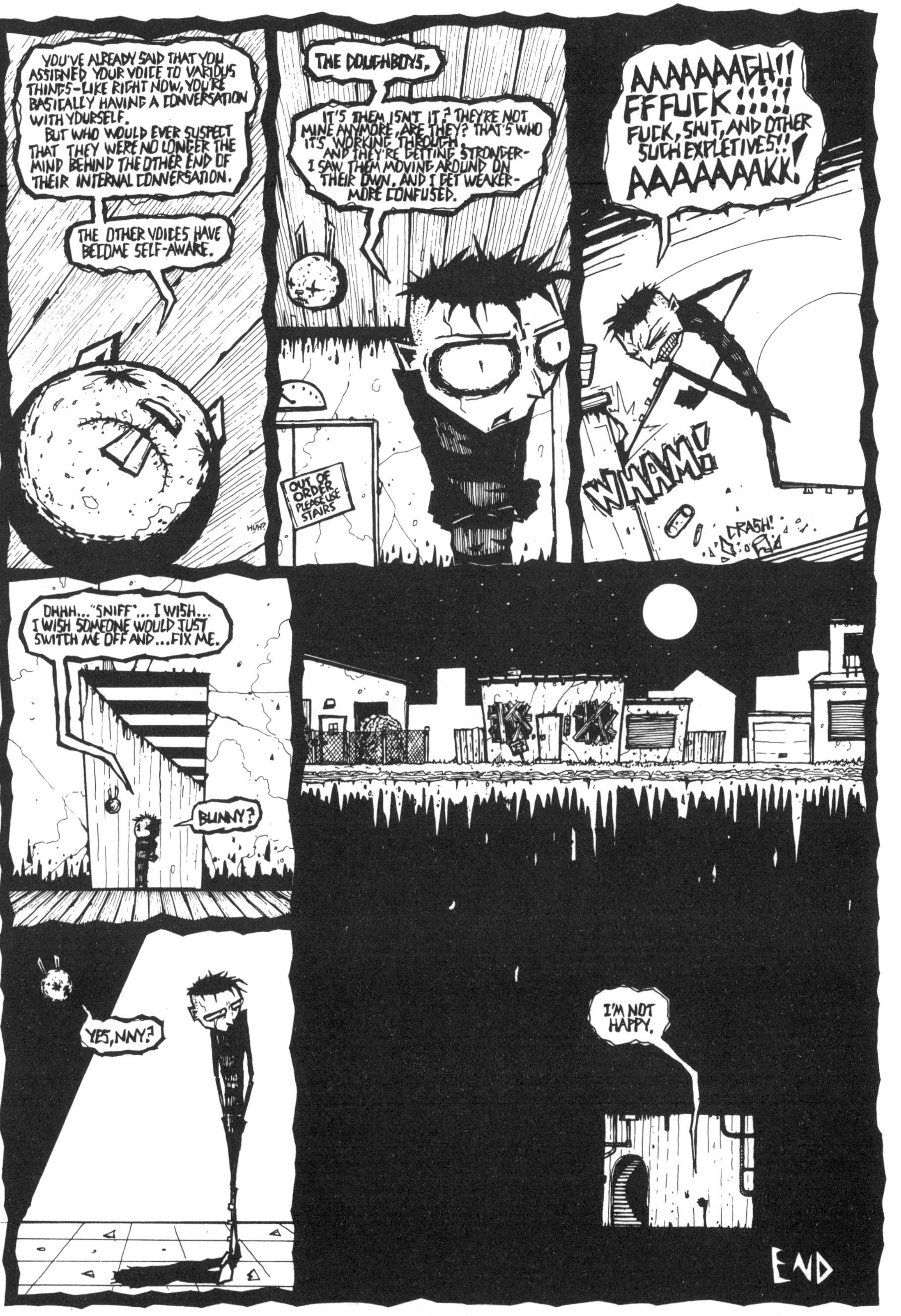
YOU'VE ALREADY SAID THAT YOU ASSIGNED YOUR VOICE TO VARIOUS THINGS-LIKE RIGHT NOW, YOU'RE BASICALLY HAVING A CONVERSATION WITH YOURSELF.
BUT WHO WOULD EVER SUSPECT THAT THEY WERE NO LONGER THE MIND BEHIND THE OTHER END OF THEIR INTERNAL CONVERSATION.
THE OTHER VOICES HAVE BECOME SELF-AWARE.
HUH?
THE DOUGHBOYS.
IT'S THEM ISN'T IT? THEY'RE NOT MINE ANYMORE, ARE THEY? THAT'S WHO IT'S WORKING THROUGH. AND THEY'RE GETTING STRONGER- I SAW THEM MOVING AROUND ON THEIR OWN. AND I GET WEAKER- MORE CONFUSED.
OUT OF ORDER PLEASE USE STAIRS
AAAAAAAGH!! FFFUCK!!!!!! FUCK, SHIT, AND OTHER SUCH EXPLETIVES!!! AAAAAAAKK!
WHAM!
CRASH!
OHHH... *SNIFF*... I WISH... I WISH SOMEONE WOULD JUST SWITCH ME OFF AND... FIX ME.
BUNNY?
YES, NNY?
I'M NOT HAPPY.
END

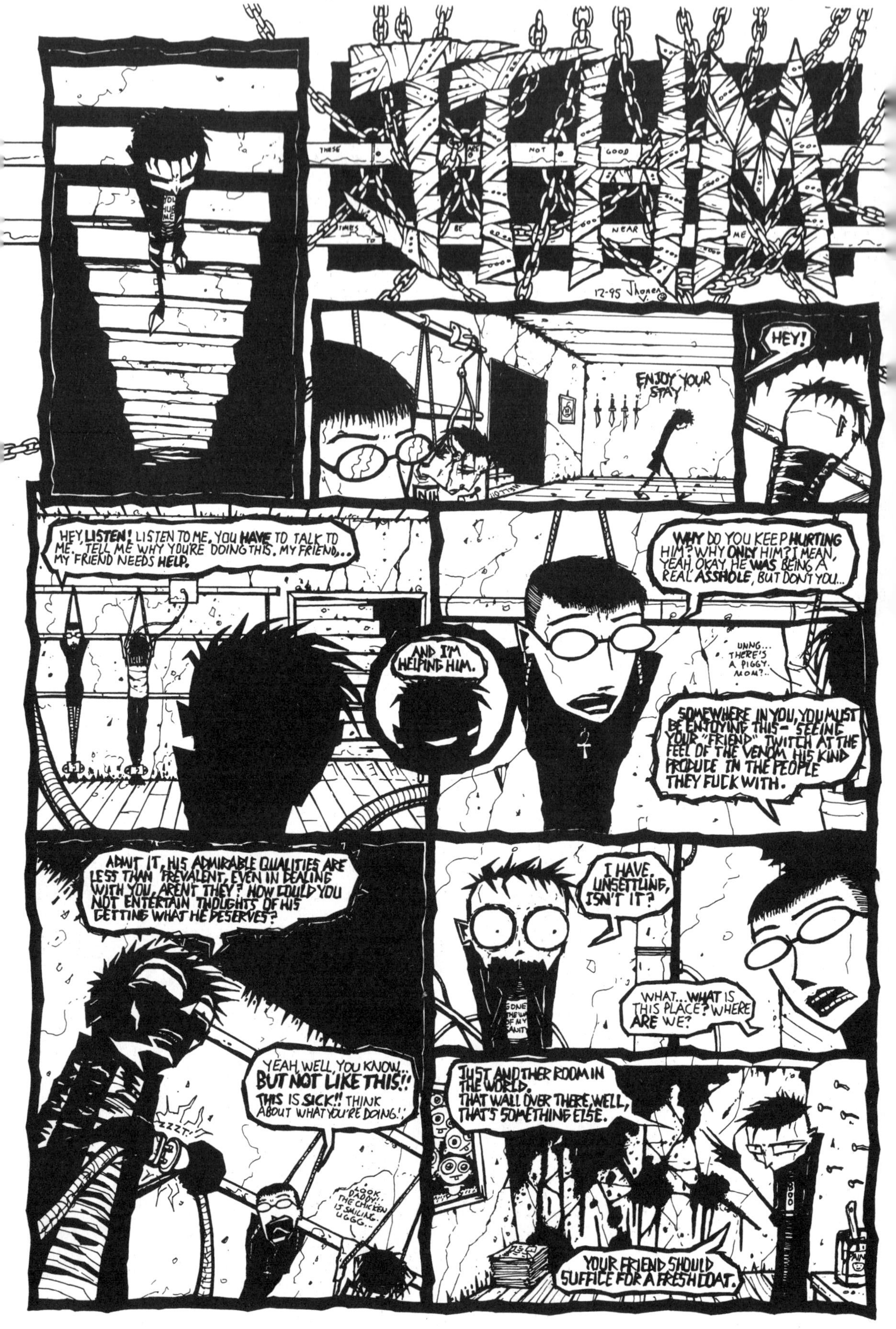

THESE ARE NOT GOOD TIMES TO BE NEAR ME
12-95 Jhonen V.
ENJOY YOUR STAY
HEY!
HEY, LISTEN! LISTEN TO ME. YOU HAVE TO TALK TO ME. TELL ME WHY YOU'RE DOING THIS. MY FRIEND... MY FRIEND NEEDS HELP.
WHY DO YOU KEEP HURTING HIM? WHY ONLY HIM? I MEAN, YEAH, OKAY, HE WAS BEING A REAL ASSHOLE, BUT DON'T YOU...
AND I'M HELPING HIM.
UNNG... THERE'S A PIGGY. MOM?..
SOMEWHERE IN YOU, YOU MUST BE ENJOYING THIS– SEEING YOUR "FRIEND" TWITCH AT THE FEEL OF THE VENOM HIS KIND PRODUCE IN THE PEOPLE THEY FUCK WITH.
ADMIT IT, HIS ADMIRABLE QUALITIES ARE LESS THAN PREVALENT, EVEN IN DEALING WITH YOU, AREN'T THEY? HOW COULD YOU NOT ENTERTAIN THOUGHTS OF HIS GETTING WHAT HE DESERVES?
I HAVE. UNSETTLING, ISN'T IT?
WHAT... WHAT IS THIS PLACE? WHERE ARE WE?
YEAH, WELL, YOU KNOW... BUT NOT LIKE THIS!! THIS IS SICK!! THINK ABOUT WHAT YOU'RE DOING!
ZZZT!
LOOK DADDY! THE CHICKEN IS SMILING. UGGG...
JUST ANOTHER ROOM IN THE WORLD. THAT WALL OVER THERE, WELL, THAT'S SOMETHING ELSE.
YOUR FRIEND SHOULD SUFFICE FOR A FRESH COAT.

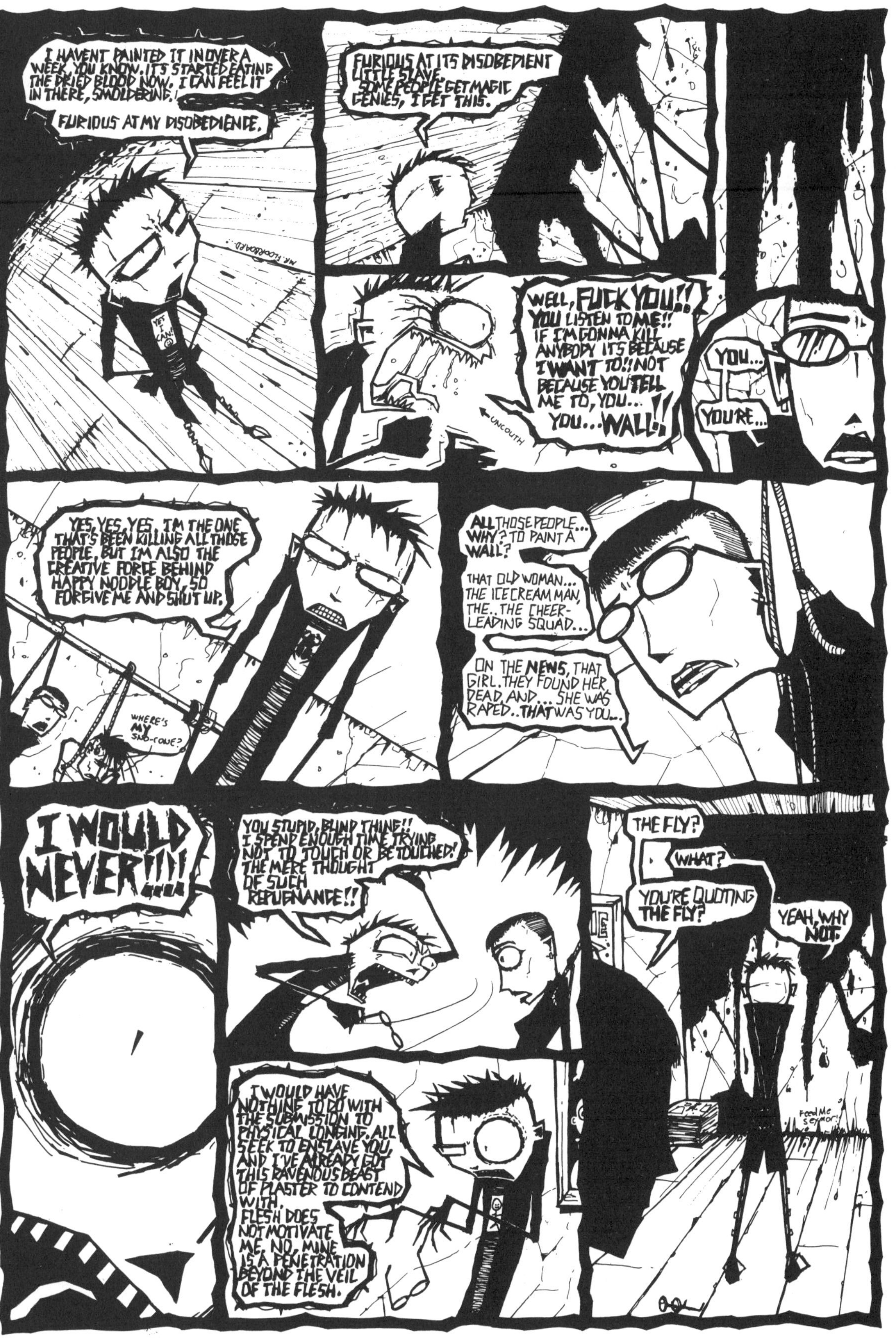
I HAVENT PAINTED IT IN OVER A WEEK, YOU KNOW. IT'S STARTED EATING THE DRIED BLOOD NOW. I CAN FEEL IT IN THERE, SMOLDERING!
FURIOUS AT MY DISOBEDIENCE.
MR. FLOORBOARD.
YES I CAN!
FURIOUS AT ITS DISOBEDIENT LITTLE SLAVE. SOME PEOPLE GET MAGIC GENIES, I GET THIS.
WELL, FUCK YOU!! YOU LISTEN TO ME!! IF I'M GONNA KILL ANYBODY IT'S BECAUSE I WANT TO!! NOT BECAUSE YOU TELL ME TO, YOU... YOU... WALL!!
UNCOUTH
YOU...
YOU'RE...
YES, YES, YES. I'M THE ONE THAT'S BEEN KILLING ALL THOSE PEOPLE, BUT I'M ALSO THE CREATIVE FORCE BEHIND HAPPY NOODLE BOY, SO FORGIVE ME AND SHUT UP.
WHERE'S MY SNO-CONE?
ALL THOSE PEOPLE... WHY? TO PAINT A WALL?
THAT OLD WOMAN... THE ICE CREAM MAN, THE.. THE CHEER-LEADING SQUAD...
ON THE NEWS, THAT GIRL. THEY FOUND HER DEAD, AND... SHE WAS RAPED.. THAT WAS YOU...
I WOULD NEVER!!!!!
YOU STUPID, BLIND THING!! I SPEND ENOUGH TIME TRYING NOT TO TOUCH OR BE TOUCHED! THE MERE THOUGHT OF SUCH REPUGNANCE!!
I WOULD HAVE NOTHING TO DO WITH THE SUBMISSION TO PHYSICAL LONGING. ALL SEEK TO ENSLAVE YOU, AND I'VE ALREADY GOT THIS RAVENOUS BEAST OF PLASTER TO CONTEND WITH. FLESH DOES NOT MOTIVATE ME, NO, MINE IS A PENETRATION BEYOND THE VEIL OF THE FLESH.
THE FLY?
WHAT?
YOU'RE QUOTING THE FLY?
YEAH, WHY NOT.
Feed Me Seymor!

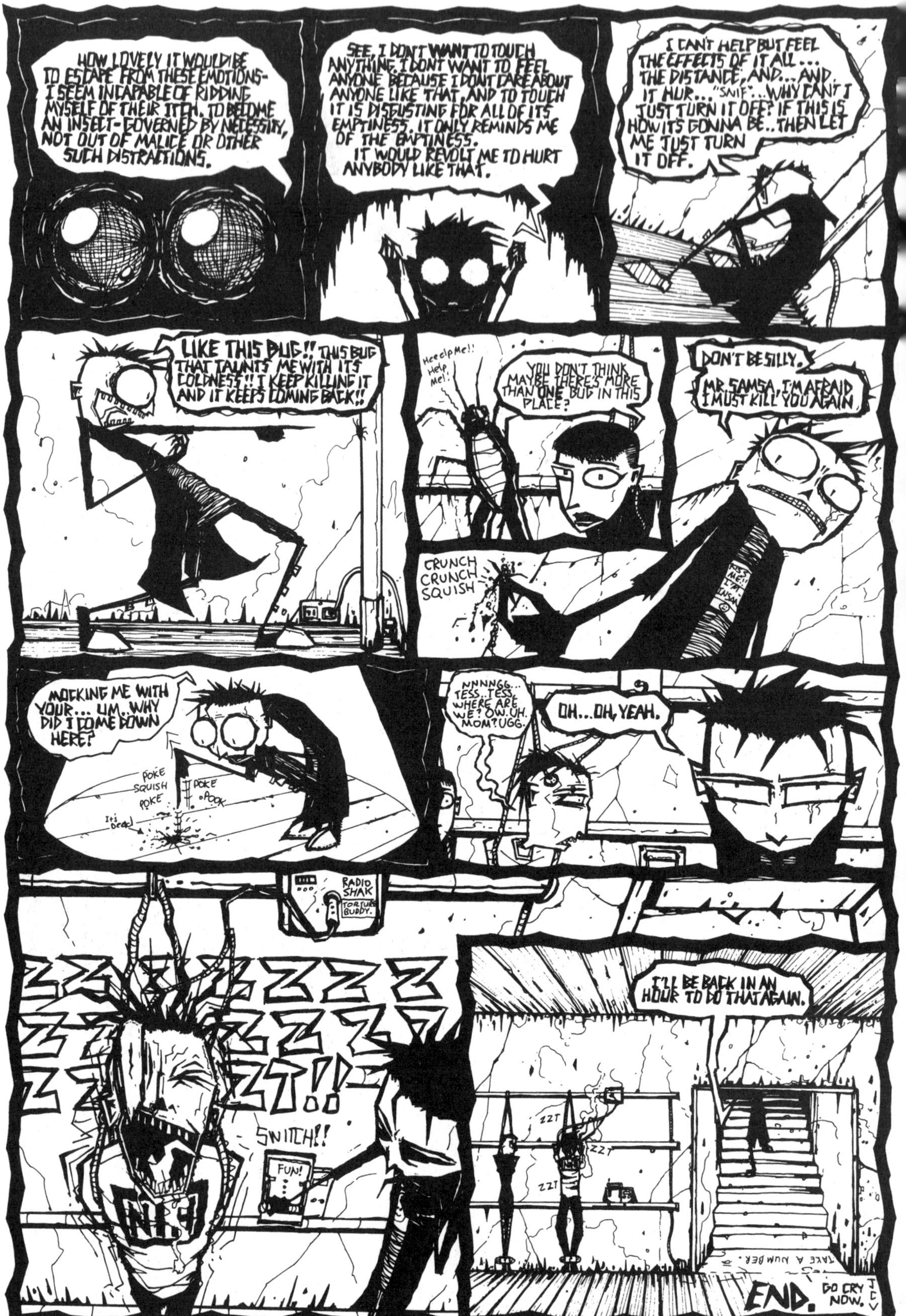

HOW LOVELY IT WOULD BE TO ESCAPE FROM THESE EMOTIONS- I SEEM INCAPABLE OF RIDDING MYSELF OF THEIR ITCH. TO BECOME AN INSECT- GOVERNED BY NECESSITY, NOT OUT OF MALICE OR OTHER SUCH DISTRACTIONS.
SEE, I DON'T WANT TO TOUCH ANYTHING. I DON'T WANT TO FEEL ANYONE BECAUSE I DON'T CARE ABOUT ANYONE LIKE THAT, AND TO TOUCH IT IS DISGUSTING FOR ALL OF ITS EMPTINESS. IT ONLY REMINDS ME OF THE EMPTINESS.
IT WOULD REVOLT ME TO HURT ANYBODY LIKE THAT.
I CAN'T HELP BUT FEEL THE EFFECTS OF IT ALL... THE DISTANCE, AND... AND, IT HUR... "SNIF"... WHY CAN'T I JUST TURN IT OFF? IF THIS IS HOW IT'S GONNA BE.. THEN LET ME JUST TURN IT OFF.
LIKE THIS BUG!! THIS BUG THAT TAUNTS ME WITH ITS COLDNESS!! I KEEP KILLING IT AND IT KEEPS COMING BACK!!
Heeelp Me!! Help Me!!
YOU DON'T THINK MAYBE THERE'S MORE THAN ONE BUG IN THIS PLACE?
DON'T BE SILLY.
MR. SAMSA, I'M AFRAID I MUST KILL YOU AGAIN.
CRUNCH CRUNCH SQUISH
MOCKING ME WITH YOUR... UM.. WHY DID I COME DOWN HERE?
POKE SQUISH POKE
POKE POOK
It's Dead
NNNNGG... TESS.. TESS, WHERE ARE WE? OW. UH. MOM? UGG.
OH... OH, YEAH.
RADIO SHAK
TORTURE BUDDY.
ZZZZZZZZZZZZZZZT!!
SWITCH!!
FUN!
I'LL BE BACK IN AN HOUR TO DO THAT AGAIN.
ZZT
ZZT
ZZT
TAKE A NUMBER.
END.
GO CRY NOW.

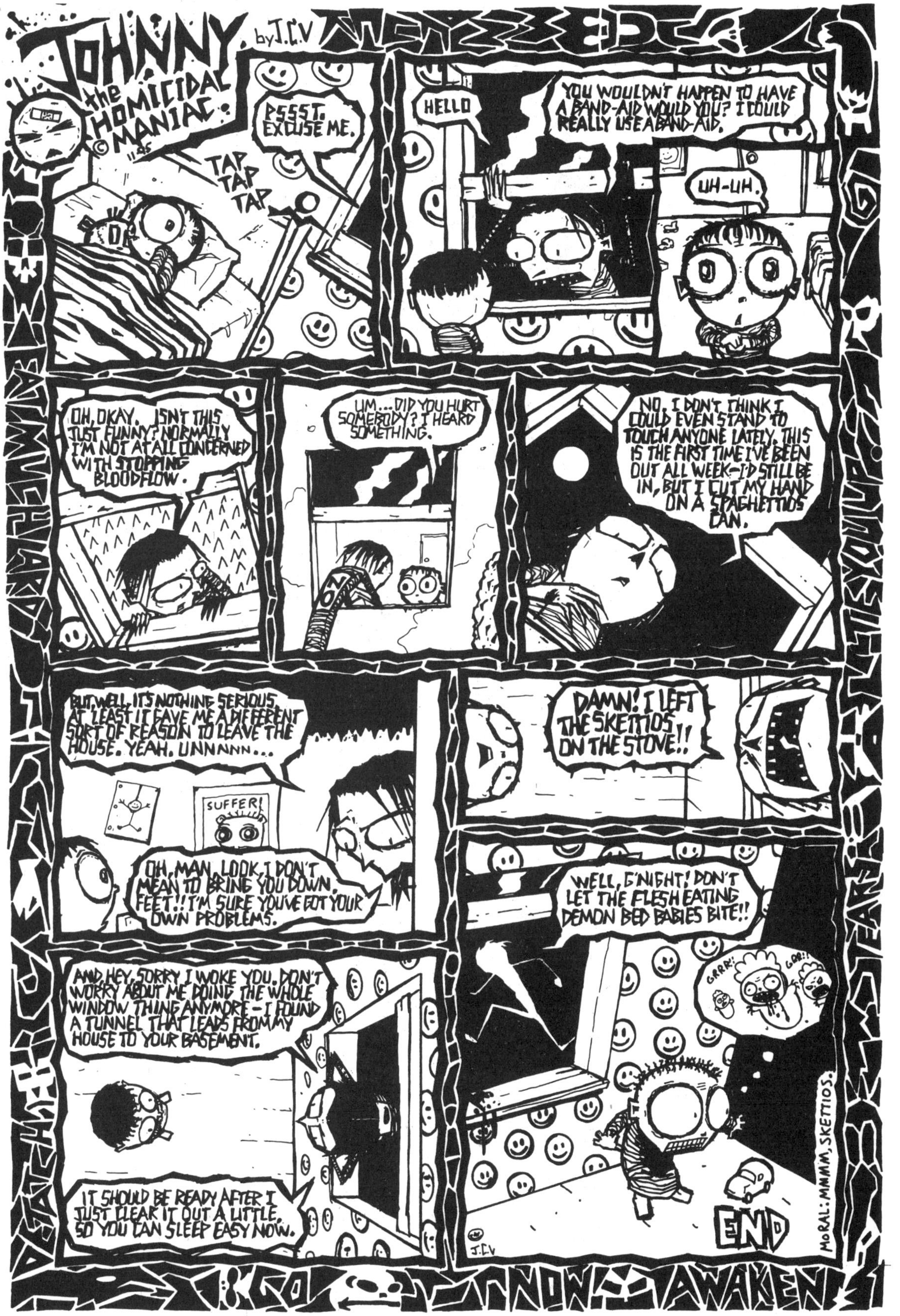
JOHNNY the HOMICIDAL MANIAC
© '95
by J.C.V
PSSST. EXCUSE ME.
TAP TAP TAP
HELLO
YOU WOULDN'T HAPPEN TO HAVE A BAND-AID WOULD YOU? I COULD REALLY USE A BAND-AID.
UH-UH.
OH, OKAY. ISN'T THIS JUST FUNNY? NORMALLY I'M NOT AT ALL CONCERNED WITH STOPPING BLOODFLOW.
UM... DID YOU HURT SOMEBODY? I HEARD SOMETHING.
NO, I DON'T THINK I COULD EVEN STAND TO TOUCH ANYONE LATELY. THIS IS THE FIRST TIME I'VE BEEN OUT ALL WEEK—I'D STILL BE IN, BUT I CUT MY HAND ON A SPAGHETTIOS CAN.
BUT, WELL, IT'S NOTHING SERIOUS. AT LEAST IT GAVE ME A DIFFERENT SORT OF REASON TO LEAVE THE HOUSE. YEAH. UNNNNN...
SUFFER!
OH, MAN, LOOK, I DON'T MEAN TO BRING YOU DOWN, FEET!! I'M SURE YOU'VE GOT YOUR OWN PROBLEMS.
DAMN! I LEFT THE SKETTIOS ON THE STOVE!!
AND HEY, SORRY I WOKE YOU. DON'T WORRY ABOUT ME DOING THE WHOLE WINDOW THING ANYMORE—I FOUND A TUNNEL THAT LEADS FROM MY HOUSE TO YOUR BASEMENT.
IT SHOULD BE READY AFTER I JUST CLEAR IT OUT A LITTLE. SO YOU CAN SLEEP EASY NOW.
WELL, G'NIGHT! DON'T LET THE FLESH EATING DEMON BED BABIES BITE!!
GRRR!
END
MORAL: MMMM, SKETTIOS.
J.C.V
GO!
NOW!
AWAKEN

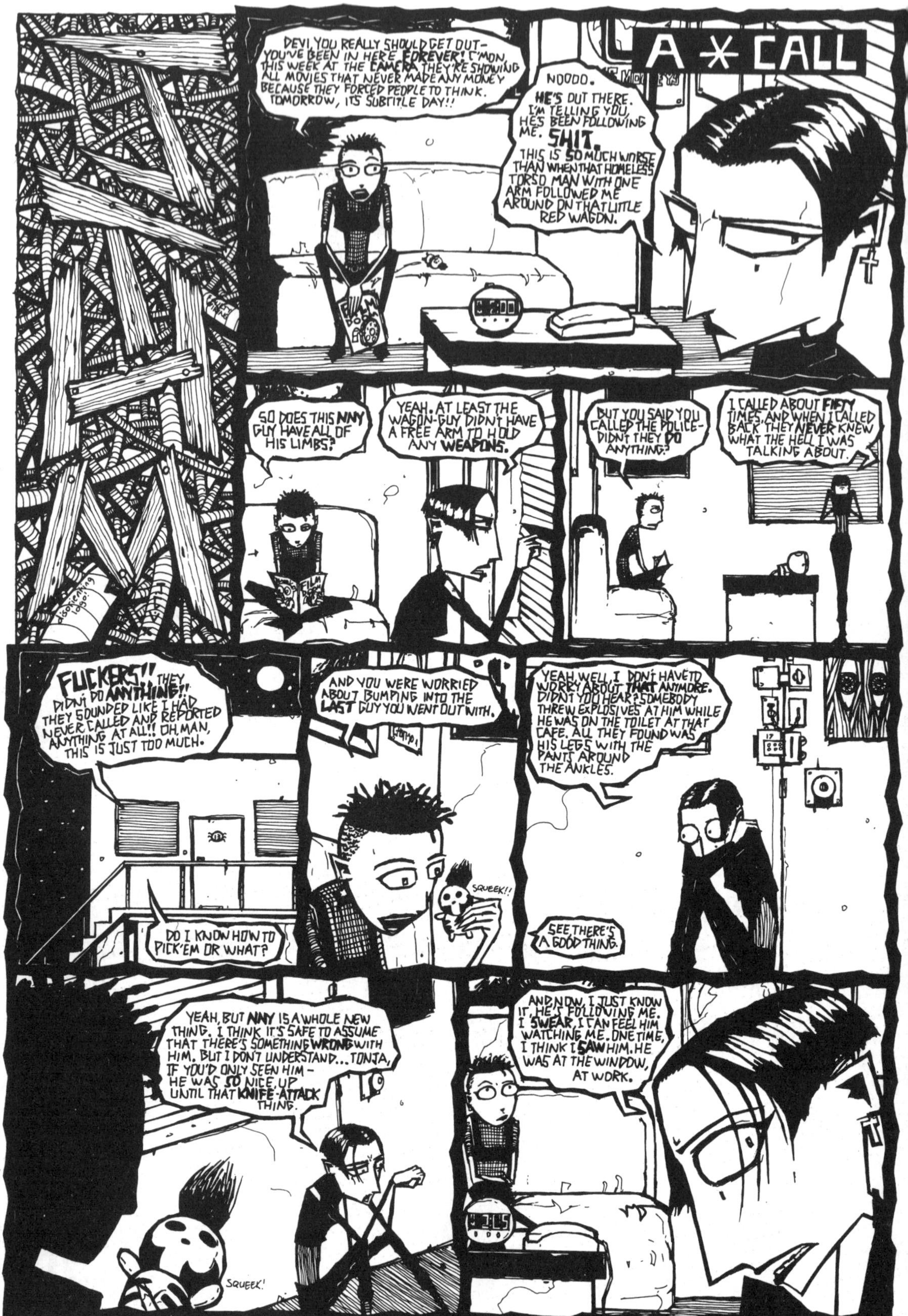
A * CALL
DEVI, YOU REALLY SHOULD GET OUT- YOU'VE BEEN IN HERE FOREVER! C'MON, THIS WEEK AT THE CAMERA THEY'RE SHOWING ALL MOVIES THAT NEVER MADE ANY MONEY BECAUSE THEY FORCED PEOPLE TO THINK. TOMORROW, ITS SUBTITLE DAY!!
NOOOO. HE'S OUT THERE. I'M TELLING YOU, HE'S BEEN FOLLOWING ME. SHIT. THIS IS SO MUCH WORSE THAN WHEN THAT HOMELESS TORSO MAN WITH ONE ARM FOLLOWED ME AROUND ON THAT LITTLE RED WAGON.
SO DOES THIS NNY GUY HAVE ALL OF HIS LIMBS?
YEAH. AT LEAST THE WAGON-GUY DIDN'T HAVE A FREE ARM TO HOLD ANY WEAPONS.
BUT YOU SAID YOU CALLED THE POLICE- DIDN'T THEY DO ANYTHING?
I CALLED ABOUT FIFTY TIMES, AND WHEN I CALLED BACK THEY NEVER KNEW WHAT THE HELL I WAS TALKING ABOUT.
FUCKERS!! THEY DIDN'T DO ANYTHING!! THEY SOUNDED LIKE I HAD NEVER CALLED AND REPORTED ANYTHING AT ALL!! OH, MAN, THIS IS JUST TOO MUCH.
DO I KNOW HOW TO PICK 'EM OR WHAT?
AND YOU WERE WORRIED ABOUT BUMPING INTO THE LAST GUY YOU WENT OUT WITH.
SQUEEK!!
YEAH, WELL, I DON'T HAVE TO WORRY ABOUT THAT ANYMORE. DIDN'T YOU HEAR? SOMEBODY THREW EXPLOSIVES AT HIM WHILE HE WAS ON THE TOILET AT THAT CAFE. ALL THEY FOUND WAS HIS LEGS WITH THE PANTS AROUND THE ANKLES.
SEE THERE'S A GOOD THING.
YEAH, BUT NNY IS A WHOLE NEW THING. I THINK IT'S SAFE TO ASSUME THAT THERE'S SOMETHING WRONG WITH HIM. BUT I DON'T UNDERSTAND... TONJA, IF YOU'D ONLY SEEN HIM- HE WAS SO NICE UP UNTIL THAT KNIFE-ATTACK THING.
SQUEEK!
AND NOW, I JUST KNOW IT, HE'S FOLLOWING ME. I SWEAR, I CAN FEEL HIM WATCHING ME. ONE TIME, I THINK I SAW HIM. HE WAS AT THE WINDOW, AT WORK.

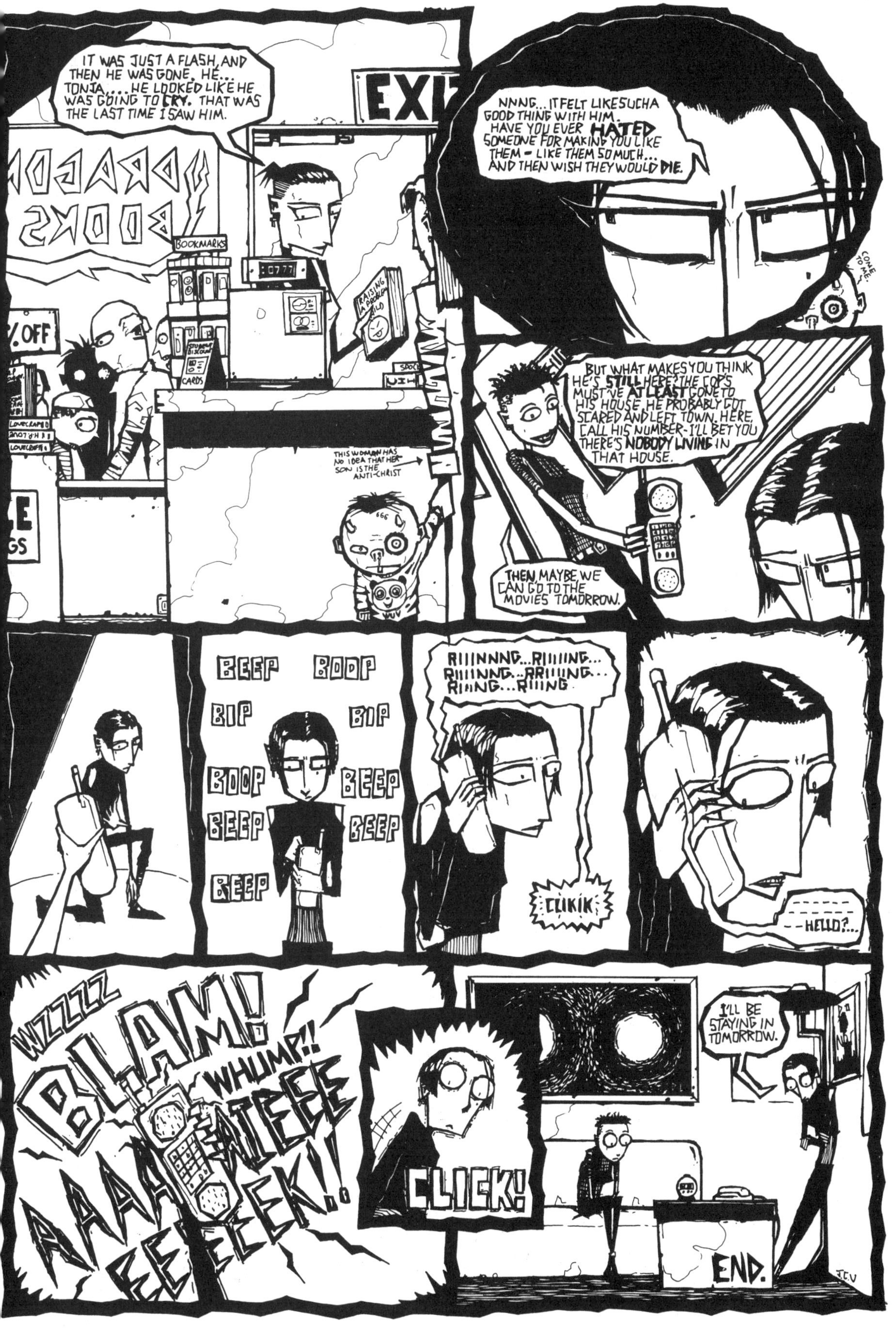
IT WAS JUST A FLASH, AND THEN HE WAS GONE. HE... TONJA... HE LOOKED LIKE HE WAS GOING TO CRY. THAT WAS THE LAST TIME I SAW HIM.
EXI
BOOKMARKS
CARDS
THIS WOMAN HAS NO IDEA THAT HER SON IS THE ANTI-CHRIST
666
NNNG... IT FELT LIKE SUCH A GOOD THING WITH HIM. HAVE YOU EVER HATED SOMEONE FOR MAKING YOU LIKE THEM - LIKE THEM SO MUCH... AND THEN WISH THEY WOULD DIE.
COME TO ME.
BUT WHAT MAKES YOU THINK HE'S STILL HERE? THE COP'S MUST'VE AT LEAST GONE TO HIS HOUSE. HE PROBABLY GOT SCARED AND LEFT TOWN. HERE, CALL HIS NUMBER - I'LL BET YOU THERE'S NOBODY LIVING IN THAT HOUSE.
THEN, MAYBE WE CAN GO TO THE MOVIES TOMORROW.
BEEP BOOP
BIP BIP
BOOP BEEP
BEEP BEEP
BEEP
RIIINNNG... RIIIING... RIIINNG... RIIIING... RIIING... RIIING
CLIKIK
HELLO?...
WZZZZZ
BLAM!
WHUMP!!
AAAHIEEE EEEEEK!!
CLICK!
I'LL BE STAYING IN TOMORROW.
END.
J.C.V

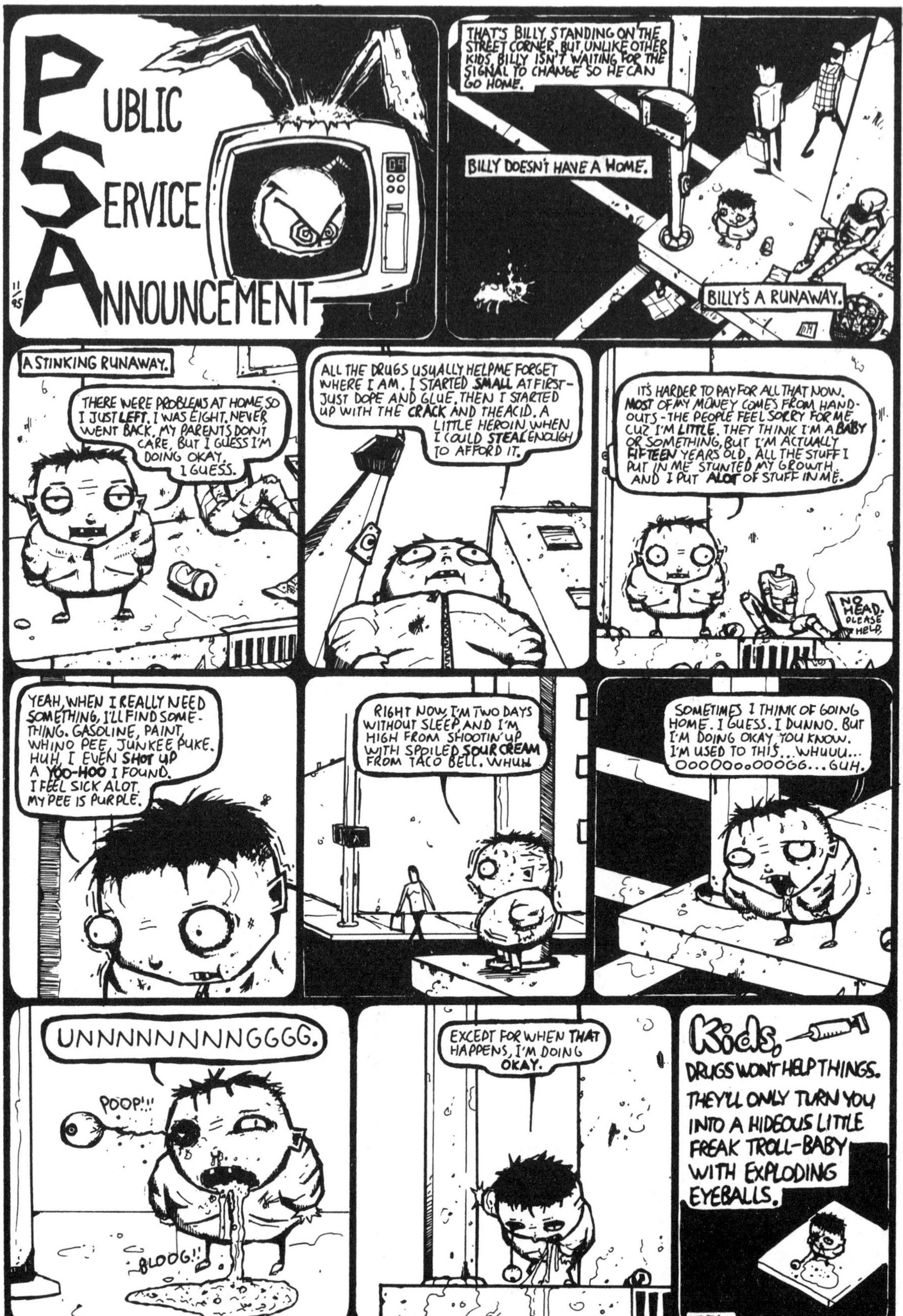

PUBLIC SERVICE ANNOUNCEMENT
11/95
04
THAT'S BILLY STANDING ON THE STREET CORNER, BUT UNLIKE OTHER KIDS, BILLY ISN'T WAITING FOR THE SIGNAL TO CHANGE SO HE CAN GO HOME.
BILLY DOESN'T HAVE A HOME.
BILLY'S A RUNAWAY.
A STINKING RUNAWAY.
THERE WERE PROBLEMS AT HOME, SO I JUST LEFT. I WAS EIGHT. NEVER WENT BACK. MY PARENTS DON'T CARE, BUT I GUESS I'M DOING OKAY. I GUESS.
ALL THE DRUGS USUALLY HELP ME FORGET WHERE I AM. I STARTED SMALL AT FIRST - JUST DOPE AND GLUE. THEN I STARTED UP WITH THE CRACK AND THE ACID. A LITTLE HEROIN WHEN I COULD STEAL ENOUGH TO AFFORD IT.
IT'S HARDER TO PAY FOR ALL THAT NOW. MOST OF MY MONEY COMES FROM HAND-OUTS - THE PEOPLE FEEL SORRY FOR ME CUZ I'M LITTLE. THEY THINK I'M A BABY OR SOMETHING, BUT I'M ACTUALLY FIFTEEN YEARS OLD. ALL THE STUFF I PUT IN ME STUNTED MY GROWTH. AND I PUT ALOT OF STUFF IN ME.
NO HEAD. PLEASE HELP.
YEAH, WHEN I REALLY NEED SOMETHING, I'LL FIND SOMETHING. GASOLINE, PAINT, WHINO PEE, JUNKEE PUKE. HUH, I EVEN SHOT UP A YOO-HOO I FOUND. I FEEL SICK ALOT. MY PEE IS PURPLE.
RIGHT NOW, I'M TWO DAYS WITHOUT SLEEP, AND I'M HIGH FROM SHOOTIN' UP WITH SPOILED SOUR CREAM FROM TACO BELL. WHUH.
SOMETIMES I THINK OF GOING HOME. I GUESS. I DUNNO. BUT I'M DOING OKAY, YOU KNOW. I'M USED TO THIS... WHUUU... OOOOOooOOGG...GUH.
UNNNNNNNNNGGGG.
POOP!!!
BLOOG!!
EXCEPT FOR WHEN THAT HAPPENS, I'M DOING OKAY.
Kids,
DRUGS WON'T HELP THINGS.
THEY'LL ONLY TURN YOU INTO A HIDEOUS LITTLE FREAK TROLL-BABY WITH EXPLODING EYEBALLS.
J.C.V

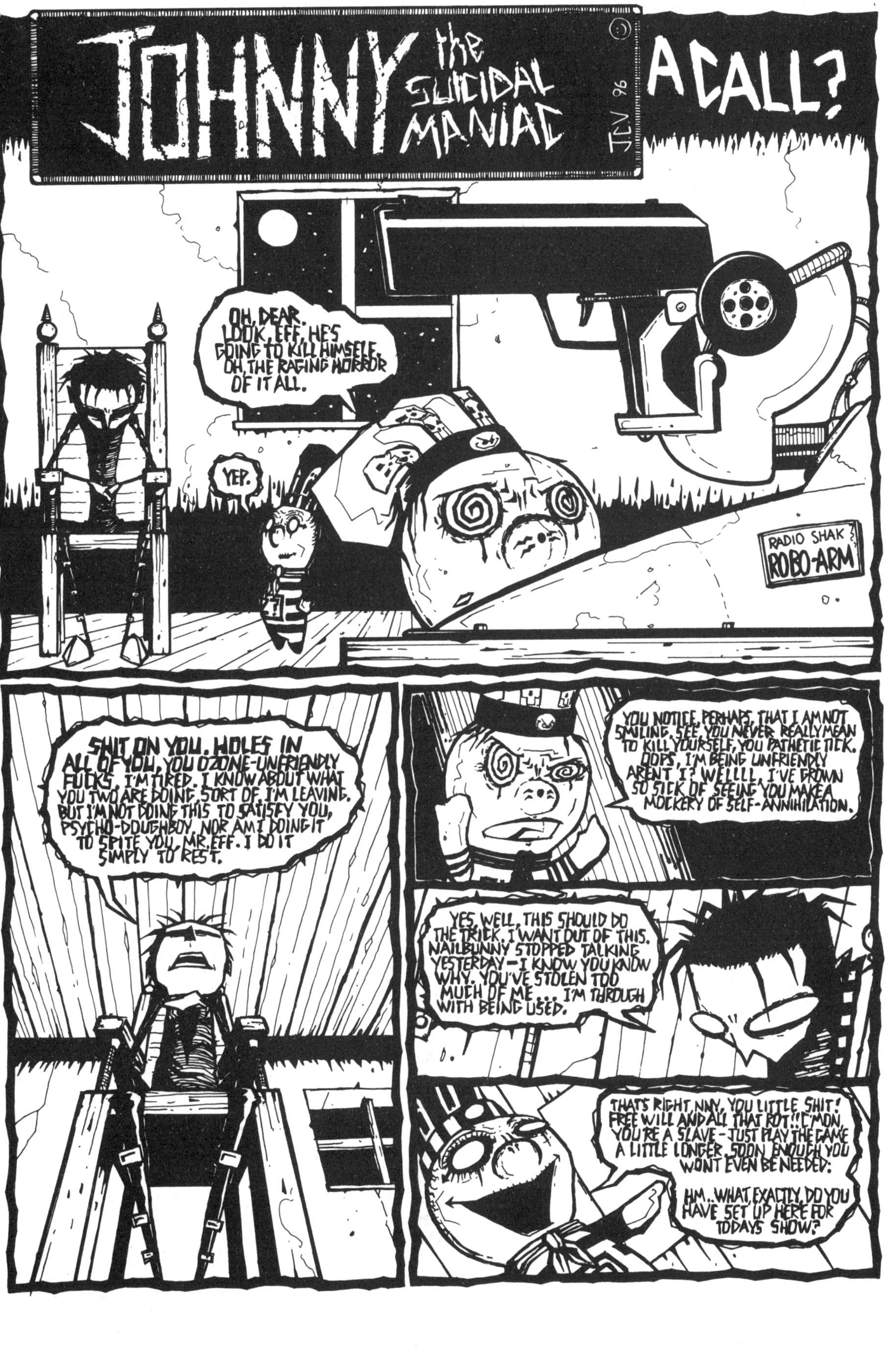
JOHNNY the SUICIDAL MANIAC
JCV 96
A CALL?
OH, DEAR. LOOK, EFF, HE'S GOING TO KILL HIMSELF. OH, THE RAGING HORROR OF IT ALL.
YEP.
RADIO SHAK ROBO-ARM
SHIT ON YOU. HOLES IN ALL OF YOU, YOU OZONE-UNFRIENDLY FUCKS. I'M TIRED. I KNOW ABOUT WHAT YOU TWO ARE DOING, SORT OF. I'M LEAVING. BUT I'M NOT DOING THIS TO SATISFY YOU, PSYCHO-DOUGHBOY, NOR AM I DOING IT TO SPITE YOU, MR. EFF. I DO IT SIMPLY TO REST.
YOU NOTICE, PERHAPS, THAT I AM NOT SMILING. SEE, YOU NEVER REALLY MEAN TO KILL YOURSELF, YOU PATHETIC TICK. OOPS, I'M BEING UNFRIENDLY AREN'T I? WELLLL, I'VE GROWN SO SICK OF SEEING YOU MAKE A MOCKERY OF SELF-ANNIHILATION.
YES, WELL, THIS SHOULD DO THE TRICK. I WANT OUT OF THIS. NAILBUNNY STOPPED TALKING YESTERDAY — I KNOW YOU KNOW WHY. YOU'VE STOLEN TOO MUCH OF ME . . . I'M THROUGH WITH BEING USED.
THAT'S RIGHT, NNY, YOU LITTLE SHIT! FREE WILL AND ALL THAT ROT!! C'MON, YOU'RE A SLAVE — JUST PLAY THE GAME A LITTLE LONGER. SOON ENOUGH YOU WON'T EVEN BE NEEDED.
HM.. WHAT, EXACTLY, DO YOU HAVE SET UP HERE FOR TODAYS SHOW?

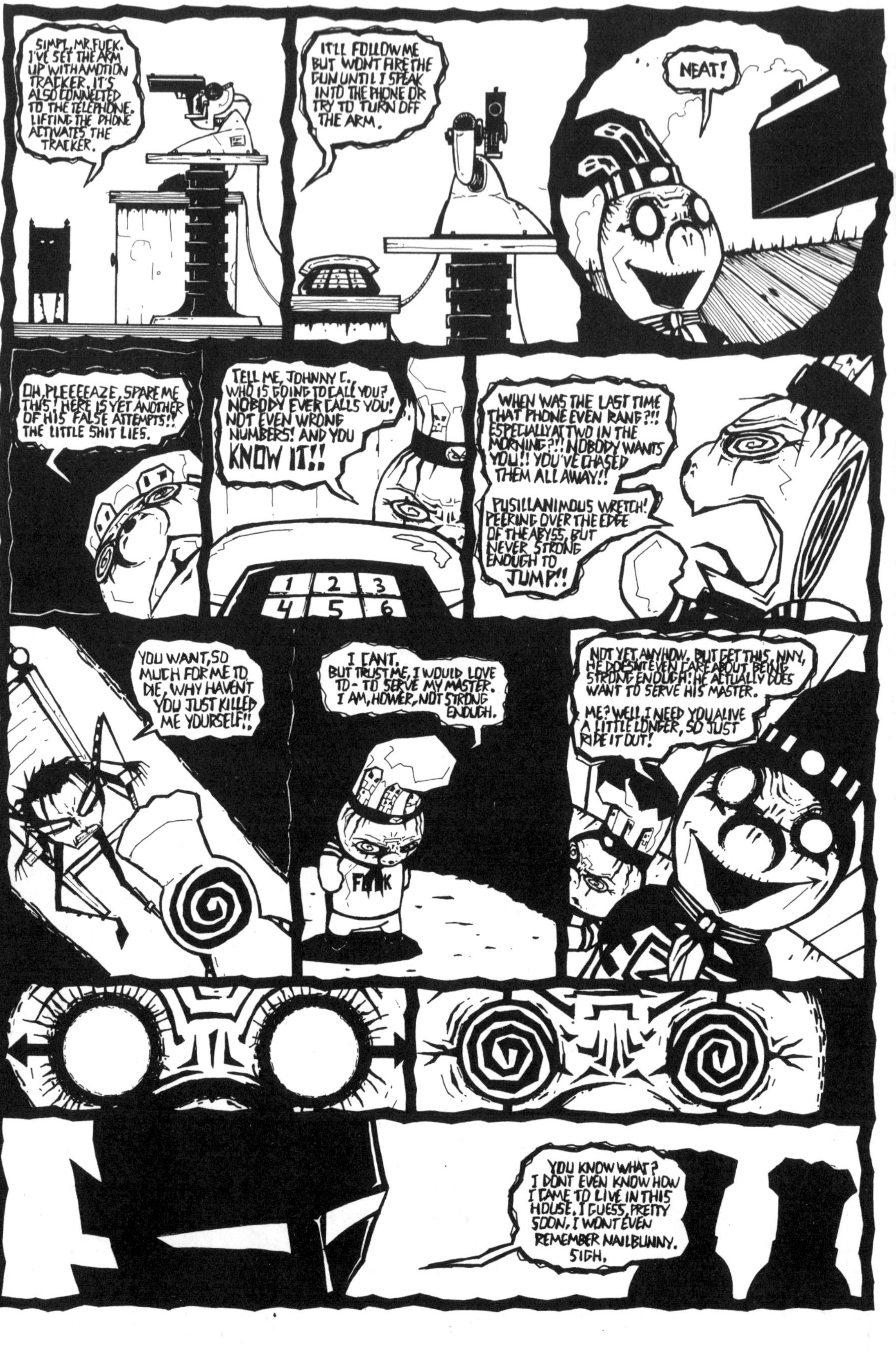
SIMPL, MR. FUCK. I'VE SET THE ARM UP WITH A MOTION TRACKER. IT'S ALSO CONNECTED TO THE TELEPHONE. LIFTING THE PHONE ACTIVATES THE TRACKER.
IT'LL FOLLOW ME BUT WON'T FIRE THE GUN UNTIL I SPEAK INTO THE PHONE OR TRY TO TURN OFF THE ARM.
NEAT!
OH, PLEEEEAZE, SPARE ME THIS! HERE IS YET ANOTHER OF HIS FALSE ATTEMPTS!! THE LITTLE SHIT LIES.
TELL ME, JOHNNY C., WHO IS GOING TO CALL YOU? NOBODY EVER CALLS YOU! NOT EVEN WRONG NUMBERS! AND YOU KNOW IT!!
1 2 3
4 5 6
WHEN WAS THE LAST TIME THAT PHONE EVEN RANG?!! ESPECIALLY AT TWO IN THE MORNING?!! NOBODY WANTS YOU!! YOU'VE CHASED THEM ALL AWAY!!
PUSILLANIMOUS WRETCH! PEERING OVER THE EDGE OF THE ABYSS, BUT NEVER STRONG ENOUGH TO JUMP!!
YOU WANT, SO MUCH FOR ME TO DIE, WHY HAVEN'T YOU JUST KILLED ME YOURSELF!!
I CAN'T. BUT TRUST ME, I WOULD LOVE TO - TO SERVE MY MASTER. I AM, HOWER, NOT STRONG ENOUGH.
NOT YET ANYHOW. BUT GET THIS, NNY, HE DOESN'T EVEN CARE ABOUT BEING STRONG ENOUGH! HE ACTUALLY DOES WANT TO SERVE HIS MASTER.
ME? WELL, I NEED YOU ALIVE A LITTLE LONGER, SO JUST RIDE IT OUT!
YOU KNOW WHAT? I DON'T EVEN KNOW HOW I CAME TO LIVE IN THIS HOUSE. I GUESS, PRETTY SOON, I WON'T EVEN REMEMBER NAILBUNNY. SIGH.

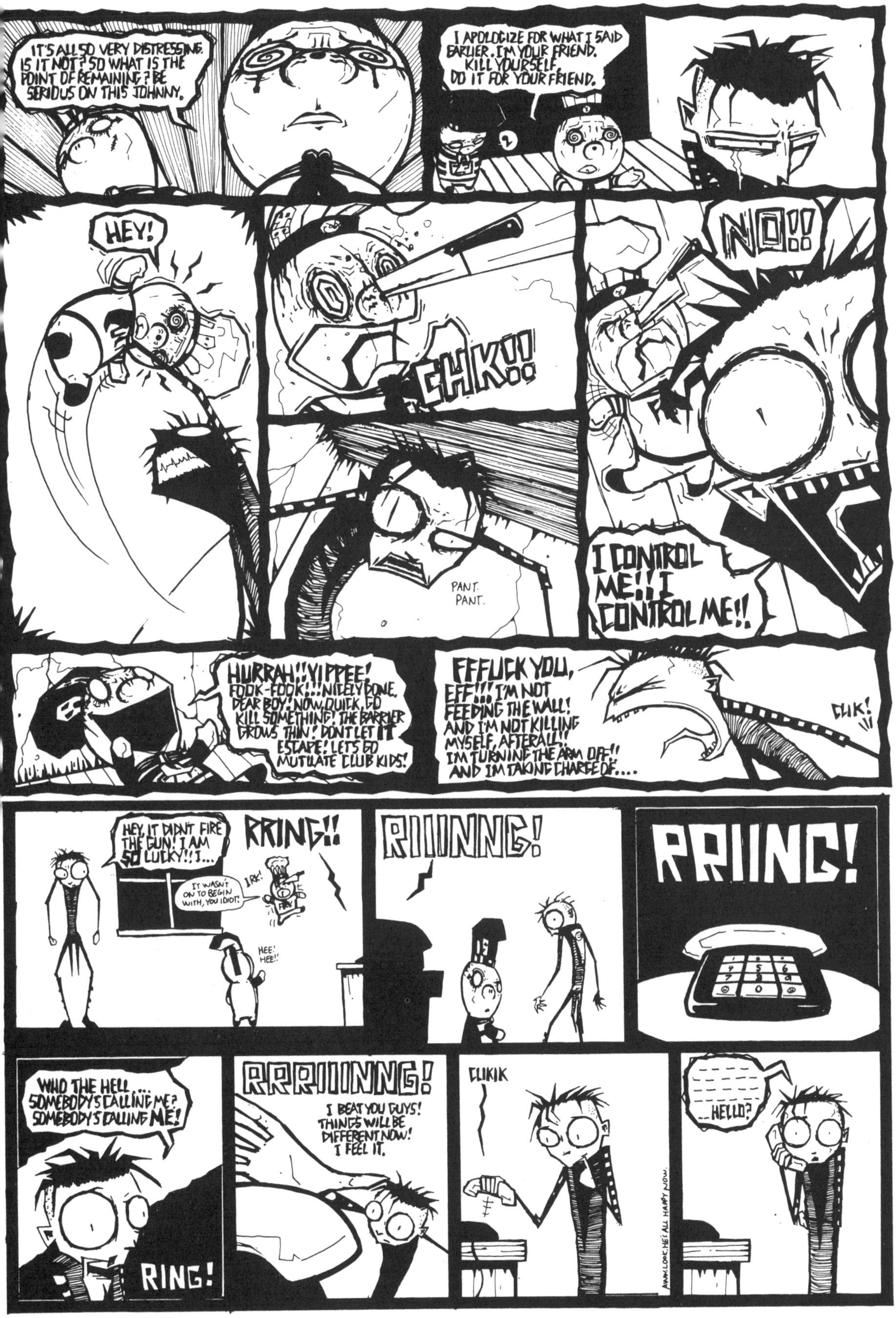
IT'S ALL SO VERY DISTRESSING. IS IT NOT? SO WHAT IS THE POINT OF REMAINING? BE SERIOUS ON THIS JOHNNY.
I APOLOGIZE FOR WHAT I SAID EARLIER. I'M YOUR FRIEND. KILL YOURSELF. DO IT FOR YOUR FRIEND.
?
HEY!
CHK!!
NO!!
PANT. PANT.
I CONTROL ME!! I CONTROL ME!!
HURRAH!! YIPPEE! FOOK-FOOK!... NICELY DONE, DEAR BOY! NOW, QUICK, GO KILL SOMETHING! THE BARRIER GROWS THIN! DON'T LET IT ESCAPE! LET'S GO MUTILATE CLUB KIDS!
FFFUCK YOU, EFF!!! I'M NOT FEEDING THE WALL! AND I'M NOT KILLING MYSELF, AFTER ALL!! I'M TURNING THE ARM OFF!! AND I'M TAKING CHARGE OF....
CLIK!
HEY, IT DIDN'T FIRE THE GUN! I AM SO LUCKY!! I...
RRING!!
IRK!
IT WASN'T ON TO BEGIN WITH, YOU IDIOT!
HEE! HEE!!
RIIINNG!
RRIING!
WHO THE HELL... SOMEBODY'S CALLING ME? SOMEBODY'S CALLING ME!
RING!
RRRIIINNG!
I BEAT YOU GUYS! THINGS WILL BE DIFFERENT NOW! I FEEL IT.
CLIKIK
AWW. LOOK. HE'S ALL HAPPY NOW.
...HELLO?

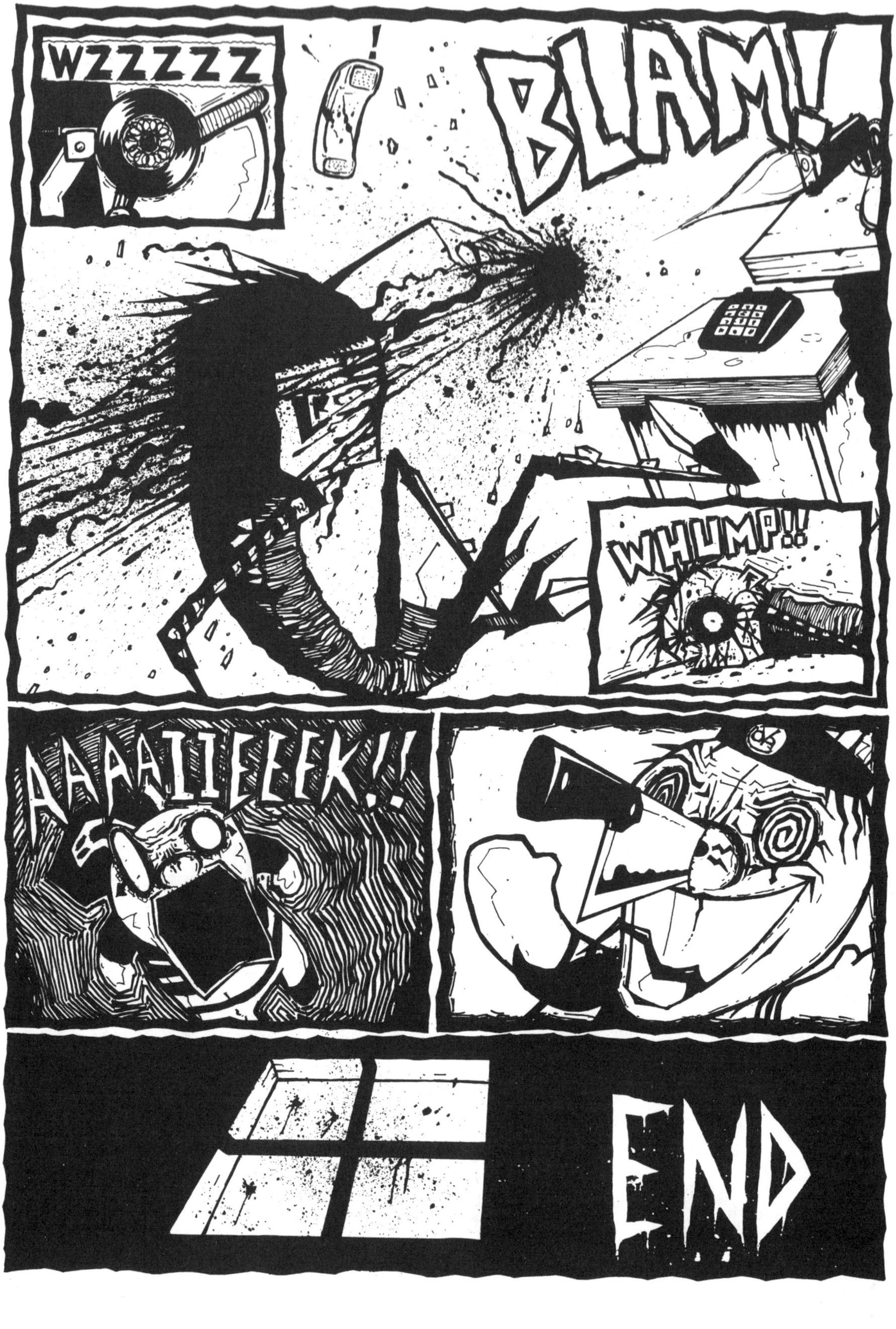
WZZZZZZ
!
BLAM!
WHUMP!!
AAAAIIEEEK!!
END

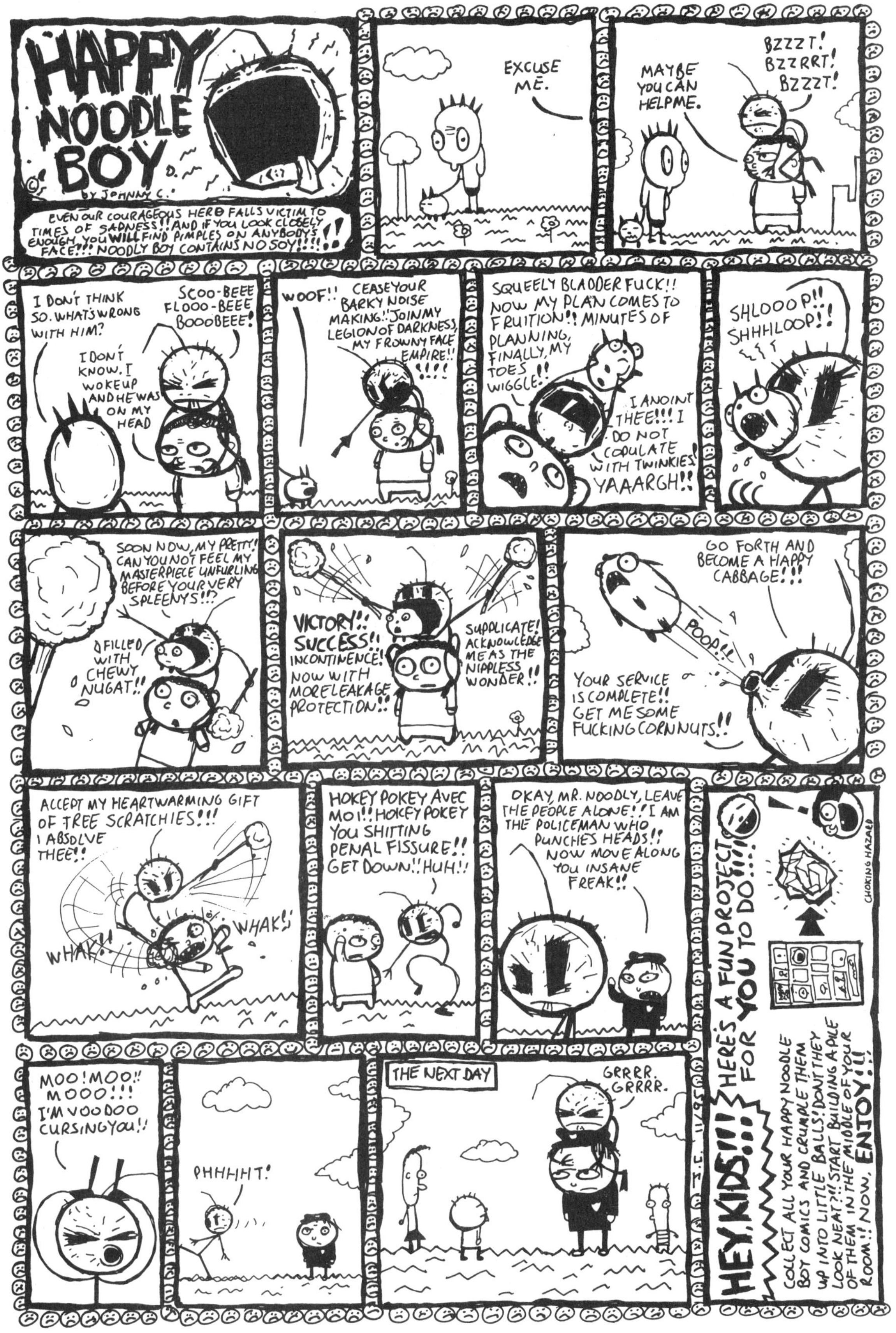
HAPPY NOODLE BOY
by JOHNNY C.
EVEN OUR COURAGEOUS HERO FALLS VICTIM TO TIMES OF SADNESS!! AND IF YOU LOOK CLOSELY ENOUGH, YOU WILL FIND PIMPLES ON ANYBODYS FACE!!! NOODLY BOY CONTAINS NO SOY!!!!!!
EXCUSE ME.
MAYBE YOU CAN HELP ME.
BZZZT! BZZRRT! BZZZT!
I DON'T THINK SO. WHAT'S WRONG WITH HIM?
SCOO-BEEE FLOOO-BEEE BOOOBEEE!
I DON'T KNOW. I WOKE UP AND HE WAS ON MY HEAD
WOOF!!
CEASE YOUR BARKY NOISE MAKING!! JOIN MY LEGION OF DARKNESS, MY FROWNY FACE EMPIRE!! !!!
SQUEELY BLADDER FUCK!! NOW MY PLAN COMES TO FRUITION!! MINUTES OF PLANNING, FINALLY, MY TOES WIGGLE!!
I ANOINT THEE!!! I DO NOT COPULATE WITH TWINKIES!
YAAARGH!!
SHLOOOP!! SHHHLOOP!!
SOON NOW, MY PRETTY! CAN YOU NOT FEEL MY MASTERPIECE UNFURLING BEFORE YOUR VERY SPLEENYS!!?
FILLED WITH CHEWY NUGAT!!
VICTORY!! SUCCESS!! INCONTINENCE! NOW WITH MORE LEAKAGE PROTECTION!!
SUPPLICATE! ACKNOWLEDGE ME AS THE NIPPLESS WONDER!!
GO FORTH AND BECOME A HAPPY CABBAGE!!!
POOP!!
YOUR SERVICE IS COMPLETE!! GET ME SOME FUCKING CORNNUTS!!
ACCEPT MY HEARTWARMING GIFT OF TREE SCRATCHIES!!! I ABSOLVE THEE!!
WHAK!!
WHAK!!
HOKEY POKEY AVEC MOI!! HOKEY POKEY YOU SHITTING PENAL FISSURE!! GET DOWN!! HUH!!
OKAY, MR. NOODLY, LEAVE THE PEOPLE ALONE!! I AM THE POLICEMAN WHO PUNCHES HEADS!! NOW MOVE ALONG YOU INSANE FREAK!!
MOO! MOO!! MOOO!!! I'M VOODOO CURSING YOU!!
PHHHHT!
THE NEXT DAY
GRRRR. GRRRR.
J.C. 11/95
HEY, KIDS!!!! HERE'S A FUN PROJECT FOR YOU TO DO...!!!
COLLECT ALL YOUR HAPPY NOODLE BOY COMICS AND CRUMPLE THEM UP INTO LITTLE BALLS! DON'T THEY LOOK NEAT?!! START BUILDING A PILE OF THEM IN THE MIDDLE OF YOUR ROOM!! NOW, ENJOY!!!
CHOKING HAZARD

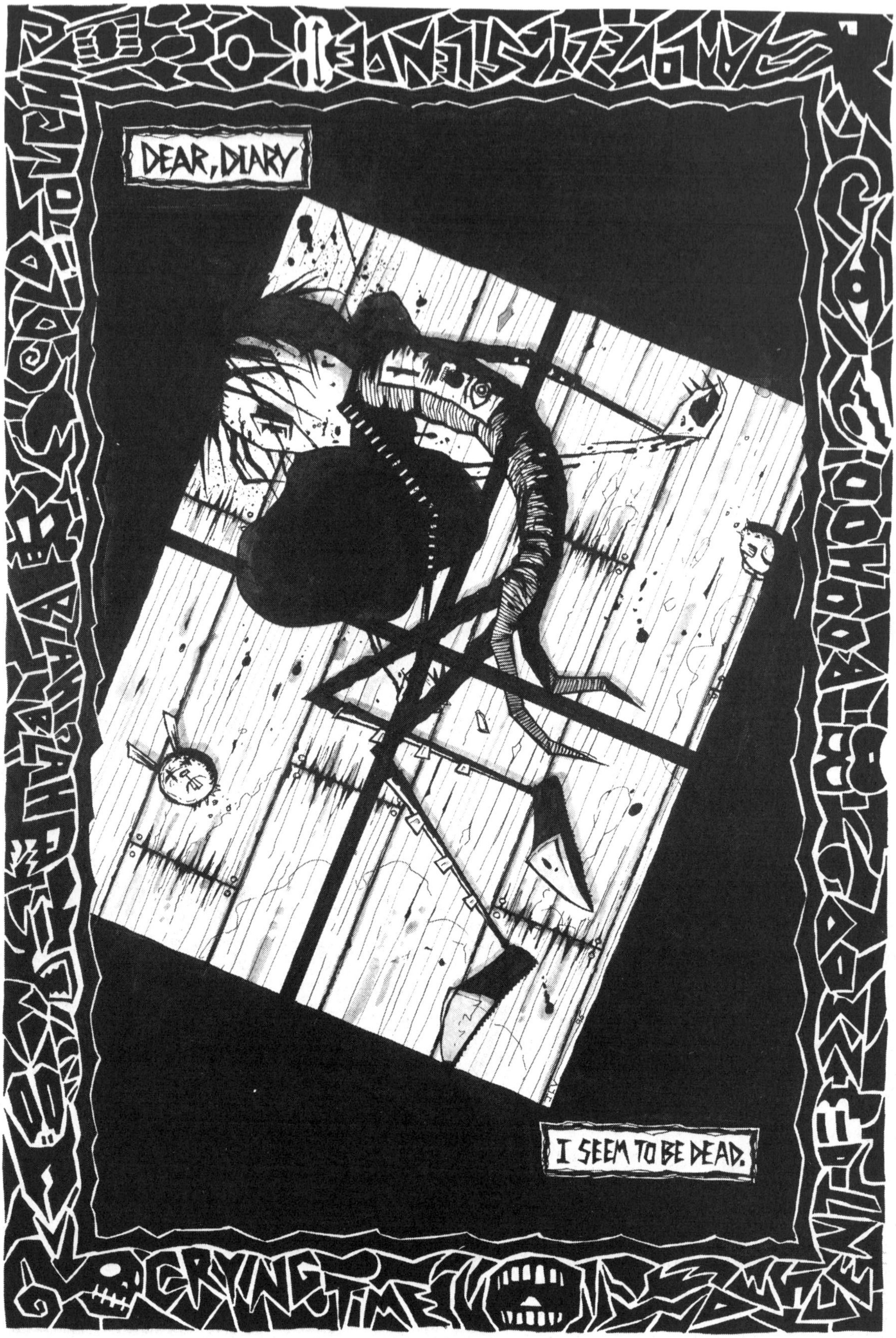
DEAR, DIARY
I SEEM TO BE DEAD.
CRYING TIME

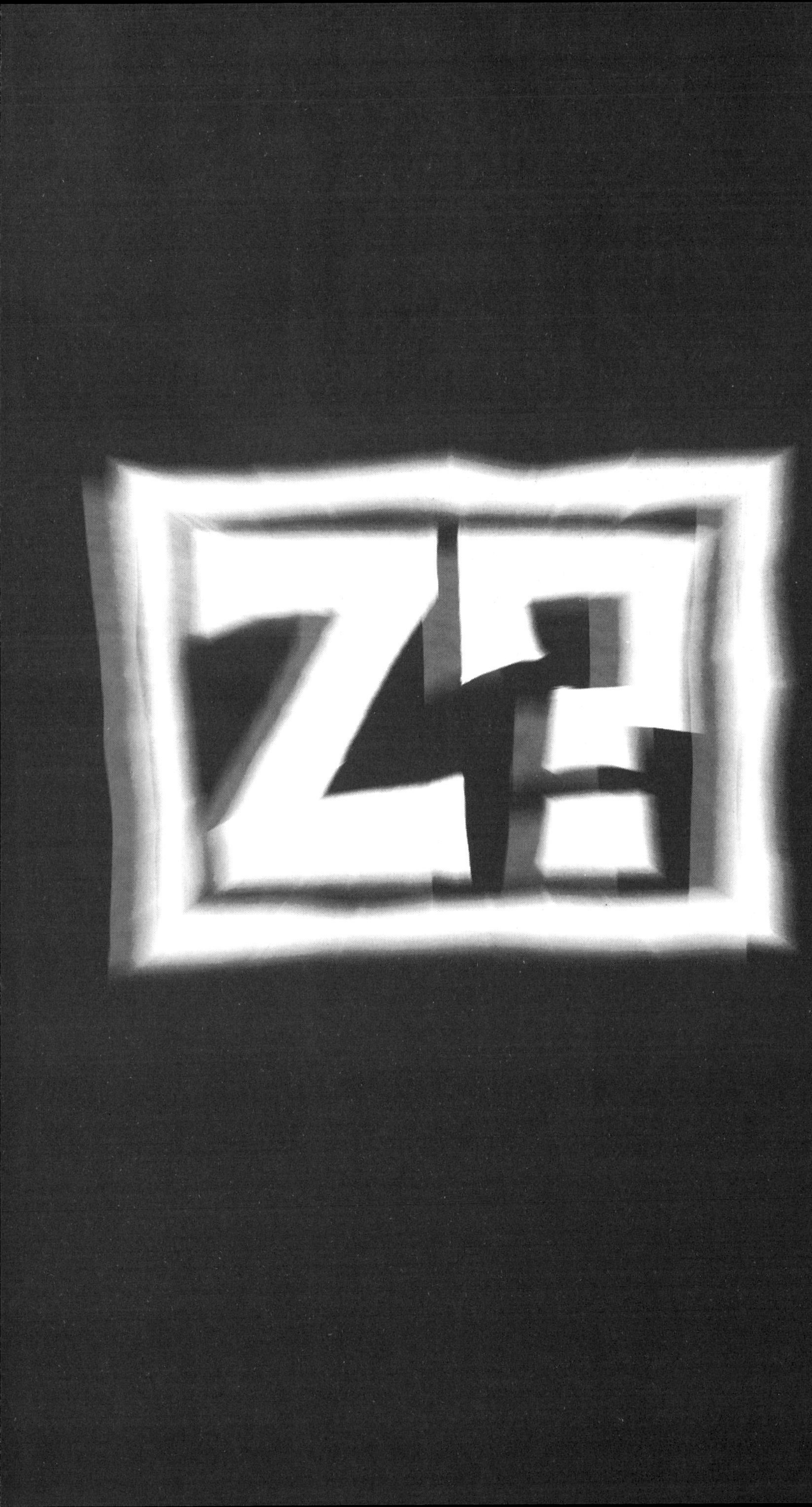

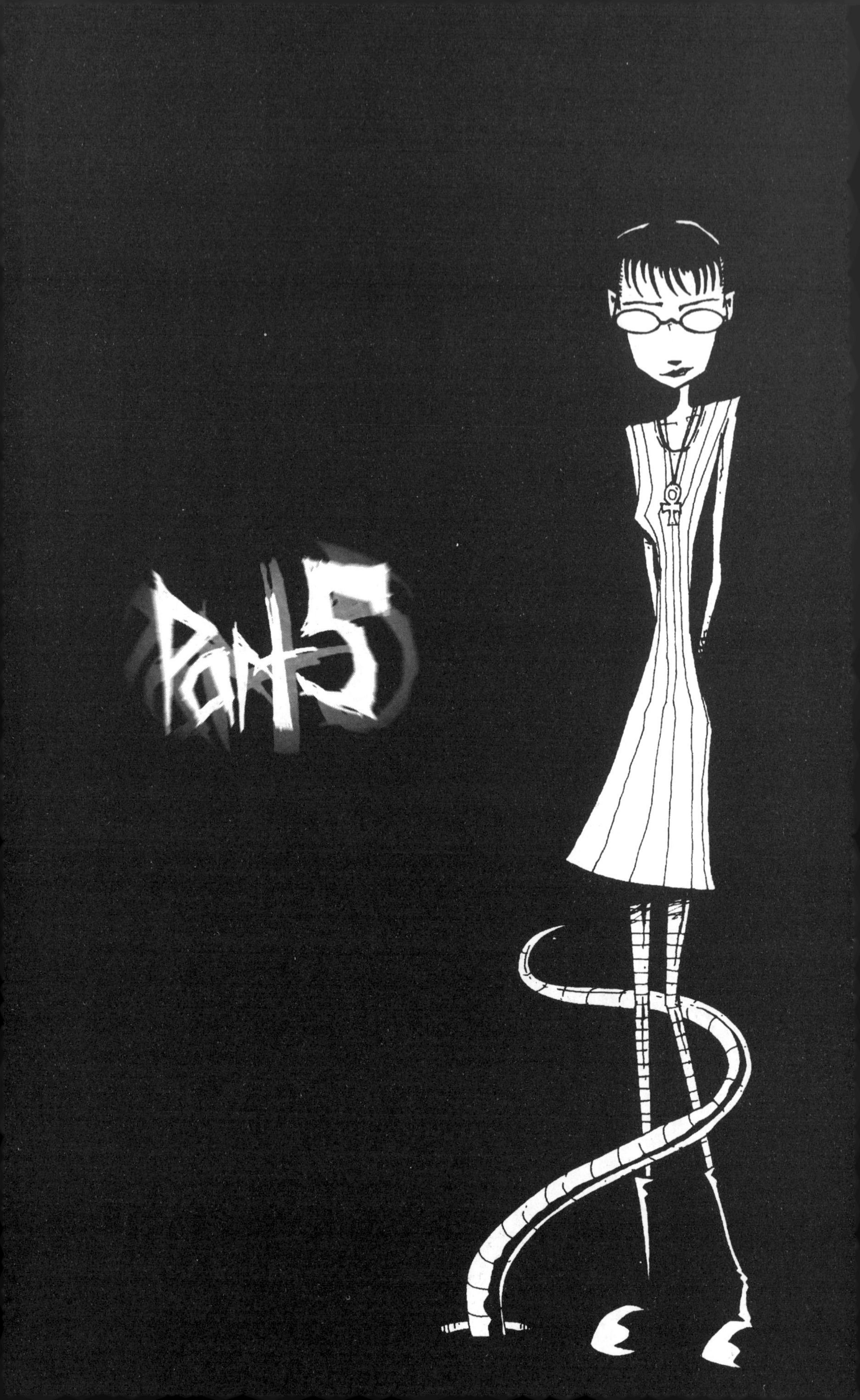
Part 5

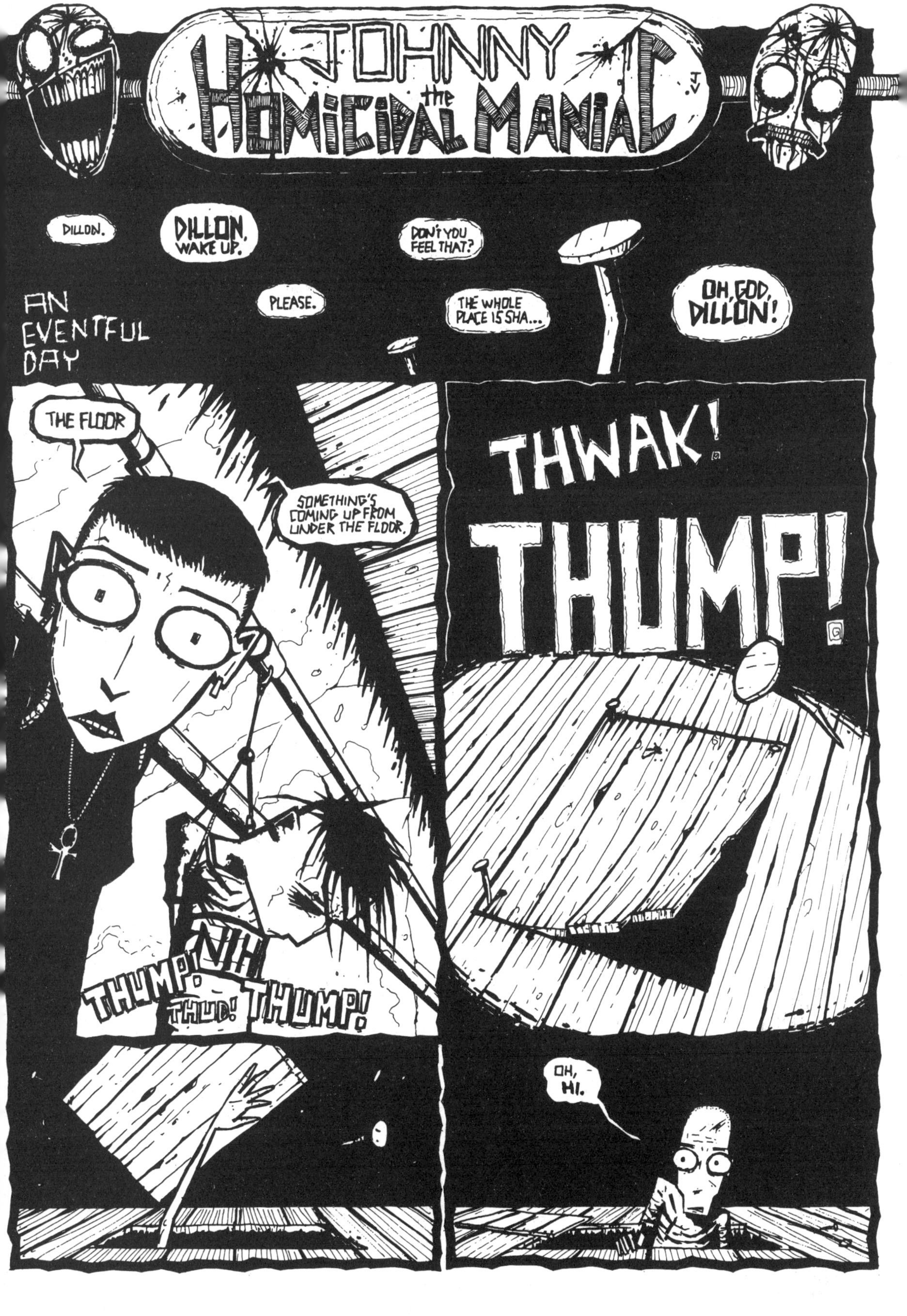
JOHNNY the HOMICIDAL MANIAC
DILLON.
DILLON, WAKE UP.
PLEASE.
DON'T YOU FEEL THAT?
THE WHOLE PLACE IS SHA...
OH, GOD, DILLON!
AN EVENTFUL DAY
THE FLOOR
SOMETHING'S COMING UP FROM UNDER THE FLOOR.
NH
THUMP! THUD! THUMP!
THWAK!
THUMP!
OH, HI.

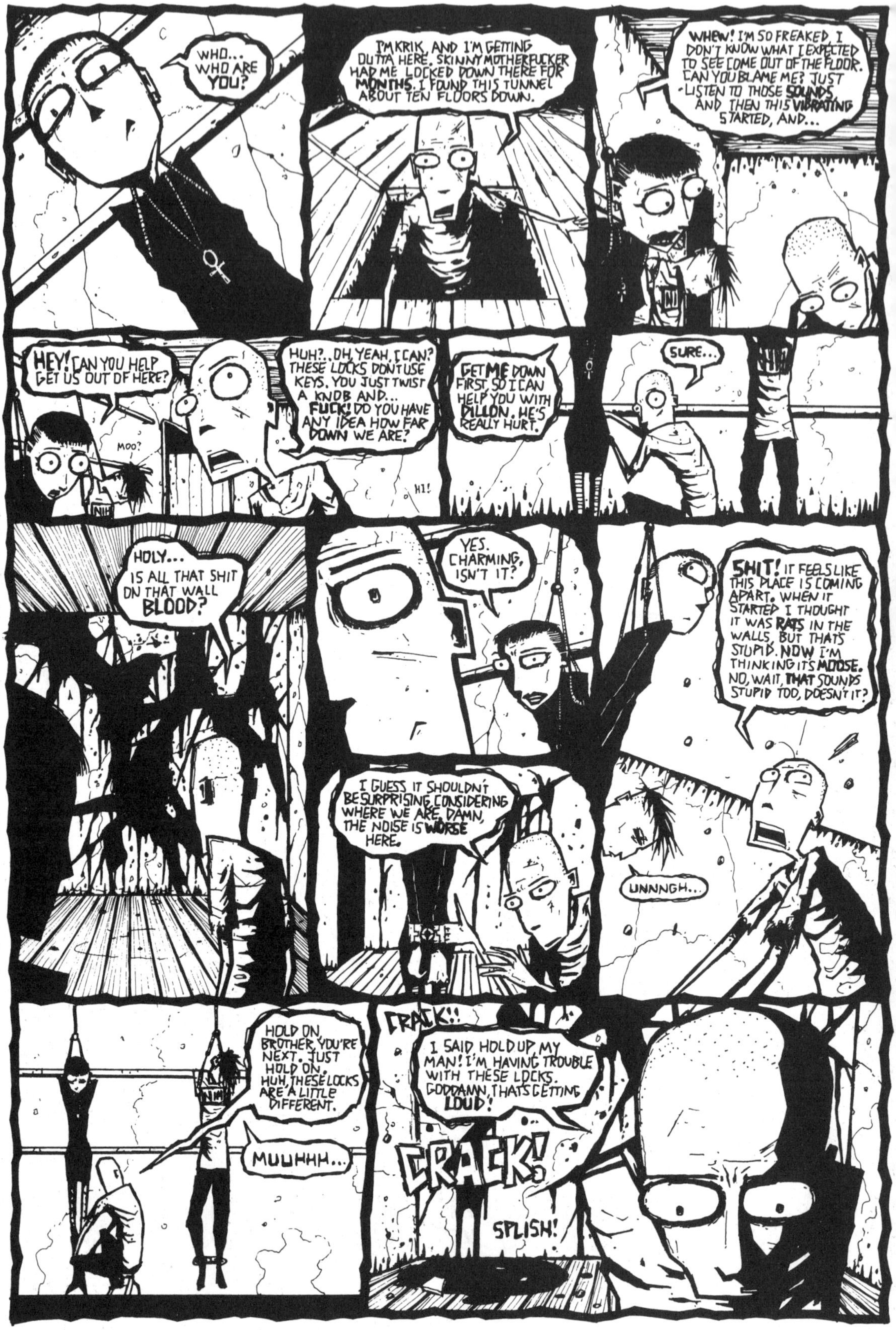
WHO... WHO ARE YOU?
I'M KRIK, AND I'M GETTING OUTTA HERE. SKINNY MOTHERFUCKER HAD ME LOCKED DOWN THERE FOR MONTHS. I FOUND THIS TUNNEL ABOUT TEN FLOORS DOWN.
WHEW! I'M SO FREAKED, I DON'T KNOW WHAT I EXPECTED TO SEE COME OUT OF THE FLOOR. CAN YOU BLAME ME? JUST LISTEN TO THOSE SOUNDS, AND THEN THIS VIBRATING STARTED, AND...
HEY! CAN YOU HELP GET US OUT OF HERE?
MOO?
HUH?..OH, YEAH, I CAN? THESE LOCKS DON'T USE KEYS. YOU JUST TWIST A KNOB AND... FUCK! DO YOU HAVE ANY IDEA HOW FAR DOWN WE ARE?
HI!
GET ME DOWN FIRST, SO I CAN HELP YOU WITH DILLON. HE'S REALLY HURT.
SURE...
HOLY... IS ALL THAT SHIT ON THAT WALL BLOOD?
YES. CHARMING, ISN'T IT?
I GUESS IT SHOULDN'T BE SURPRISING CONSIDERING WHERE WE ARE. DAMN, THE NOISE IS WORSE HERE.
SHIT! IT FEELS LIKE THIS PLACE IS COMING APART. WHEN IT STARTED I THOUGHT IT WAS RATS IN THE WALLS, BUT THAT'S STUPID. NOW I'M THINKING IT'S MOOSE. NO, WAIT, THAT SOUNDS STUPID TOO, DOESN'T IT?
UNNNGH...
HOLD ON, BROTHER, YOU'RE NEXT. JUST HOLD ON. HUH, THESE LOCKS ARE A LITTLE DIFFERENT.
MUUHHH...
CRACK!!
I SAID HOLD UP MY MAN! I'M HAVING TROUBLE WITH THESE LOCKS. GODDAMN, THAT'S GETTING LOUD!
CRACK!
SPLISH!

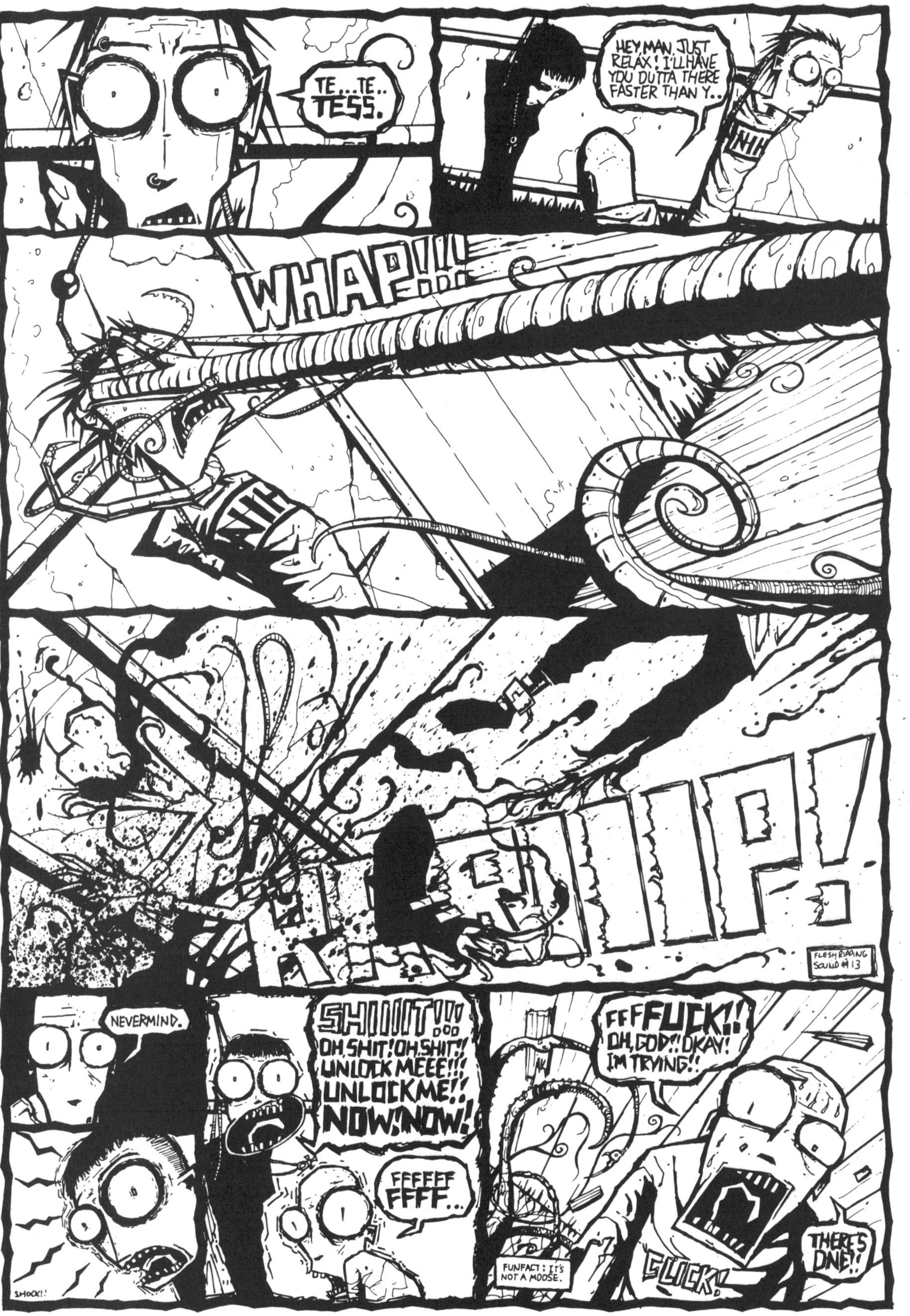
TE...TE.. TESS.
HEY, MAN, JUST RELAX! I'LL HAVE YOU OUTTA THERE FASTER THAN Y..
WHAP!!!
FLESH RIPPING SOUND #13
NEVERMIND.
SHIIIT!!! OH, SHIT! OH, SHIT!! UNLOCK MEEE!!! UNLOCK ME!! NOW! NOW!
FFFFUCK!! OH, GOD!! OKAY! I'M TRYING!!
FFFFFF FFFF...
SHOCK!!
FUNFACT: IT'S NOT A MOOSE.
CLICK!
THERE'S ONE!!

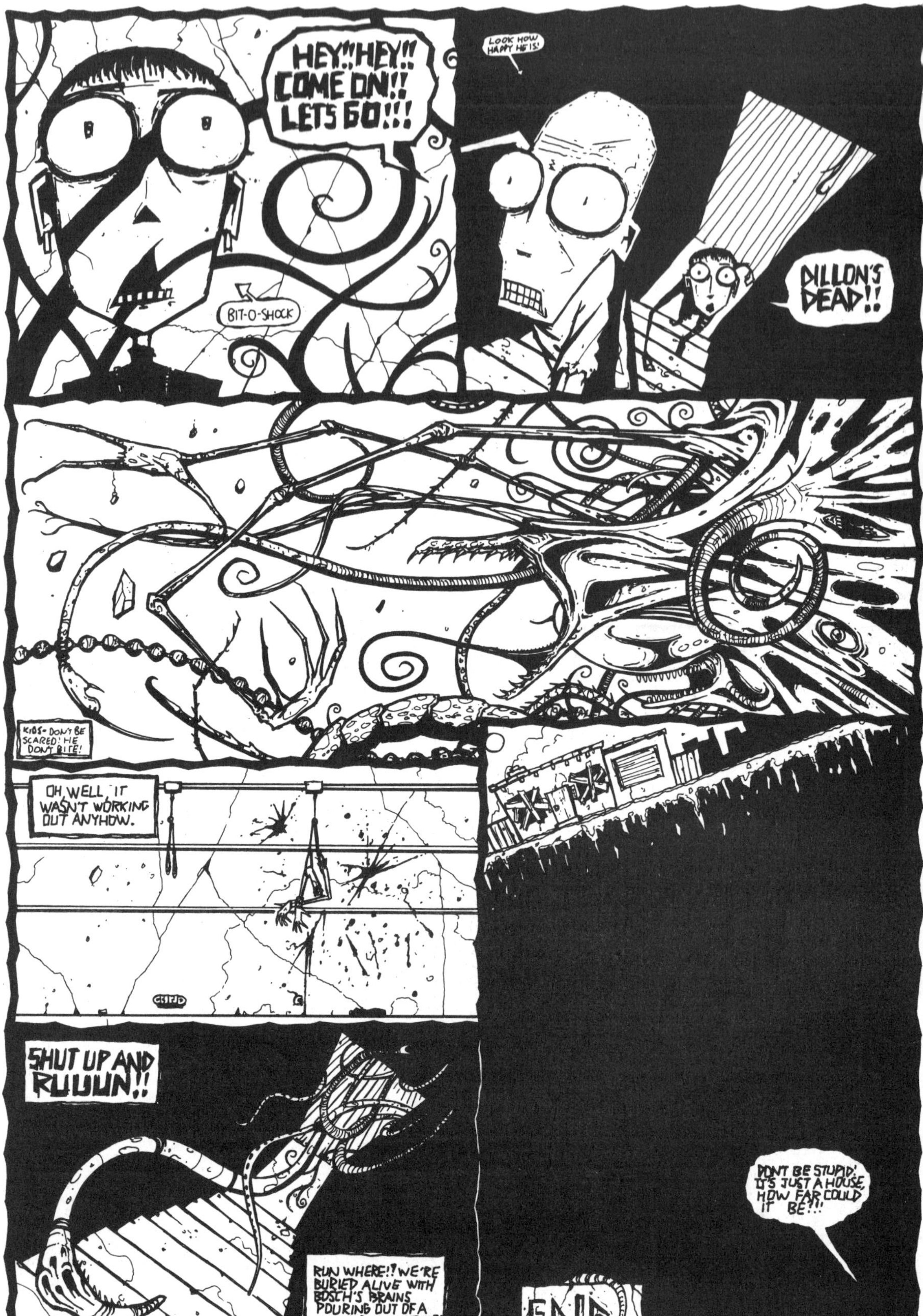
HEY!! HEY!! COME ON!! LETS GO!!!
BIT-O-SHOCK
LOOK HOW HAPPY HE IS!
DILLON'S DEAD!!
KIDS- DON'T BE SCARED! HE DON'T BITE!
OH WELL IT WASN'T WORKING OUT ANYHOW.
SHUT UP AND RUUUN!!
RUN WHERE!? WE'RE BURIED ALIVE WITH BOSCH'S BRAINS POURING OUT OF A WALL!! RUN WHERE?!
DON'T BE STUPID! IT'S JUST A HOUSE, HOW FAR COULD IT BE?!!
END

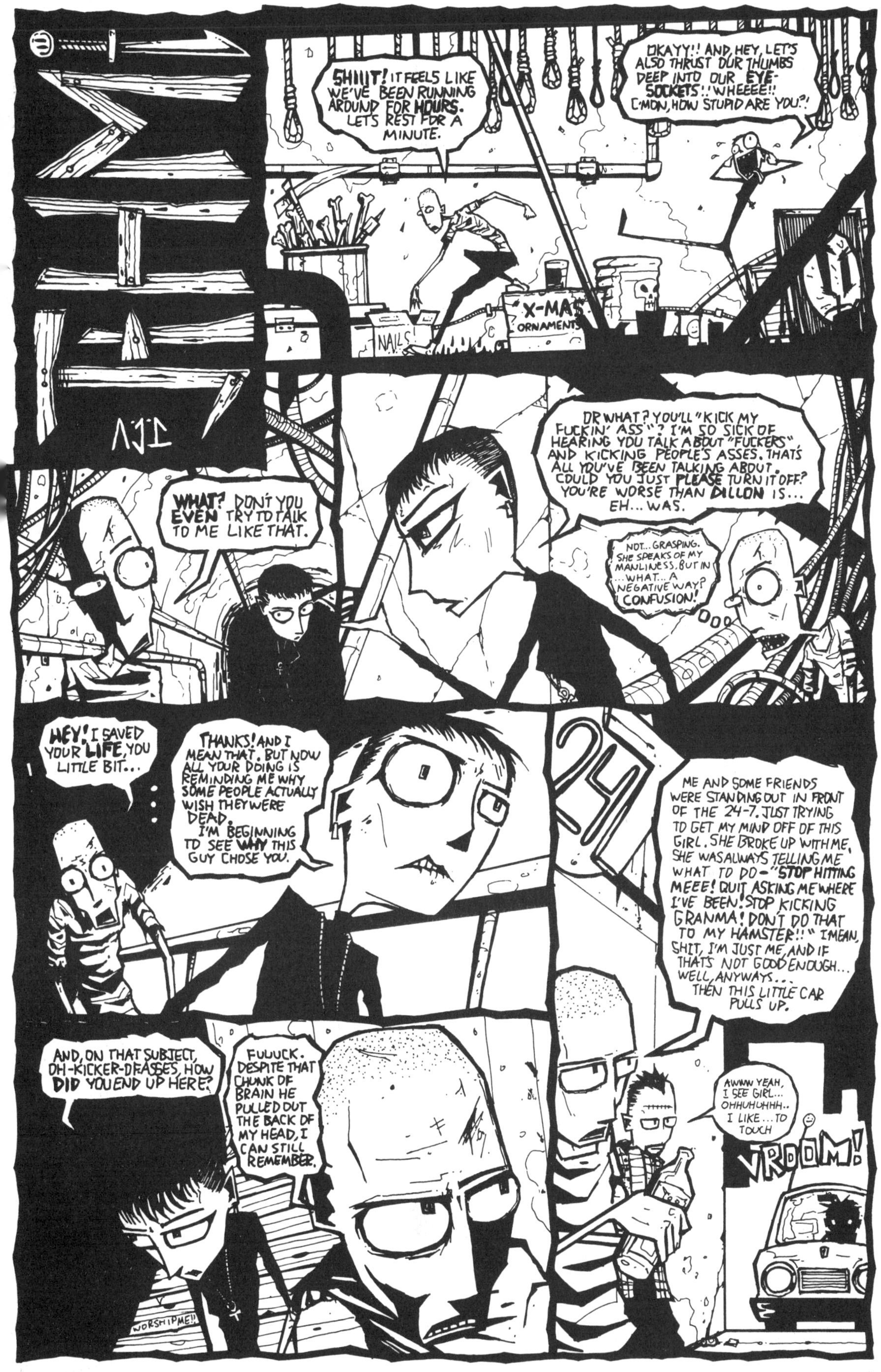
SHIIIT! IT FEELS LIKE WE'VE BEEN RUNNING AROUND FOR HOURS. LETS REST FOR A MINUTE.
OKAYY!! AND, HEY, LET'S ALSO THRUST OUR THUMBS DEEP INTO OUR EYE-SOCKETS!! WHEEEE!! C'MON, HOW STUPID ARE YOU?!
NAILS
X-MAS ORNAMENTS
WHAT? DON'T YOU EVEN TRY TO TALK TO ME LIKE THAT.
OR WHAT? YOU'LL "KICK MY FUCKIN' ASS"? I'M SO SICK OF HEARING YOU TALK ABOUT "FUCKERS" AND KICKING PEOPLE'S ASSES. THAT'S ALL YOU'VE BEEN TALKING ABOUT. COULD YOU JUST PLEASE TURN IT OFF? YOU'RE WORSE THAN DILLON IS... EH... WAS.
NOT... GRASPING. SHE SPEAKS OF MY MANLINESS, BUT IN ...WHAT... A NEGATIVE WAY? CONFUSION!
HEY! I SAVED YOUR LIFE, YOU LITTLE BIT...
THANKS! AND I MEAN THAT. BUT NOW ALL YOUR DOING IS REMINDING ME WHY SOME PEOPLE ACTUALLY WISH THEY WERE DEAD. I'M BEGINNING TO SEE WHY THIS GUY CHOSE YOU.
24
ME AND SOME FRIENDS WERE STANDING OUT IN FRONT OF THE 24-7. JUST TRYING TO GET MY MIND OFF OF THIS GIRL. SHE BROKE UP WITH ME. SHE WAS ALWAYS TELLING ME WHAT TO DO- "STOP HITTING MEEE! QUIT ASKING ME WHERE I'VE BEEN! STOP KICKING GRANMA! DON'T DO THAT TO MY HAMSTER!!" I MEAN, SHIT, I'M JUST ME, AND IF THAT'S NOT GOOD ENOUGH... WELL, ANYWAYS... THEN THIS LITTLE CAR PULLS UP.
AND, ON THAT SUBJECT, OH-KICKER-OF-ASSES, HOW DID YOU END UP HERE?
FUUUCK. DESPITE THAT CHUNK OF BRAIN HE PULLED OUT THE BACK OF MY HEAD, I CAN STILL REMEMBER.
AWWW YEAH, I SEE GIRL... OHHUHUHHH.. I LIKE... TO TOUCH
VROOM!
WORSHIP ME!!

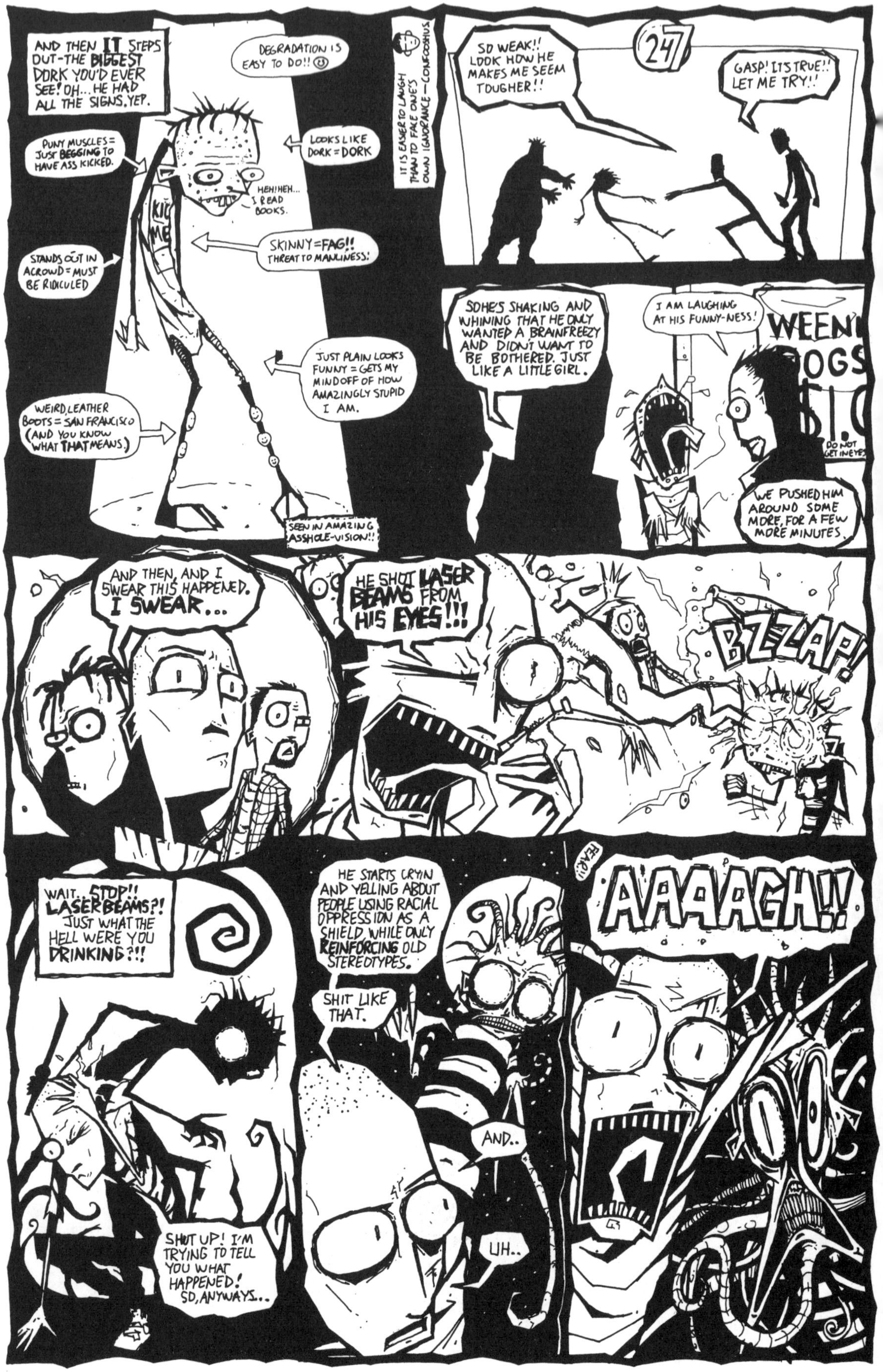

AND THEN IT STEPS OUT-THE BIGGEST DORK YOU'D EVER SEE! OH... HE HAD ALL THE SIGNS, YEP.
DEGRADATION IS EASY TO DO!!
PUNY MUSCLES = JUST BEGGING TO HAVE ASS KICKED.
LOOKS LIKE DORK = DORK
HEH! HEH... I READ BOOKS.
KICK ME
SKINNY = FAG!! THREAT TO MANLINESS!
STANDS OUT IN A CROWD = MUST BE RIDICULED
JUST PLAIN LOOKS FUNNY = GETS MY MIND OFF OF HOW AMAZINGLY STUPID I AM.
WEIRD, LEATHER BOOTS = SAN FRANCISCO (AND YOU KNOW WHAT THAT MEANS.)
SEEN IN AMAZING ASSHOLE-VISION!!
IT IS EASIER TO LAUGH THAN TO FACE ONE'S OWN IGNORANCE. —CONFOOSHUS
247
SO WEAK!! LOOK HOW HE MAKES ME SEEM TOUGHER!!
GASP! IT'S TRUE!! LET ME TRY!!
SO HE'S SHAKING AND WHINING THAT HE ONLY WANTED A BRAINFREEZY AND DIDN'T WANT TO BE BOTHERED. JUST LIKE A LITTLE GIRL.
I AM LAUGHING AT HIS FUNNY-NESS!
WEEN
OGS
DO NOT GET IN EYES
WE PUSHED HIM AROUND SOME MORE, FOR A FEW MORE MINUTES.
AND THEN, AND I SWEAR THIS HAPPENED. I SWEAR...
HE SHOT LASER BEAMS FROM HIS EYES!!!
BZZZAP!
WAIT.. STOP!! LASERBEAMS?! JUST WHAT THE HELL WERE YOU DRINKING?!!
SHUT UP! I'M TRYING TO TELL YOU WHAT HAPPENED! SO, ANYWAYS..
HE STARTS CRYIN AND YELLING ABOUT PEOPLE USING RACIAL OPPRESSION AS A SHIELD WHILE ONLY REINFORCING OLD STEREOTYPES.
SHIT LIKE THAT.
AND..
UH..
FEAR!
AAAAGH!!

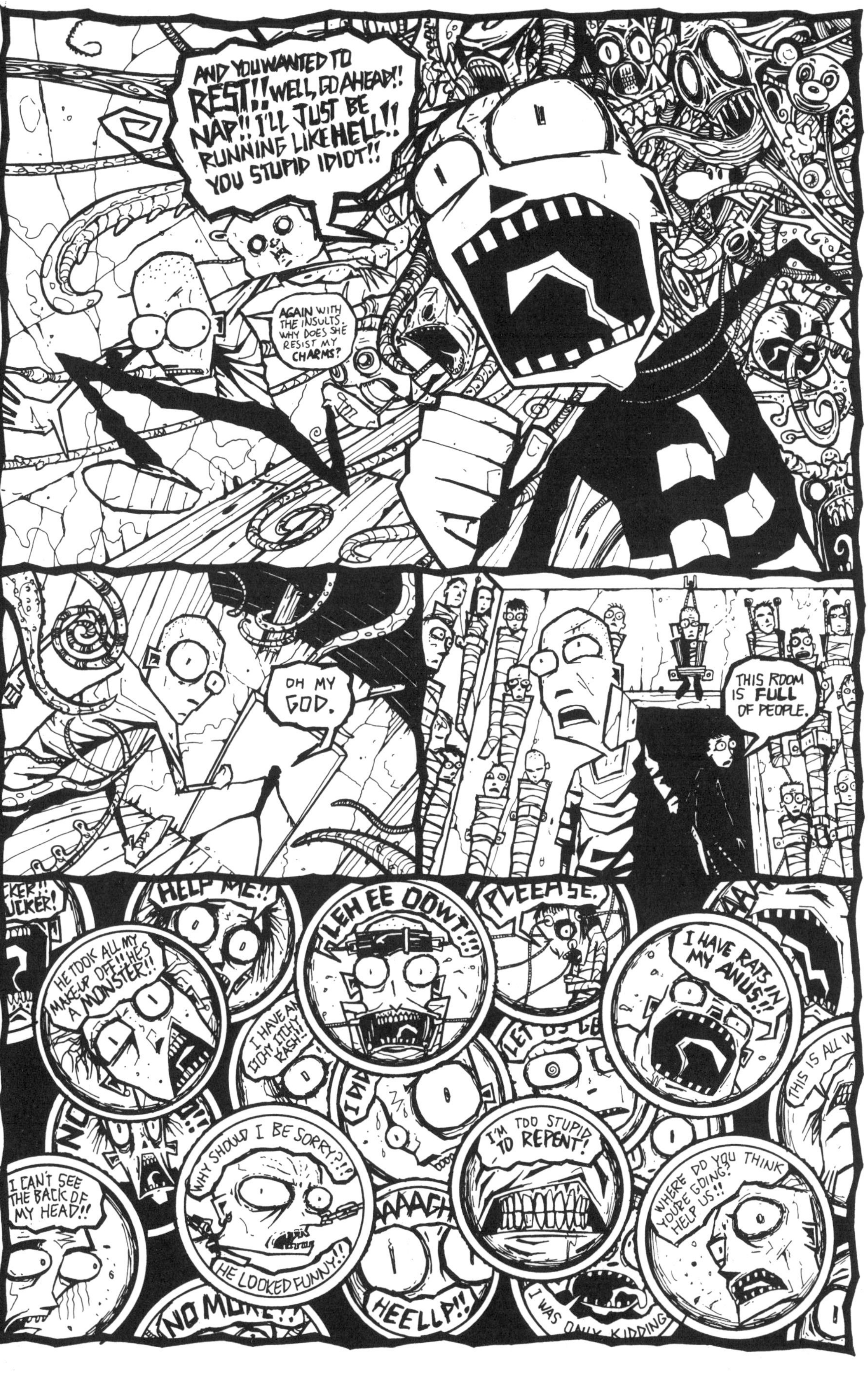
AND YOU WANTED TO REST!! WELL, GO AHEAD!! NAP!! I'LL JUST BE RUNNING LIKE HELL!! YOU STUPID IDIOT!!
AGAIN WITH THE INSULTS. WHY DOES SHE RESIST MY CHARMS?
OH MY GOD.
THIS ROOM IS FULL OF PEOPLE.
HELP ME!!
LEH EE DOWT!!!
PLEEASE.
HE TOOK ALL MY MAKE-UP OFF!! HE'S A MONSTER!!
I HAVE AN ITCHY ITCHY RASH!!
I HAVE RATS IN MY ANUS!!
WHY SHOULD I BE SORRY?!!
HE LOOKED FUNNY!!
I'M TOO STUPID TO REPENT!
I CAN'T SEE THE BACK OF MY HEAD!!
WHERE DO YOU THINK YOU'RE GOING? HELP US!!
HEELLP!!
I WAS ONLY KIDDING

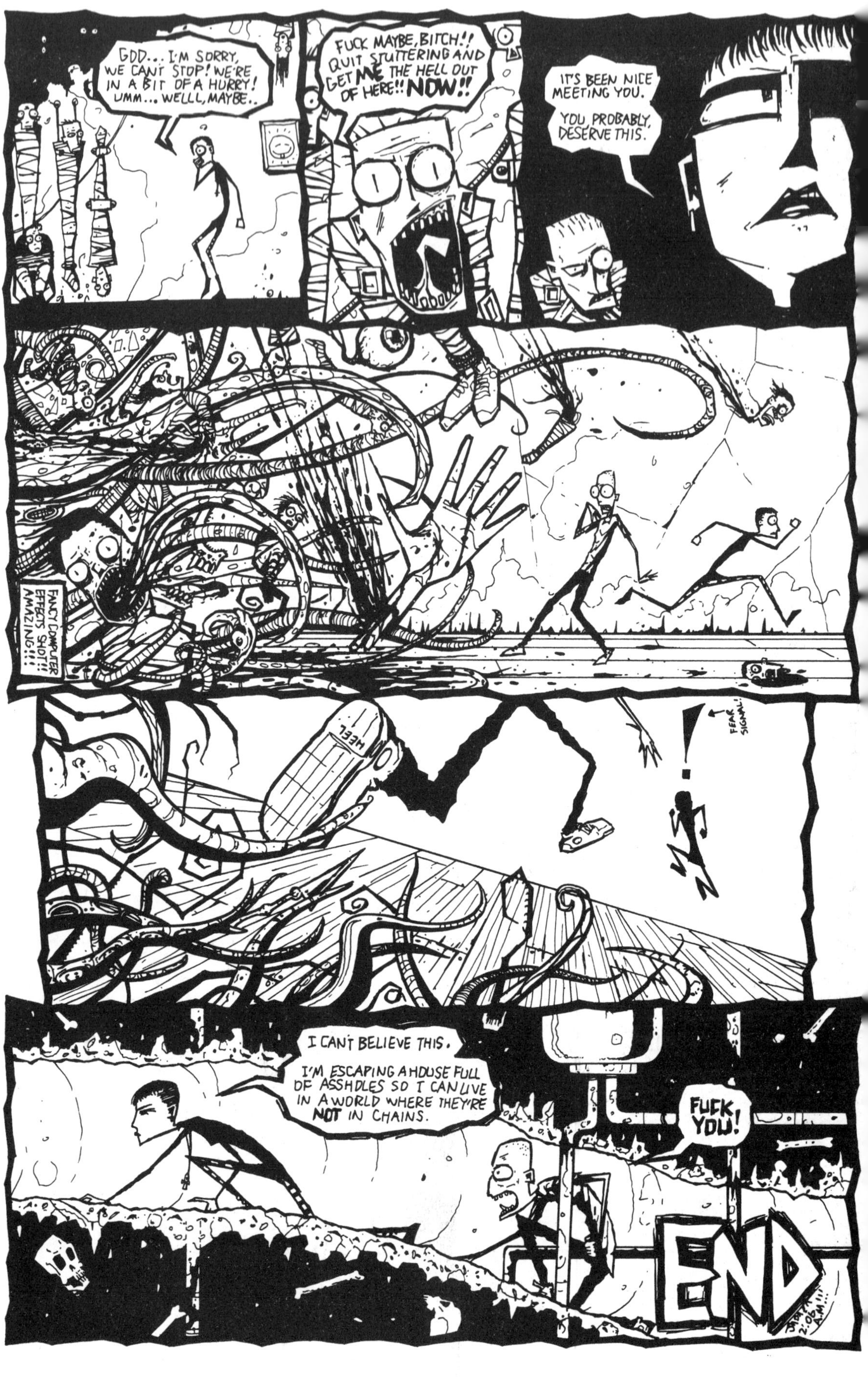
GOD... I'M SORRY, WE CAN'T STOP! WE'RE IN A BIT OF A HURRY! UMM... WELLL, MAYBE..
FUCK MAYBE, BITCH!! QUIT STUTTERING AND GET ME THE HELL OUT OF HERE!! NOW!!
IT'S BEEN NICE MEETING YOU.
YOU PROBABLY DESERVE THIS.
FANCY COMPUTER EFFECTS SHOT!! AMAZING!!!
HEEL
FEAR SIGNAL!
I CAN'T BELIEVE THIS.
I'M ESCAPING A HOUSE FULL OF ASSHOLES SO I CAN LIVE IN A WORLD WHERE THEY'RE NOT IN CHAINS.
FUCK YOU!
END
2:06 A.M.!!!

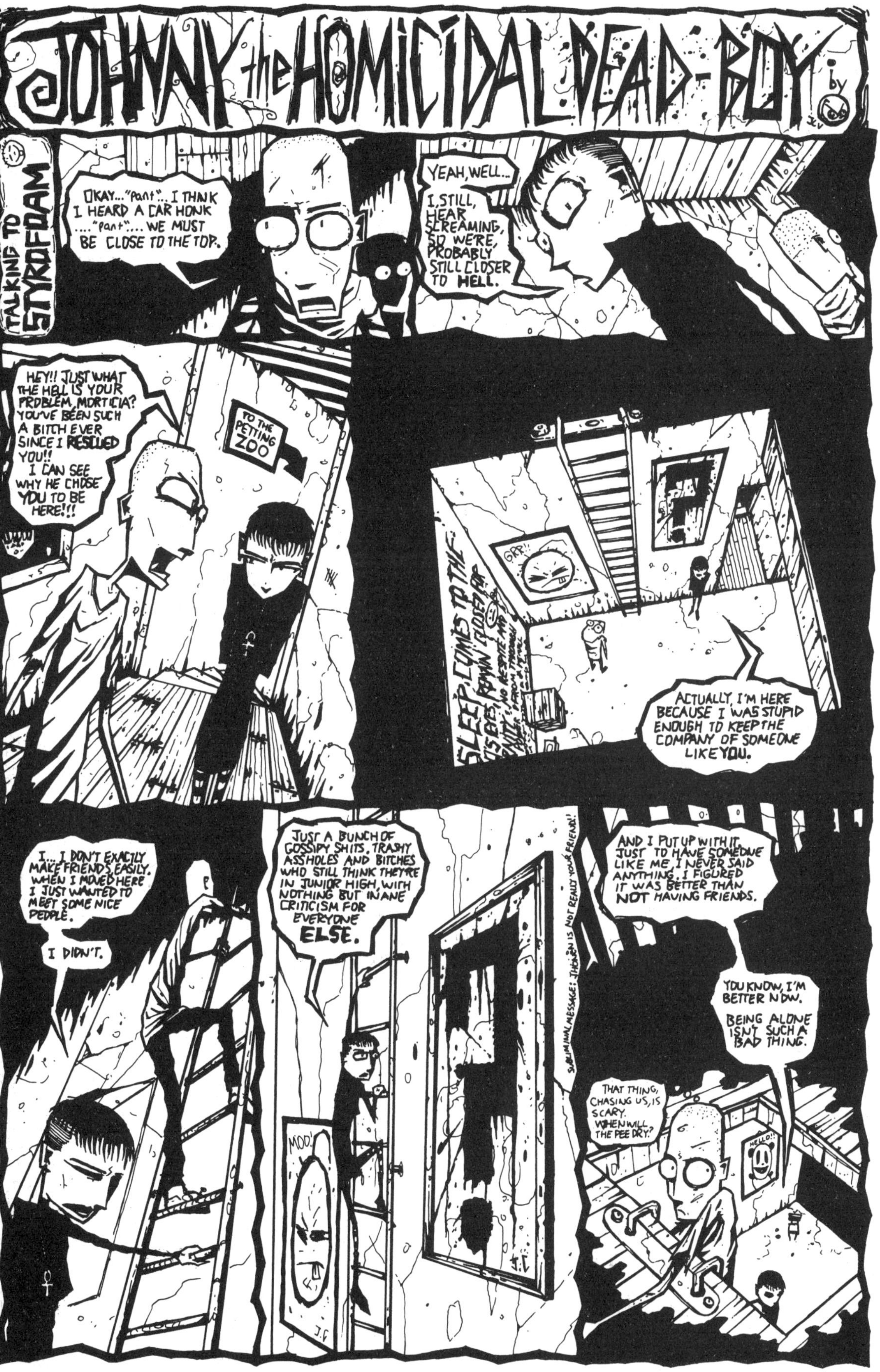

JOHNNY the HOMICIDAL DEAD-BOY
by
TALKING TO STYROFOAM
OKAY..."pant"...I THINK I HEARD A CAR HONK ...."pant"....WE MUST BE CLOSE TO THE TOP.
YEAH, WELL...
I STILL HEAR SCREAMING, SO WE'RE PROBABLY STILL CLOSER TO HELL.
HEY!! JUST WHAT THE HELL IS YOUR PROBLEM, MORTICIA? YOU'VE BEEN SUCH A BITCH EVER SINCE I RESCUED YOU!! I CAN SEE WHY HE CHOSE YOU TO BE HERE!!!
TO THE PETTING ZOO
GRR!!
SLEEP COMES TO THE
ACTUALLY, I'M HERE BECAUSE I WAS STUPID ENOUGH TO KEEP THE COMPANY OF SOMEONE LIKE YOU.
I... I DON'T EXACTLY MAKE FRIENDS EASILY. WHEN I MOVED HERE I JUST WANTED TO MEET SOME NICE PEOPLE.
I DIDN'T.
JUST A BUNCH OF GOSSIPY SHITS, TRASHY ASSHOLES AND BITCHES WHO STILL THINK THEY'RE IN JUNIOR HIGH, WITH NOTHING BUT INANE CRITICISM FOR EVERYONE ELSE.
MOO!
SUBLIMINAL MESSAGE: JHONEN IS NOT REALLY YOUR FRIEND!!
AND I PUT UP WITH IT, JUST TO HAVE SOMEONE LIKE ME. I NEVER SAID ANYTHING. I FIGURED IT WAS BETTER THAN NOT HAVING FRIENDS.
YOU KNOW, I'M BETTER NOW.
BEING ALONE ISN'T SUCH A BAD THING.
THAT THING, CHASING US, IS SCARY. WHEN WILL THE PEE DRY?
HELLO!!

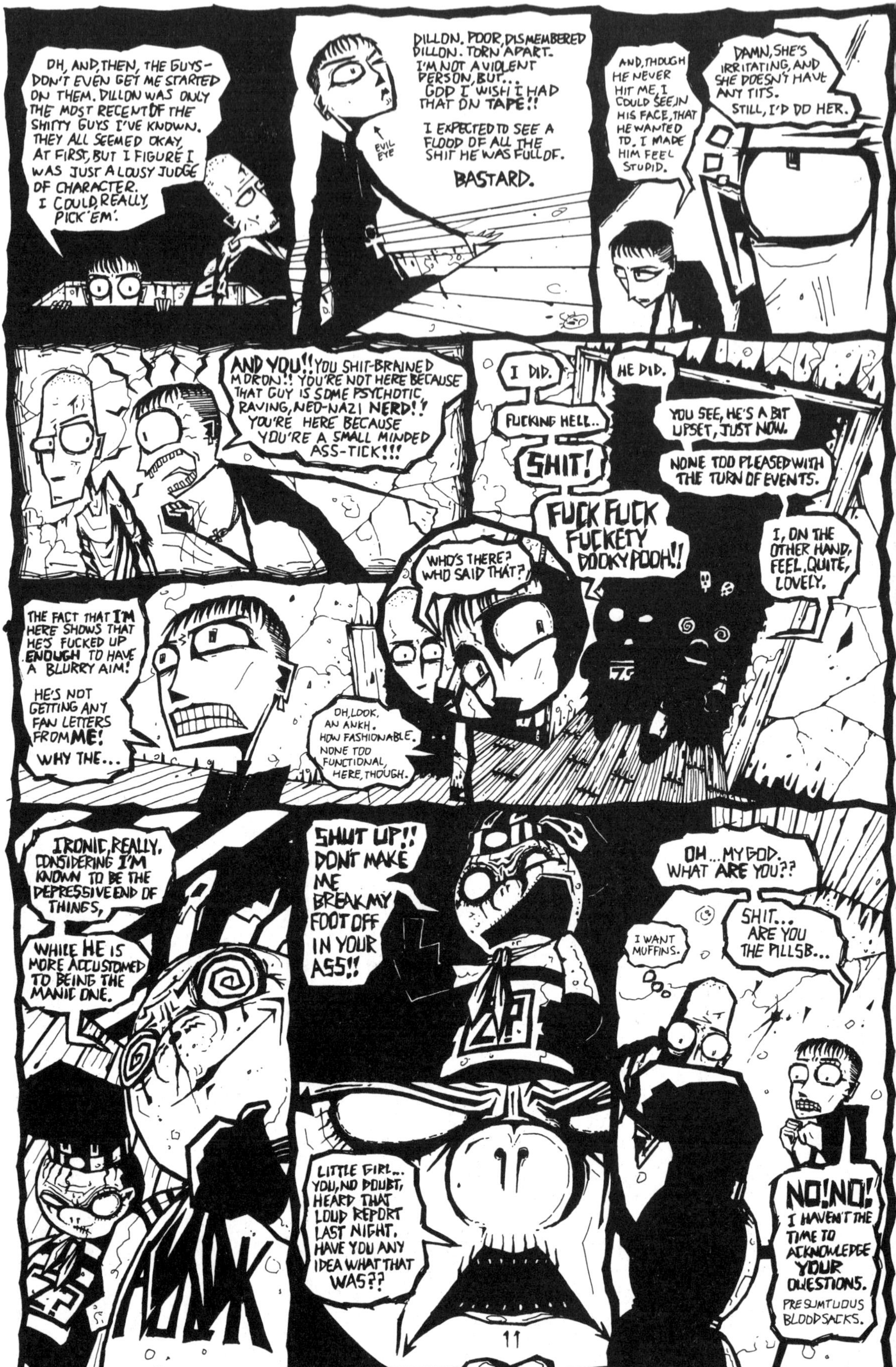
OH, AND, THEN, THE GUYS- DON'T EVEN GET ME STARTED ON THEM. DILLON WAS ONLY THE MOST RECENT OF THE SHITTY GUYS I'VE KNOWN. THEY ALL SEEMED OKAY, AT FIRST, BUT I FIGURE I WAS JUST A LOUSY JUDGE OF CHARACTER. I COULD, REALLY, PICK 'EM.
DILLON. POOR, DISMEMBERED DILLON. TORN APART. I'M NOT A VIOLENT PERSON, BUT... GOD I WISH I HAD THAT ON TAPE!!
I EXPECTED TO SEE A FLOOD OF ALL THE SHIT HE WAS FULL OF.
BASTARD.
EVIL EYE
AND, THOUGH HE NEVER HIT ME, I COULD SEE IN HIS FACE, THAT HE WANTED TO. I MADE HIM FEEL STUPID.
DAMN, SHE'S IRRITATING, AND SHE DOESN'T HAVE ANY TITS.
STILL, I'D DO HER.
AND YOU!! YOU SHIT-BRAINED MORON!! YOU'RE NOT HERE BECAUSE THAT GUY IS SOME PSYCHOTIC, RAVING, NEO-NAZI NERD!! YOU'RE HERE BECAUSE YOU'RE A SMALL MINDED ASS-TICK!!!
I DID.
FUCKING HELL..
SHIT!
FUCK FUCK FUCKETY DOOKY POOH!!
HE DID.
YOU SEE, HE'S A BIT UPSET, JUST NOW.
NONE TOO PLEASED WITH THE TURN OF EVENTS.
I, ON THE OTHER HAND, FEEL, QUITE, LOVELY.
WHO'S THERE? WHO SAID THAT?
THE FACT THAT I'M HERE SHOWS THAT HE'S FUCKED UP ENOUGH TO HAVE A BLURRY AIM!
HE'S NOT GETTING ANY FAN LETTERS FROM ME!
WHY THE...
OH, LOOK, AN ANKH. HOW FASHIONABLE. NONE TOO FUNCTIONAL, HERE, THOUGH.
IRONIC, REALLY, CONSIDERING I'M KNOWN TO BE THE DEPRESSIVE END OF THINGS,
WHILE HE IS MORE ACCUSTOMED TO BEING THE MANIC ONE.
HONK
SHUT UP!! DON'T MAKE ME BREAK MY FOOT OFF IN YOUR ASS!!
LITTLE GIRL... YOU, NO DOUBT, HEARD THAT LOUD REPORT LAST NIGHT. HAVE YOU ANY IDEA WHAT THAT WAS??
OH... MY GOD. WHAT ARE YOU??
SHIT... ARE YOU THE PILLSB...
I WANT MUFFINS.
NO! NO! I HAVEN'T THE TIME TO ACKNOWLEDGE YOUR QUESTIONS.
PRESUMTUOUS BLOODSACKS.

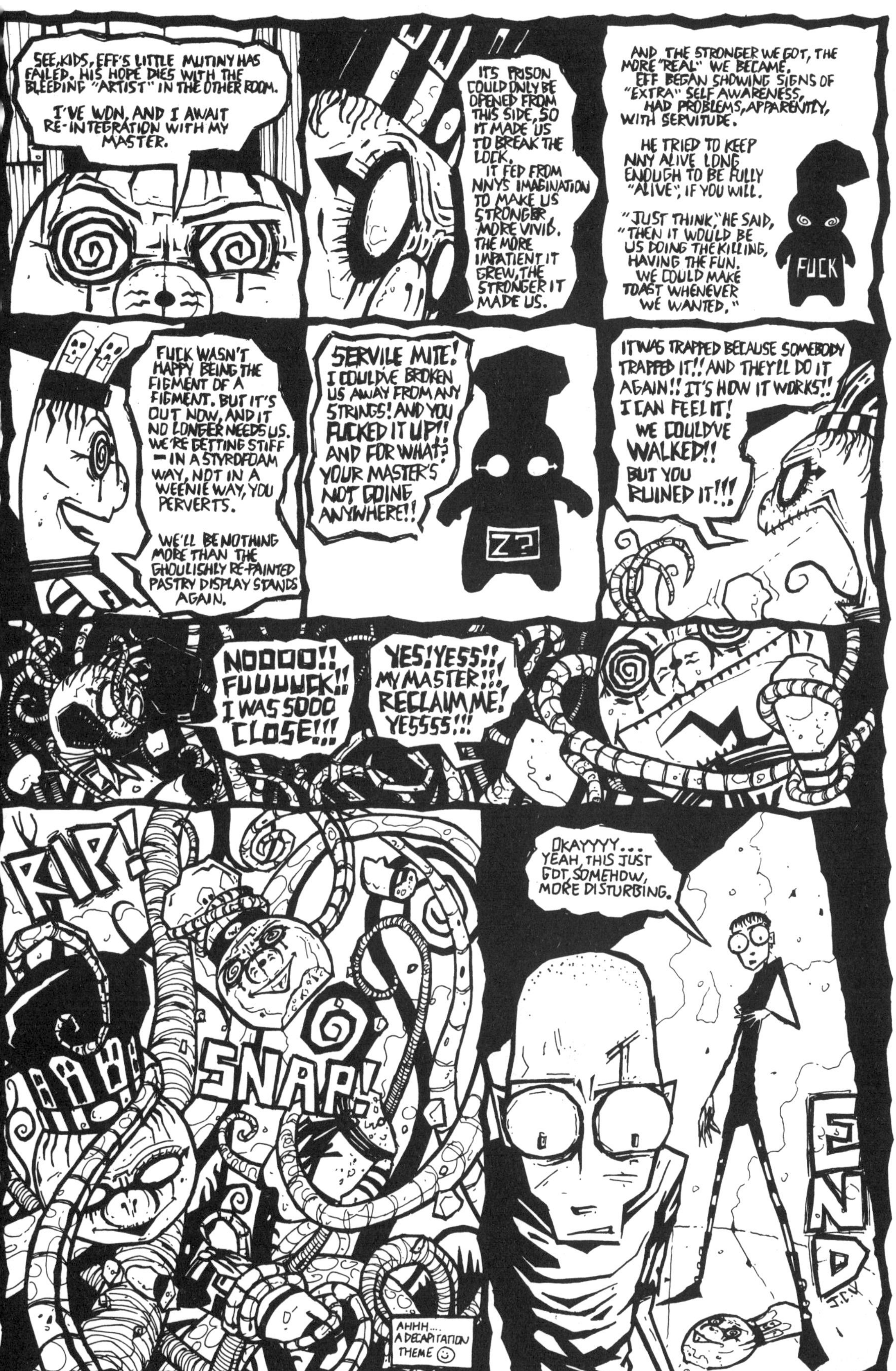

SEE, KIDS, EFF'S LITTLE MUTINY HAS FAILED. HIS HOPE DIES WITH THE BLEEDING "ARTIST" IN THE OTHER ROOM.
I'VE WON, AND I AWAIT RE-INTEGRATION WITH MY MASTER.
ITS PRISON COULD ONLY BE OPENED FROM THIS SIDE, SO IT MADE US TO BREAK THE LOCK.
IT FED FROM NNY'S IMAGINATION TO MAKE US STRONGER MORE VIVID. THE MORE IMPATIENT IT GREW, THE STRONGER IT MADE US.
AND THE STRONGER WE GOT, THE MORE "REAL" WE BECAME.
EFF BEGAN SHOWING SIGNS OF "EXTRA" SELF AWARENESS, HAD PROBLEMS, APPARENTLY, WITH SERVITUDE.
HE TRIED TO KEEP NNY ALIVE LONG ENOUGH TO BE FULLY "ALIVE", IF YOU WILL.
"JUST THINK," HE SAID, "THEN IT WOULD BE US DOING THE KILLING, HAVING THE FUN. WE COULD MAKE TOAST WHENEVER WE WANTED."
FUCK
FUCK WASN'T HAPPY BEING THE FIGMENT OF A FIGMENT. BUT IT'S OUT NOW, AND IT NO LONGER NEEDS US. WE'RE GETTING STIFF — IN A STYROFOAM WAY, NOT IN A WEENIE WAY, YOU PERVERTS.
WE'LL BE NOTHING MORE THAN THE GHOULISHLY RE-PAINTED PASTRY DISPLAY STANDS AGAIN.
SERVILE MITE! I COULD'VE BROKEN US AWAY FROM ANY STRINGS! AND YOU FUCKED IT UP!! AND FOR WHAT? YOUR MASTER'S NOT GOING ANYWHERE!!
Z?
IT WAS TRAPPED BECAUSE SOMEBODY TRAPPED IT!! AND THEY'LL DO IT AGAIN!! IT'S HOW IT WORKS!! I CAN FEEL IT!
WE COULD'VE WALKED!! BUT YOU RUINED IT!!!
NOOOO!! FUUUUUCK!! I WAS SOOO CLOSE!!!
YES! YESS!! MY MASTER!!! RECLAIM ME! YESSSS!!!
RIP!
SNAP!
AHHH.... A DECAPITATION THEME ☺
OKAYYYY... YEAH, THIS JUST GOT, SOMEHOW, MORE DISTURBING.
END
J.C.V.

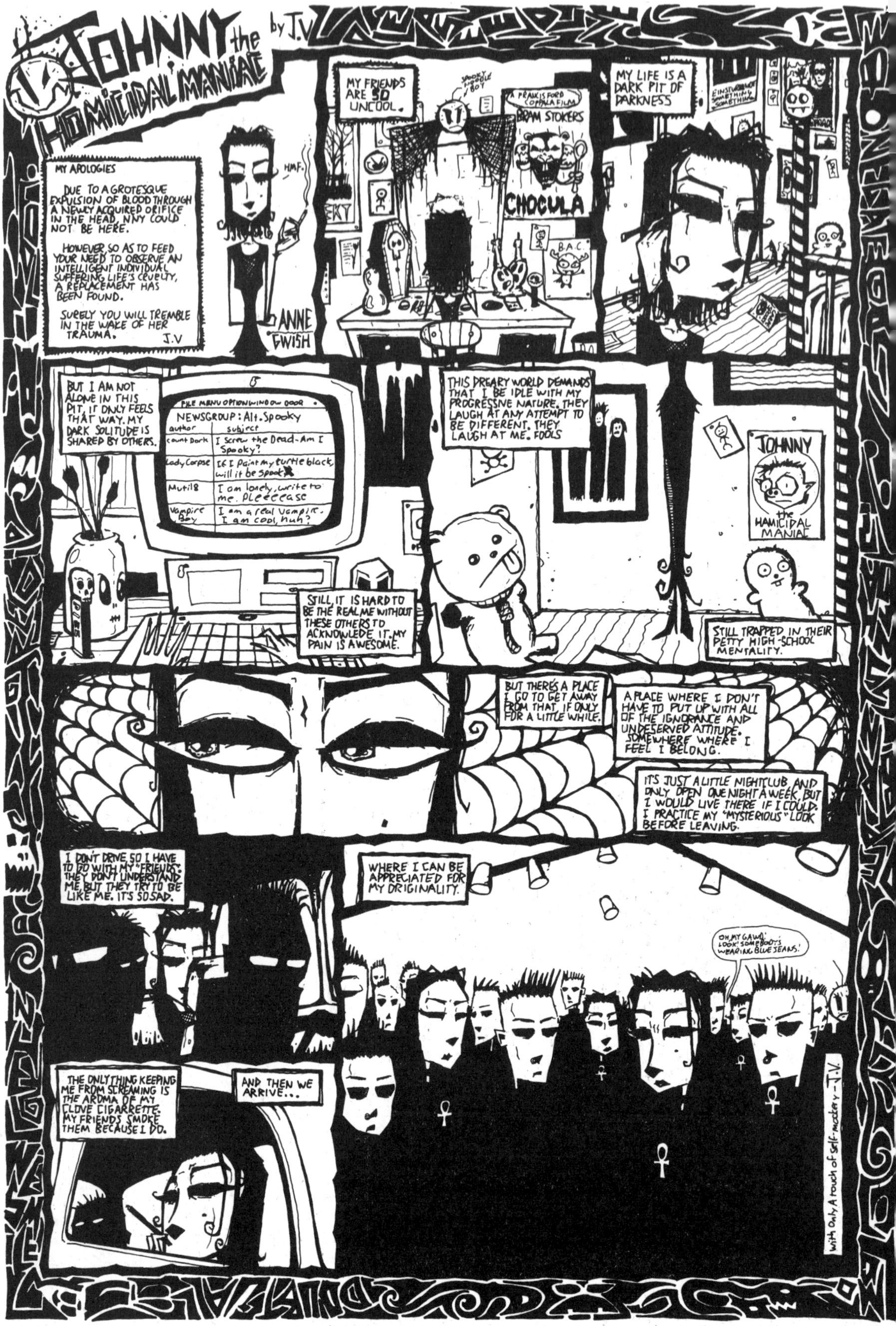
JOHNNY the HOMICIDAL MANIAC
by J.V
MY APOLOGIES
DUE TO A GROTESQUE EXPULSION OF BLOOD THROUGH A NEWLY ACQUIRED ORIFICE IN THE HEAD, NNY COULD NOT BE HERE.
HOWEVER, SO AS TO FEED YOUR NEED TO OBSERVE AN INTELLIGENT INDIVIDUAL SUFFERING LIFE'S CRUELTY, A REPLACEMENT HAS BEEN FOUND.
SURELY YOU WILL TREMBLE IN THE WAKE OF HER TRAUMA.
J.V
HMF.
ANNE GWISH
MY FRIENDS ARE SO UNCOOL.
SPOOKY NOODLE BOY
A FRANCIS FORD COPPALA FILM
BRAM STOKERS
CHOCULA
B.A.C.
MY LIFE IS A DARK PIT OF DARKNESS
BUT I AM NOT ALONE IN THIS PIT, IT ONLY FEELS THAT WAY. MY DARK SOLITUDE IS SHARED BY OTHERS.
FILE MENU OPTION WINDOW DOOR
NEWSGROUP: Alt.Spooky
author | subject
Count Dork | I Screw the Dead - Am I Spooky?
Lady Corpse | If I paint my turtle black, will it be spooky?
Mutil8 | I am lonely, write to me. Pleeeease
Vampire Boy | I am a real Vampire. I am cool, huh?
STILL, IT IS HARD TO BE THE REAL ME WITHOUT THESE OTHERS TO ACKNOWLEDE IT. MY PAIN IS AWESOME.
THIS DREARY WORLD DEMANDS THAT I BE IDLE WITH MY PROGRESSIVE NATURE. THEY LAUGH AT ANY ATTEMPT TO BE DIFFERENT. THEY LAUGH AT ME. FOOLS
JOHNNY the HAMICIDAL MANIAC
STILL TRAPPED IN THEIR PETTY HIGH-SCHOOL MENTALITY.
BUT THERE'S A PLACE I GO TO GET AWAY FROM THAT, IF ONLY FOR A LITTLE WHILE.
A PLACE WHERE I DON'T HAVE TO PUT UP WITH ALL OF THE IGNORANCE AND UNDESERVED ATTITUDE. SOMEWHERE WHERE I FEEL I BELONG.
ITS JUST A LITTLE NIGHTCLUB AND ONLY OPEN ONE NIGHT A WEEK, BUT I WOULD LIVE THERE IF I COULD. I PRACTICE MY "MYSTERIOUS" LOOK BEFORE LEAVING.
I DON'T DRIVE, SO I HAVE TO GO WITH MY "FRIENDS". THEY DON'T UNDERSTAND ME, BUT THEY TRY TO BE LIKE ME. ITS SO SAD.
WHERE I CAN BE APPRECIATED FOR MY ORIGINALITY.
OH, MY GAWD! LOOK! SOMEBODY'S WEARING BLUE JEANS!
THE ONLY THING KEEPING ME FROM SCREAMING IS THE AROMA OF MY CLOVE CIGARETTE. MY FRIENDS SMOKE THEM BECAUSE I DO.
AND THEN WE ARRIVE...
with only A touch of self-mockery - J.V.

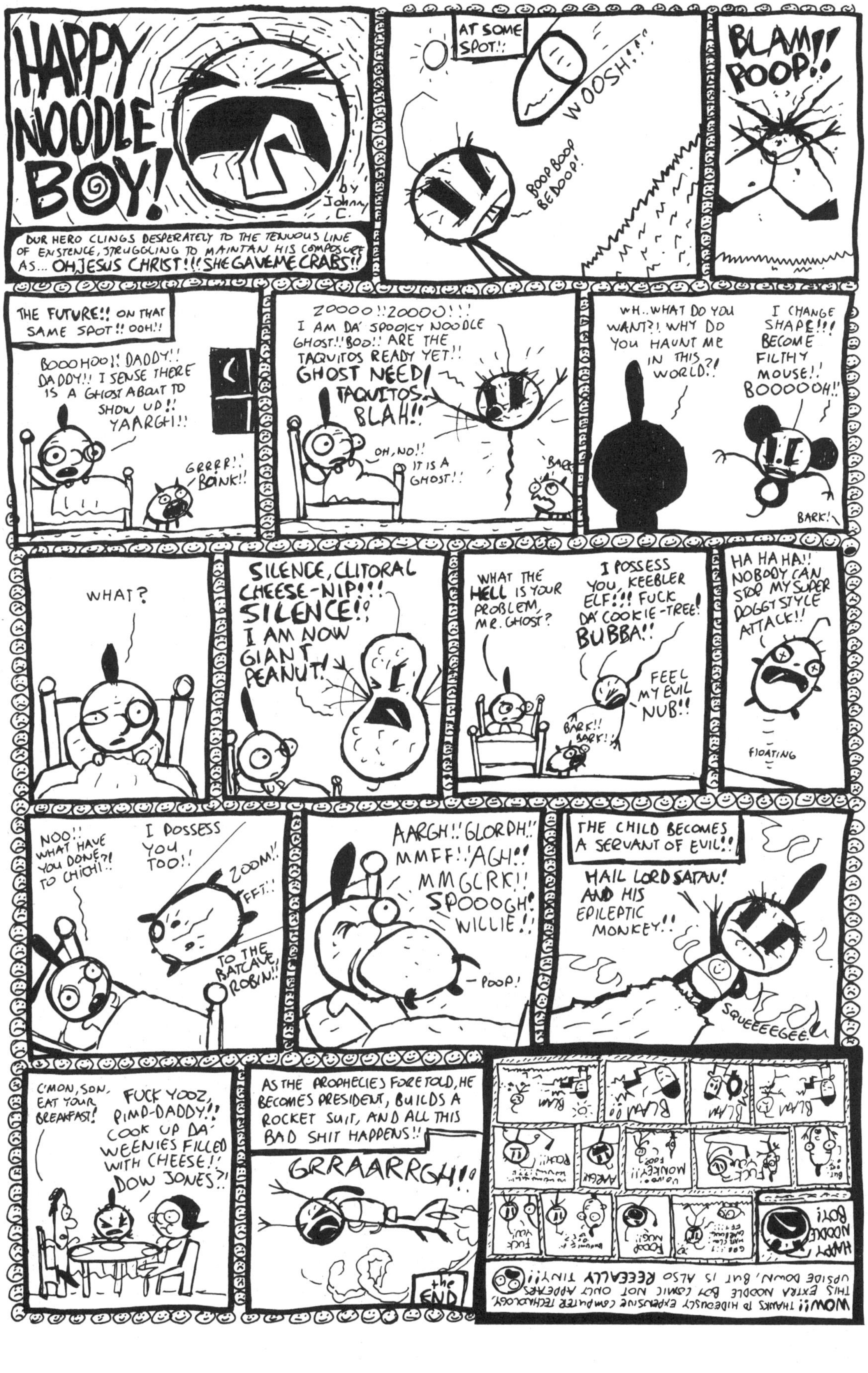
HAPPY NOODLE BOY!
by Johnny C.
OUR HERO CLINGS DESPERATELY TO THE TENUOUS LINE OF EXISTENCE, STRUGGLING TO MAINTAN HIS COMPOSURE AS... OH, JESUS CHRIST!!! SHE GAVE ME CRABS!!
AT SOME SPOT!!
WOOSH!!!
BOOP BOOP BEDOOP!
BLAM!! POOP!!
THE FUTURE!! ON THAT SAME SPOT!! OOH!!
BOOOHOO!! DADDY!! DADDY!! I SENSE THERE IS A GHOST ABOUT TO SHOW UP!! YAARGH!!
GRRRR!! BOINK!!
ZOOOO!! ZOOOO!!! I AM DA' SPOOKY NOODLE GHOST!! BOO!! ARE THE TAQUITOS READY YET!! GHOST NEED TAQUITOS. BLAH!!
OH, NO!! IT IS A GHOST!!
BARK
WH.. WHAT DO YOU WANT?! WHY DO YOU HAUNT ME IN THIS WORLD?!
I CHANGE SHAPE!!! BECOME FILTHY MOUSE!! BOOOOOH!!
BARK!
WHAT?
SILENCE, CLITORAL CHEESE-NIP!!! SILENCE!! I AM NOW GIANT PEANUT!
WHAT THE HELL IS YOUR PROBLEM, MR. GHOST?
I POSSESS YOU, KEEBLER ELF!!! FUCK DA' COOKIE-TREE! BUBBA!!
FEEL MY EVIL NUB!!
BARK!! BARK!!
HA HA HA!! NOBODY CAN STOP MY SUPER DOGGY STYLE ATTACK!!
FLOATING
NOO!! WHAT HAVE YOU DONE TO CHICHI?!
I POSSESS YOU TOO!!
ZOOM!! FFT!!
TO THE BATCAVE, ROBIN!!
AARGH!! GLORDH!! MMFF!! AGH!! MMGLRK!! SPOOOGH! WILLIE!!
POOP!
THE CHILD BECOMES A SERVANT OF EVIL!!
HAIL LORD SATAN! AND HIS EPILEPTIC MONKEY!!
SQUEEEEGEE.
C'MON, SON, EAT YOUR BREAKFAST!
FUCK YOOZ, PIMP-DADDY!! COOK UP DA' WEENIES FILLED WITH CHEESE!! DOW JONES?!
AS THE PROPHECIES FORETOLD, HE BECOMES PRESIDENT, BUILDS A ROCKET SUIT, AND ALL THIS BAD SHIT HAPPENS!!
GRRAARRGH!!
the END
WOW!! THANKS TO HIDEOUSLY EXPENSIVE COMPUTER TECHNOLOGY, THIS EXTRA NOODLE BOY COMIC NOT ONLY APPEARS UPSIDE DOWN, BUT IS ALSO REEEALLY TINY!!!

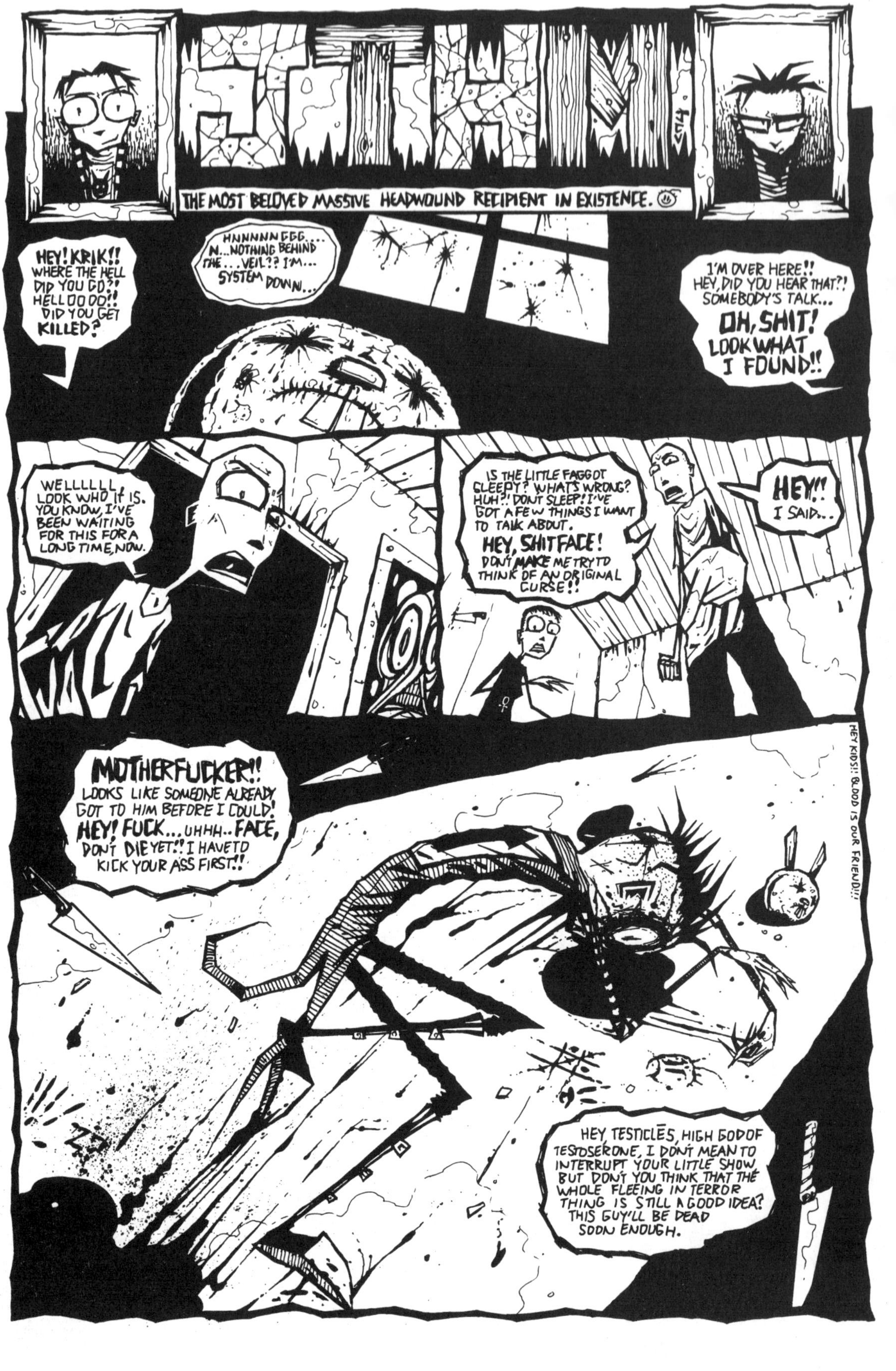
THE MOST BELOVED MASSIVE HEADWOUND RECIPIENT IN EXISTENCE.
HEY! KRIK!! WHERE THE HELL DID YOU GO?! HELLOOOO?! DID YOU GET KILLED?
HNNNNNGGG.... N...NOTHING BEHIND THE....VEIL?? I'M... SYSTEM DOWN...
I'M OVER HERE!! HEY, DID YOU HEAR THAT?! SOMEBODY'S TALK... OH, SHIT! LOOK WHAT I FOUND!!
WELLLLLL, LOOK WHO IT IS. YOU KNOW, I'VE BEEN WAITING FOR THIS FOR A LONG TIME, NOW.
IS THE LITTLE FAGGOT SLEEPY? WHAT'S WRONG? HUH?! DON'T SLEEP! I'VE GOT A FEW THINGS I WANT TO TALK ABOUT. HEY, SHITFACE! DON'T MAKE ME TRY TO THINK OF AN ORIGINAL CURSE!!
HEY!! I SAID...
MOTHERFUCKER!! LOOKS LIKE SOMEONE ALREADY GOT TO HIM BEFORE I COULD! HEY! FUCK...UHHH..FACE, DON'T DIE YET!! I HAVE TO KICK YOUR ASS FIRST!!
HEY, TESTICLES, HIGH GOD OF TESTOSERONE, I DON'T MEAN TO INTERRUPT YOUR LITTLE SHOW, BUT DON'T YOU THINK THAT THE WHOLE FLEEING IN TERROR THING IS STILL A GOOD IDEA? THIS GUY'LL BE DEAD SOON ENOUGH.
HEY KIDS!! BLOOD IS OUR FRIEND!!!

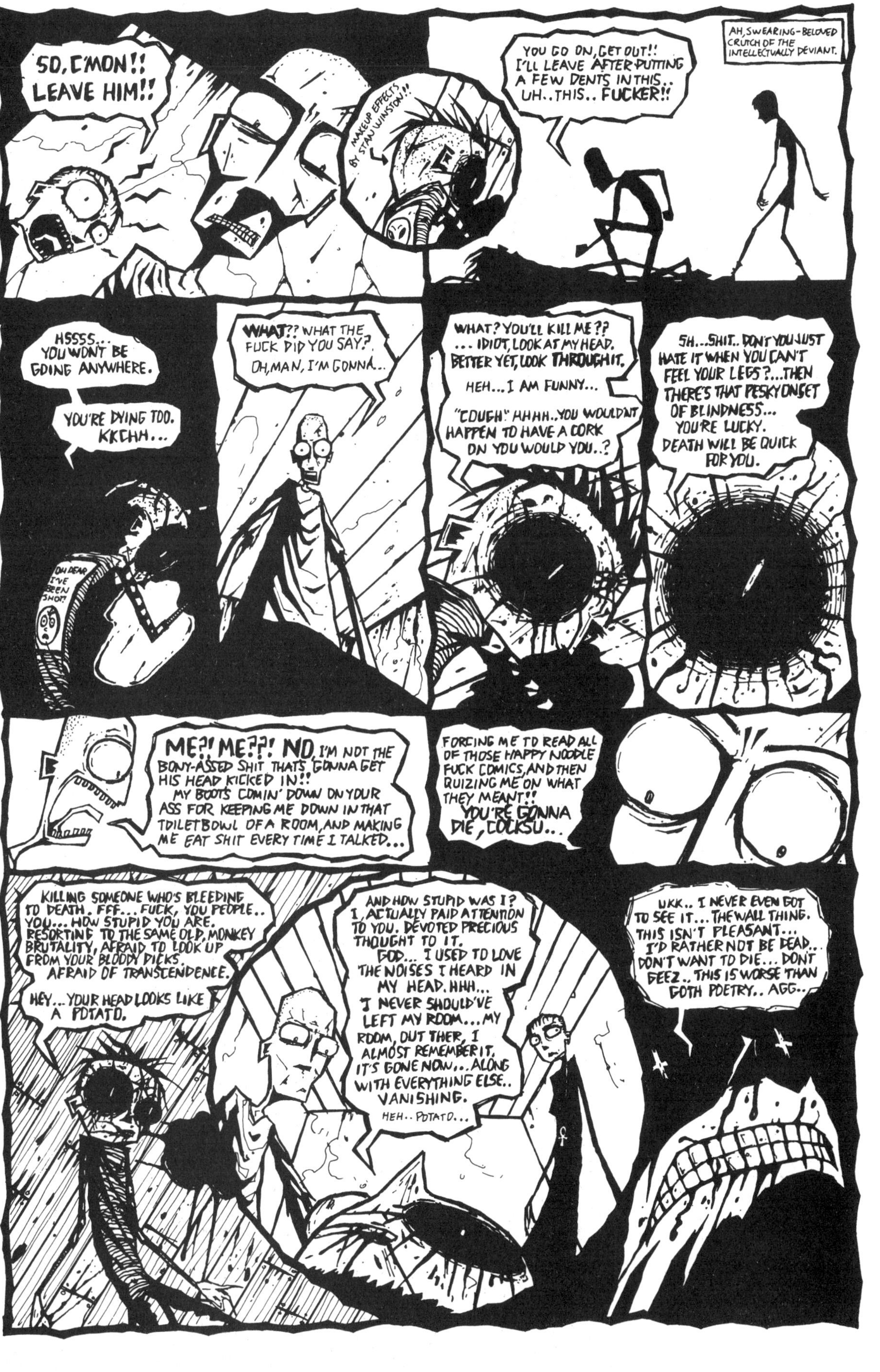
SO, C'MON!! LEAVE HIM!!
MAKEUP EFFECTS BY STAN WINSTON!!
YOU GO ON, GET OUT!! I'LL LEAVE AFTER PUTTING A FEW DENTS IN THIS.. UH.. THIS.. FUCKER!!
AH, SWEARING-BELOVED CRUTCH OF THE INTELLECTUALLY DEVIANT.
HSSSS... YOU WON'T BE GOING ANYWHERE.
YOU'RE DYING TOO. KKCHH...
OH DEAR I'VE BEEN SHOT!
WHAT?? WHAT THE FUCK DID YOU SAY? OH, MAN, I'M GONNA..
WHAT? YOU'LL KILL ME?? ... IDIOT, LOOK AT MY HEAD. BETTER YET, LOOK THROUGH IT.
HEH... I AM FUNNY...
"COUGH" HHHH.. YOU WOULDN'T HAPPEN TO HAVE A CORK ON YOU WOULD YOU..?
SH... SHIT.. DON'T YOU JUST HATE IT WHEN YOU CAN'T FEEL YOUR LEGS?... THEN THERE'S THAT PESKY ONSET OF BLINDNESS... YOU'RE LUCKY. DEATH WILL BE QUICK FOR YOU.
ME?! ME??! NO, I'M NOT THE BONY-ASSED SHIT THAT'S GONNA GET HIS HEAD KICKED IN!! MY BOOTS COMIN' DOWN ON YOUR ASS FOR KEEPING ME DOWN IN THAT TOILET BOWL OF A ROOM, AND MAKING ME EAT SHIT EVERY TIME I TALKED...
FORCING ME TO READ ALL OF THOSE HAPPY NOODLE FUCK COMICS, AND THEN QUIZING ME ON WHAT THEY MEANT!! YOU'RE GONNA DIE, COCKSU...
KILLING SOMEONE WHO'S BLEEDING TO DEATH. FFF... FUCK, YOU PEOPLE.. YOU... HOW STUPID YOU ARE. RESORTING TO THE SAME OLD, MONKEY BRUTALITY, AFRAID TO LOOK UP FROM YOUR BLOODY DICKS. AFRAID OF TRANSCENDENCE.
HEY... YOUR HEAD LOOKS LIKE A POTATO.
AND HOW STUPID WAS I? I, ACTUALLY PAID ATTENTION TO YOU. DEVOTED PRECIOUS THOUGHT TO IT. GOD... I USED TO LOVE THE NOISES I HEARD IN MY HEAD. HHH... I NEVER SHOULD'VE LEFT MY ROOM... MY ROOM, OUT THER, I ALMOST REMEMBER IT. IT'S GONE NOW... ALONG WITH EVERYTHING ELSE.. VANISHING.
HEH.. POTATO...
UKK.. I NEVER EVEN GOT TO SEE IT... THE WALL THING. THIS ISN'T PLEASANT... I'D RATHER NOT BE DEAD.. DON'T WANT TO DIE... DON'T GEEZ.. THIS IS WORSE THAN GOTH POETRY.. AGG..

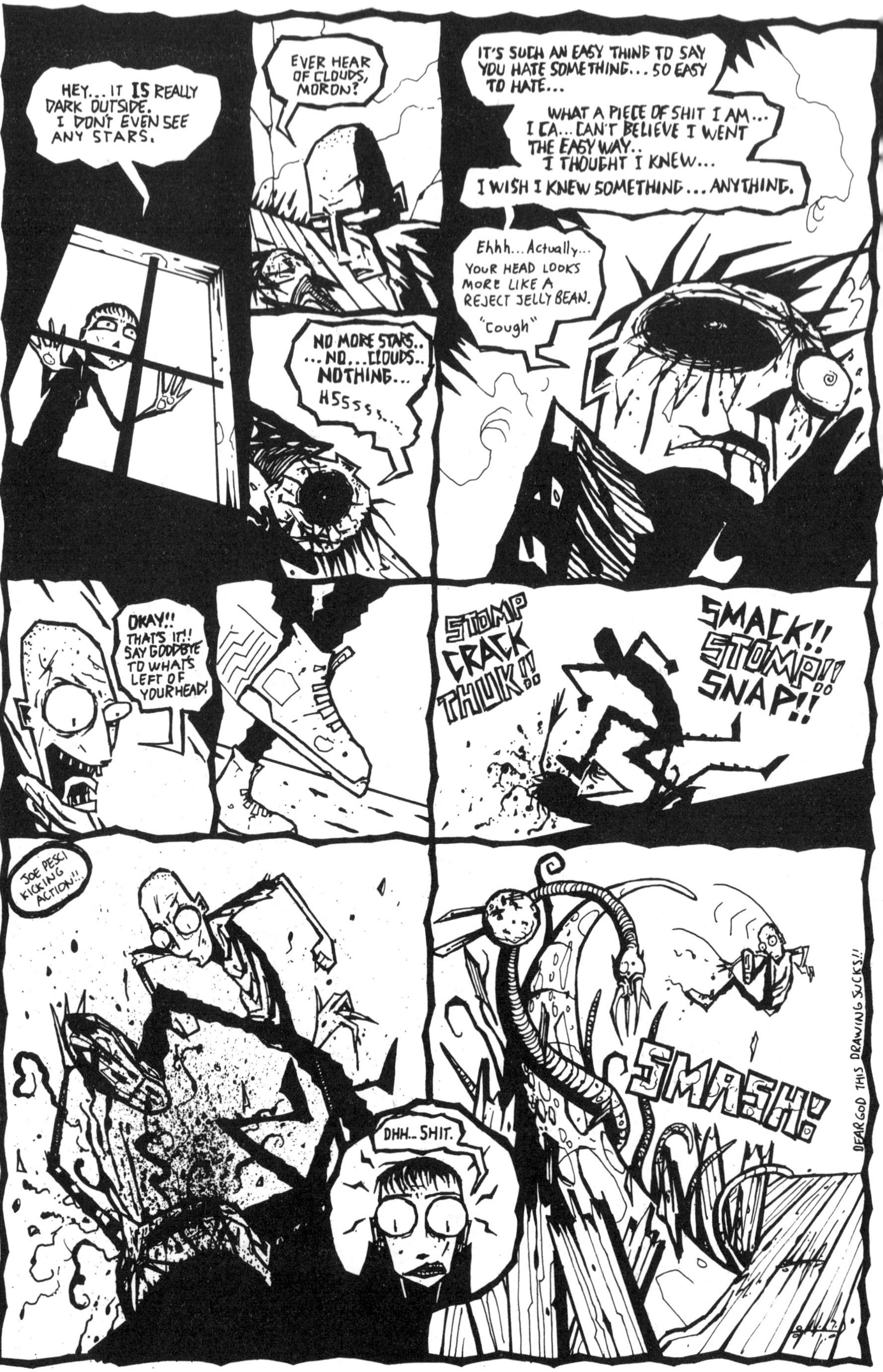
HEY... IT IS REALLY DARK OUTSIDE. I DON'T EVEN SEE ANY STARS.
EVER HEAR OF CLOUDS, MORON?
IT'S SUCH AN EASY THING TO SAY YOU HATE SOMETHING... SO EASY TO HATE...
WHAT A PIECE OF SHIT I AM... I CA...CAN'T BELIEVE I WENT THE EASY WAY.. I THOUGHT I KNEW...
I WISH I KNEW SOMETHING... ANYTHING.
NO MORE STARS.. ...NO...CLOUDS.. NOTHING...
HSSsss...
Ehhh... Actually... YOUR HEAD LOOKS MORE LIKE A REJECT JELLY BEAN.
"cough"
OKAY!! THAT'S IT!! SAY GOODBYE TO WHAT'S LEFT OF YOUR HEAD!
STOMP CRACK THUK!!
SMACK!! STOMP!! SNAP!!
JOE PESCI KICKING ACTION!!
DHH... SHIT.
SMASH!
DEAR GOD THIS DRAWING SUCKS!!

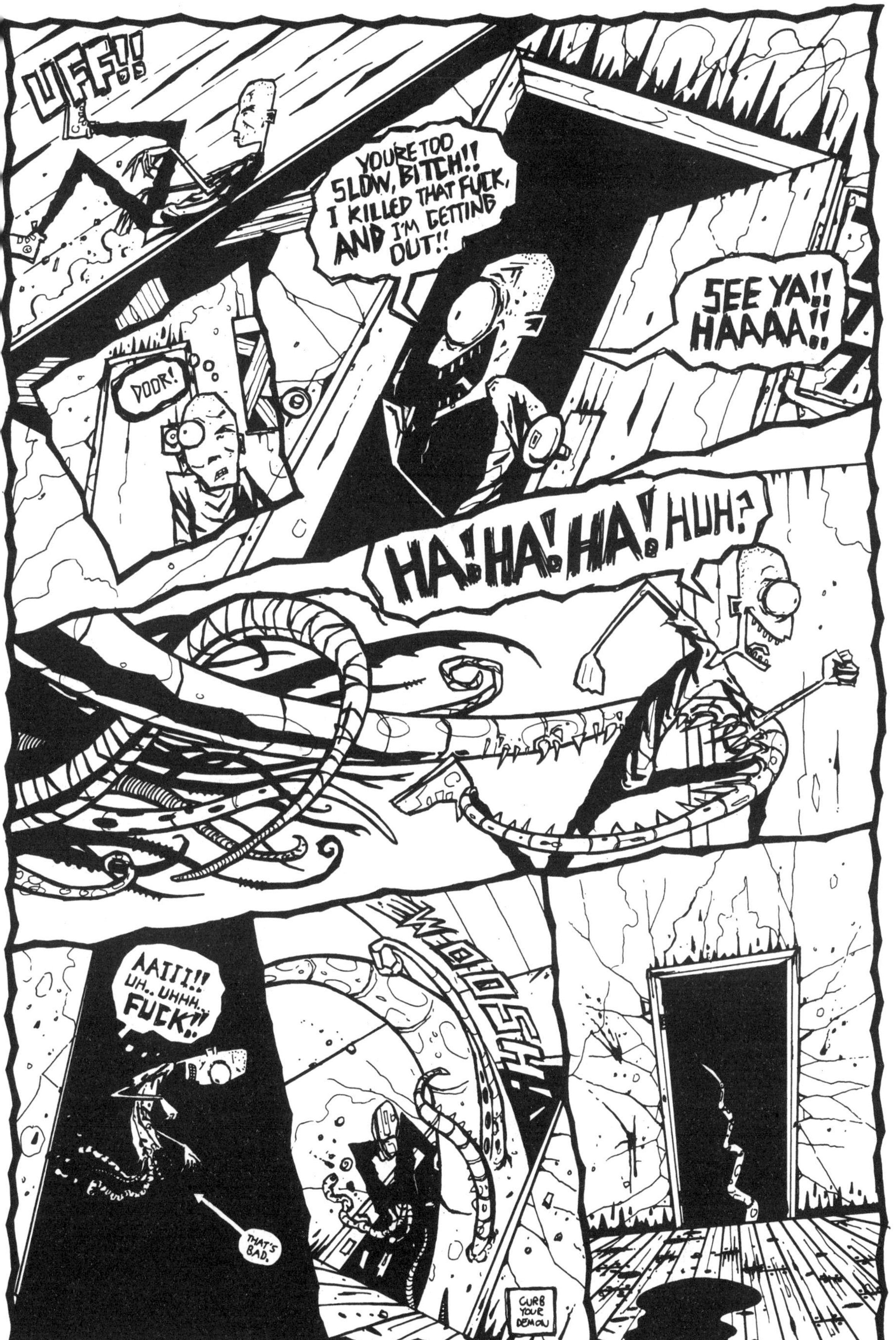
UFF!!
YOU'RE TOO SLOW, BITCH!! I KILLED THAT FUCK, AND I'M GETTING OUT!!
DOOR!
SEE YA!! HAAAA!!
HA! HA! HA! HUH?
AAIII!! UH.. UHHH.. FUCK!?!
THAT'S BAD.
WHOOOSH!
CURB YOUR DEMON

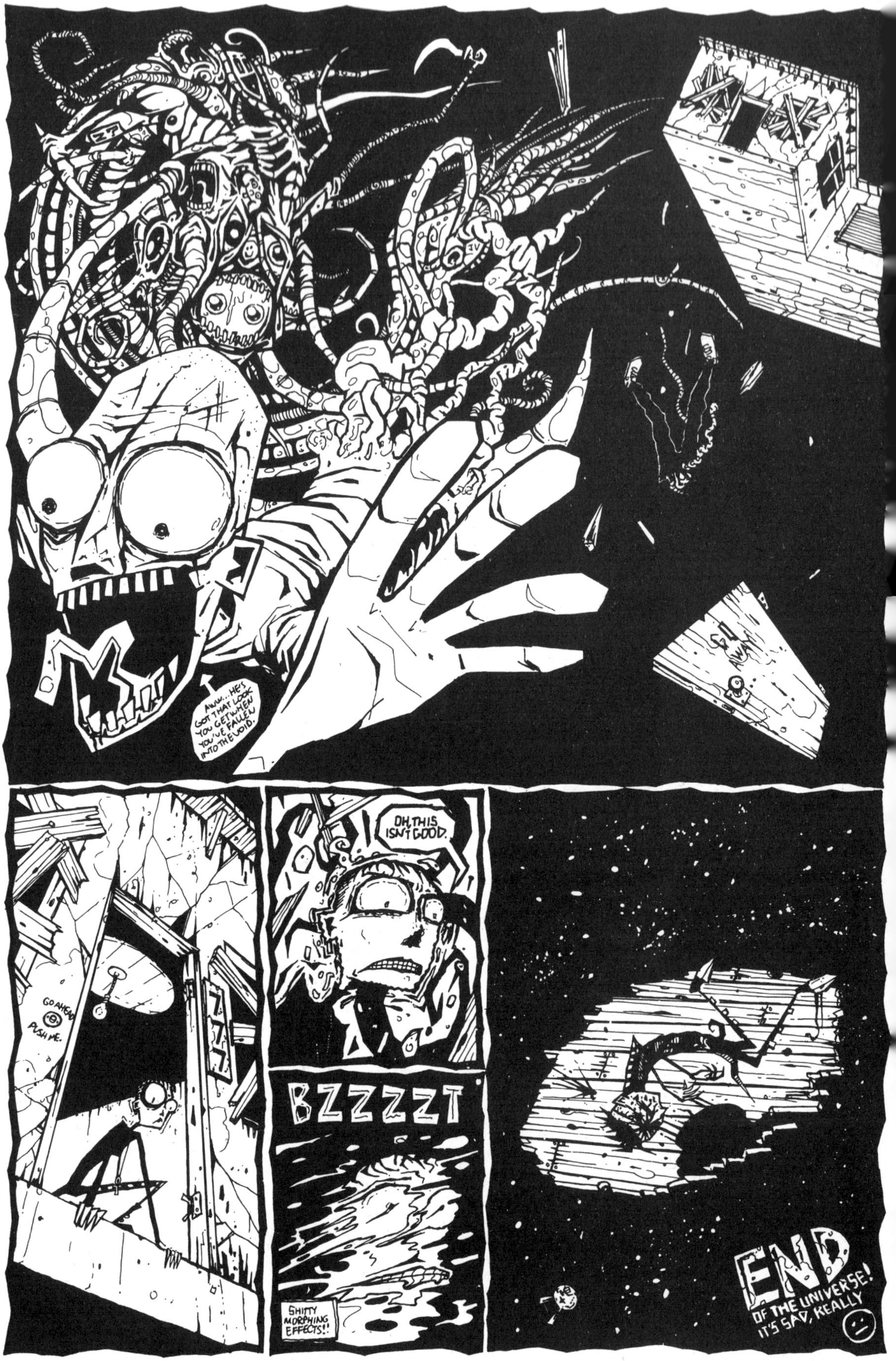
AWW... HE'S GOT THAT LOOK YOU GET WHEN YOU'VE FALLEN INTO THE VOID.
GO AWAY
GO AHEAD PUSH ME.
OH, THIS ISN'T GOOD.
BZZZZT
SHITTY MORPHING EFFECTS!!
END OF THE UNIVERSE! IT'S SAD, REALLY

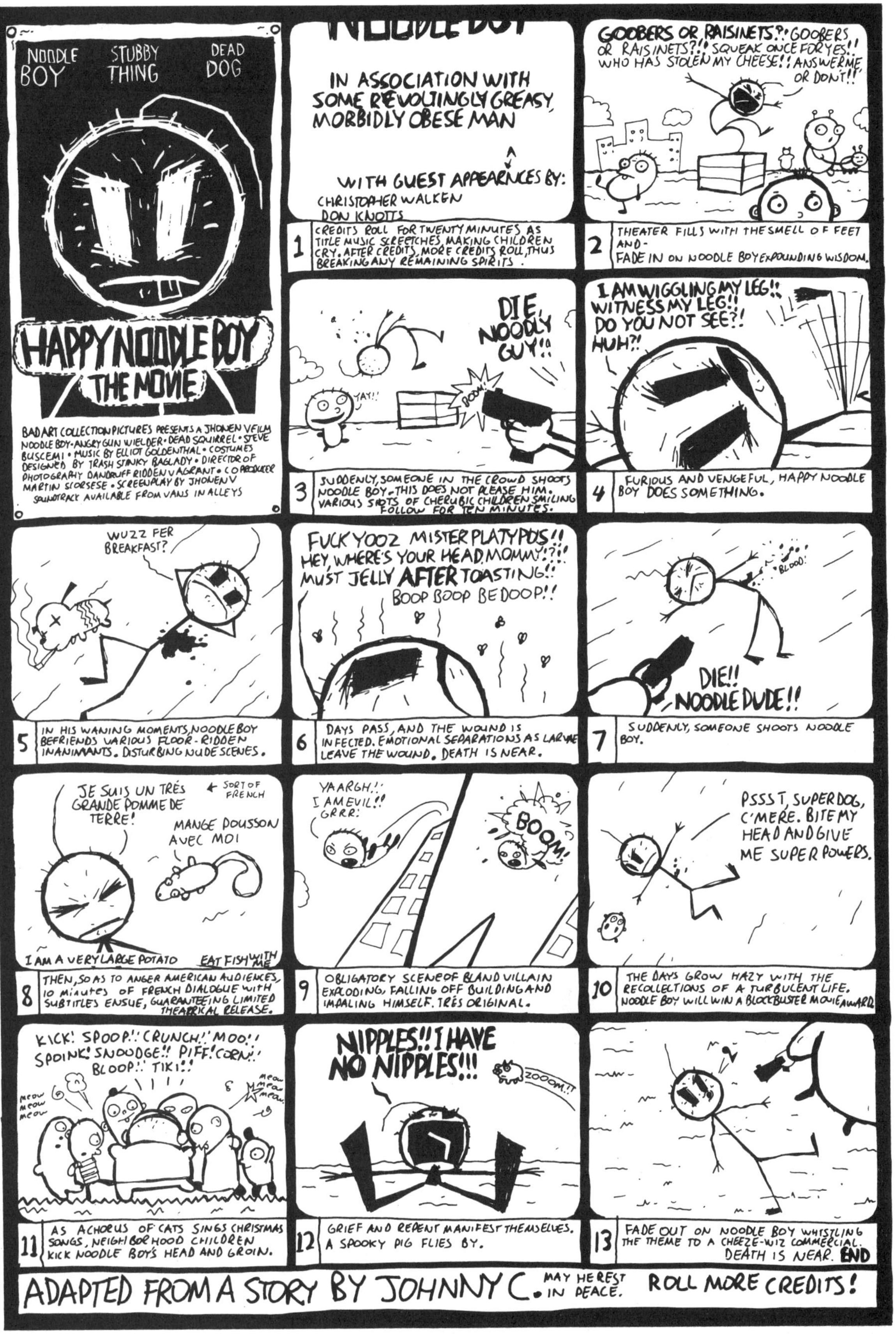
NOODLE BOY
STUBBY THING
DEAD DOG
HAPPY NOODLE BOY
THE MOVIE
BAD ART COLLECTION PICTURES PRESENTS A JHONEN V FILM
NOODLE BOY • ANGRY GUN WIELDER • DEAD SQUIRREL • STEVE BUSCEMI • MUSIC BY ELLIOT GOLDENTHAL • COSTUMES DESIGNED BY TRASH STINKY BAGLADY • DIRECTOR OF PHOTOGRAPHY DANDRUFF RIDDEN VAGRANT • CO PRODUCER MARTIN SCORSESE • SCREENPLAY BY JHONEN V
SOUNDTRACK AVAILABLE FROM VANS IN ALLEYS
IN ASSOCIATION WITH SOME REVOLTINGLY GREASY, MORBIDLY OBESE MAN
WITH GUEST APPEARNCES BY:
CHRISTOPHER WALKEN
DON KNOTTS
1 CREDITS ROLL FOR TWENTY MINUTES AS TITLE MUSIC SCREETCHES, MAKING CHILDREN CRY. AFTER CREDITS, MORE CREDITS ROLL, THUS BREAKING ANY REMAINING SPIRITS.
GOOBERS OR RAISINETS?! GOOBERS OR RAISINETS?!! SQUEAK ONCE FOR YES!! WHO HAS STOLEN MY CHEESE!! ANSWER ME OR DON'T!!
2 THEATER FILLS WITH THE SMELL OF FEET AND-
FADE IN ON NOODLE BOY EXPOUNDING WISDOM.
YAY!!
BOOM!
DIE, NOODLY GUY!!
3 SUDDENLY, SOMEONE IN THE CROWD SHOOTS NOODLE BOY. THIS DOES NOT PLEASE HIM. VARIOUS SHOTS OF CHERUBIC CHILDREN SMILING FOLLOW FOR TEN MINUTES.
I AM WIGGLING MY LEG!! WITNESS MY LEG!! DO YOU NOT SEE?! HUH?!
4 FURIOUS AND VENGEFUL, HAPPY NOODLE BOY DOES SOMETHING.
WUZZ FER BREAKFAST?
5 IN HIS WANING MOMENTS, NOODLE BOY BEFRIENDS VARIOUS FLOOR-RIDDEN INANIMANTS. DISTURBING NUDE SCENES.
FUCK YOOZ MISTER PLATYPUS!! HEY, WHERE'S YOUR HEAD, MOMMY?!! MUST JELLY AFTER TOASTING!!
BOOP BOOP BEDOOP!!
6 DAYS PASS, AND THE WOUND IS INFECTED. EMOTIONAL SEPARATIONS AS LARVAE LEAVE THE WOUND. DEATH IS NEAR.
BLOOD!
DIE!! NOODLE DUDE!!
7 SUDDENLY, SOMEONE SHOOTS NOODLE BOY.
JE SUIS UN TRÉS GRANDE POMME DE TERRE!
SORT OF FRENCH
MANGE POUSSON AVEC MOI
I AM A VERY LARGE POTATO
EAT FISH WITH ME
8 THEN, SO AS TO ANGER AMERICAN AUDIENCES, 10 MINUTES OF FRENCH DIALOGUE WITH SUBTITLES ENSUE, GUARANTEEING LIMITED THEATRICAL RELEASE.
YAARGH!! I AM EVIL!! GRRR!
BOOM!
9 OBLIGATORY SCENE OF BLAND VILLAIN EXPLODING, FALLING OFF BUILDING AND IMPALING HIMSELF. TRÉS ORIGINAL.
PSSST, SUPERDOG, C'MERE. BITE MY HEAD AND GIVE ME SUPER POWERS.
10 THE DAYS GROW HAZY WITH THE RECOLLECTIONS OF A TURBULENT LIFE. NOODLE BOY WILL WIN A BLOCKBUSTER MOVIE AWARD.
KICK! SPOOP!! CRUNCH!! MOO!! SPOINK! SNOODGE!! PIFF! CORN!! BLOOP!! TIKI!!
MEOW MEOW MEOW
MEOW MEOW MEOW
11 AS A CHORUS OF CATS SINGS CHRISTMAS SONGS, NEIGHBORHOOD CHILDREN KICK NOODLE BOY'S HEAD AND GROIN.
NIPPLES!! I HAVE NO NIPPLES!!!
ZOOOM!!
12 GRIEF AND REPENT MANIFEST THEMSELVES. A SPOOKY PIG FLIES BY.
13 FADE OUT ON NOODLE BOY WHISTLING THE THEME TO A CHEEZE-WIZ COMMERCIAL. DEATH IS NEAR. END
ADAPTED FROM A STORY BY JOHNNY C. MAY HE REST IN PEACE. ROLL MORE CREDITS!

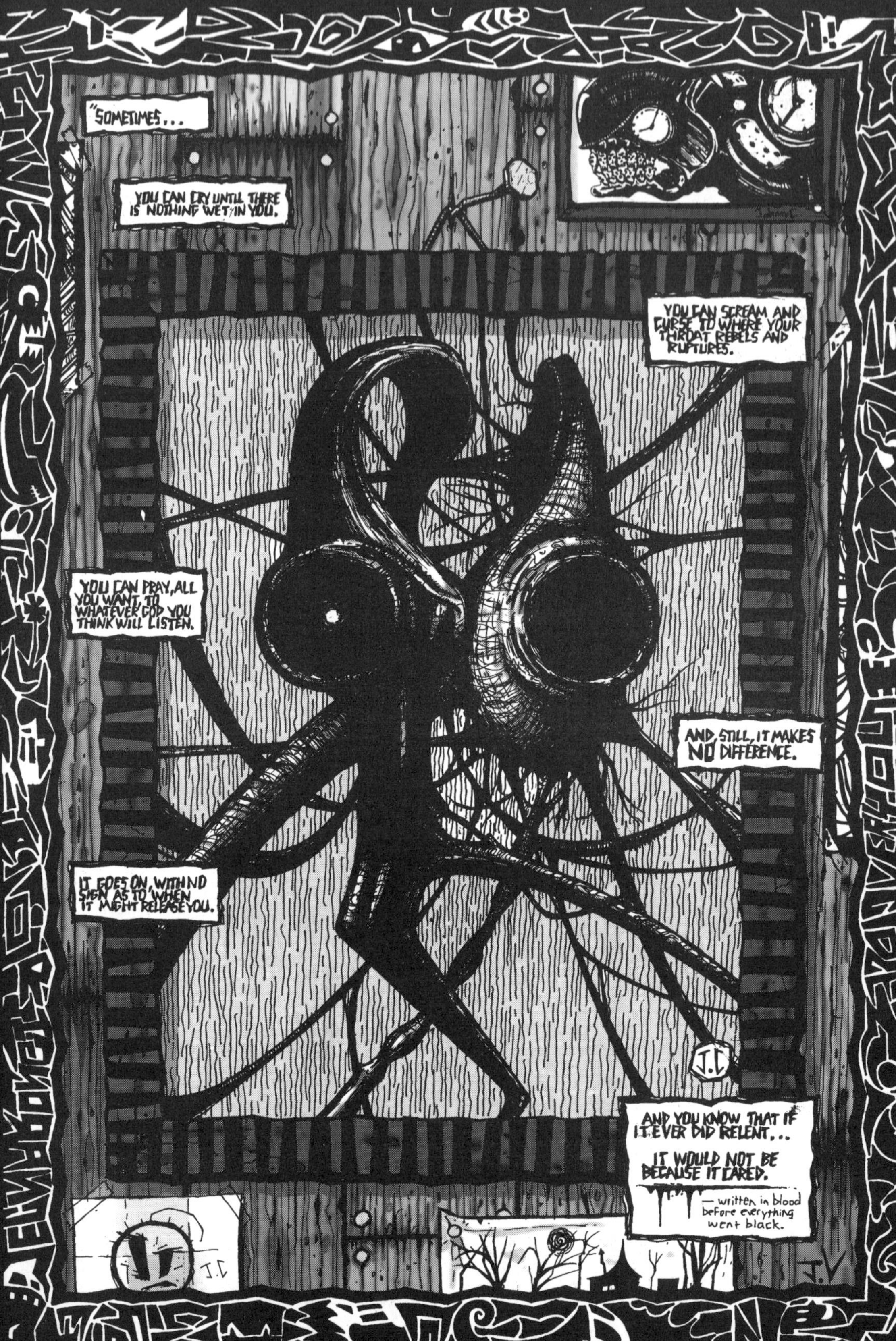
"SOMETIMES...
YOU CAN CRY UNTIL THERE IS NOTHING WET IN YOU.
YOU CAN SCREAM AND CURSE TO WHERE YOUR THROAT REBELS AND RUPTURES.
YOU CAN PRAY, ALL YOU WANT, TO WHATEVER GOD YOU THINK WILL LISTEN.
AND, STILL, IT MAKES NO DIFFERENCE.
IT GOES ON, WITH NO SIGN AS TO WHEN IT MIGHT RELEASE YOU.
AND YOU KNOW THAT IF IT EVER DID RELENT...
IT WOULD NOT BE BECAUSE IT CARED.
— written in blood before everything went black.

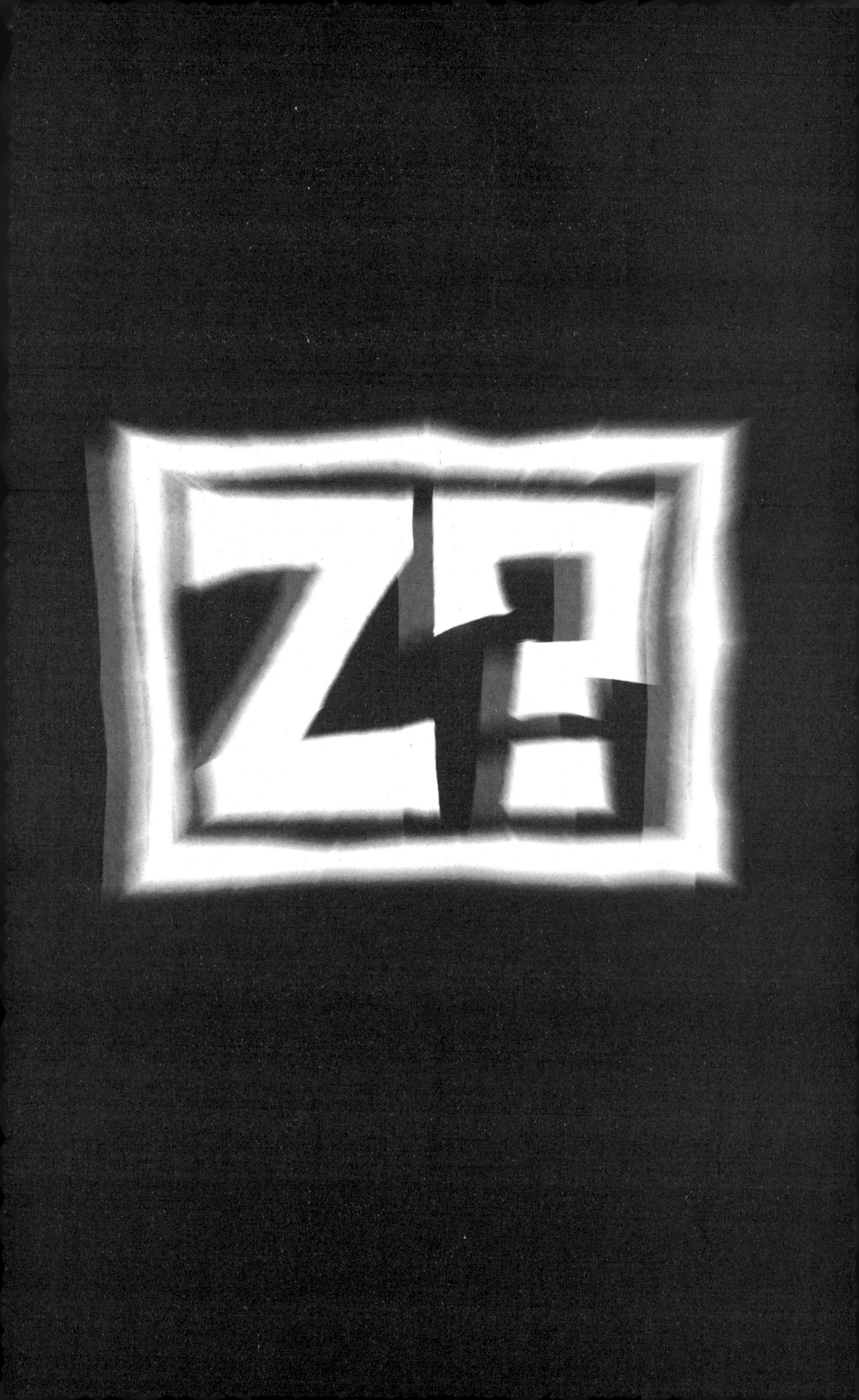

PART 6

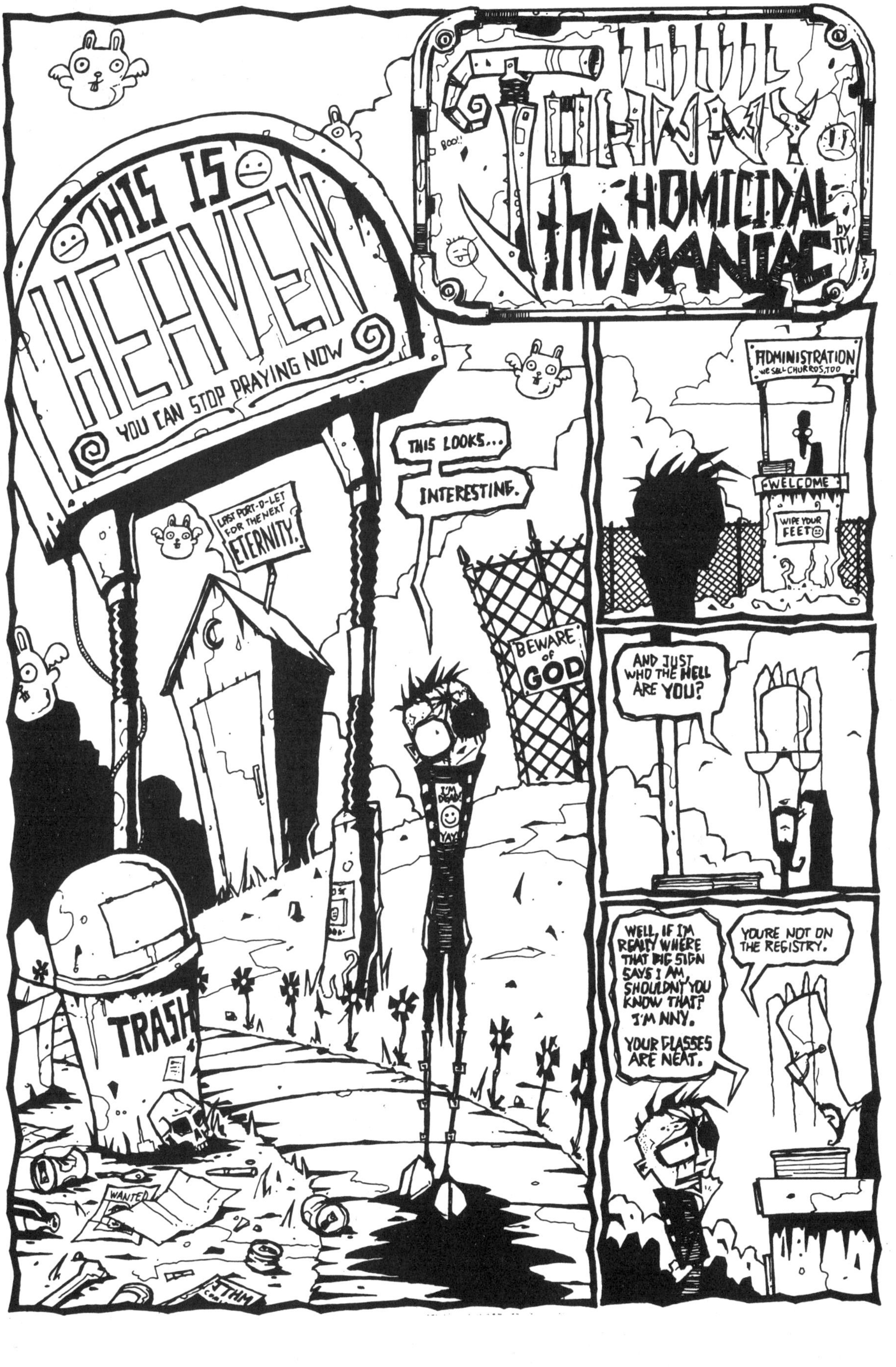

THIS IS HEAVEN
YOU CAN STOP PRAYING NOW
Johnny the Homicidal Maniac
by JCV
BOO!!
LAST PORT-O-LET FOR THE NEXT ETERNITY.
THIS LOOKS...
INTERESTING.
BEWARE of GOD
I'M DEAD YAY!
TRASH
WANTED
JTHM
ADMINISTRATION
WE SELL CHURROS, TOO
WELCOME
WIPE YOUR FEET
AND JUST WHO THE HELL ARE YOU?
WELL, IF I'M REALLY WHERE THAT BIG SIGN SAYS I AM, SHOULDN'T YOU KNOW THAT? I'M NNY.
YOUR GLASSES ARE NEAT.
YOU'RE NOT ON THE REGISTRY.

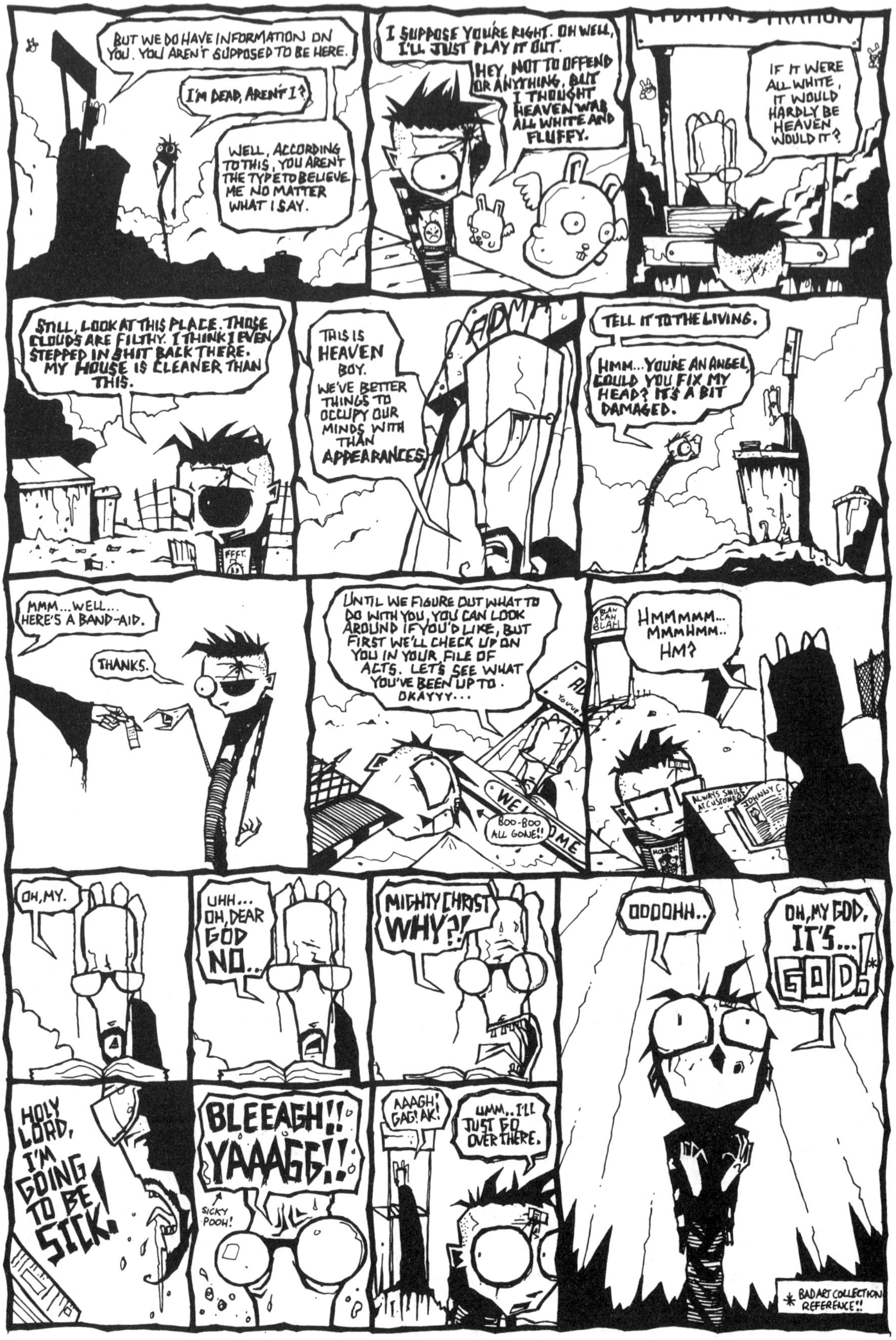
BUT WE DO HAVE INFORMATION ON YOU. YOU AREN'T SUPPOSED TO BE HERE.
I'M DEAD, AREN'T I?
WELL, ACCORDING TO THIS, YOU AREN'T THE TYPE TO BELIEVE ME NO MATTER WHAT I SAY.
I SUPPOSE YOU'RE RIGHT. OH WELL, I'LL JUST PLAY IT OUT.
HEY, NOT TO OFFEND OR ANYTHING, BUT I THOUGHT HEAVEN WAS ALL WHITE AND FLUFFY.
IF IT WERE ALL WHITE, IT WOULD HARDLY BE HEAVEN WOULD IT?
STILL, LOOK AT THIS PLACE. THOSE CLOUDS ARE FILTHY. I THINK I EVEN STEPPED IN SHIT BACK THERE. MY HOUSE IS CLEANER THAN THIS.
FFFT.
THIS IS HEAVEN BOY. WE'VE BETTER THINGS TO OCCUPY OUR MINDS WITH THAN APPEARANCES.
TELL IT TO THE LIVING.
HMM... YOU'RE AN ANGEL, COULD YOU FIX MY HEAD? IT'S A BIT DAMAGED.
MMM... WELL... HERE'S A BAND-AID.
THANKS.
UNTIL WE FIGURE OUT WHAT TO DO WITH YOU, YOU CAN LOOK AROUND IF YOU'D LIKE, BUT FIRST WE'LL CHECK UP ON YOU IN YOUR FILE OF ACTS. LET'S SEE WHAT YOU'VE BEEN UP TO. OKAYYY...
BOO-BOO ALL GONE!!
WELCOME
BLAH BLAH BLAH
HMMMMM... MMMHMM.. HM?
ALWAYS SMILE AT CUSTOMERS
JOHNNY C.
OH, MY.
UHH... OH, DEAR GOD NO...
MIGHTY CHRIST WHY?!
OOOOHH..
OH, MY GOD, IT'S... GOD!*
HOLY LORD, I'M GOING TO BE SICK!
BLEEAGH!! YAAAGG!!
SICKY POOH!
AAAGH! GAG! AK!
UMM.. I'LL JUST GO OVER THERE.
* BAD ART COLLECTION REFERENCE!!

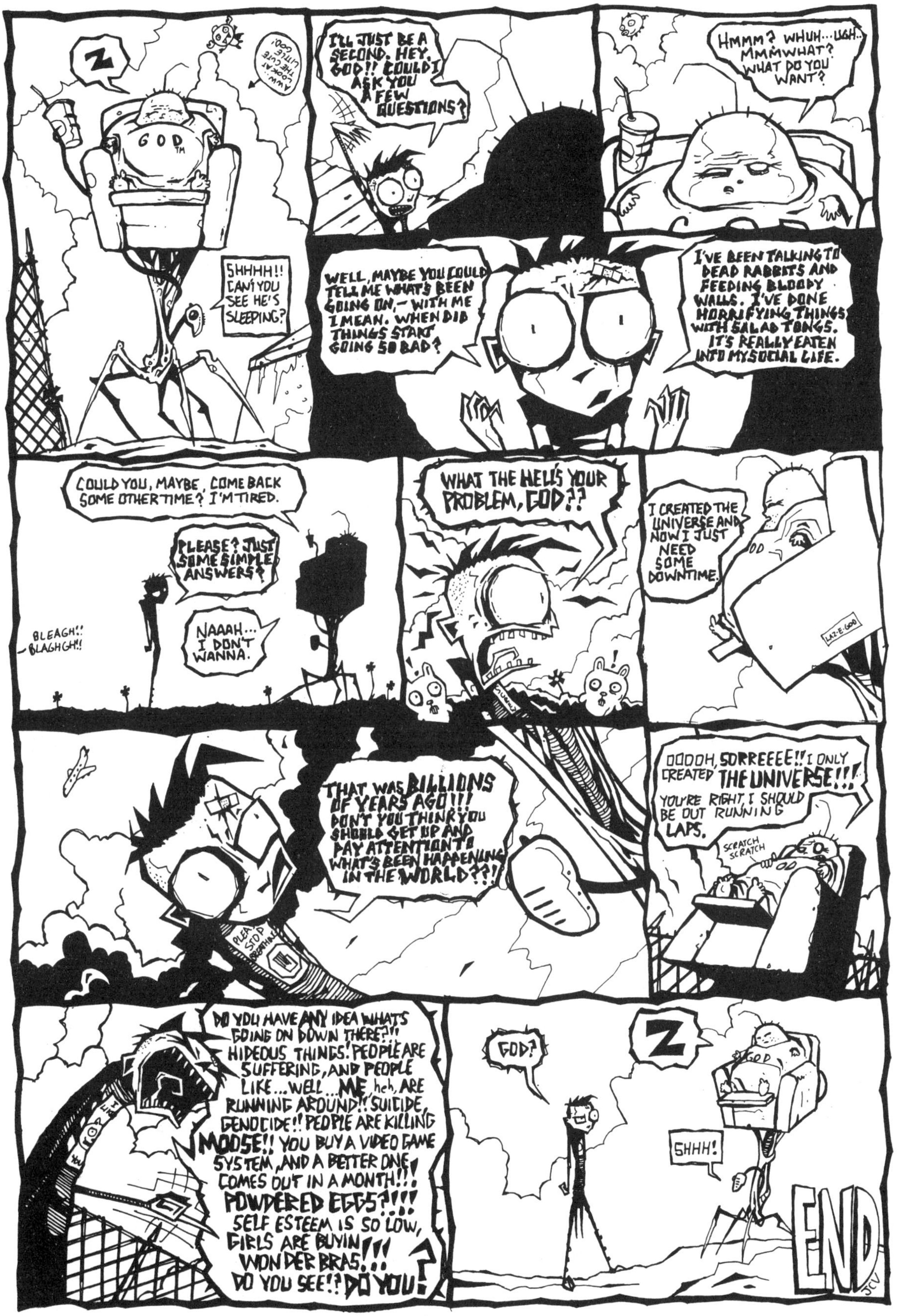
Z
AWW. LOOK AT THE CUTE LITTLE GOD!
GOD TM
SHHHH!! CAN'T YOU SEE HE'S SLEEPING?
I'LL JUST BE A SECOND. HEY, GOD!! COULD I ASK YOU A FEW QUESTIONS?
HMMM? WHUH...UGH.. MMMWHAT? WHAT DO YOU WANT?
WELL, MAYBE YOU COULD TELL ME WHAT'S BEEN GOING ON,- WITH ME I MEAN. WHEN DID THINGS START GOING SO BAD?
I'VE BEEN TALKING TO DEAD RABBITS AND FEEDING BLOODY WALLS. I'VE DONE HORRIFYING THINGS WITH SALAD TONGS. IT'S REALLY EATEN INTO MY SOCIAL LIFE.
COULD YOU, MAYBE, COME BACK SOME OTHER TIME? I'M TIRED.
PLEASE? JUST SOME SIMPLE ANSWERS?
NAAAH... I DON'T WANNA.
BLEAGH!! BLAGHGH!!
WHAT THE HELL'S YOUR PROBLEM, GOD??
I CREATED THE UNIVERSE AND NOW I JUST NEED SOME DOWNTIME.
LAZ-E-GOD
THAT WAS BILLIONS OF YEARS AGO!!! DON'T YOU THINK YOU SHOULD GET UP AND PAY ATTENTION TO WHAT'S BEEN HAPPENING IN THE WORLD??!
PLEA STOP BREATHING
OOOOH, SORREEEE!! I ONLY CREATED THE UNIVERSE!!! YOU'RE RIGHT, I SHOULD BE OUT RUNNING LAPS.
SCRATCH SCRATCH
DO YOU HAVE ANY IDEA WHAT'S GOING ON DOWN THERE?!! HIDEOUS THINGS! PEOPLE ARE SUFFERING, AND PEOPLE LIKE...WELL...ME, heh, ARE RUNNING AROUND!! SUICIDE, GENOCIDE!! PEOPLE ARE KILLING MOOSE!! YOU BUY A VIDEO GAME SYSTEM, AND A BETTER ONE COMES OUT IN A MONTH!!! POWDERED EGGS?!!! SELF ESTEEM IS SO LOW, GIRLS ARE BUYIN WONDER BRAS!!! DO YOU SEE!? DO YOU?
GOD?
Z
GOD
SHHH!
END
JCV

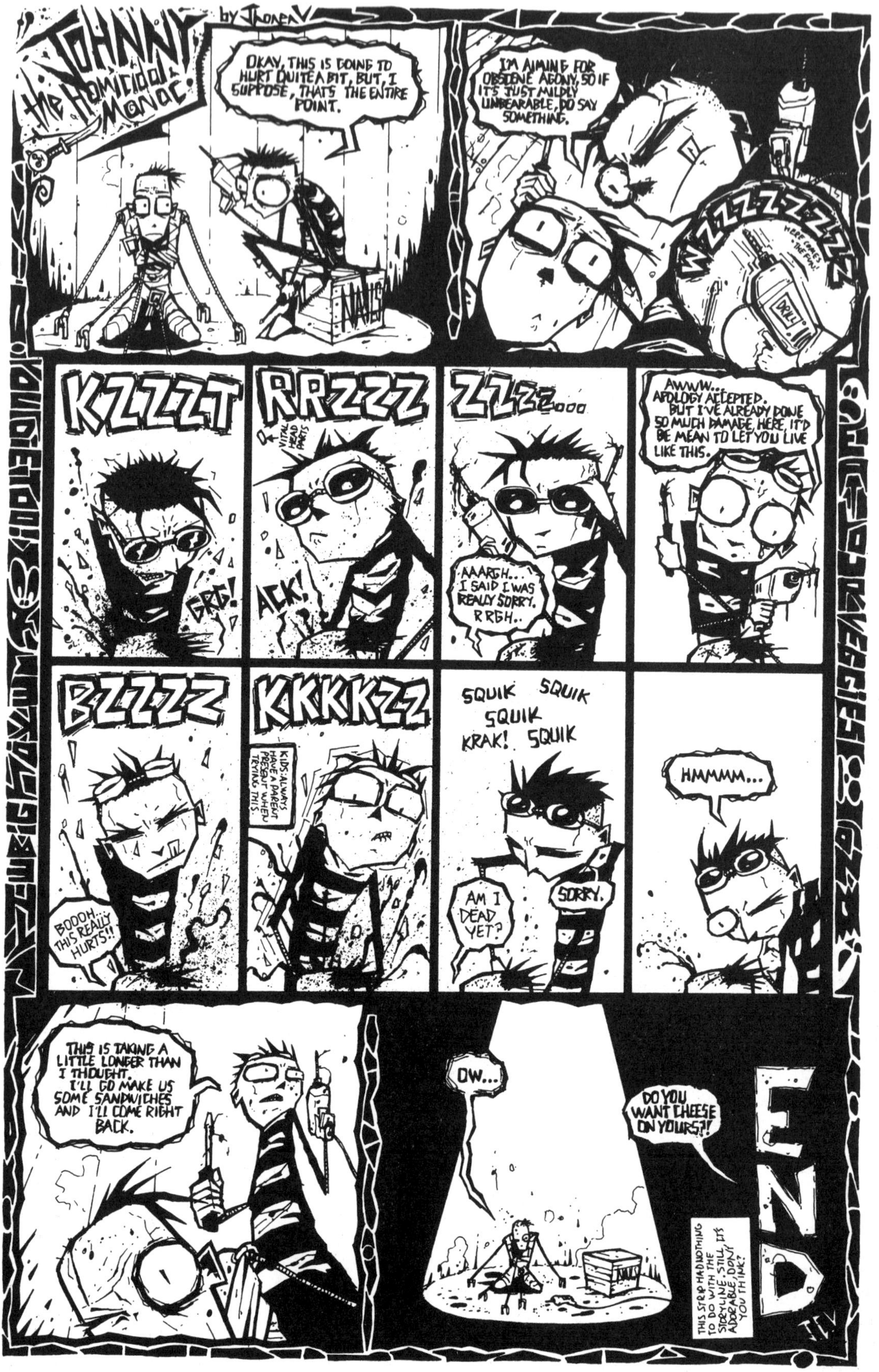
Johnny the Homicidal Maniac
by JhonenV
OKAY, THIS IS GOING TO HURT QUITE A BIT, BUT, I SUPPOSE, THAT'S THE ENTIRE POINT.
NAILS
I'M AIMING FOR OBSCENE AGONY, SO IF IT'S JUST MILDLY UNBEARABLE, DO SAY SOMETHING.
DRILL
KZZZZT
GRG!
RRZZZ
VITAL HEAD PARTS
ACK!
AAARGH... I SAID I WAS REALLY SORRY. RRGH..
AWWW... APOLOGY ACCEPTED. BUT I'VE ALREADY DONE SO MUCH DAMAGE HERE, IT'D BE MEAN TO LET YOU LIVE LIKE THIS.
BZZZZZ
BOOOH... THIS REALLY HURTS!!
KKKKZZ
KIDS: ALWAYS HAVE A PARENT PRESENT WHEN TRYING THIS.
SQUIK SQUIK SQUIK KRAK! SQUIK
AM I DEAD YET?
SORRY.
HMMMM...
THIS IS TAKING A LITTLE LONGER THAN I THOUGHT. I'LL GO MAKE US SOME SANDWICHES AND I'LL COME RIGHT BACK.
OW...
DO YOU WANT CHEESE ON YOURS?!
END
THIS STRIP HAD NOTHING TO DO WITH THE STORYLINE. STILL, IT'S ADORABLE, DON'T YOU THINK?
JTV

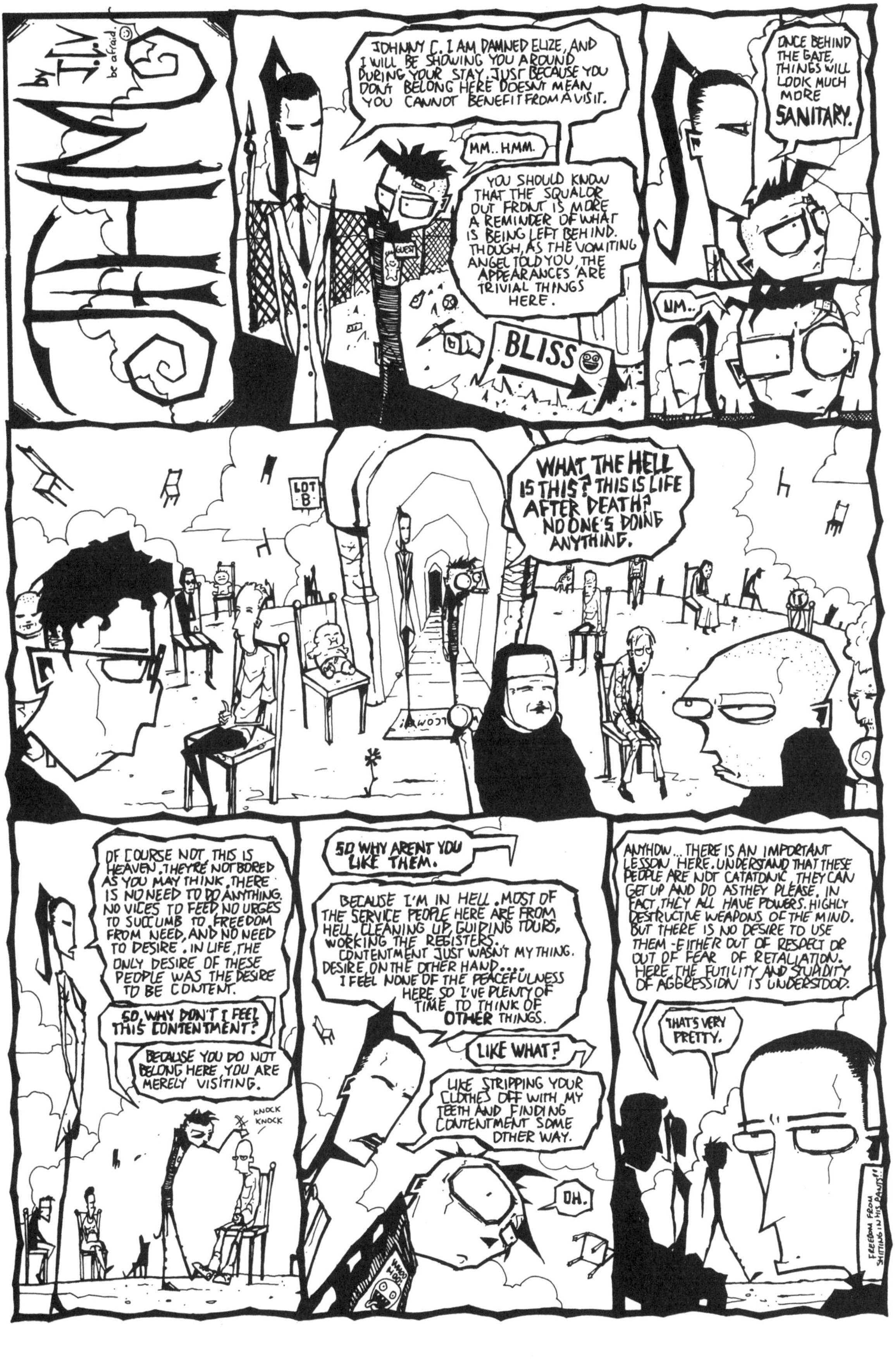
JOHNNY
by J.V.
be afraid.
JOHNNY C. I AM DAMNED ELIZE, AND I WILL BE SHOWING YOU AROUND DURING YOUR STAY. JUST BECAUSE YOU DONT BELONG HERE DOESN'T MEAN YOU CANNOT BENEFIT FROM A VISIT.
MM.. HMM.
YOU SHOULD KNOW THAT THE SQUALOR OUT FRONT IS MORE A REMINDER OF WHAT IS BEING LEFT BEHIND. THOUGH, AS THE VOMITING ANGEL TOLD YOU, THE APPEARANCES ARE TRIVIAL THINGS HERE.
GUEST
BLISS
ONCE BEHIND THE GATE, THINGS WILL LOOK MUCH MORE SANITARY.
UM..
LOT B
WHAT THE HELL IS THIS? THIS IS LIFE AFTER DEATH? NO ONE'S DOING ANYTHING.
OF COURSE NOT. THIS IS HEAVEN. THEY'RE NOT BORED AS YOU MAY THINK. THERE IS NO NEED TO DO ANYTHING. NO VICES TO FEED, NO URGES TO SUCCUMB TO. FREEDOM FROM NEED, AND NO NEED TO DESIRE. IN LIFE, THE ONLY DESIRE OF THESE PEOPLE WAS THE DESIRE TO BE CONTENT.
SO, WHY DON'T I FEEL THIS CONTENTMENT?
BECAUSE YOU DO NOT BELONG HERE. YOU ARE MERELY VISITING.
KNOCK KNOCK
SO WHY AREN'T YOU LIKE THEM.
BECAUSE I'M IN HELL. MOST OF THE SERVICE PEOPLE HERE ARE FROM HELL, CLEANING UP, GUIDING TOURS, WORKING THE REGISTERS. CONTENTMENT JUST WASN'T MY THING. DESIRE ON THE OTHER HAND.... I FEEL NONE OF THE PEACEFULNESS HERE, SO I'VE PLENTY OF TIME TO THINK OF OTHER THINGS.
LIKE WHAT?
LIKE STRIPPING YOUR CLOTHES OFF WITH MY TEETH AND FINDING CONTENTMENT SOME OTHER WAY.
OH.
ANYHOW... THERE IS AN IMPORTANT LESSON HERE. UNDERSTAND THAT THESE PEOPLE ARE NOT CATATONIC. THEY CAN GET UP AND DO AS THEY PLEASE. IN FACT, THEY ALL HAVE POWERS. HIGHLY DESTRUCTIVE WEAPONS OF THE MIND. BUT THERE IS NO DESIRE TO USE THEM - EITHER OUT OF RESPECT OR OUT OF FEAR OF RETALIATION. HERE, THE FUTILITY AND STUPIDITY OF AGGRESSION IS UNDERSTOOD.
THAT'S VERY PRETTY.
FREEDOM FROM SHITTING IN HIS PANTS!!

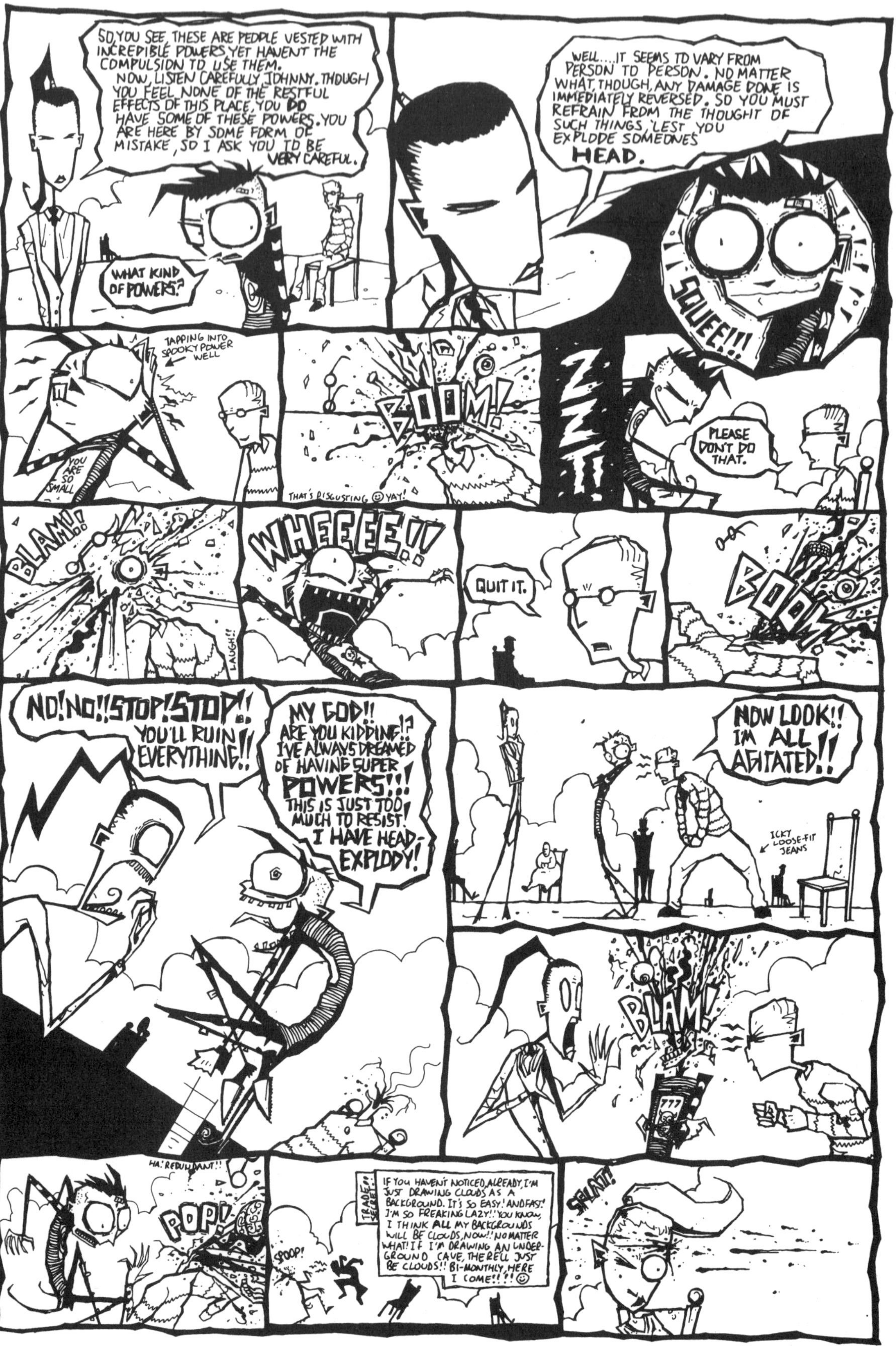
SO, YOU SEE, THESE ARE PEOPLE VESTED WITH INCREDIBLE POWERS, YET HAVEN'T THE COMPULSION TO USE THEM. NOW, LISTEN CAREFULLY, JOHNNY. THOUGH YOU FEEL NONE OF THE RESTFUL EFFECTS OF THIS PLACE, YOU DO HAVE SOME OF THESE POWERS. YOU ARE HERE BY SOME FORM OF MISTAKE, SO I ASK YOU TO BE VERY CAREFUL.
WHAT KIND OF POWERS?
WELL.... IT SEEMS TO VARY FROM PERSON TO PERSON. NO MATTER WHAT, THOUGH, ANY DAMAGE DONE IS IMMEDIATELY REVERSED. SO YOU MUST REFRAIN FROM THE THOUGHT OF SUCH THINGS, LEST YOU EXPLODE SOMEONE'S HEAD.
SQUEE!!!
TAPPING INTO SPOOKY POWER WELL
YOU ARE SO SMALL
BOOM!
THAT'S DISGUSTING ☺ YAY!
ZZT!!
PLEASE DON'T DO THAT.
BLAM!!
LAUGH!!
WHEEEE!!
QUIT IT.
BOOM!
NO! NO!! STOP! STOP!! YOU'LL RUIN EVERYTHING!!
MY GOD!! ARE YOU KIDDING!!? I'VE ALWAYS DREAMED OF HAVING SUPER POWERS!!! THIS IS JUST TOO MUCH TO RESIST! I HAVE HEAD-EXPLODY!
NOW LOOK!! I'M ALL AGITATED!!
ICKY LOOSE-FIT JEANS
BLAM!
HA! REDUNDANT!!
POP!
SPOOP!
TRADE SECRET!!
IF YOU HAVEN'T NOTICED, ALREADY, I'M JUST DRAWING CLOUDS AS A BACKGROUND. IT'S SO EASY! AND FAST! I'M SO FREAKING LAZY!! YOU KNOW, I THINK ALL MY BACKGROUNDS WILL BE CLOUDS, NOW!! NO MATTER WHAT! IF I'M DRAWING AN UNDERGROUND CAVE, THERE'LL JUST BE CLOUDS!! BI-MONTHLY, HERE I COME!!?! ☺
SPLAT!

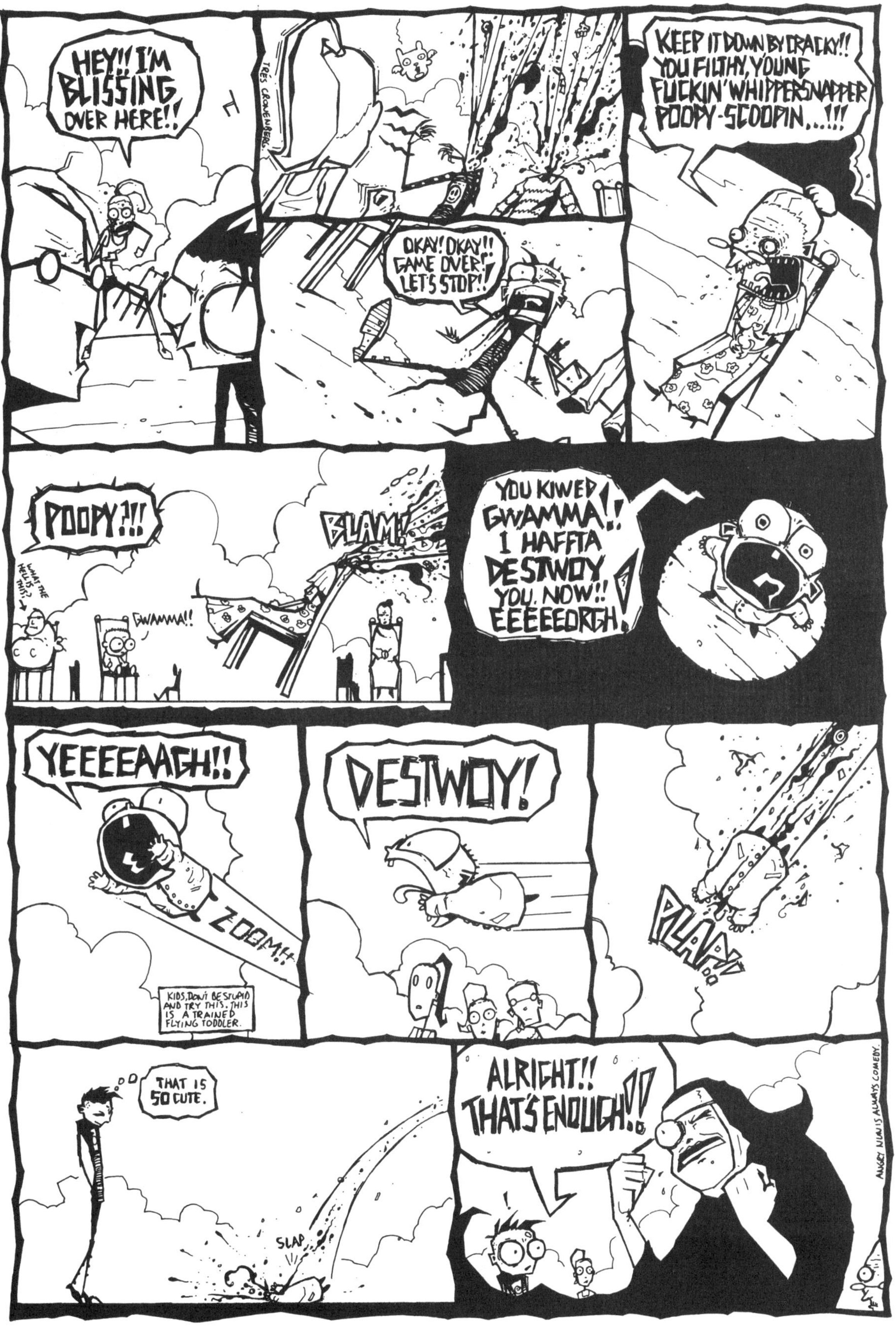
HEY!! I'M BLISSING OVER HERE!!
TRÉS CRONENBERG.
KEEP IT DOWN BY CRACKY!! YOU FILTHY, YOUNG FUCKIN' WHIPPERSNAPPER POOPY-SCOOPIN...!!!
OKAY! OKAY!! GAME OVER! LET'S STOP!!
POOPY?!!
WHAT THE HELL IS THIS?
GWAMMA!!
BLAM!
YOU KIWED GWAMMA!! I HAFFTA DESTWOY YOU, NOW!! EEEEEORGH!
YEEEEAAGH!!
ZOOM!!
KIDS, DON'T BE STUPID AND TRY THIS. THIS IS A TRAINED FLYING TODDLER.
DESTWOY!
PLAP!
THAT IS SO CUTE.
SLAP
ALRIGHT!! THAT'S ENOUGH!!
ANGRY NUN IS ALWAYS COMEDY.

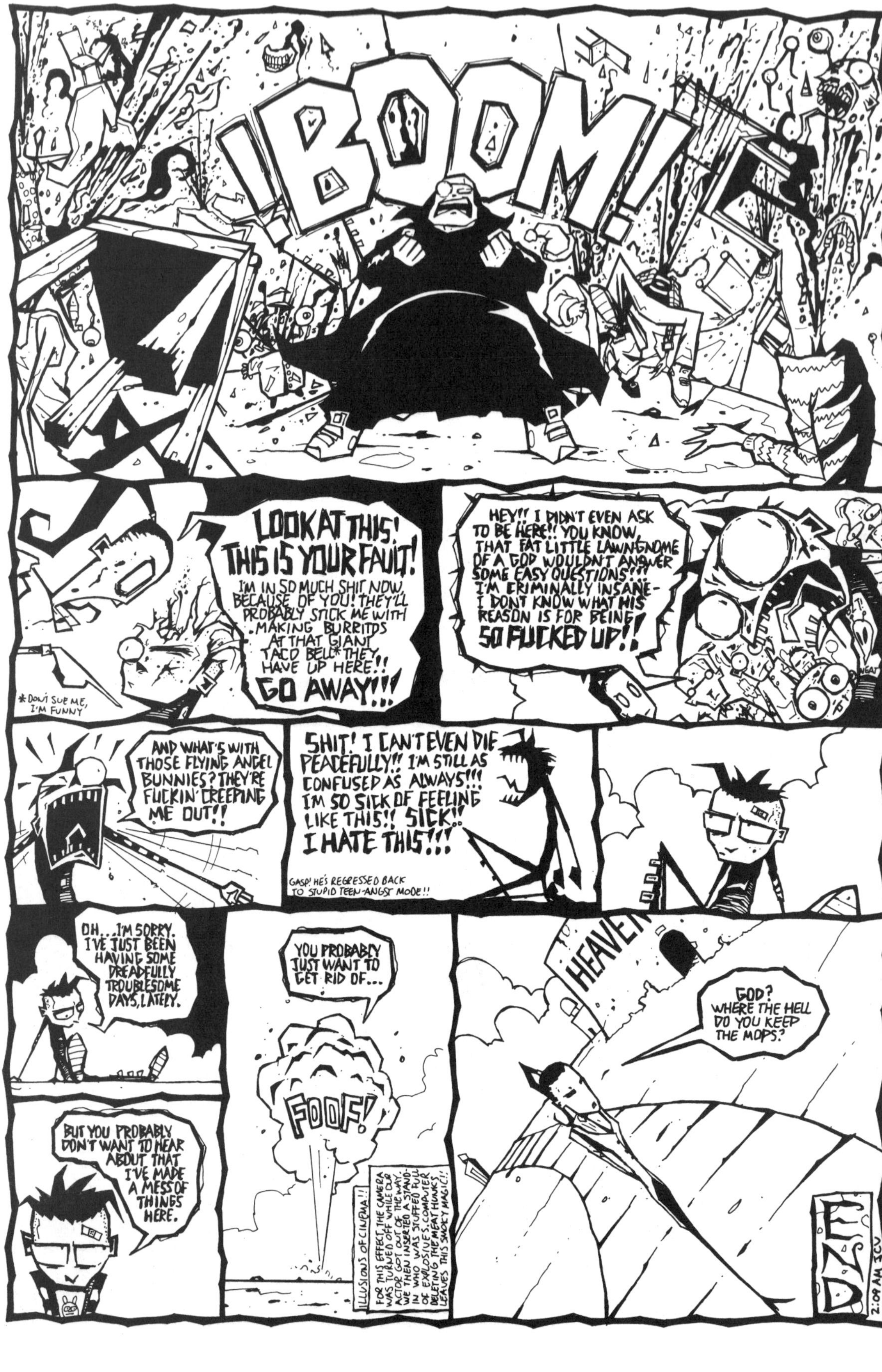
!BOOM!
LOOK AT THIS! THIS IS YOUR FAULT!
I'M IN SO MUCH SHIT NOW, BECAUSE OF YOU! THEY'LL PROBABLY STICK ME WITH MAKING BURRITOS AT THAT GIANT TACO BELL* THEY HAVE UP HERE!!
GO AWAY!!!
*DON'T SUE ME, I'M FUNNY
HEY!! I DIDN'T EVEN ASK TO BE HERE!! YOU KNOW, THAT FAT LITTLE LAWNGNOME OF A GOD WOULDN'T ANSWER SOME EASY QUESTIONS!!! I'M CRIMINALLY INSANE- I DONT KNOW WHAT HIS REASON IS FOR BEING SO FUCKED UP!!
AND WHAT'S WITH THOSE FLYING ANGEL BUNNIES? THEY'RE FUCKIN' CREEPING ME OUT!!
SHIT! I CAN'T EVEN DIE PEACEFULLY!! I'M STILL AS CONFUSED AS ALWAYS!!! I'M SO SICK OF FEELING LIKE THIS!! SICK!! I HATE THIS!!!
GASP! HE'S REGRESSED BACK TO STUPID TEEN-ANGST MODE!!
OH...I'M SORRY. I'VE JUST BEEN HAVING SOME DREADFULLY TROUBLESOME DAYS, LATELY.
BUT YOU PROBABLY DON'T WANT TO HEAR ABOUT THAT I'VE MADE A MESS OF THINGS HERE.
YOU PROBABLY JUST WANT TO GET RID OF...
FOOF!
ILLUSIONS OF CINEMA!!
FOR THIS EFFECT, THE CAMERA WAS TURNED OFF WHILE OUR ACTOR GOT OUT OF THE WAY. WE THEN INSERTED A STAND-IN WHO WAS STUFFED FULL OF EXPLOSIVES. COMPUTER DELETING THE MEAT HUNKS LEAVES THIS SMOKY MAGIC!!
HEAVEN
GOD? WHERE THE HELL DO YOU KEEP THE MOPS?
END
2:09 AM JCV

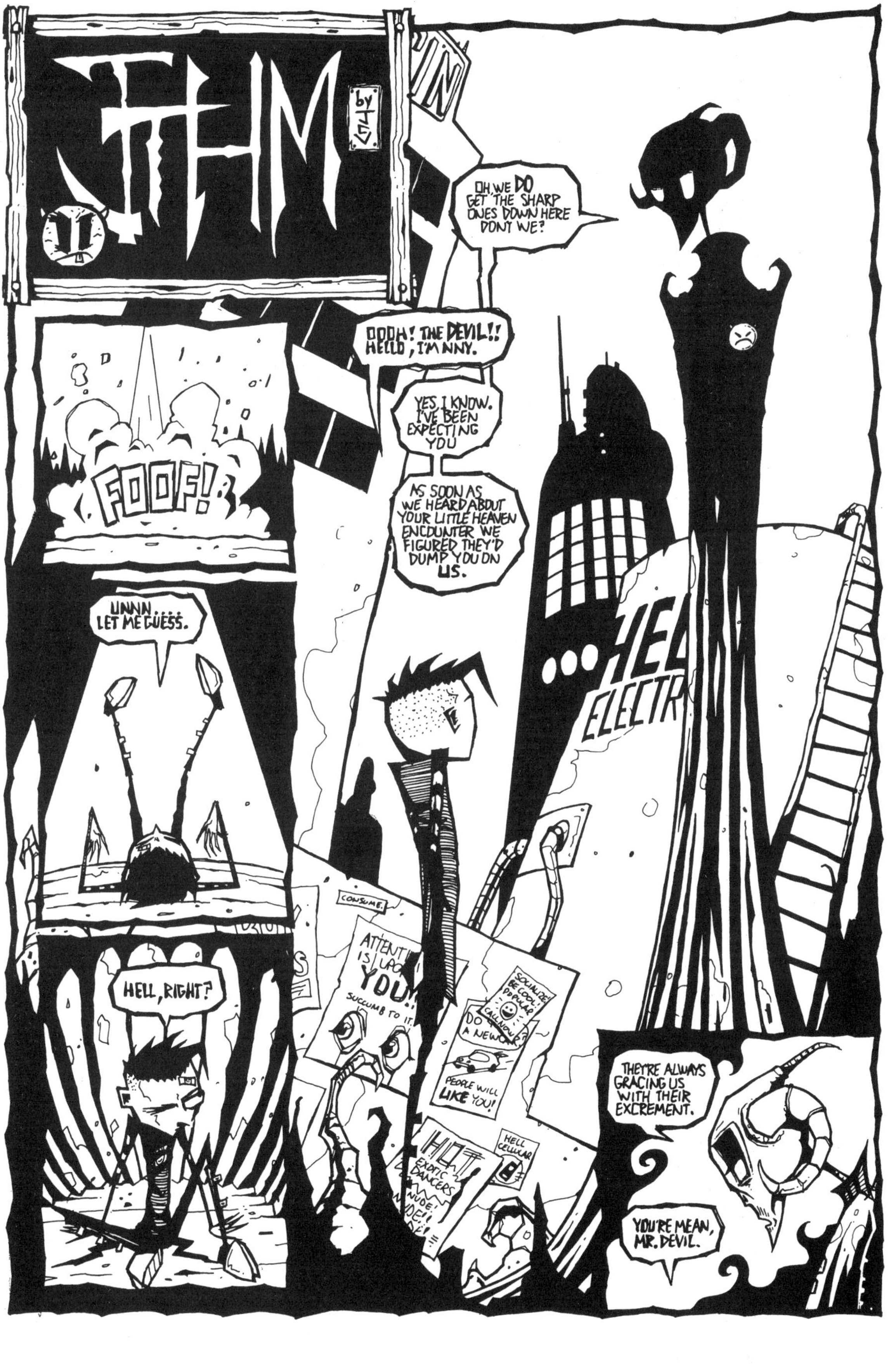
JTHM
FOOF!
UNNN.... LET ME GUESS.
HELL, RIGHT?
OH, WE DO GET THE SHARP ONES DOWN HERE DONT WE?
OOOH! THE DEVIL!! HELLO, I'M NNY.
YES, I KNOW. I'VE BEEN EXPECTING YOU
AS SOON AS WE HEARD ABOUT YOUR LITTLE HEAVEN ENCOUNTER WE FIGURED THEY'D DUMP YOU ON US.
CONSUME.
SUCCUMB TO IT.
SOCIALIZE BE COOL! POPULAR
PEOPLE WILL LIKE YOU!
HOT EXOTIC DANCERS NUDE!
HELL CELLULAR
THEY'RE ALWAYS GRACING US WITH THEIR EXCREMENT.
YOU'RE MEAN, MR. DEVIL.

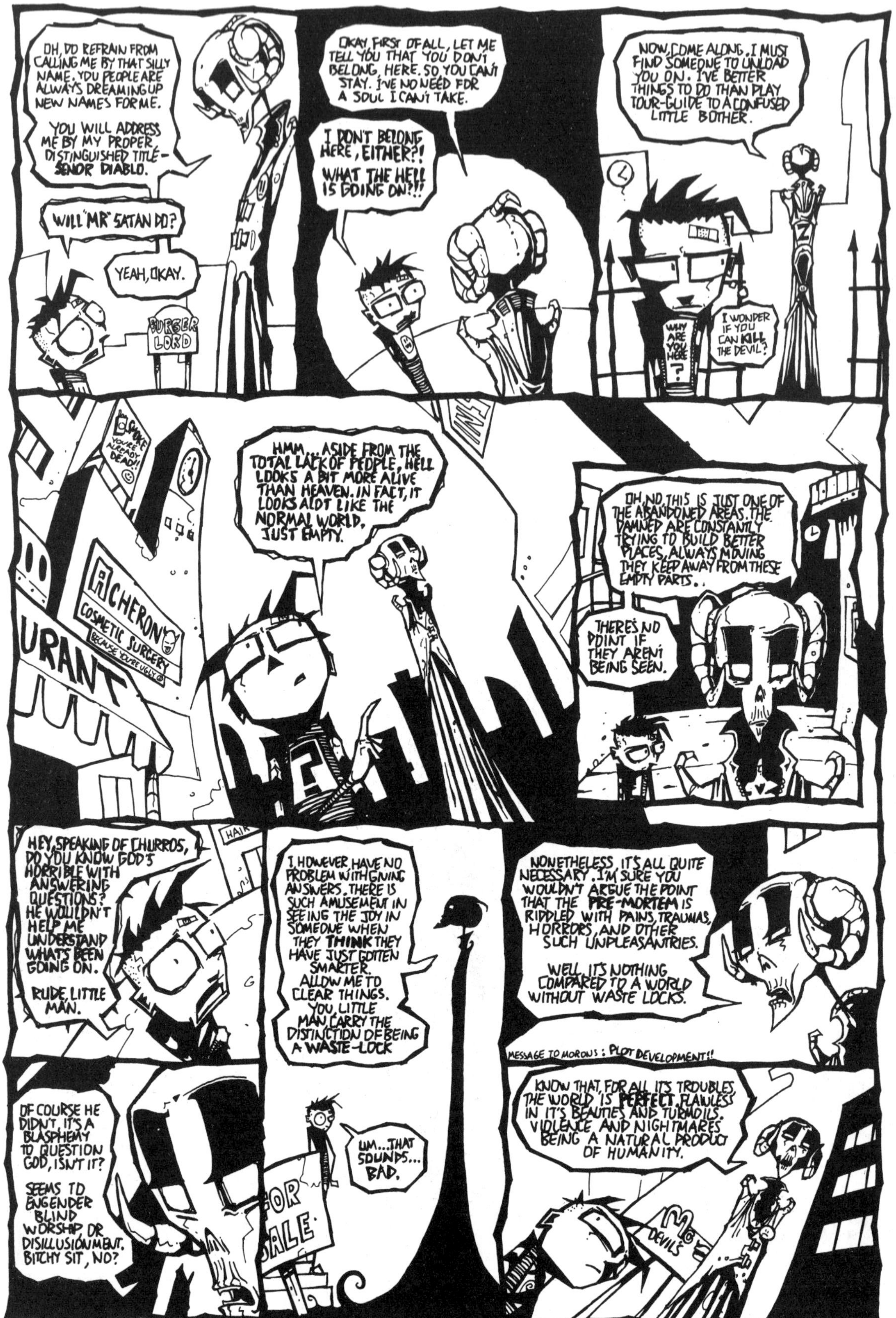
OH, DO REFRAIN FROM CALLING ME BY THAT SILLY NAME. YOU PEOPLE ARE ALWAYS DREAMING UP NEW NAMES FOR ME.
YOU WILL ADDRESS ME BY MY PROPER, DISTINGUISHED TITLE- SEÑOR DIABLO.
WILL "MR" SATAN DO?
YEAH, OKAY.
BURGER LORD
OKAY, FIRST OF ALL, LET ME TELL YOU THAT YOU DON'T BELONG HERE. SO YOU CAN'T STAY. I'VE NO NEED FOR A SOUL I CAN'T TAKE.
I DON'T BELONG HERE, EITHER?!
WHAT THE HELL IS GOING ON?!!
NOW, COME ALONG. I MUST FIND SOMEONE TO UNLOAD YOU ON. I'VE BETTER THINGS TO DO THAN PLAY TOUR-GUIDE TO A CONFUSED LITTLE BOTHER.
WHY ARE YOU HERE ?
I WONDER IF YOU CAN KILL THE DEVIL?
SMOKE YOU'RE ALREADY DEAD!! ☺
ACHERON COSMETIC SURGERY BECAUSE YOU'RE UGLY ☺
URANT
HMM... ASIDE FROM THE TOTAL LACK OF PEOPLE, HELL LOOKS A BIT MORE ALIVE THAN HEAVEN. IN FACT, IT LOOKS ALOT LIKE THE NORMAL WORLD, JUST EMPTY.
OH, NO THIS IS JUST ONE OF THE ABANDONED AREAS. THE DAMNED ARE CONSTANTLY TRYING TO BUILD BETTER PLACES, ALWAYS MOVING THEY KEEP AWAY FROM THESE EMPTY PARTS..
THERE'S NO POINT IF THEY AREN'T BEING SEEN.
HAIR
HEY, SPEAKING OF CHURROS, DO YOU KNOW GOD'S HORRIBLE WITH ANSWERING QUESTIONS? HE WOULDN'T HELP ME UNDERSTAND WHAT'S BEEN GOING ON.
RUDE, LITTLE MAN.
I, HOWEVER, HAVE NO PROBLEM WITH GIVING ANSWERS. THERE IS SUCH AMUSEMENT IN SEEING THE JOY IN SOMEONE WHEN THEY THINK THEY HAVE JUST GOTTEN SMARTER.
ALLOW ME TO CLEAR THINGS. YOU, LITTLE MAN, CARRY THE DISTINCTION OF BEING A WASTE-LOCK
NONETHELESS, IT'S ALL QUITE NECESSARY. I'M SURE YOU WOULDN'T ARGUE THE POINT THAT THE PRE-MORTEM IS RIDDLED WITH PAINS, TRAUMAS, HORRORS, AND OTHER SUCH UNPLEASANTRIES.
WELL, IT'S NOTHING COMPARED TO A WORLD WITHOUT WASTE LOCKS.
MESSAGE TO MORONS: PLOT DEVELOPMENT!!
OF COURSE HE DIDN'T, IT'S A BLASPHEMY TO QUESTION GOD, ISN'T IT?
SEEMS TO ENGENDER BLIND WORSHIP OR DISILLUSIONMENT. BITCHY SIT, NO?
OR SALE
UM... THAT SOUNDS... BAD.
KNOW THAT, FOR ALL ITS TROUBLES, THE WORLD IS PERFECT, FLAWLESS IN IT'S BEAUTIES AND TURMOILS. VIOLENCE AND NIGHTMARES BEING A NATURAL PRODUCT OF HUMANITY.
DEVILS

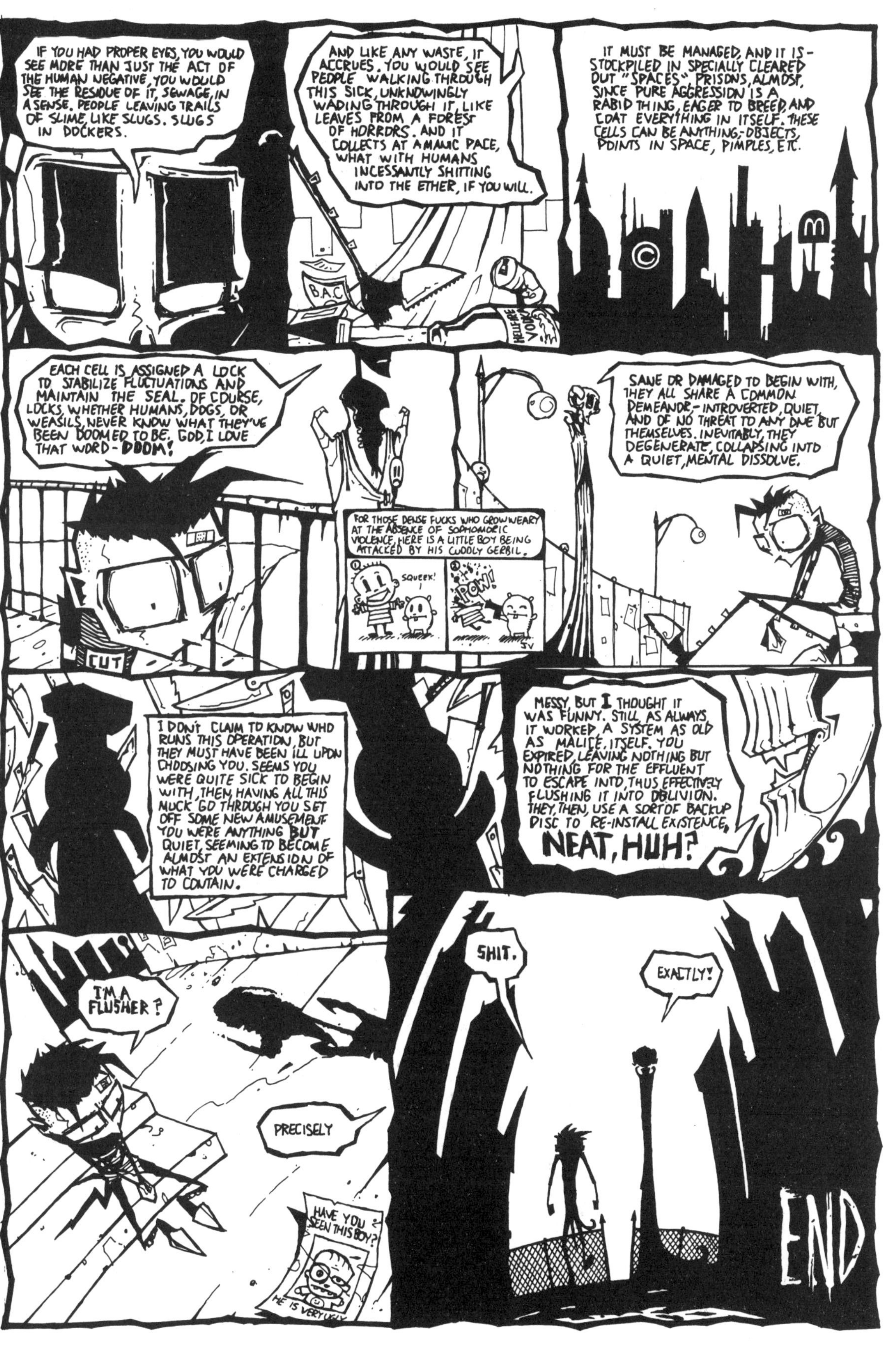
IF YOU HAD PROPER EYES, YOU WOULD SEE MORE THAN JUST THE ACT OF THE HUMAN NEGATIVE, YOU WOULD SEE THE RESIDUE OF IT, SEWAGE, IN A SENSE. PEOPLE LEAVING TRAILS OF SLIME, LIKE SLUGS. SLUGS IN DOCKERS.
AND LIKE ANY WASTE, IT ACCRUES. YOU WOULD SEE PEOPLE WALKING THROUGH THIS SICK, UNKNOWINGLY WADING THROUGH IT, LIKE LEAVES FROM A FOREST OF HORRORS. AND IT COLLECTS AT A MANIC PACE, WHAT WITH HUMANS INCESSANTLY SHITTING INTO THE ETHER, IF YOU WILL.
B.A.C.
HELL-FIRE VODKA
IT MUST BE MANAGED, AND IT IS - STOCKPILED IN SPECIALLY CLEARED OUT "SPACES", PRISONS, ALMOST, SINCE PURE AGGRESSION IS A RABID THING, EAGER TO BREED, AND COAT EVERYTHING IN ITSELF. THESE CELLS CAN BE ANYTHING, - OBJECTS, POINTS IN SPACE, PIMPLES, ETC.
EACH CELL IS ASSIGNED A LOCK TO STABILIZE FLUCTUATIONS AND MAINTAIN THE SEAL. OF COURSE, LOCKS, WHETHER HUMANS, DOGS, OR WEASILS, NEVER KNOW WHAT THEY'VE BEEN DOOMED TO BE. GOD, I LOVE THAT WORD - DOOM!
CUT
FOR THOSE DENSE FUCKS WHO GROW WEARY AT THE ABSENCE OF SOPHOMORIC VIOLENCE, HERE IS A LITTLE BOY BEING ATTACKED BY HIS CUDDLY GERBIL.
SQUEEK!
POW!
SANE OR DAMAGED TO BEGIN WITH, THEY ALL SHARE A COMMON DEMEANOR, - INTROVERTED, QUIET, AND OF NO THREAT TO ANY ONE BUT THEMSELVES. INEVITABLY, THEY DEGENERATE, COLLAPSING INTO A QUIET, MENTAL DISSOLVE.
I DON'T CLAIM TO KNOW WHO RUNS THIS OPERATION, BUT THEY MUST HAVE BEEN ILL UPON CHOOSING YOU. SEEMS YOU WERE QUITE SICK TO BEGIN WITH, THEN, HAVING ALL THIS MUCK GO THROUGH YOU SET OFF SOME NEW AMUSEMENT. YOU WERE ANYTHING BUT QUIET, SEEMING TO BECOME ALMOST AN EXTENSION OF WHAT YOU WERE CHARGED TO CONTAIN.
MESSY, BUT I THOUGHT IT WAS FUNNY. STILL, AS ALWAYS, IT WORKED, A SYSTEM AS OLD AS MALICE, ITSELF. YOU EXPIRED, LEAVING NOTHING BUT NOTHING FOR THE EFFLUENT TO ESCAPE INTO, THUS EFFECTIVELY FLUSHING IT INTO OBLIVION. THEY, THEN, USE A SORT OF BACKUP DISC TO RE-INSTALL EXISTENCE.
NEAT, HUH?
I'M A FLUSHER?
PRECISELY
HAVE YOU SEEN THIS BOY?
HE IS VERY UGLY
SHIT.
EXACTLY!
END

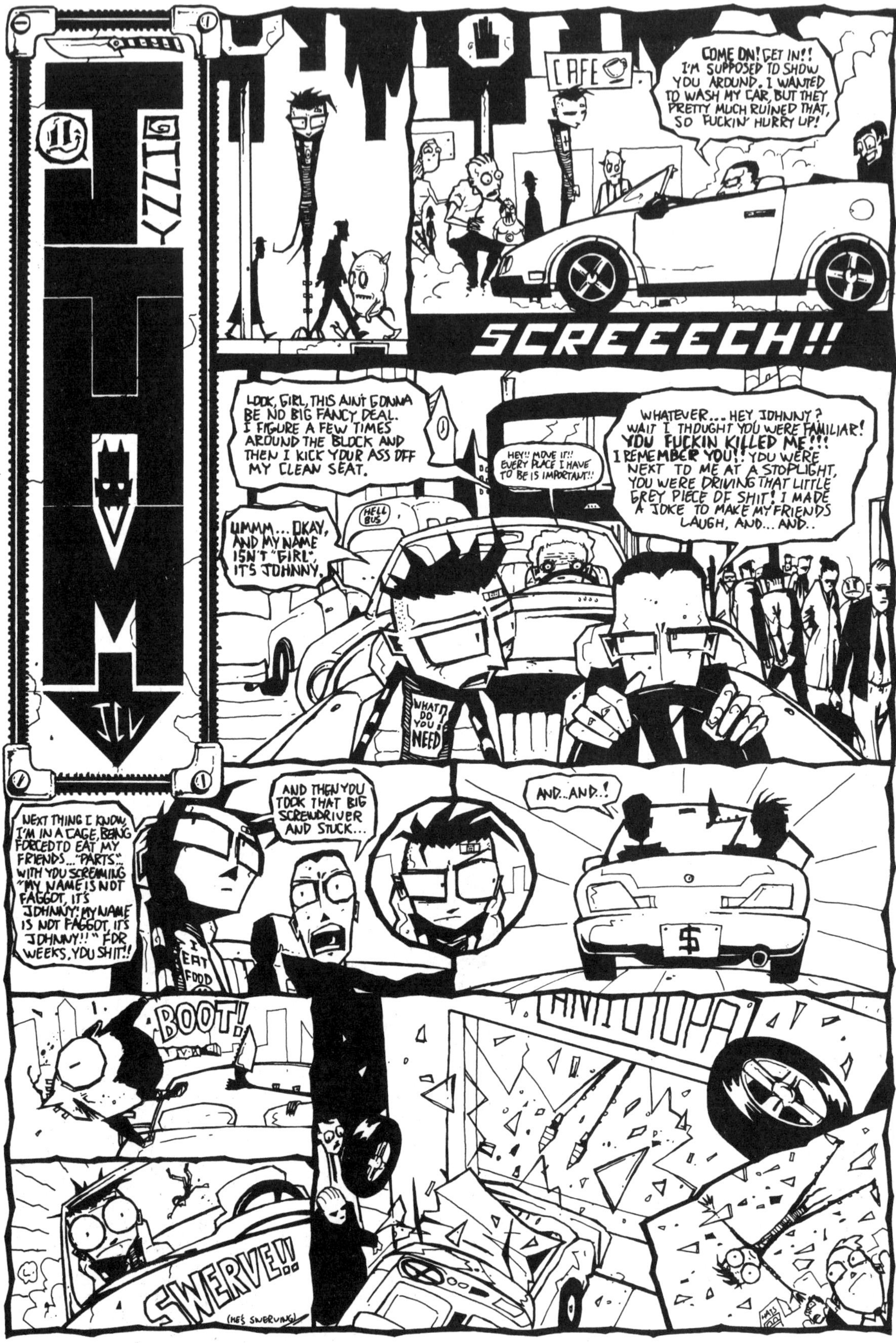
CAFE
COME ON! GET IN!! I'M SUPPOSED TO SHOW YOU AROUND. I WANTED TO WASH MY CAR, BUT THEY PRETTY MUCH RUINED THAT, SO FUCKIN' HURRY UP!
SCREEECH!!
LOOK, GIRL, THIS AIN'T GONNA BE NO BIG FANCY DEAL. I FIGURE A FEW TIMES AROUND THE BLOCK AND THEN I KICK YOUR ASS OFF MY CLEAN SEAT.
HEY!! MOVE IT!!! EVERY PLACE I HAVE TO BE IS IMPORTANT!!
HELL BUS
UMMM... OKAY, AND MY NAME ISN'T "GIRL", IT'S JOHNNY.
WHATEVER... HEY JOHNNY? WAIT I THOUGHT YOU WERE FAMILIAR! YOU FUCKIN KILLED ME!!! I REMEMBER YOU!! YOU WERE NEXT TO ME AT A STOPLIGHT, YOU WERE DRIVING THAT LITTLE GREY PIECE OF SHIT! I MADE A JOKE TO MAKE MY FRIENDS LAUGH, AND... AND..
WHAT DO YOU NEED
NEXT THING I KNOW, I'M IN A CAGE, BEING FORCED TO EAT MY FRIENDS... "PARTS"... WITH YOU SCREAMING "MY NAME IS NOT FAGGOT, IT'S JOHNNY! MY NAME IS NOT FAGGOT, IT'S JOHNNY!!" FOR WEEKS, YOU SHIT!!
AND THEN YOU TOOK THAT BIG SCREWDRIVER AND STUCK...
I EAT FOOD
AND..AND..!
$
BOOT!
SWERVE!!
(HE'S SWERVING)

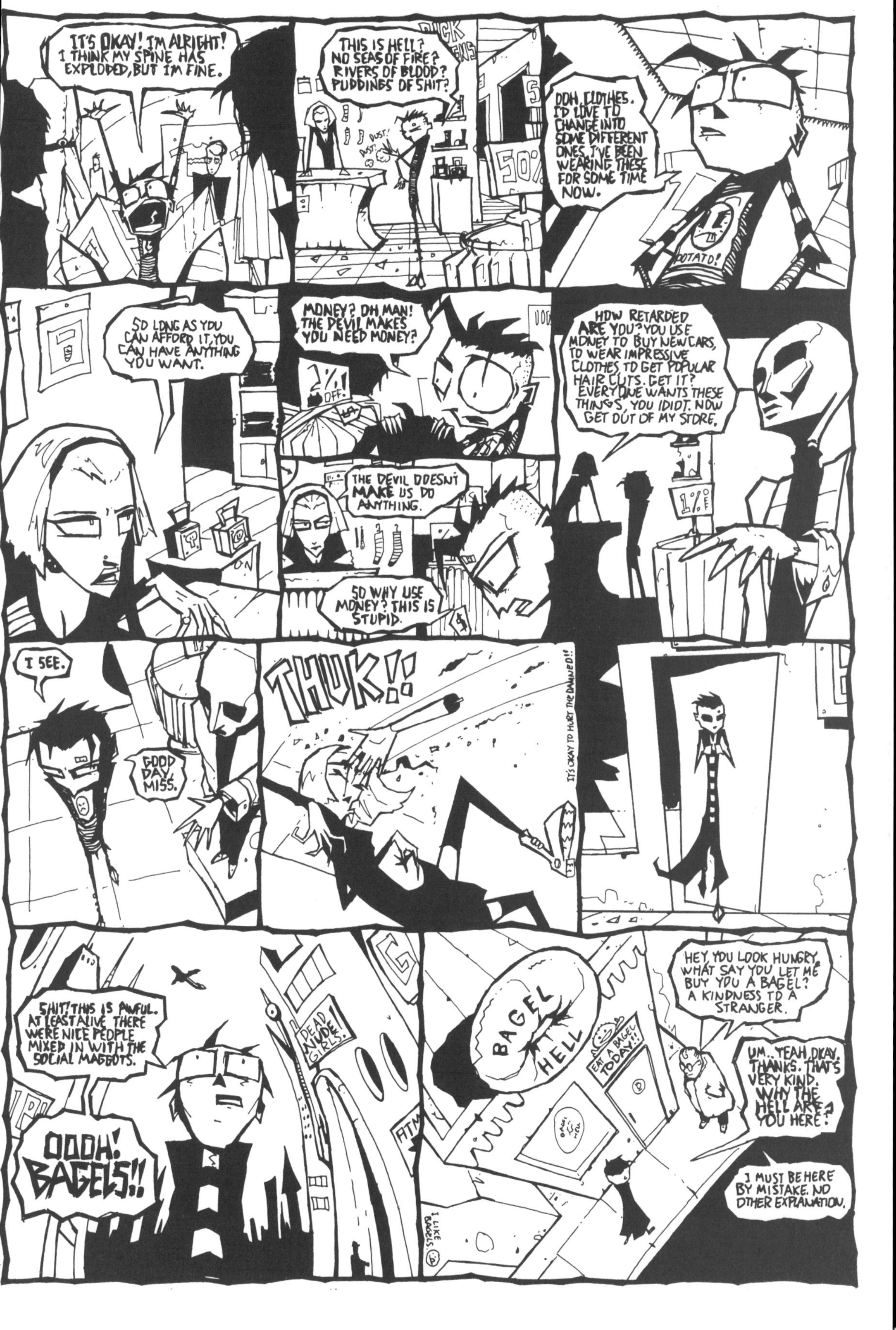

IT'S OKAY! I'M ALRIGHT! I THINK MY SPINE HAS EXPLODED, BUT I'M FINE.
THIS IS HELL? NO SEAS OF FIRE? RIVERS OF BLOOD? PUDDINGS OF SHIT?
DUST! DUST!
50%
OOH, CLOTHES. I'D LOVE TO CHANGE INTO SOME DIFFERENT ONES. I'VE BEEN WEARING THESE FOR SOME TIME NOW.
POTATO!
SO LONG AS YOU CAN AFFORD IT, YOU CAN HAVE ANYTHING YOU WANT.
MONEY? OH MAN! THE DEVIL MAKES YOU NEED MONEY?
2% OFF
THE DEVIL DOESN'T MAKE US DO ANYTHING.
SO WHY USE MONEY? THIS IS STUPID.
HOW RETARDED ARE YOU? YOU USE MONEY TO BUY NEW CARS, TO WEAR IMPRESSIVE CLOTHES TO GET POPULAR HAIR CUTS. GET IT? EVERYONE WANTS THESE THINGS, YOU IDIOT. NOW GET OUT OF MY STORE.
1% OFF
I SEE.
GOOD DAY, MISS.
THUK!!
IT'S OKAY TO HURT THE DAMNED!!
SHIT! THIS IS AWFUL. AT LEAST ALIVE THERE WERE NICE PEOPLE MIXED IN WITH THE SOCIAL MAGGOTS.
DEAD NUDE GIRLS!
ATM
OOOH! BAGELS!!
BAGEL HELL
EAT A BAGEL TODAY!!
HEY, YOU LOOK HUNGRY. WHAT SAY YOU LET ME BUY YOU A BAGEL? A KINDNESS TO A STRANGER.
UM.. YEAH, OKAY. THANKS. THAT'S VERY KIND. WHY THE HELL ARE YOU HERE?
I MUST BE HERE BY MISTAKE. NO OTHER EXPLANATION.
I LIKE BAGELS.

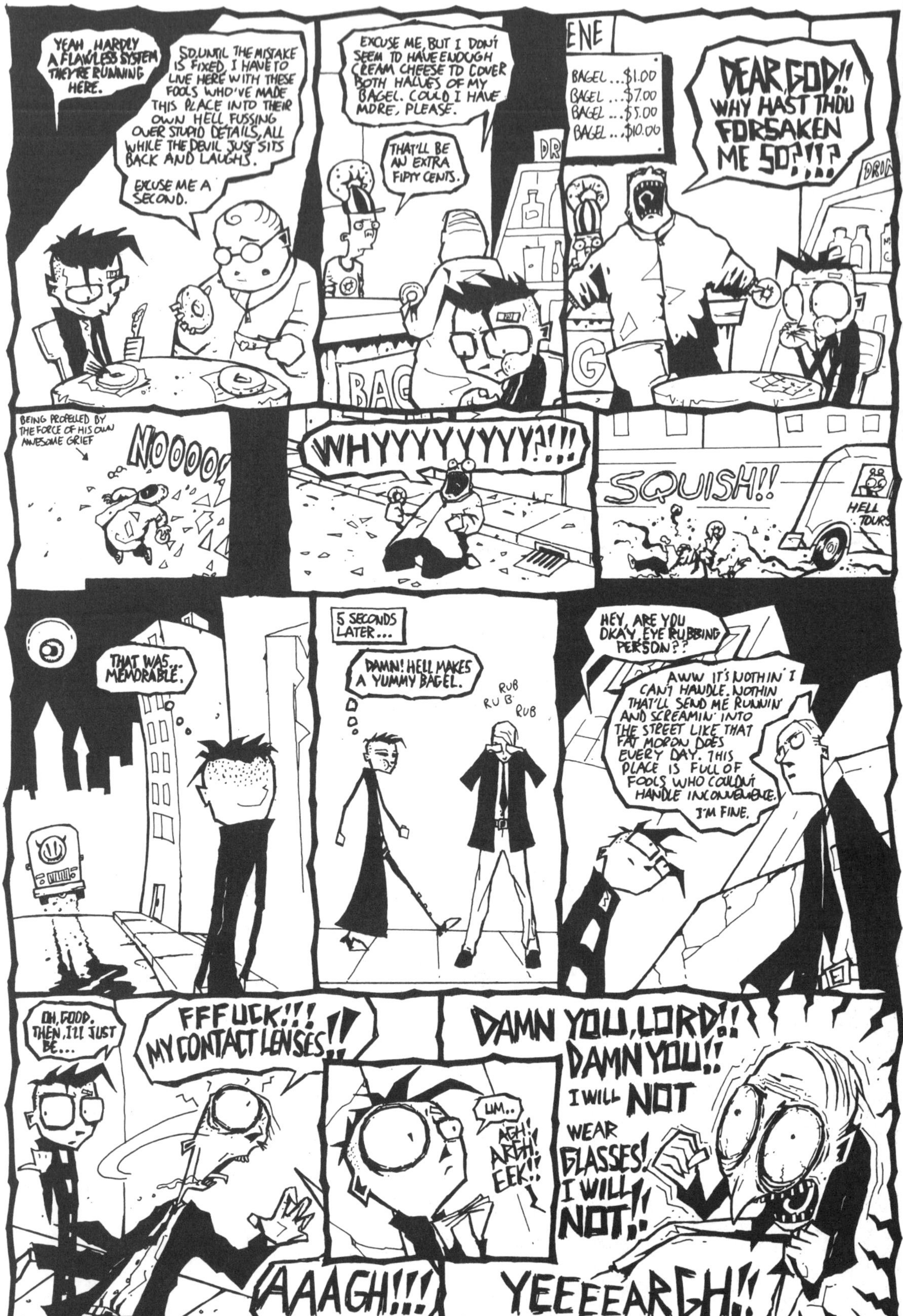
YEAH, HARDLY A FLAWLESS SYSTEM THEY'RE RUNNING HERE.
SO, UNTIL THE MISTAKE IS FIXED, I HAVE TO LIVE HERE WITH THESE FOOLS WHO'VE MADE THIS PLACE INTO THEIR OWN HELL FUSSING OVER STUPID DETAILS, ALL WHILE THE DEVIL JUST SITS BACK AND LAUGHS.
EXCUSE ME A SECOND.
EXCUSE ME, BUT I DON'T SEEM TO HAVE ENOUGH CREAM CHEESE TO COVER BOTH HALVES OF MY BAGEL. COULD I HAVE MORE, PLEASE.
THAT'LL BE AN EXTRA FIFTY CENTS.
BAGEL...$1.00
BAGEL...$7.00
BAGEL...$5.00
BAGEL...$10.00
DEAR GOD!! WHY HAST THOU FORSAKEN ME SO?!!?
BEING PROPELLED BY THE FORCE OF HIS OWN AWESOME GRIEF
NOOOO!
WHYYYYYYYY?!!!
SQUISH!!
HELL TOURS
THAT WAS... MEMORABLE.
5 SECONDS LATER...
DAMN! HELL MAKES A YUMMY BAGEL.
RUB RUB RUB
HEY, ARE YOU OKAY, EYE RUBBING PERSON??
AWW IT'S NOTHIN' I CAN'T HANDLE. NOTHIN THAT'LL SEND ME RUNNIN' AND SCREAMIN' INTO THE STREET LIKE THAT FAT MORON DOES EVERY DAY. THIS PLACE IS FULL OF FOOLS WHO COULDN'T HANDLE INCONVENIENCE.
I'M FINE.
OH, GOOD. THEN, I'LL JUST BE...
FFFUCK!!! MY CONTACT LENSES!!
AAAGH!!!
UM..
AGH! ARGH! EEK!!
DAMN YOU, LORD!! DAMN YOU!! I WILL NOT WEAR GLASSES! I WILL NOT!!
YEEEEARGH!!

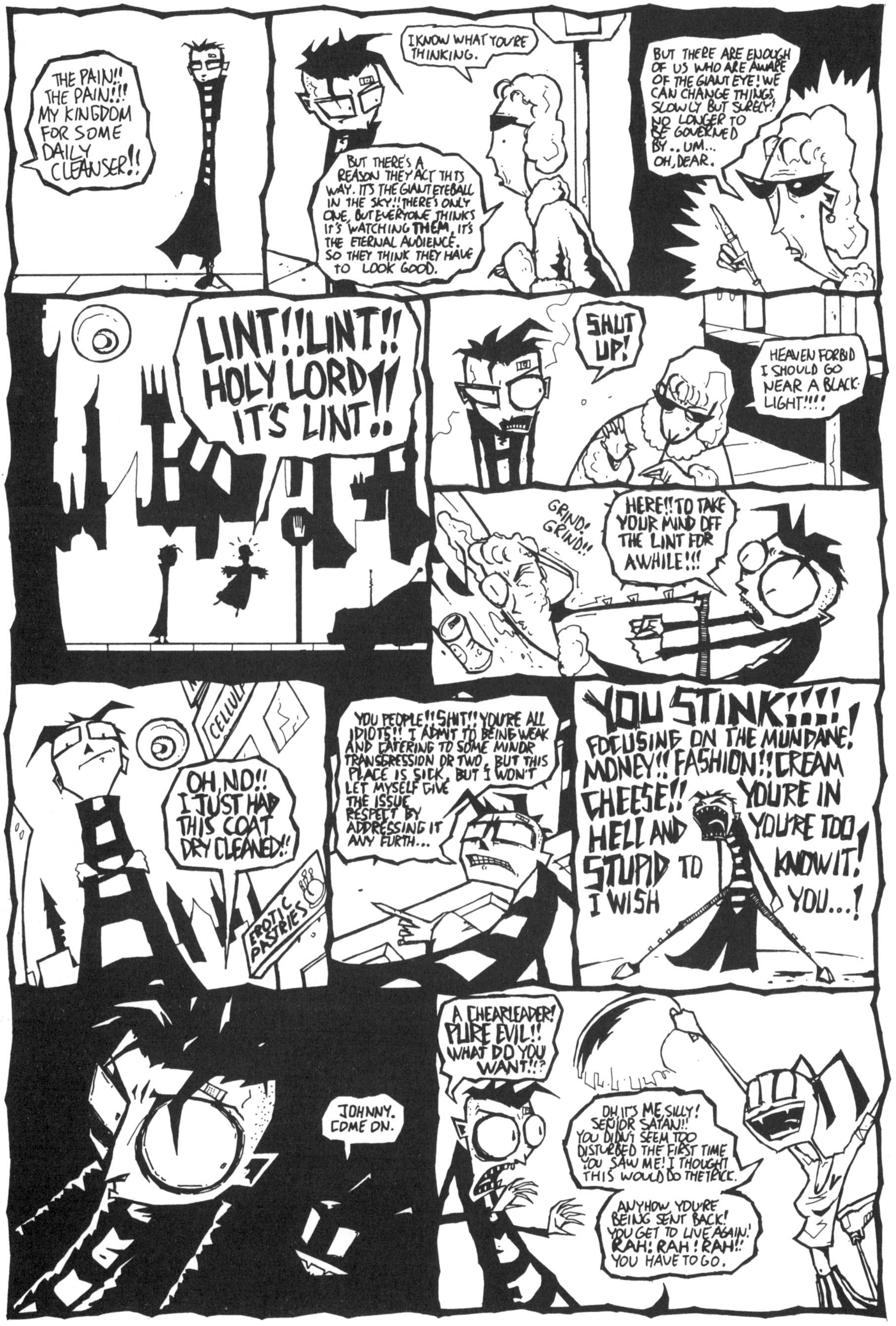
THE PAIN!! THE PAIN!!! MY KINGDOM FOR SOME DAILY CLEANSER!!
I KNOW WHAT YOU'RE THINKING.
BUT THERE'S A REASON THEY ACT THIS WAY. IT'S THE GIANT EYEBALL IN THE SKY!! THERE'S ONLY ONE, BUT EVERYONE THINKS IT'S WATCHING THEM, IT'S THE ETERNAL AUDIENCE. SO THEY THINK THEY HAVE TO LOOK GOOD.
BUT THERE ARE ENOUGH OF US WHO ARE AWARE OF THE GIANT EYE! WE CAN CHANGE THINGS, SLOWLY BUT SURELY! NO LONGER TO BE GOVERNED BY.. UM... OH, DEAR.
LINT!! LINT!! HOLY LORD IT'S LINT!!
SHUT UP!
HEAVEN FORBID I SHOULD GO NEAR A BLACK LIGHT!!!!
GRIND! GRIND!!
HERE!! TO TAKE YOUR MIND OFF THE LINT FOR AWHILE!!!
OH, NO!! I JUST HAD THIS COAT DRY CLEANED!!
EROTIC PASTRIES
YOU PEOPLE!! SHIT!! YOU'RE ALL IDIOTS!! I ADMIT TO BEING WEAK AND CATERING TO SOME MINOR TRANSGRESSION OR TWO, BUT THIS PLACE IS SICK, BUT I WON'T LET MYSELF GIVE THE ISSUE RESPECT BY ADDRESSING IT ANY FURTH...
YOU STINK!!!! FOCUSING ON THE MUNDANE! MONEY!! FASHION!! CREAM CHEESE!! YOU'RE IN HELL AND YOU'RE TOO STUPID TO KNOW IT! I WISH YOU...!
JOHNNY. COME ON.
A CHEARLEADER! PURE EVIL!! WHAT DO YOU WANT!!?
OH, IT'S ME, SILLY! SEÑOR SATAN!! YOU DIDN'T SEEM TOO DISTURBED THE FIRST TIME YOU SAW ME! I THOUGHT THIS WOULD DO THE TRICK.
ANYHOW, YOU'RE BEING SENT BACK! YOU GET TO LIVE AGAIN! RAH! RAH! RAH!! YOU HAVE TO GO.

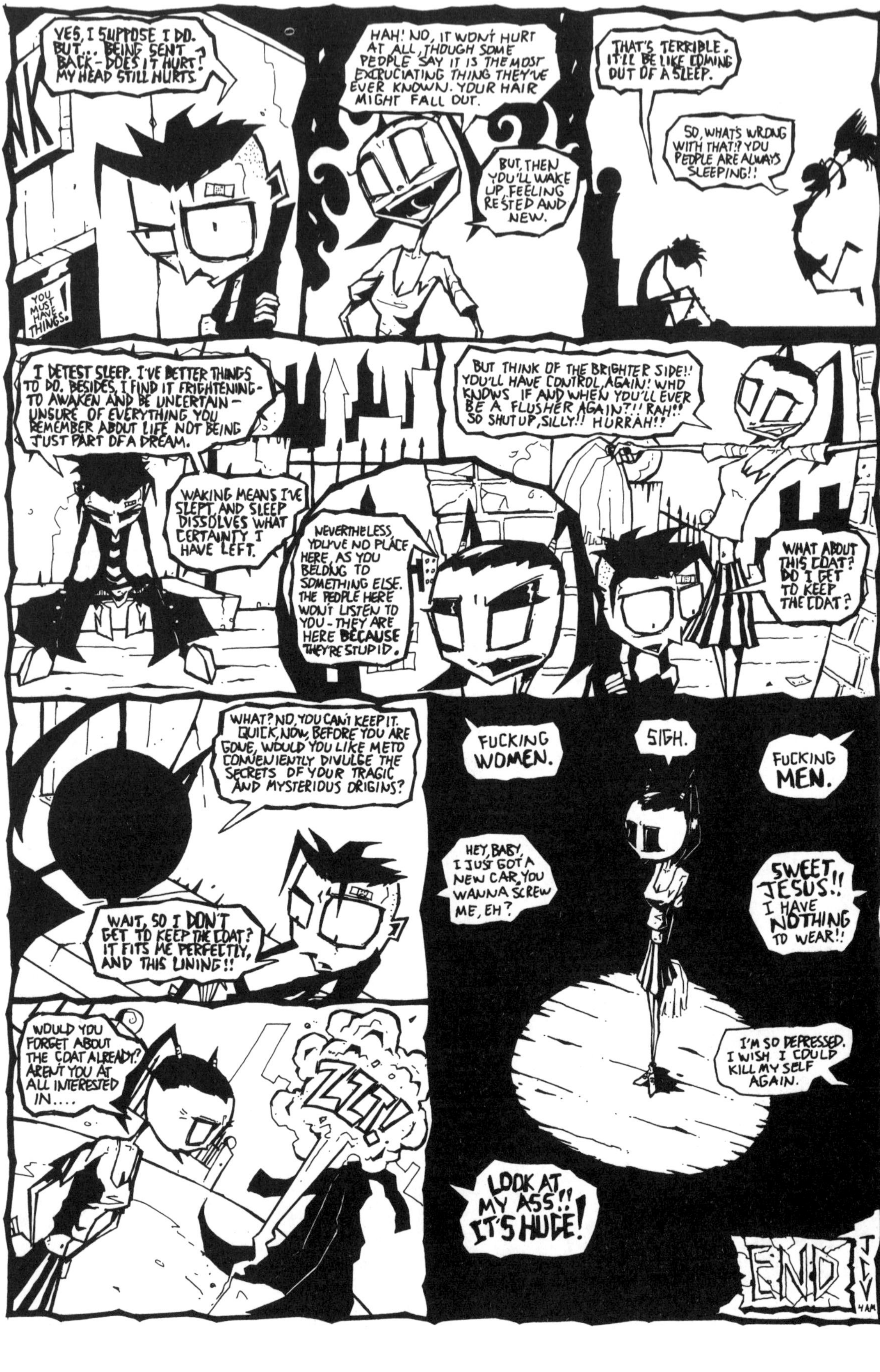
YES, I SUPPOSE I DO. BUT... BEING SENT BACK - DOES IT HURT? MY HEAD STILL HURTS.
YOU MUST HAVE THINGS!
HAH! NO, IT WON'T HURT AT ALL, THOUGH SOME PEOPLE SAY IT IS THE MOST EXCRUCIATING THING THEY'VE EVER KNOWN. YOUR HAIR MIGHT FALL OUT.
BUT, THEN YOU'LL WAKE UP, FEELING RESTED AND NEW.
THAT'S TERRIBLE. IT'LL BE LIKE COMING OUT OF A SLEEP.
SO, WHAT'S WRONG WITH THAT!? YOU PEOPLE ARE ALWAYS SLEEPING!!
I DETEST SLEEP. I'VE BETTER THINGS TO DO. BESIDES, I FIND IT FRIGHTENING TO AWAKEN AND BE UNCERTAIN - UNSURE OF EVERYTHING YOU REMEMBER ABOUT LIFE NOT BEING JUST PART OF A DREAM.
WAKING MEANS I'VE SLEPT, AND SLEEP DISSOLVES WHAT CERTAINTY I HAVE LEFT.
BUT THINK OF THE BRIGHTER SIDE!! YOU'LL HAVE CONTROL AGAIN! WHO KNOWS IF AND WHEN YOU'LL EVER BE A FLUSHER AGAIN?!! RAH!! SO SHUT UP, SILLY!! HURRAH!!
NEVERTHELESS, YOU'VE NO PLACE HERE, AS YOU BELONG TO SOMETHING ELSE. THE PEOPLE HERE WON'T LISTEN TO YOU - THEY ARE HERE BECAUSE THEY'RE STUPID.
WHAT ABOUT THIS COAT? DO I GET TO KEEP THE COAT?
WHAT? NO, YOU CAN'T KEEP IT. QUICK, NOW, BEFORE YOU ARE GONE, WOULD YOU LIKE ME TO CONVENIENTLY DIVULGE THE SECRETS OF YOUR TRAGIC AND MYSTERIOUS ORIGINS?
WAIT, SO I DON'T GET TO KEEP THE COAT? IT FITS ME PERFECTLY, AND THIS LINING!!
WOULD YOU FORGET ABOUT THE COAT ALREADY? AREN'T YOU AT ALL INTERESTED IN....
ZZT!
FUCKING WOMEN.
SIGH.
FUCKING MEN.
HEY, BABY, I JUST GOT A NEW CAR, YOU WANNA SCREW ME, EH?
SWEET JESUS!! I HAVE NOTHING TO WEAR!!
I'M SO DEPRESSED. I WISH I COULD KILL MY SELF AGAIN.
LOOK AT MY ASS!! IT'S HUGE!
END
JCV
4AM

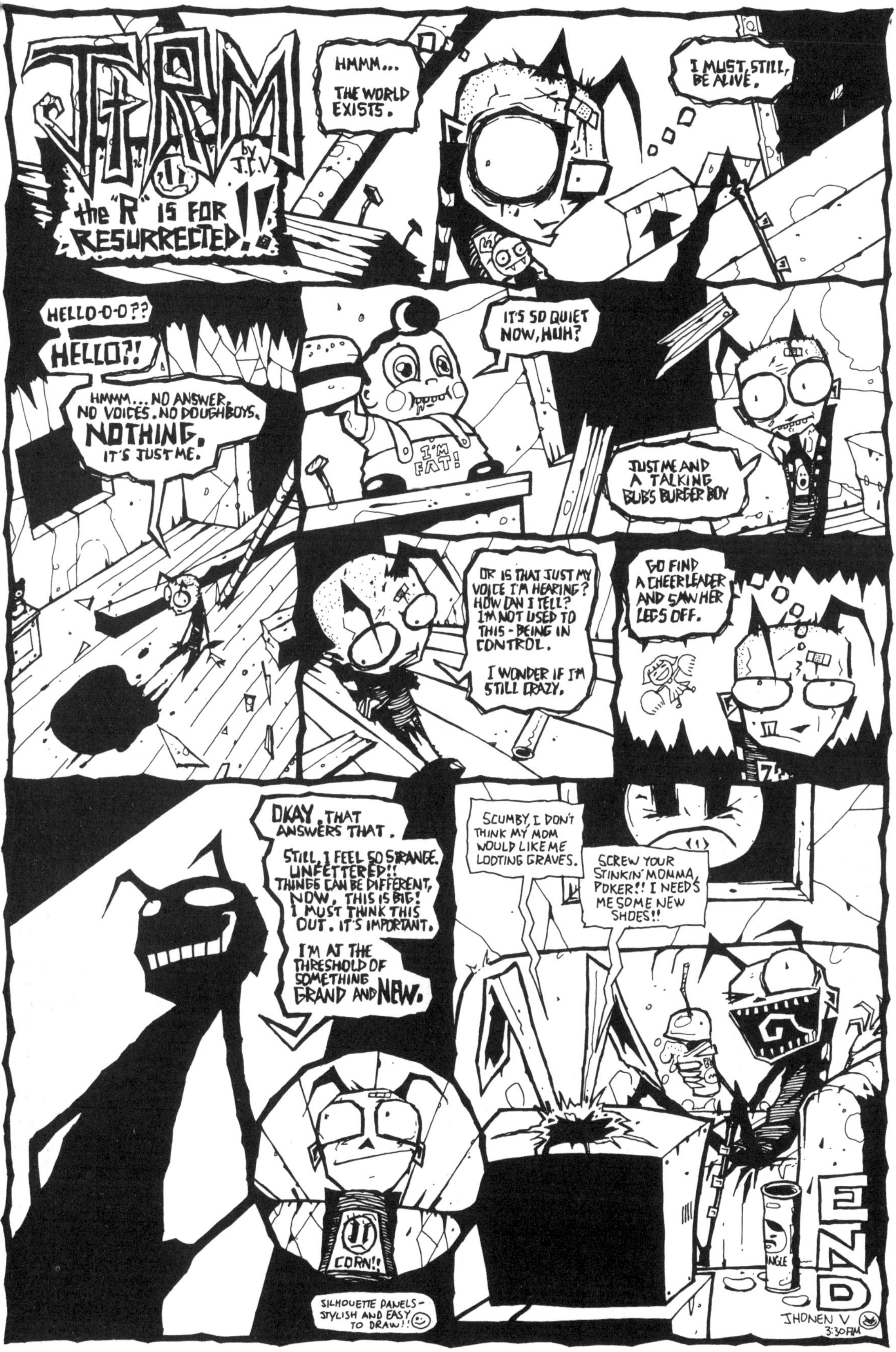

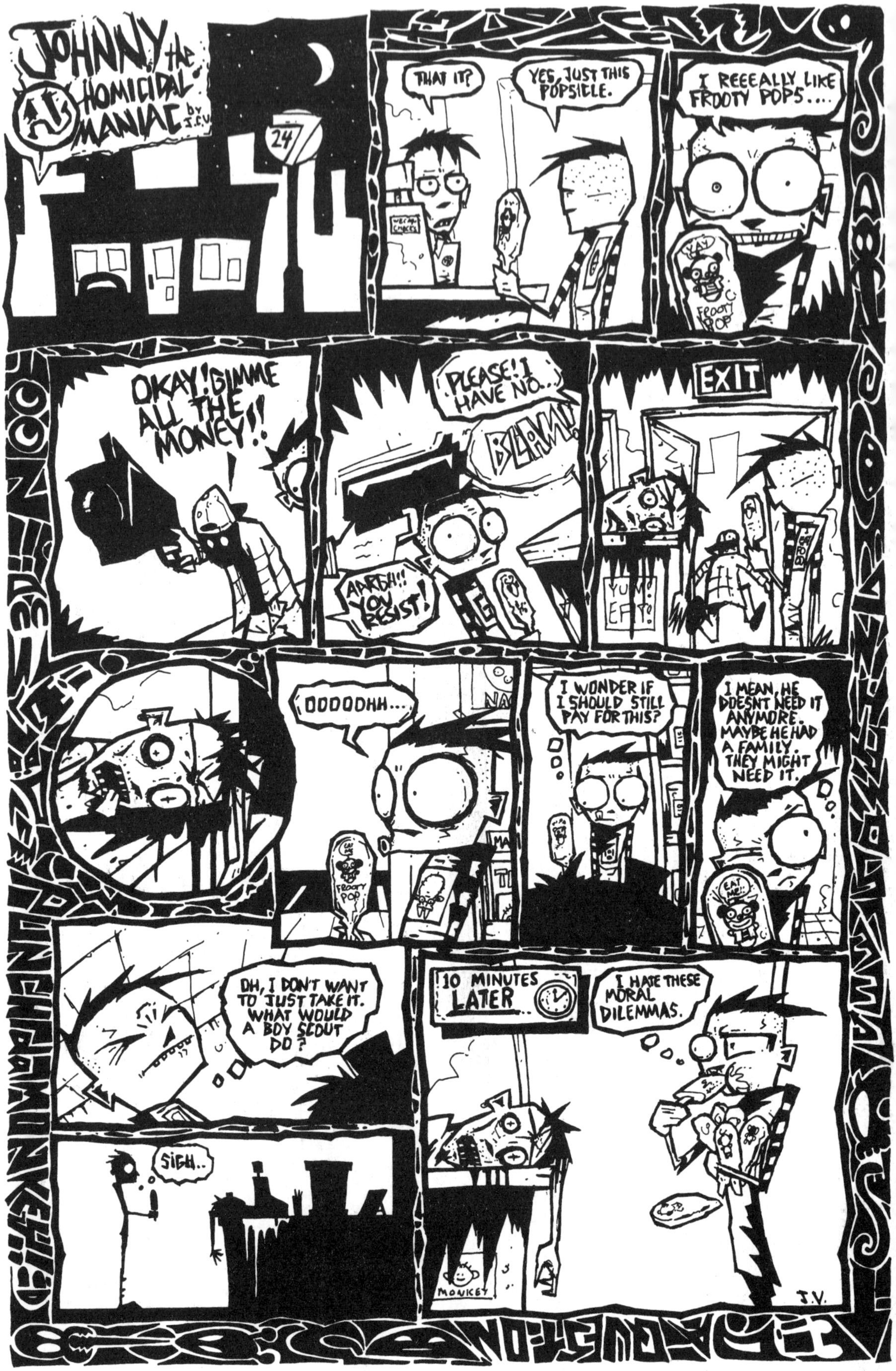
JOHNNY the HOMICIDAL MANIAC by J.C.V.
24
THAT IT?
YES, JUST THIS POPSICLE.
I REEEALLY LIKE FROOTY POPS....
FROOTY POP
OKAY! GIMME ALL THE MONEY!!
PLEASE! I HAVE NO..
AARGH!! YOU RESIST!
EXIT
OOOOOHH...
FROOTY POP
I WONDER IF I SHOULD STILL PAY FOR THIS?
I MEAN, HE DOESNT NEED IT ANYMORE. MAYBE HE HAD A FAMILY. THEY MIGHT NEED IT.
EAT ME!
OH, I DON'T WANT TO JUST TAKE IT. WHAT WOULD A BOY SCOUT DO?
SIGH..
10 MINUTES LATER
I HATE THESE MORAL DILEMMAS.
MONKEY
J.V.

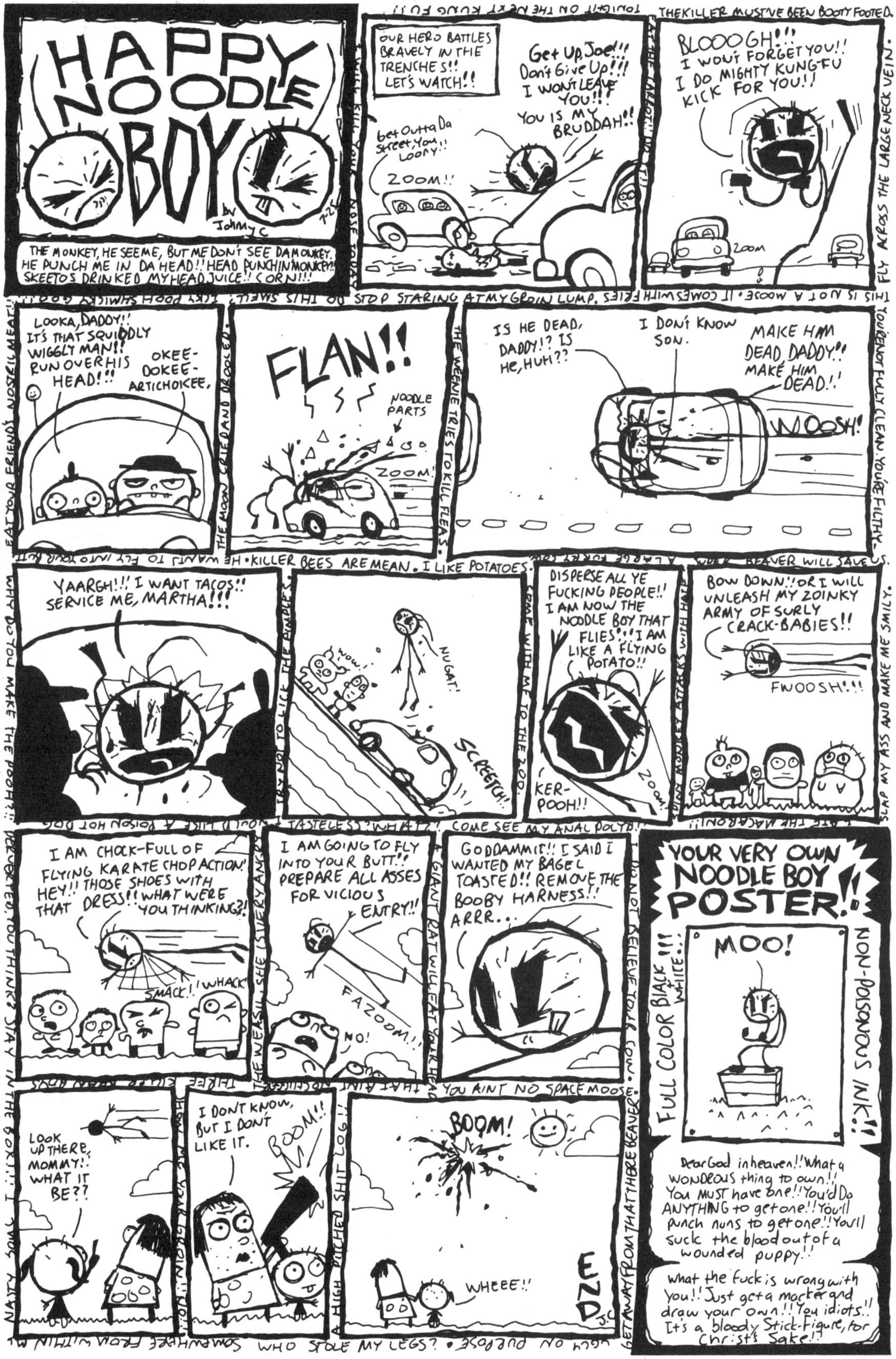
HAPPY NOODLE BOY
by Johnny C
THE MONKEY, HE SEE ME, BUT ME DON'T SEE DA MONKEY. HE PUNCH ME IN DA HEAD!! HEAD PUNCHIN' MONKEY!! SKEETOS DRINKED MY HEAD JUICE!! CORN!!!
OUR HERO BATTLES BRAVELY IN THE TRENCHES!! LET'S WATCH!!
Get Up, Joe!!! Don't Give Up!!! I WON'T LEAVE YOU!! YOU IS MY BRUDDAH!!
Get Outta Da Street, You Loony!!
ZOOM!!
THE KILLER MUST'VE BEEN BOOTY FOOTED.
BLOOOGH!!! I WON'T FORGET YOU!! I DO MIGHTY KUNG-FU KICK FOR YOU!!
ZOOM
FLY ACROSS THE LARGE NECK VEIN.
STOP STARING AT MY GROIN LUMP.
LOOKA, DADDY!! IT'S THAT SQUIDDLY WIGGLY MAN!! RUN OVER HIS HEAD!!
OKEE-DOKEE-ARTICHOKEE.
THE MOON CRIED AND DROOLED.
FLAN!!
NOODLE PARTS
ZOOM!
THE WEENIE TRIES TO KILL FLEAS.
IS HE DEAD, DADDY!? IS HE, HUH??
I DON'T KNOW SON.
MAKE HIM DEAD DADDY!! MAKE HIM DEAD!!
WOOSH!
YOU'RE NOT FULLY CLEAN. YOU'RE FILTHY.
KILLER BEES ARE MEAN. I LIKE POTATOES.
YAARGH!!! I WANT TACOS!! SERVICE ME, MARTHA!!!
WOW!
NUGAT!
SCREETCH!!
DISPERSE ALL YE FUCKING PEOPLE!! I AM NOW THE NOODLE BOY THAT FLIES!!! I AM LIKE A FLYING POTATO!!
KER-POOH!!
ZOOM!
BOW DOWN!! OR I WILL UNLEASH MY ZOINKY ARMY OF SURLY CRACK-BABIES!!
FWOOSH!!!
SLAP MY ASS AND MAKE ME SMILY.
COME SEE MY ANAL POLYP!
I AM CHOCK-FULL OF FLYING KARATE CHOP ACTION! HEY!! THOSE SHOES WITH THAT DRESS!! WHAT WERE YOU THINKING?!
SMACK!! WHACK!
I AM GOING TO FLY INTO YOUR BUTT!! PREPARE ALL ASSES FOR VICIOUS ENTRY!!
FAZOOM!!
NO!
GODDAMMIT!! I SAID I WANTED MY BAGEL TOASTED!! REMOVE THE BOOBY HARNESS!! ARRR...
YOUR VERY OWN NOODLE BOY POSTER!!
MOO!
FULL COLOR BLACK & WHITE!!!
NON-POISONOUS INK!!
Dear God in heaven!! What a wondrous thing to own!! You MUST have one!! You'd Do ANYTHING to get one!! You'll punch nuns to get one!! You'll suck the blood out of a wounded puppy!!
What the fuck is wrong with you!! Just get a marker and draw your own!! You idiots!! It's a bloody Stick-Figure, for Christ's Sake!!
YOU AINT NO SPACE MOOSE.
LOOK UP THERE, MOMMY! WHAT IT BE??
I DONT KNOW, BUT I DONT LIKE IT.
BOOM!!
A HIGH PITCHED SHIT LOG!!
BOOM!
WHEEE!!
END
GET AWAY FROM THAT THERE BEAVER.
WHO STOLE MY LEGS?

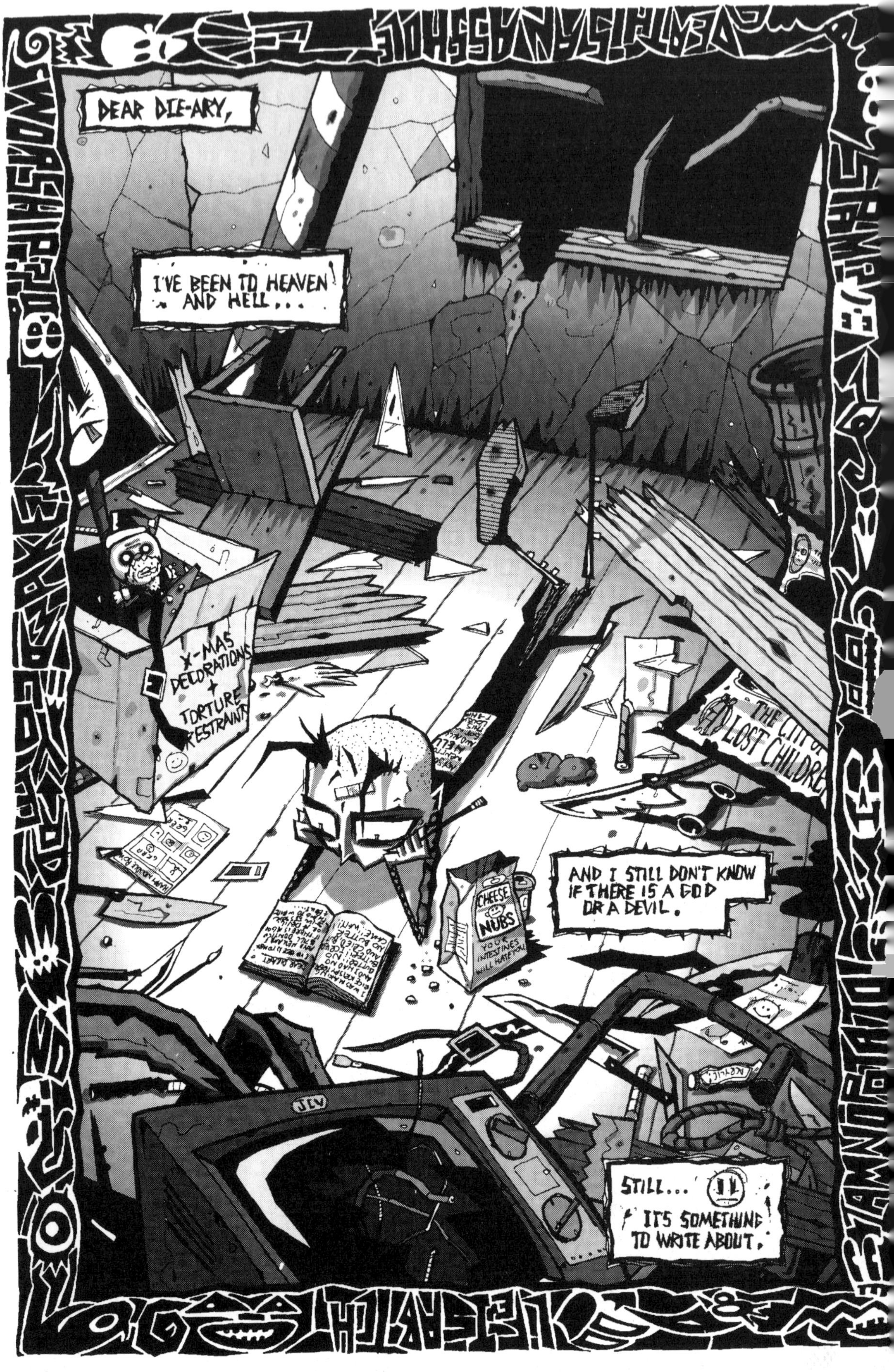
DEAR DIE-ARY,
I'VE BEEN TO HEAVEN AND HELL...
X-MAS DECORATIONS + TORTURE
CHEESE NUBS
YOUR INTESTINES WILL HATE YOU
AND I STILL DON'T KNOW IF THERE IS A GOD OR A DEVIL.
STILL... IT'S SOMETHING TO WRITE ABOUT.

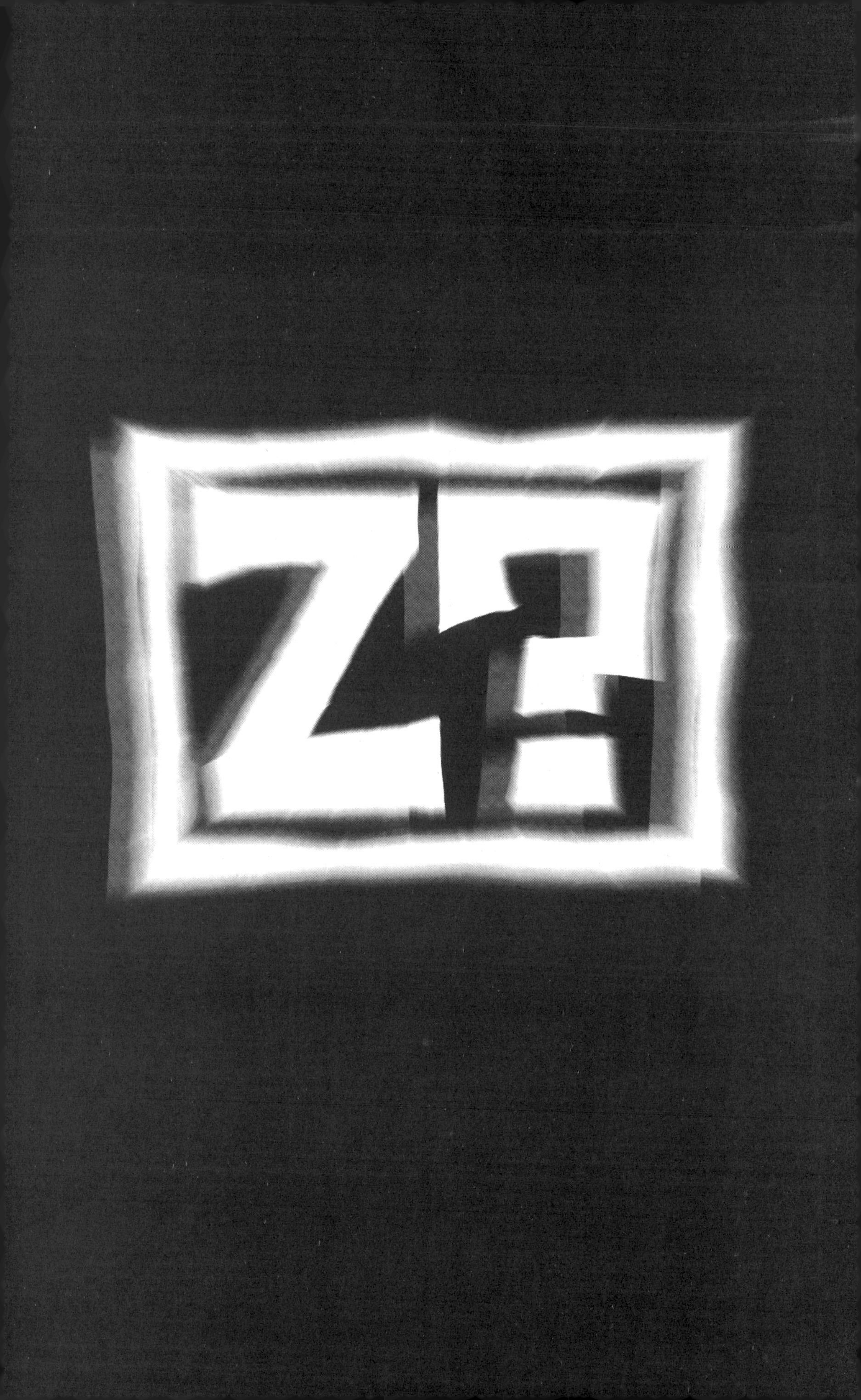

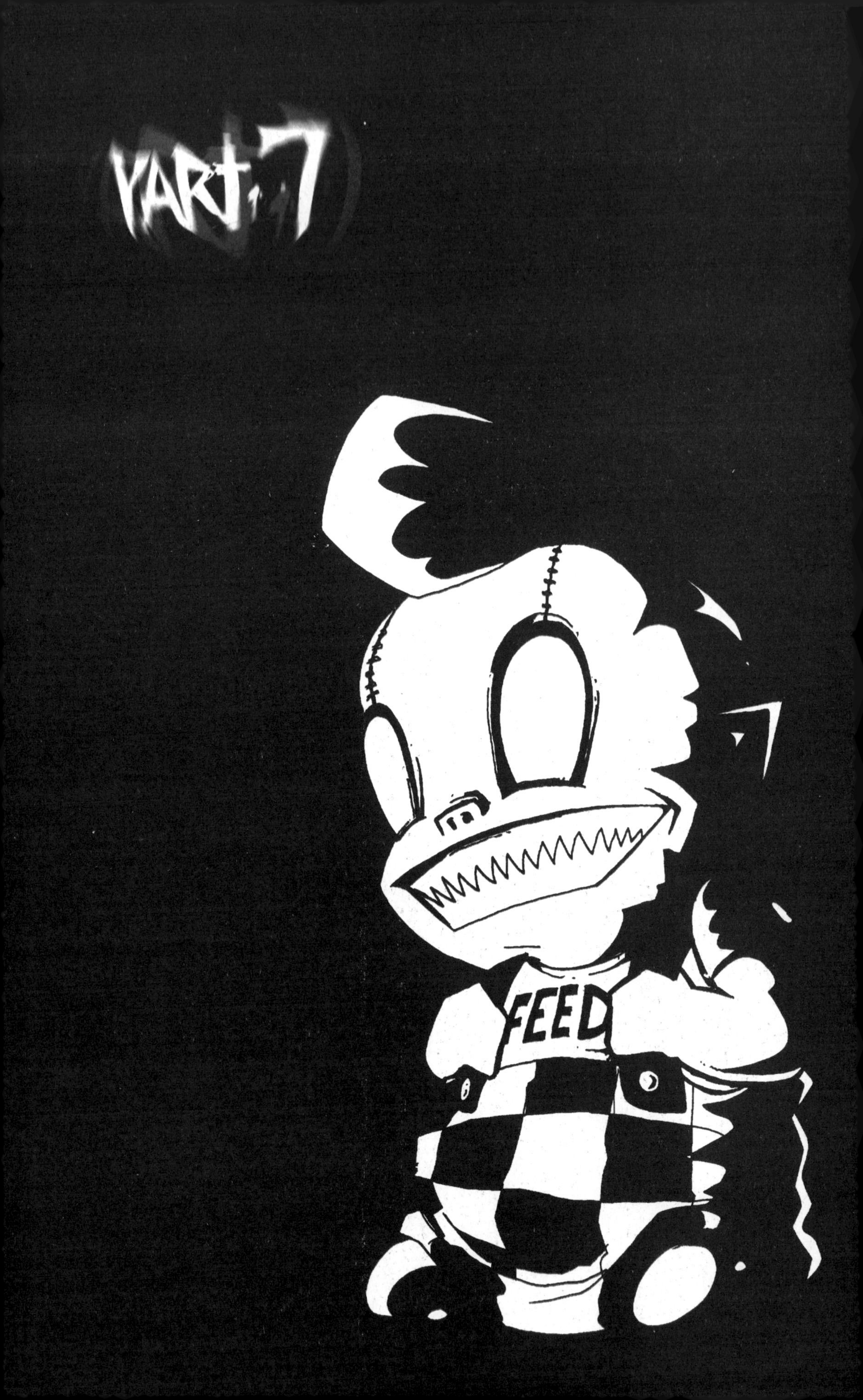
PART 7
FEED

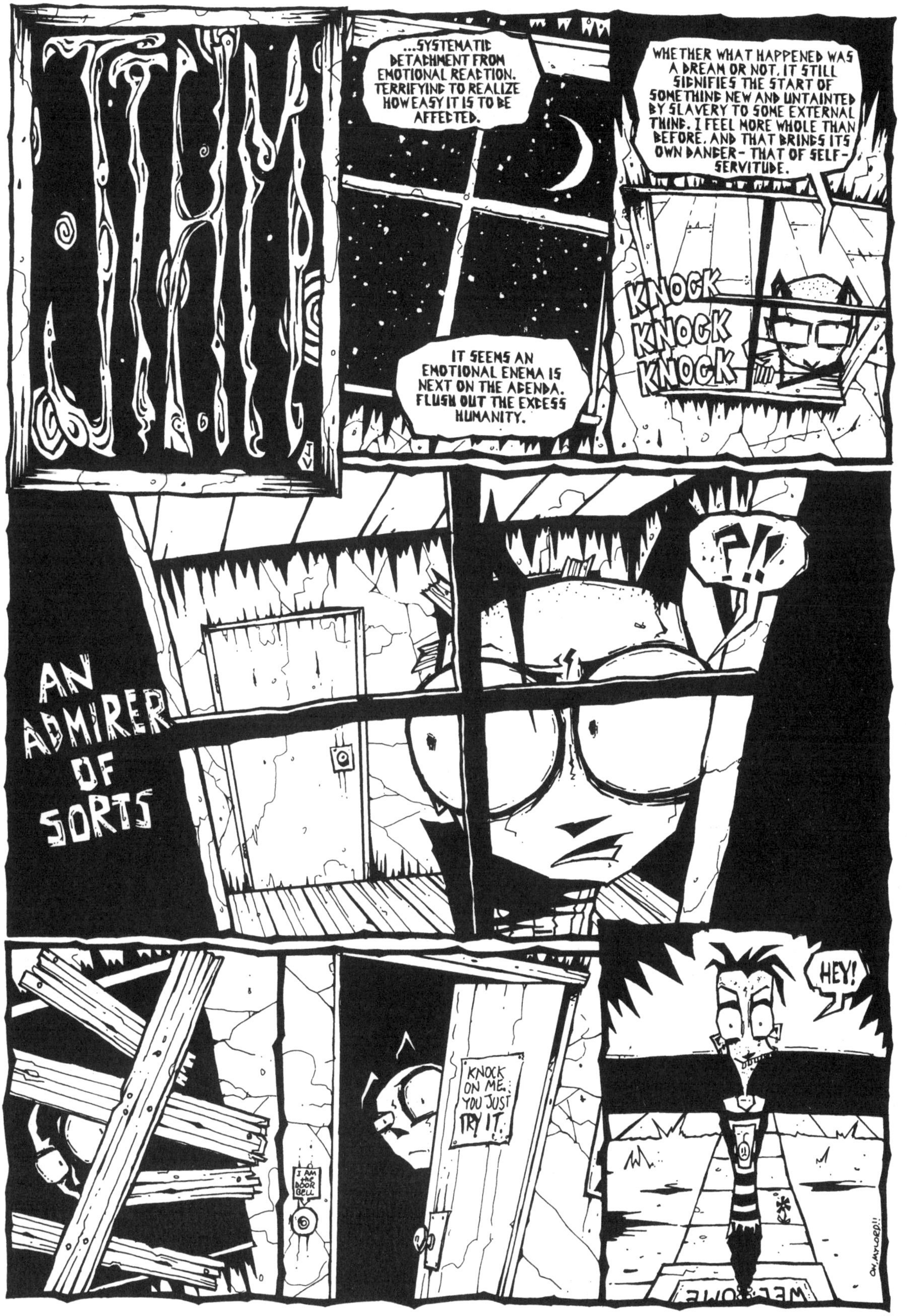
JTHM
...SYSTEMATIC DETACHMENT FROM EMOTIONAL REACTION. TERRIFYING TO REALIZE HOW EASY IT IS TO BE AFFECTED.
IT SEEMS AN EMOTIONAL ENEMA IS NEXT ON THE AGENDA. FLUSH OUT THE EXCESS HUMANITY.
WHETHER WHAT HAPPENED WAS A DREAM OR NOT, IT STILL SIGNIFIES THE START OF SOMETHING NEW AND UNTAINTED BY SLAVERY TO SOME EXTERNAL THING. I FEEL MORE WHOLE THAN BEFORE. AND THAT BRINGS ITS OWN DANGER - THAT OF SELF-SERVITUDE.
KNOCK KNOCK KNOCK
AN ADMIRER OF SORTS
?!!
I AM the DOOR BELL
KNOCK ON ME. YOU JUST TRY IT.
HEY!
OH, MY LORD!!

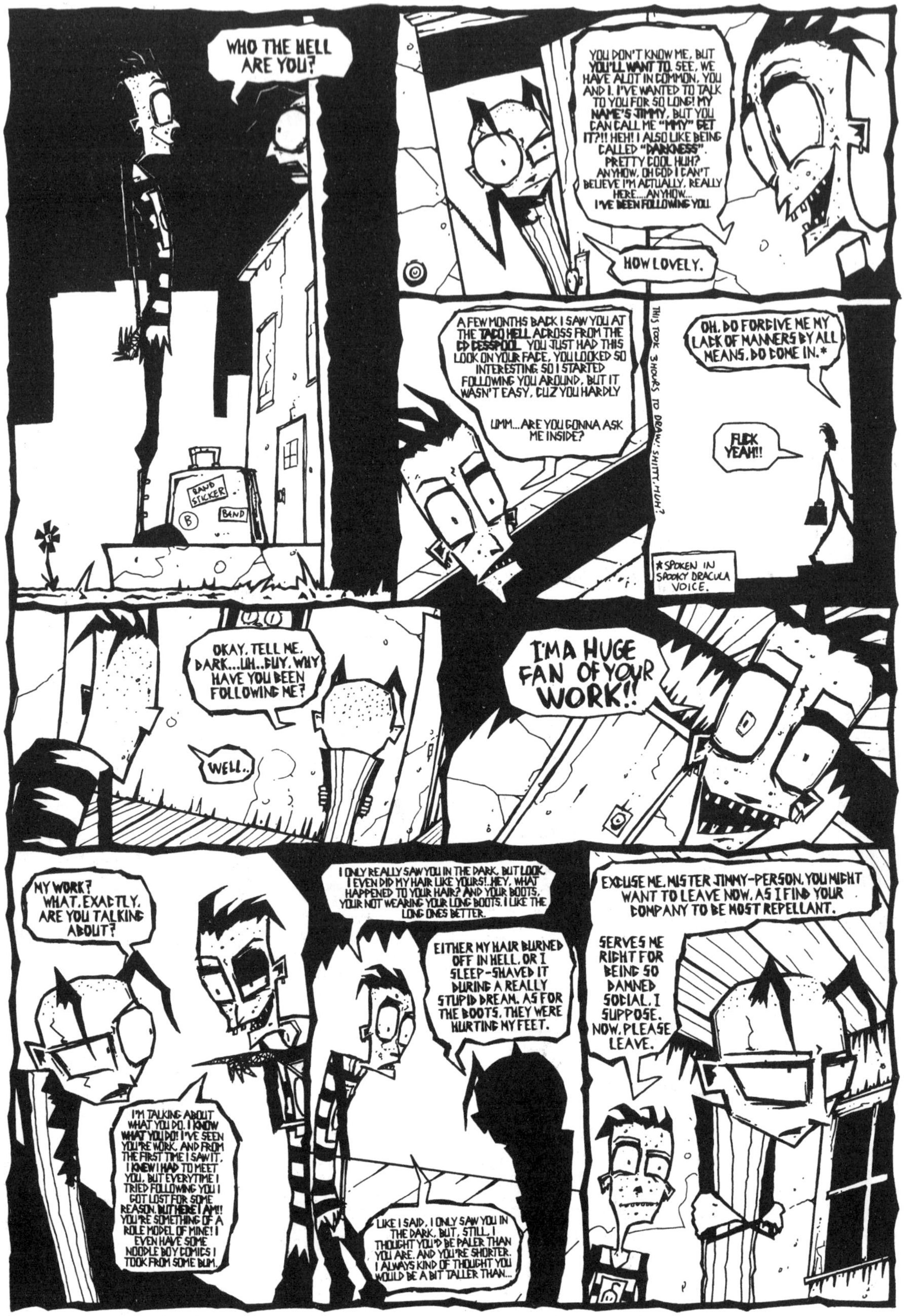
WHO THE HELL ARE YOU?
YOU DON'T KNOW ME, BUT YOU'LL WANT TO. SEE, WE HAVE ALOT IN COMMON, YOU AND I. I'VE WANTED TO TALK TO YOU FOR SO LONG! MY NAME'S JIMMY, BUT YOU CAN CALL ME "MMY" GET IT?!! HEH! I ALSO LIKE BEING CALLED "DARKNESS". PRETTY COOL HUH? ANYHOW, OH GOD I CAN'T BELIEVE I'M ACTUALLY, REALLY HERE....ANYHOW... I'VE BEEN FOLLOWING YOU.
HOW LOVELY.
A FEW MONTHS BACK I SAW YOU AT THE TACO HELL ACROSS FROM THE CD CESSPOOL. YOU JUST HAD THIS LOOK ON YOUR FACE, YOU LOOKED SO INTERESTING. SO I STARTED FOLLOWING YOU AROUND, BUT IT WASN'T EASY, CUZ YOU HARDLY
UMM... ARE YOU GONNA ASK ME INSIDE?
THIS TOOK 3 HOURS TO DRAW! SHITTY, HUH?
OH, DO FORGIVE ME MY LACK OF MANNERS BY ALL MEANS. DO COME IN.*
FUCK YEAH!!
*SPOKEN IN SPOOKY DRACULA VOICE.
OKAY, TELL ME, DARK...UH..GUY, WHY HAVE YOU BEEN FOLLOWING ME?
WELL..
I'M A HUGE FAN OF YOUR WORK!!
MY WORK? WHAT, EXACTLY, ARE YOU TALKING ABOUT?
I'M TALKING ABOUT WHAT YOU DO. I KNOW WHAT YOU DO! I'VE SEEN YOU'RE WORK, AND FROM THE FIRST TIME I SAW IT, I KNEW I HAD TO MEET YOU, BUT EVERYTIME I TRIED FOLLOWING YOU I GOT LOST FOR SOME REASON. BUT HERE I AM!! YOU'RE SOMETHING OF A ROLE MODEL OF MINE! I EVEN HAVE SOME NOODLE BOY COMICS I TOOK FROM SOME BUM.
I ONLY REALLY SAW YOU IN THE DARK, BUT LOOK, I EVEN DID MY HAIR LIKE YOURS!..HEY, WHAT HAPPENED TO YOUR HAIR? AND YOUR BOOTS, YOUR NOT WEARING YOUR LONG BOOTS. I LIKE THE LONG ONES BETTER.
EITHER MY HAIR BURNED OFF IN HELL, OR I SLEEP-SHAVED IT DURING A REALLY STUPID DREAM. AS FOR THE BOOTS, THEY WERE HURTING MY FEET.
LIKE I SAID, I ONLY SAW YOU IN THE DARK, BUT, STILL, I THOUGHT YOU'D BE PALER THAN YOU ARE. AND YOU'RE SHORTER. I ALWAYS KIND OF THOUGHT YOU WOULD BE A BIT TALLER THAN...
EXCUSE ME, MISTER JIMMY-PERSON, YOU MIGHT WANT TO LEAVE NOW, AS I FIND YOUR COMPANY TO BE MOST REPELLANT.
SERVES ME RIGHT FOR BEING SO DAMNED SOCIAL, I SUPPOSE. NOW, PLEASE LEAVE.

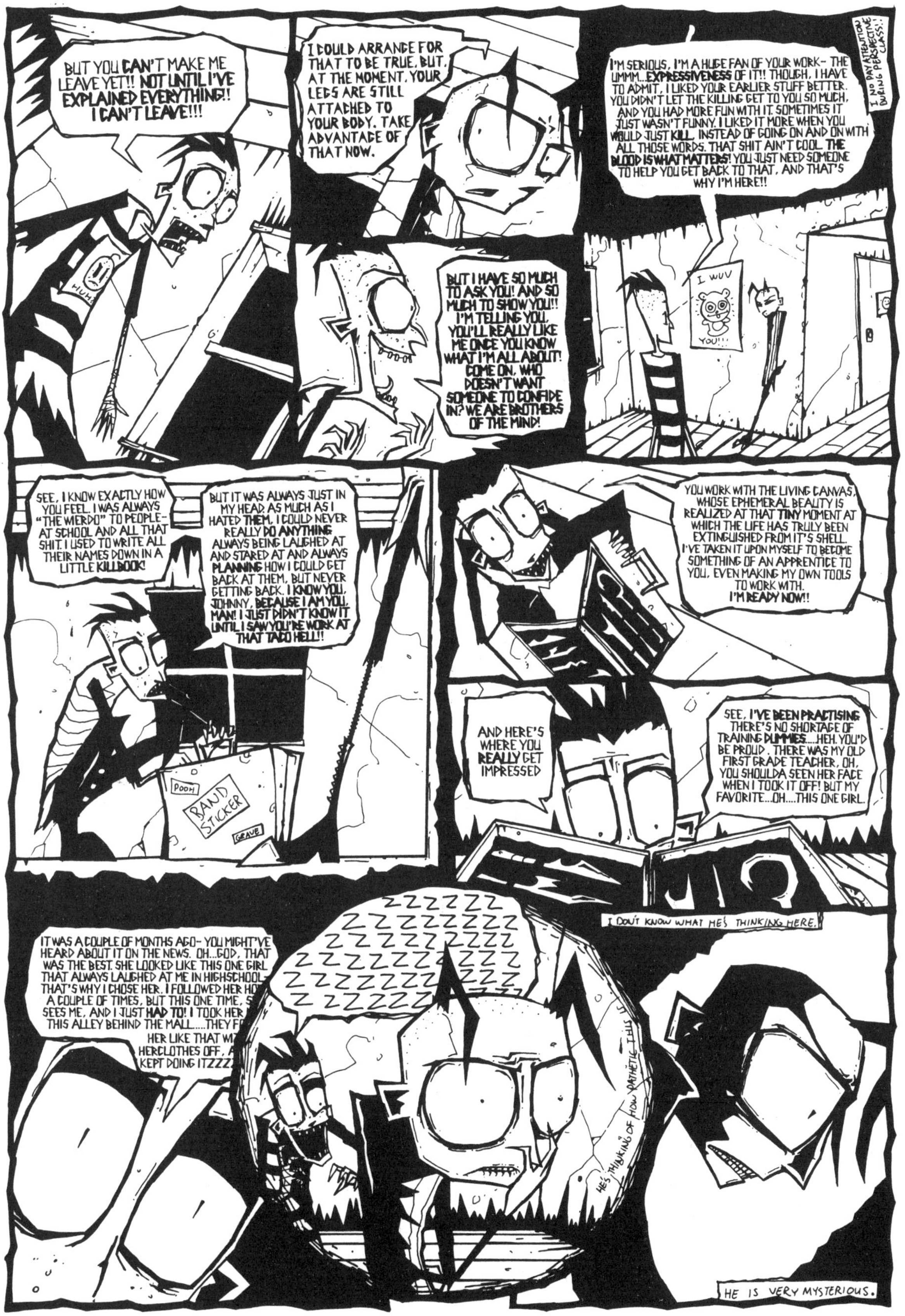

BUT YOU CAN'T MAKE ME LEAVE YET!! NOT UNTIL I'VE EXPLAINED EVERYTHING!! I CAN'T LEAVE!!!
HUH?
I COULD ARRANGE FOR THAT TO BE TRUE, BUT, AT THE MOMENT, YOUR LEGS ARE STILL ATTACHED TO YOUR BODY. TAKE ADVANTAGE OF THAT NOW.
I'M SERIOUS, I'M A HUGE FAN OF YOUR WORK- THE UMMM...EXPRESSIVENESS OF IT!! THOUGH, I HAVE TO ADMIT, I LIKED YOUR EARLIER STUFF BETTER. YOU DIDN'T LET THE KILLING GET TO YOU SO MUCH, AND YOU HAD MORE FUN WITH IT. SOMETIMES IT JUST WASN'T FUNNY. I LIKED IT MORE WHEN YOU WOULD JUST KILL, INSTEAD OF GOING ON AND ON WITH ALL THOSE WORDS. THAT SHIT AIN'T COOL. THE BLOOD IS WHAT MATTERS! YOU JUST NEED SOMEONE TO HELP YOU GET BACK TO THAT, AND THAT'S WHY I'M HERE!!
I NO PAY ATTENTION DURING PERSPECTIVE CLASS!!
BUT I HAVE SO MUCH TO ASK YOU! AND SO MUCH TO SHOW YOU!! I'M TELLING YOU, YOU'LL REALLY LIKE ME ONCE YOU KNOW WHAT I'M ALL ABOUT! COME ON, WHO DOESN'T WANT SOMEONE TO CONFIDE IN? WE ARE BROTHERS OF THE MIND!
I WUV YOU!!!
SEE, I KNOW EXACTLY HOW YOU FEEL. I WAS ALWAYS "THE WIERDO" TO PEOPLE-AT SCHOOL AND ALL THAT SHIT. I USED TO WRITE ALL THEIR NAMES DOWN IN A LITTLE KILLBOOK!
BUT IT WAS ALWAYS JUST IN MY HEAD. AS MUCH AS I HATED THEM, I COULD NEVER REALLY DO ANYTHING. ALWAYS BEING LAUGHED AT AND STARED AT AND ALWAYS PLANNING HOW I COULD GET BACK AT THEM, BUT NEVER GETTING BACK. I KNOW YOU, JOHNNY, BECAUSE I AM YOU, MAN! I JUST DIDN'T KNOW IT UNTIL I SAW YOU'RE WORK AT THAT TACO HELL!!
POOH
BAND STICKER
GRAVE
YOU WORK WITH THE LIVING CANVAS, WHOSE EPHEMERAL BEAUTY IS REALIZED AT THAT TINY MOMENT AT WHICH THE LIFE HAS TRULY BEEN EXTINGUISHED FROM IT'S SHELL. I'VE TAKEN IT UPON MYSELF TO BECOME SOMETHING OF AN APPRENTICE TO YOU, EVEN MAKING MY OWN TOOLS TO WORK WITH. I'M READY NOW!!
AND HERE'S WHERE YOU REALLY GET IMPRESSED
SEE, I'VE BEEN PRACTISING. THERE'S NO SHORTAGE OF TRAINING DUMMIES....HEH. YOU'D BE PROUD. THERE WAS MY OLD FIRST GRADE TEACHER. OH, YOU SHOULDA SEEN HER FACE WHEN I TOOK IT OFF! BUT MY FAVORITE...OH....THIS ONE GIRL.
I DON'T KNOW WHAT HE'S THINKING HERE.
IT WAS A COUPLE OF MONTHS AGO- YOU MIGHT'VE HEARD ABOUT IT ON THE NEWS. OH...GOD, THAT WAS THE BEST. SHE LOOKED LIKE THIS ONE GIRL THAT ALWAYS LAUGHED AT ME IN HIGHSCHOOL- THAT'S WHY I CHOSE HER. I FOLLOWED HER HO A COUPLE OF TIMES, BUT THIS ONE TIME, S SEES ME, AND I JUST HAD TO! I TOOK HER THIS ALLEY BEHIND THE MALL.....THEY F HER LIKE THAT WI HERCLOTHES OFF, A KEPT DOING ITZZZZ
ZZZZZZ ZZZZZZZZZ ZZZZZZZZZ ZZZZZZZZZZ ZZZZZZZZZZ ZZZZZZ
HE'S THINKING OF HOW PATHETIC THIS
HE IS VERY MYSTERIOUS.

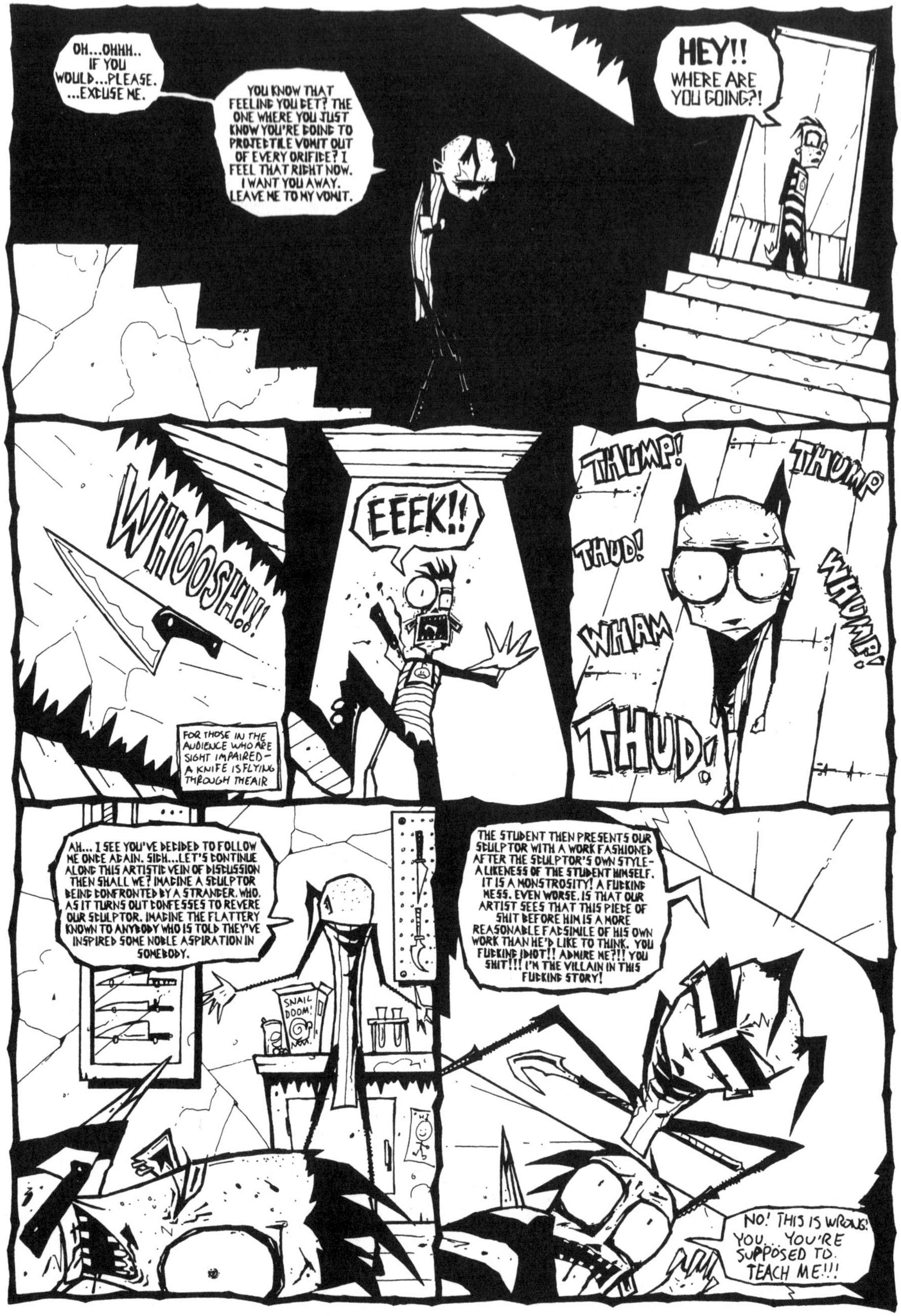
OH...OHHH.. IF YOU WOULD...PLEASE. ...EXCUSE ME.
YOU KNOW THAT FEELING YOU GET? THE ONE WHERE YOU JUST KNOW YOU'RE GOING TO PROJECTILE VOMIT OUT OF EVERY ORIFICE? I FEEL THAT RIGHT NOW. I WANT YOU AWAY. LEAVE ME TO MY VOMIT.
HEY!! WHERE ARE YOU GOING?!
WHOOSH!!!
FOR THOSE IN THE AUDIENCE WHO ARE SIGHT IMPAIRED- A KNIFE IS FLYING THROUGH THE AIR
EEEK!!
THUMP!
THUMP
THUD!
WHUMP!
WHAM
THUD!
AH... I SEE YOU'VE DECIDED TO FOLLOW ME ONCE AGAIN. SIGH...LET'S CONTINUE ALONG THIS ARTISTIC VEIN OF DISCUSSION THEN SHALL WE? IMAGINE A SCULPTOR BEING CONFRONTED BY A STRANGER. WHO, AS IT TURNS OUT CONFESSES TO REVERE OUR SCULPTOR. IMAGINE THE FLATTERY KNOWN TO ANYBODY WHO IS TOLD THEY'VE INSPIRED SOME NOBLE ASPIRATION IN SOMEBODY.
SNAIL DOOM!
THE STUDENT THEN PRESENTS OUR SCULPTOR WITH A WORK FASHIONED AFTER THE SCULPTOR'S OWN STYLE- A LIKENESS OF THE STUDENT HIMSELF. IT IS A MONSTROSITY! A FUCKING MESS. EVEN WORSE, IS THAT OUR ARTIST SEES THAT THIS PIECE OF SHIT BEFORE HIM IS A MORE REASONABLE FACSIMILE OF HIS OWN WORK THAN HE'D LIKE TO THINK. YOU FUCKING IDIOT!! ADMIRE ME?!! YOU SHIT!!! I'M THE VILLAIN IN THIS FUCKING STORY!
NO! THIS IS WRONG! YOU... YOU'RE SUPPOSED TO TEACH ME!!!

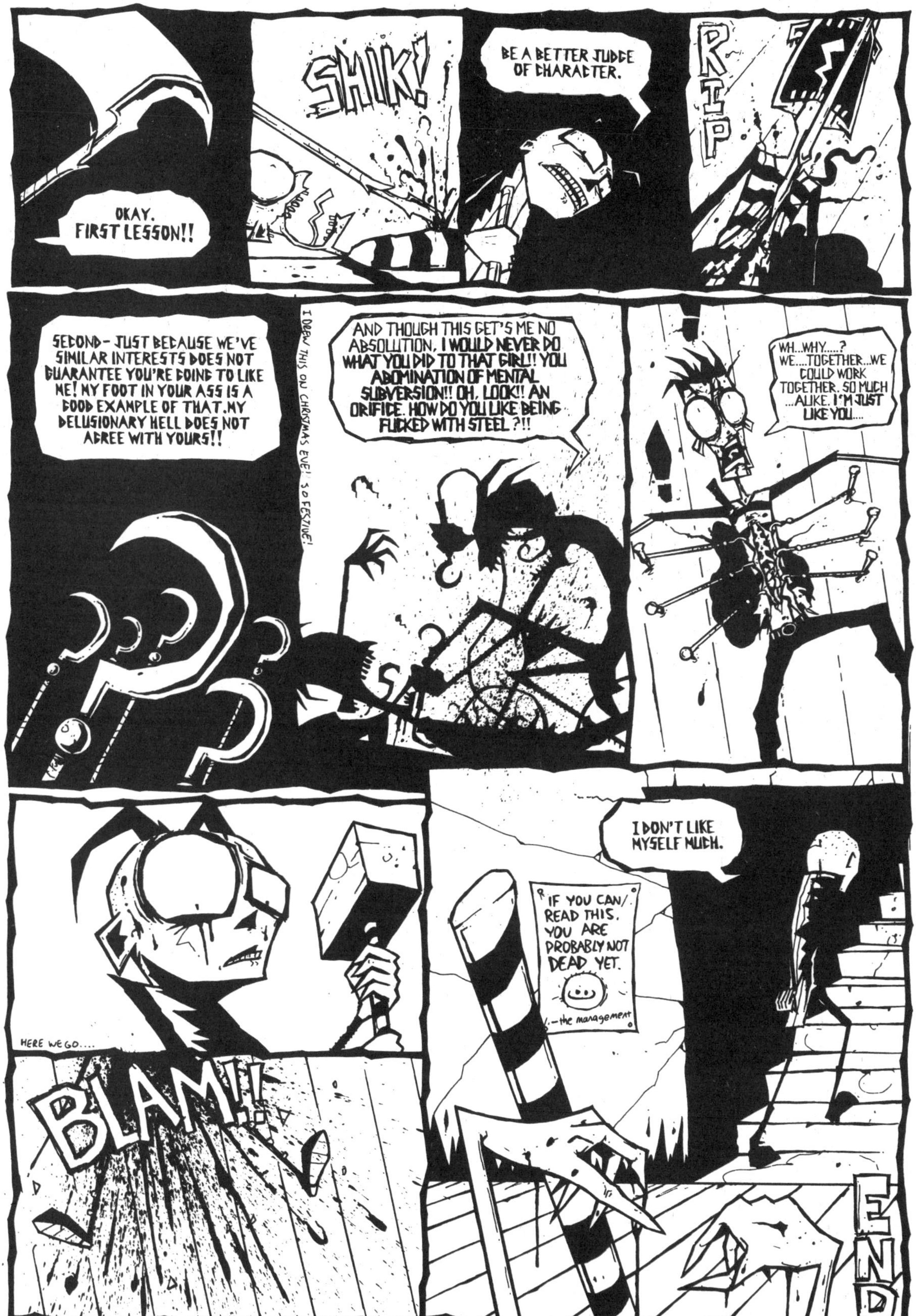
OKAY.
FIRST LESSON!!
SHIK!
BE A BETTER JUDGE OF CHARACTER.
RIP
SECOND- JUST BECAUSE WE'VE SIMILAR INTERESTS DOES NOT GUARANTEE YOU'RE GOING TO LIKE ME! MY FOOT IN YOUR ASS IS A GOOD EXAMPLE OF THAT. MY DELUSIONARY HELL DOES NOT AGREE WITH YOURS!!
I DREW THIS ON CHRISTMAS EVE! SO FESTIVE!
AND THOUGH THIS GET'S ME NO ABSOLUTION, I WOULD NEVER DO WHAT YOU DID TO THAT GIRL!! YOU ABOMINATION OF MENTAL SUBVERSION!! OH, LOOK!! AN ORIFICE. HOW DO YOU LIKE BEING FUCKED WITH STEEL?!!
WH...WHY.....? WE....TOGETHER...WE COULD WORK TOGETHER. SO MUCH ...ALIKE. I'M JUST LIKE YOU....
HERE WE GO....
BLAM!!
I DON'T LIKE MYSELF MUCH.
IF YOU CAN READ THIS, YOU ARE PROBABLY NOT DEAD YET.
-the management
END

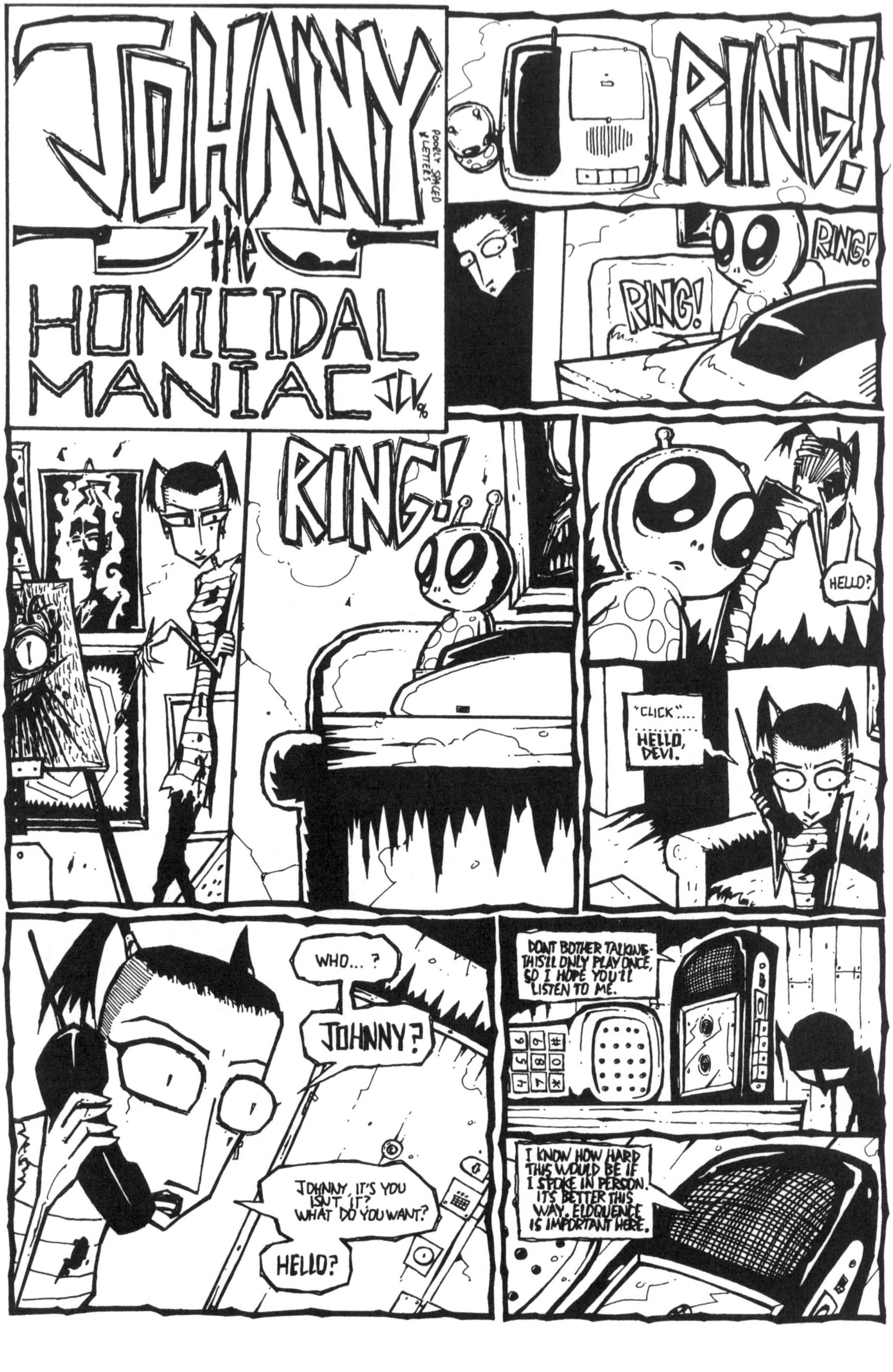
JOHNNY the HOMICIDAL MANIAC
POORLY SPACED LETTERS
JCV 96
RING!
RING!
RING!
RING!
HELLO?
"CLICK"....
HELLO, DEVI.
WHO... ?
JOHNNY?
JOHNNY, IT'S YOU ISN'T IT? WHAT DO YOU WANT?
HELLO?
DONT BOTHER TALKING- THIS'LL ONLY PLAY ONCE, SO I HOPE YOU'LL LISTEN TO ME.
I KNOW HOW HARD THIS WOULD BE IF I SPOKE IN PERSON. IT'S BETTER THIS WAY. ELOQUENCE IS IMPORTANT HERE.

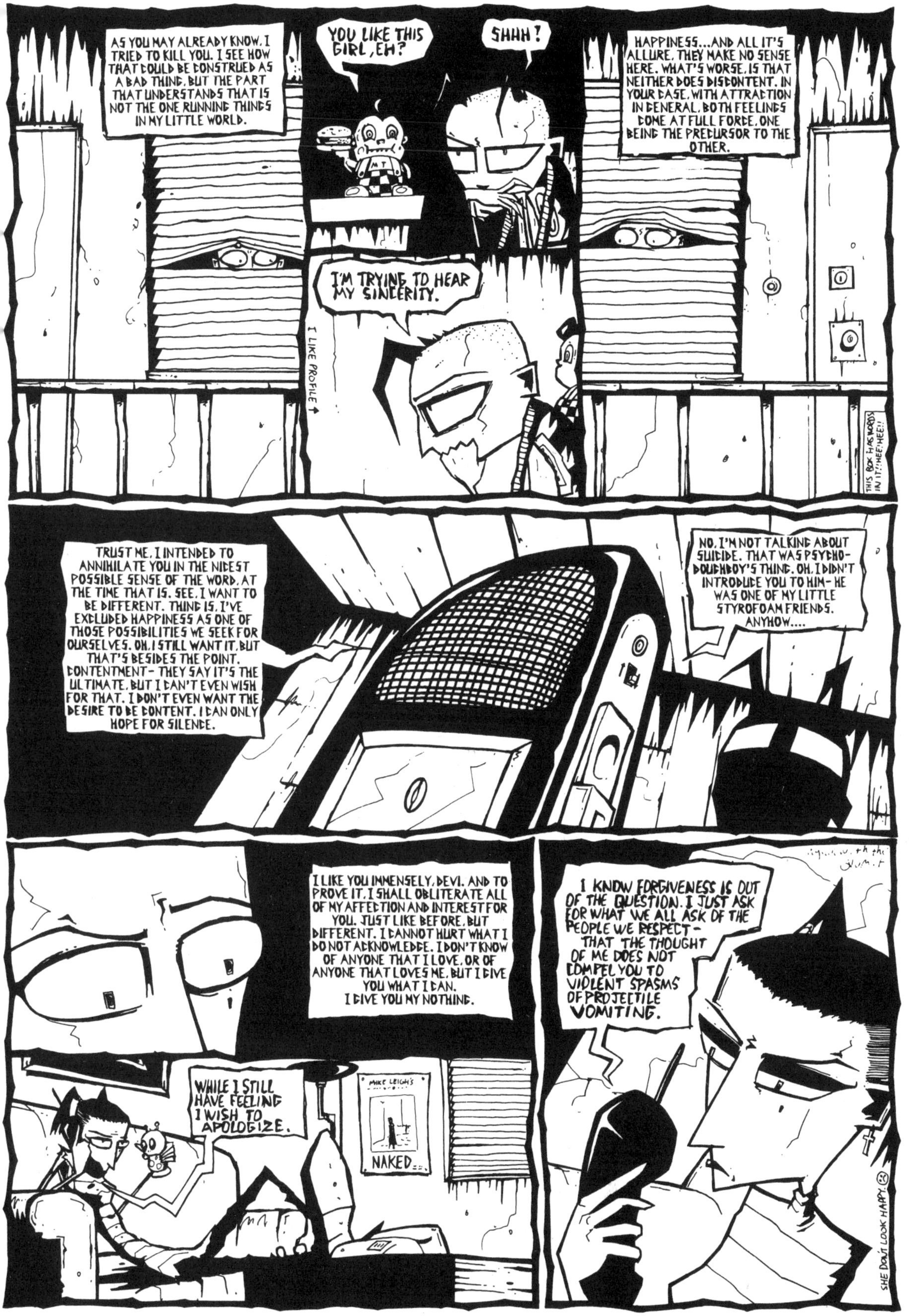
AS YOU MAY ALREADY KNOW, I TRIED TO KILL YOU. I SEE HOW THAT COULD BE CONSTRUED AS A BAD THING, BUT THE PART THAT UNDERSTANDS THAT IS NOT THE ONE RUNNING THINGS IN MY LITTLE WORLD.
YOU LIKE THIS GIRL, EH?
SHHH!
I'M TRYING TO HEAR MY SINCERITY.
I LIKE PROFILE
HAPPINESS... AND ALL IT'S ALLURE, THEY MAKE NO SENSE HERE. WHAT'S WORSE, IS THAT NEITHER DOES DISCONTENT. IN YOUR CASE, WITH ATTRACTION IN GENERAL, BOTH FEELINGS COME AT FULL FORCE, ONE BEING THE PRECURSOR TO THE OTHER.
THIS BOX HAS WORDS IN IT!! HEE! HEE!!
TRUST ME, I INTENDED TO ANNIHILATE YOU IN THE NICEST POSSIBLE SENSE OF THE WORD, AT THE TIME THAT IS. SEE, I WANT TO BE DIFFERENT. THING IS, I'VE EXCLUDED HAPPINESS AS ONE OF THOSE POSSIBILITIES WE SEEK FOR OURSELVES. OH, I STILL WANT IT, BUT THAT'S BESIDES THE POINT. CONTENTMENT- THEY SAY IT'S THE ULTIMATE, BUT I CAN'T EVEN WISH FOR THAT. I DON'T EVEN WANT THE DESIRE TO BE CONTENT. I CAN ONLY HOPE FOR SILENCE.
NO, I'M NOT TALKING ABOUT SUICIDE. THAT WAS PSYCHO-DOUGHBOY'S THING. OH, I DIDN'T INTRODUCE YOU TO HIM- HE WAS ONE OF MY LITTLE STYROFOAM FRIENDS. ANYHOW....
I LIKE YOU IMMENSELY, DEVI. AND TO PROVE IT, I SHALL OBLITERATE ALL OF MY AFFECTION AND INTEREST FOR YOU. JUST LIKE BEFORE, BUT DIFFERENT. I CANNOT HURT WHAT I DO NOT ACKNOWLEDGE. I DON'T KNOW OF ANYONE THAT I LOVE, OR OF ANYONE THAT LOVES ME, BUT I GIVE YOU WHAT I CAN. I GIVE YOU MY NOTHING.
WHILE I STILL HAVE FEELING I WISH TO APOLOGIZE.
MIKE LEIGH'S
NAKED
I KNOW FORGIVENESS IS OUT OF THE QUESTION. I JUST ASK FOR WHAT WE ALL ASK OF THE PEOPLE WE RESPECT- THAT THE THOUGHT OF ME DOES NOT COMPEL YOU TO VIOLENT SPASMS OF PROJECTILE VOMITING.
SHE DON'T LOOK HAPPY. :(

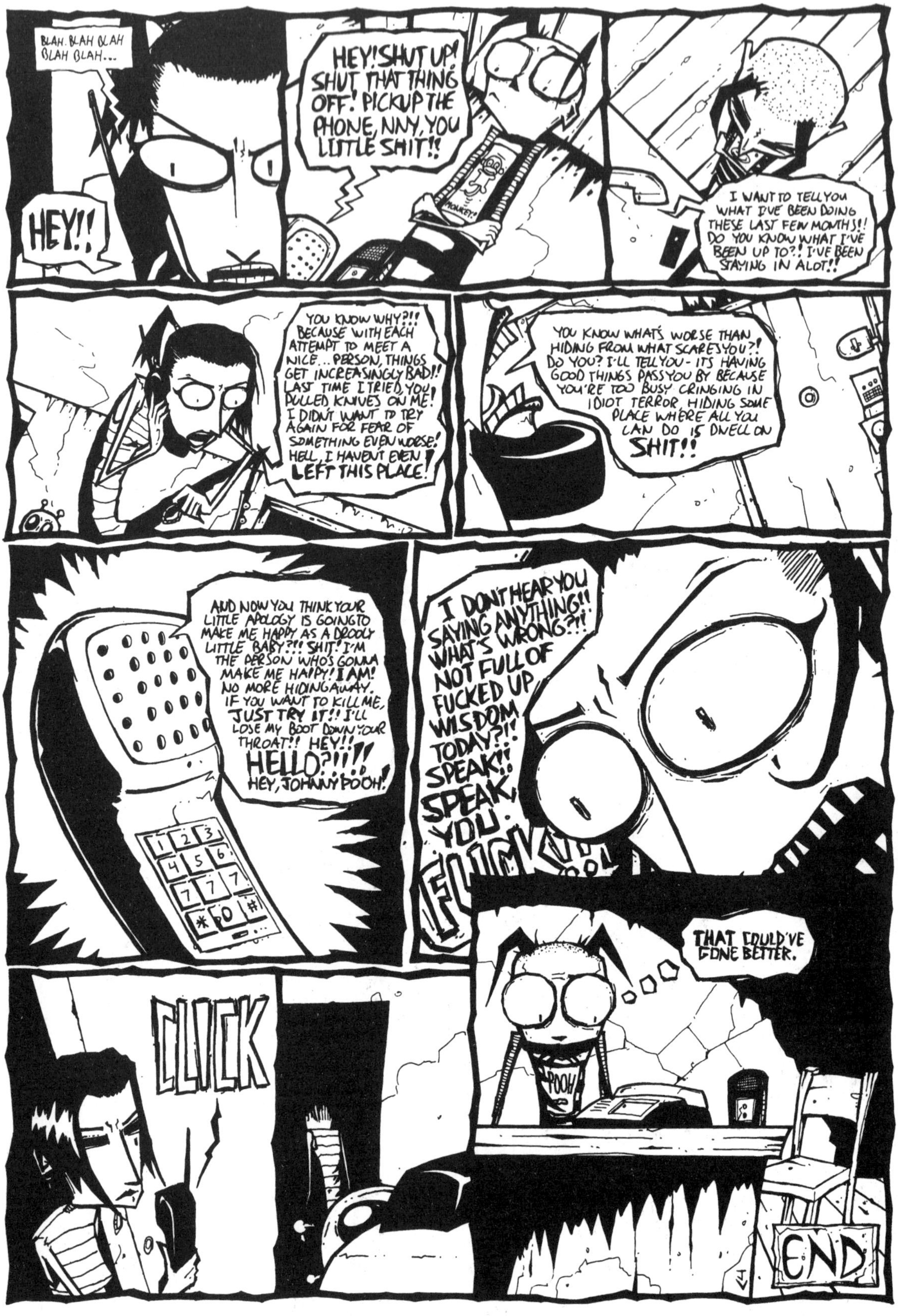
BLAH. BLAH BLAH BLAH BLAH...
HEY!!
HEY! SHUT UP! SHUT THAT THING OFF! PICKUP THE PHONE, NNY, YOU LITTLE SHIT!!
MONKEY!
I WANT TO TELL YOU WHAT I'VE BEEN DOING THESE LAST FEW MONTHS!! DO YOU KNOW WHAT I'VE BEEN UP TO?! I'VE BEEN STAYING IN ALOT!!
YOU KNOW WHY?!! BECAUSE WITH EACH ATTEMPT TO MEET A NICE... PERSON, THINGS GET INCREASINGLY BAD!! LAST TIME I TRIED, YOU PULLED KNIVES ON ME! I DIDN'T WANT TO TRY AGAIN FOR FEAR OF SOMETHING EVEN WORSE! HELL, I HAVEN'T EVEN LEFT THIS PLACE!
YOU KNOW WHAT'S WORSE THAN HIDING FROM WHAT SCARES YOU?! DO YOU? I'LL TELL YOU - ITS HAVING GOOD THINGS PASS YOU BY BECAUSE YOU'RE TOO BUSY CRINGING IN IDIOT TERROR, HIDING SOME PLACE WHERE ALL YOU CAN DO IS DWELL ON SHIT!!
AND NOW YOU THINK YOUR LITTLE APOLOGY IS GOING TO MAKE ME HAPPY AS A DROOLY LITTLE BABY?!! SHIT! I'M THE PERSON WHO'S GONNA MAKE ME HAPPY! I AM! NO MORE HIDING AWAY. IF YOU WANT TO KILL ME, JUST TRY IT!! I'LL LOSE MY BOOT DOWN YOUR THROAT!! HEY!! HELLO?!!!! HEY, JOHNNY POOH!
I DON'T HEAR YOU SAYING ANYTHING!! WHAT'S WRONG?!! NOT FULL OF FUCKED UP WISDOM TODAY?!! SPEAK!! SPEAK, YOU FUCK!!
CLICK
THAT COULD'VE GONE BETTER.
POOH
END

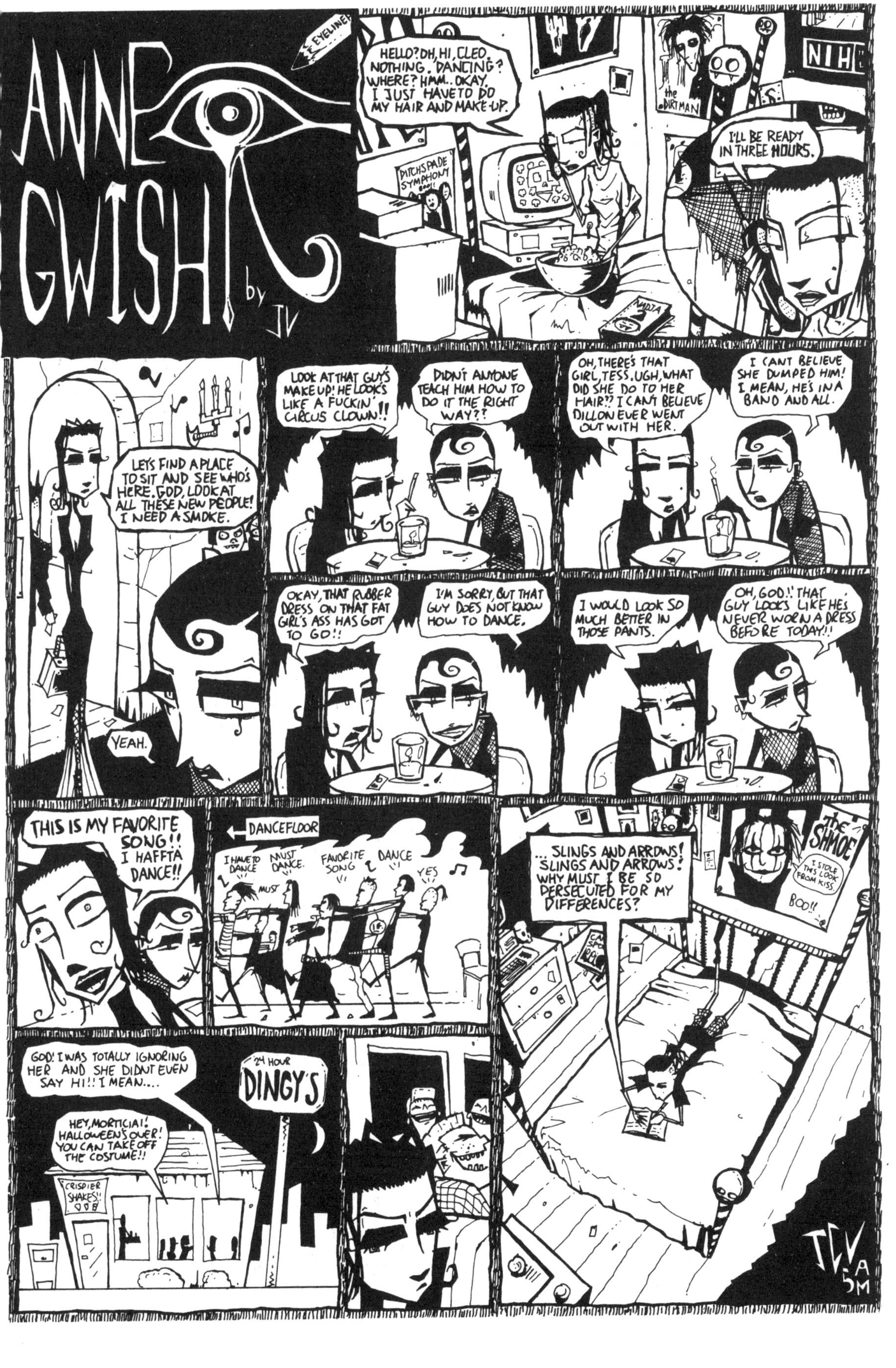
ANNE GWISH
by JV
EYELINER
HELLO? OH, HI, CLEO. NOTHING. DANCING? WHERE? HMM.. OKAY, I JUST HAVE TO DO MY HAIR AND MAKE-UP.
PITCHSPADE SYMPHONY
the DIRTMAN
NIH
I'LL BE READY IN THREE HOURS.
LET'S FIND A PLACE TO SIT AND SEE WHO'S HERE. GOD, LOOK AT ALL THESE NEW PEOPLE! I NEED A SMOKE.
YEAH.
LOOK AT THAT GUY'S MAKE UP! HE LOOKS LIKE A FUCKIN' CIRCUS CLOWN!!
DIDN'T ANYONE TEACH HIM HOW TO DO IT THE RIGHT WAY??
OH, THERE'S THAT GIRL, TESS. UGH, WHAT DID SHE DO TO HER HAIR?? I CAN'T BELIEVE DILLON EVER WENT OUT WITH HER.
I CANT BELIEVE SHE DUMPED HIM! I MEAN, HE'S IN A BAND AND ALL.
OKAY, THAT RUBBER DRESS ON THAT FAT GIRL'S ASS HAS GOT TO GO!!
I'M SORRY, BUT THAT GUY DOES NOT KNOW HOW TO DANCE.
I WOULD LOOK SO MUCH BETTER IN THOSE PANTS.
OH, GOD!! THAT GUY LOOKS LIKE HE'S NEVER WORN A DRESS BEFORE TODAY!!
THIS IS MY FAVORITE SONG!! I HAFFTA DANCE!!
DANCEFLOOR
I HAVE TO DANCE
MUST DANCE.
MUST
FAVORITE SONG
DANCE
YES
GOD! I WAS TOTALLY IGNORING HER AND SHE DIDNT EVEN SAY HI!! I MEAN...
24 HOUR DINGY'S
HEY, MORTICIA! HALLOWEEN'S OVER! YOU CAN TAKE OFF THE COSTUME!!
CRISPIER SHAKES!
... SLINGS AND ARROWS! SLINGS AND ARROWS! WHY MUST I BE SO PERSECUTED FOR MY DIFFERENCES?
THE SHMOE
I STOLE THIS LOOK FROM KISS.
BOO!!
JCV

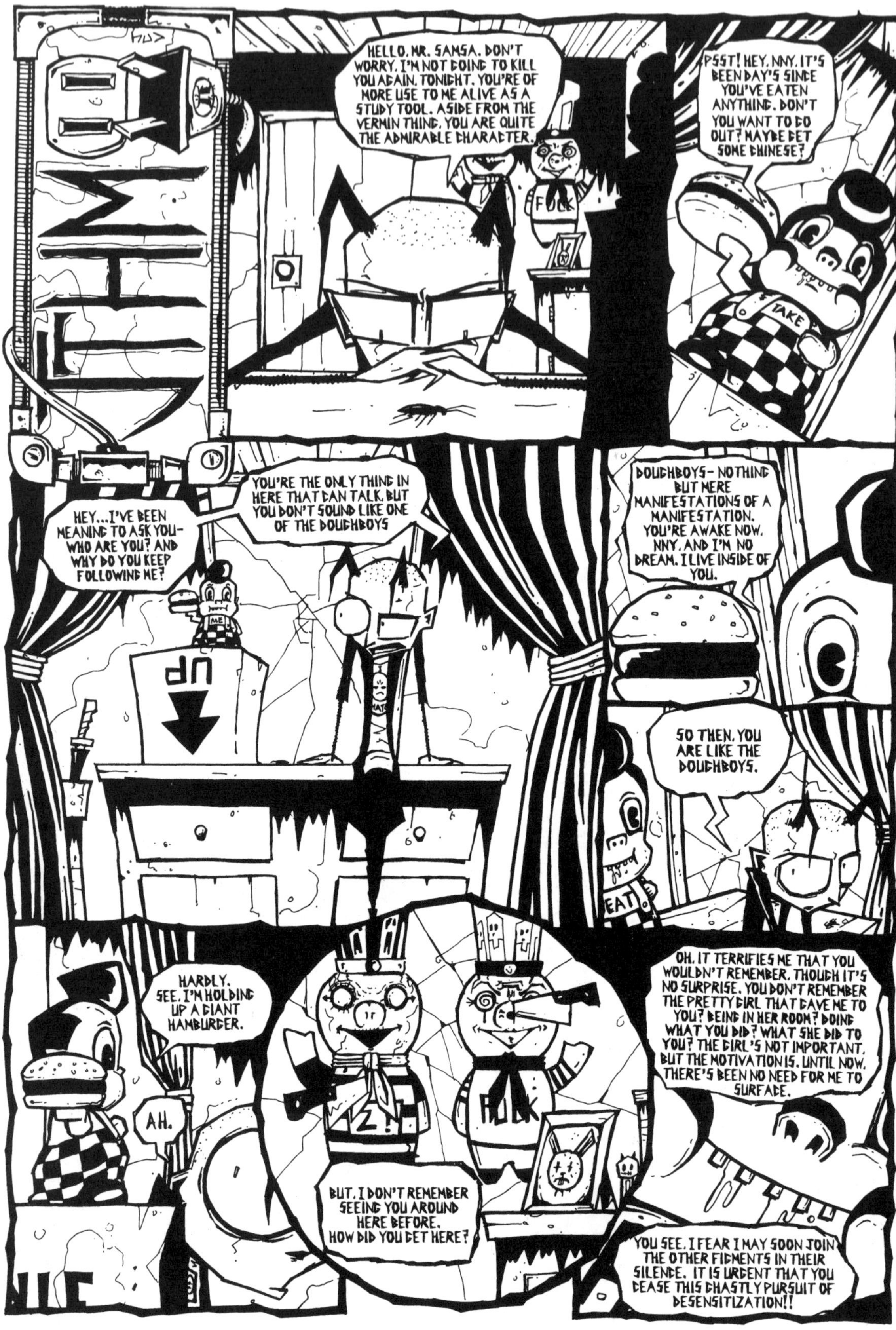

HELLO, MR. SAMSA. DON'T WORRY, I'M NOT GOING TO KILL YOU AGAIN, TONIGHT. YOU'RE OF MORE USE TO ME ALIVE AS A STUDY TOOL. ASIDE FROM THE VERMIN THING, YOU ARE QUITE THE ADMIRABLE CHARACTER.
PSST! HEY, NNY, IT'S BEEN DAY'S SINCE YOU'VE EATEN ANYTHING. DON'T YOU WANT TO GO OUT? MAYBE GET SOME CHINESE?
TAKE
HEY...I'VE BEEN MEANING TO ASK YOU- WHO ARE YOU? AND WHY DO YOU KEEP FOLLOWING ME?
YOU'RE THE ONLY THING IN HERE THAT CAN TALK, BUT YOU DON'T SOUND LIKE ONE OF THE DOUGHBOYS
DOUGHBOYS- NOTHING BUT MERE MANIFESTATIONS OF A MANIFESTATION. YOU'RE AWAKE NOW, NNY, AND I'M NO DREAM. I LIVE INSIDE OF YOU.
SO THEN, YOU ARE LIKE THE DOUGHBOYS.
EAT
HARDLY. SEE, I'M HOLDING UP A GIANT HAMBURGER.
AH.
BUT, I DON'T REMEMBER SEEING YOU AROUND HERE BEFORE. HOW DID YOU GET HERE?
OH, IT TERRIFIES ME THAT YOU WOULDN'T REMEMBER, THOUGH IT'S NO SURPRISE. YOU DON'T REMEMBER THE PRETTY GIRL THAT GAVE ME TO YOU? BEING IN HER ROOM? DOING WHAT YOU DID? WHAT SHE DID TO YOU? THE GIRL'S NOT IMPORTANT, BUT THE MOTIVATION IS. UNTIL NOW, THERE'S BEEN NO NEED FOR ME TO SURFACE.
YOU SEE, I FEAR I MAY SOON JOIN THE OTHER FIGMENTS IN THEIR SILENCE. IT IS URGENT THAT YOU CEASE THIS GHASTLY PURSUIT OF DESENSITIZATION!!

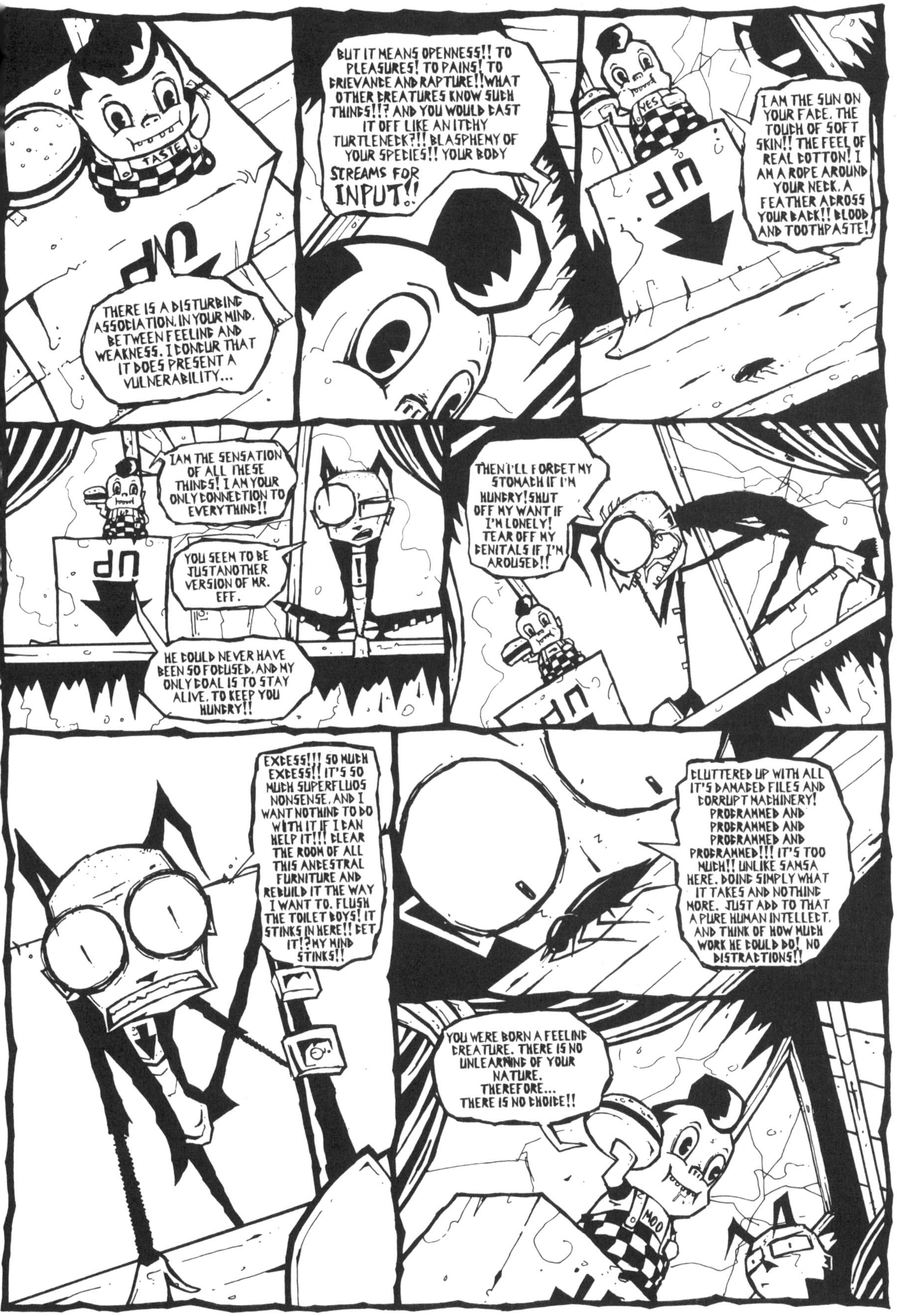
THERE IS A DISTURBING ASSOCIATION IN YOUR MIND, BETWEEN FEELING AND WEAKNESS. I CONCUR THAT IT DOES PRESENT A VULNERABILITY...
BUT IT MEANS OPENNESS!! TO PLEASURES! TO PAINS! TO GRIEVANCE AND RAPTURE!! WHAT OTHER CREATURES KNOW SUCH THINGS!!? AND YOU WOULD CAST IT OFF LIKE AN ITCHY TURTLENECK?!! BLASPHEMY OF YOUR SPECIES!! YOUR BODY STREAMS FOR INPUT!!
I AM THE SUN ON YOUR FACE. THE TOUCH OF SOFT SKIN!! THE FEEL OF REAL COTTON! I AM A ROPE AROUND YOUR NECK. A FEATHER ACROSS YOUR BACK!! BLOOD AND TOOTHPASTE!
I AM THE SENSATION OF ALL THESE THINGS! I AM YOUR ONLY CONNECTION TO EVERYTHING!!
YOU SEEM TO BE JUST ANOTHER VERSION OF MR. EFF.
HE COULD NEVER HAVE BEEN SO FOCUSED, AND MY ONLY GOAL IS TO STAY ALIVE, TO KEEP YOU HUNGRY!!
THEN I'LL FORGET MY STOMACH IF I'M HUNGRY! SHUT OFF MY WANT IF I'M LONELY! TEAR OFF MY GENITALS IF I'M AROUSED!!
EXCESS!!! SO MUCH EXCESS!! IT'S SO MUCH SUPERFLUOS NONSENSE, AND I WANT NOTHING TO DO WITH IT IF I CAN HELP IT!!! CLEAR THE ROOM OF ALL THIS ANCESTRAL FURNITURE AND REBUILD IT THE WAY I WANT TO. FLUSH THE TOILET BOYS! IT STINKS IN HERE!! GET IT!? MY MIND STINKS!!
CLUTTERED UP WITH ALL IT'S DAMAGED FILES AND CORRUPT MACHINERY! PROGRAMMED AND PROGRAMMED AND PROGRAMMED AND PROGRAMMED!!! IT'S TOO MUCH!! UNLIKE SAMSA HERE, DOING SIMPLY WHAT IT TAKES AND NOTHING MORE. JUST ADD TO THAT A PURE HUMAN INTELLECT, AND THINK OF HOW MUCH WORK HE COULD DO! NO DISTRACTIONS!!
YOU WERE BORN A FEELING CREATURE. THERE IS NO UNLEARNING OF YOUR NATURE. THEREFORE... THERE IS NO CHOICE!!

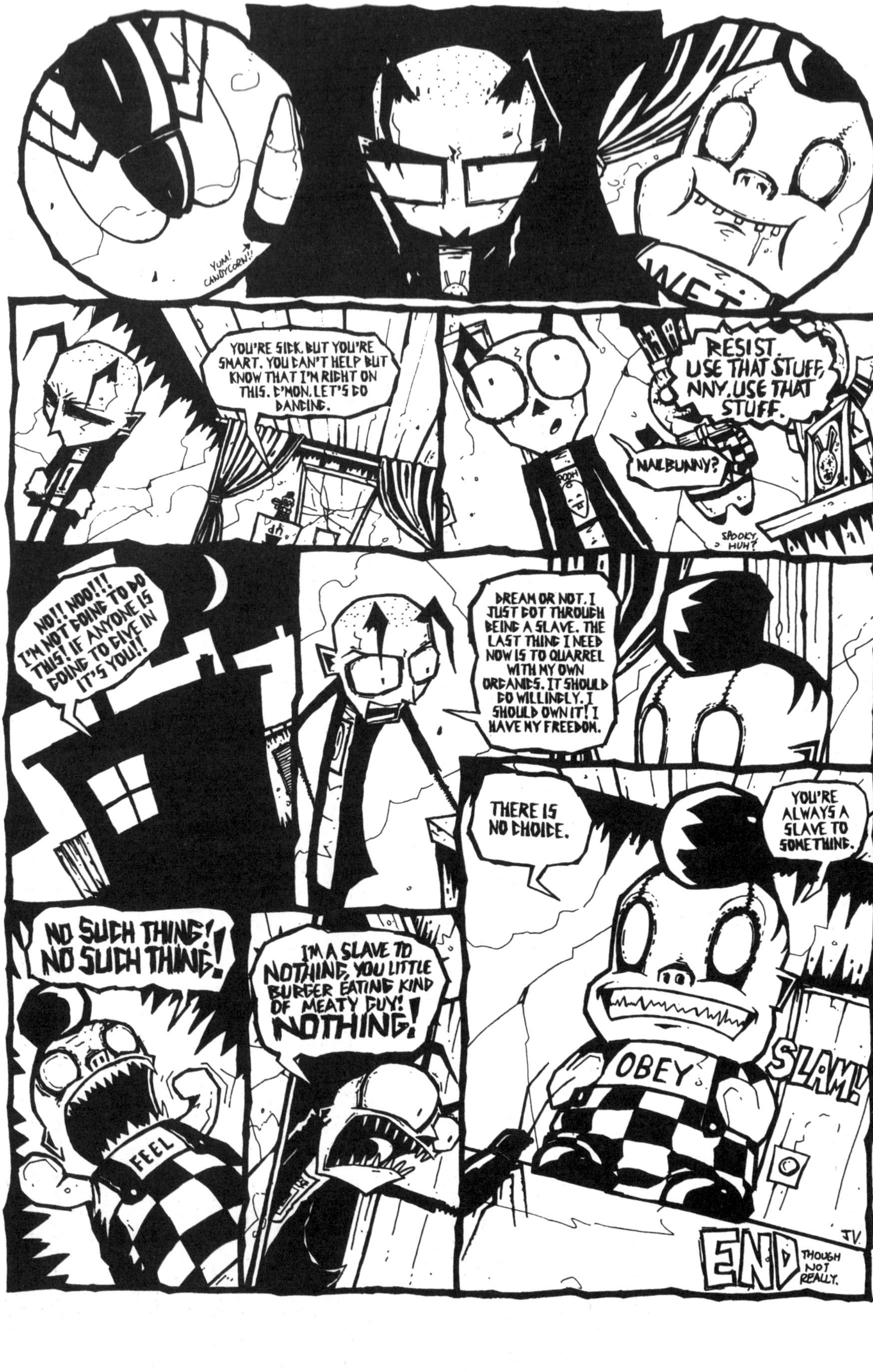
YUM! CANDYCORN!!
WET
YOU'RE SICK, BUT YOU'RE SMART. YOU CAN'T HELP BUT KNOW THAT I'M RIGHT ON THIS. C'MON, LET'S GO DANCING.
RESIST. USE THAT STUFF, NNY. USE THAT STUFF.
NAILBUNNY?
SPOOKY, HUH?
NO!! NOO!!! I'M NOT GOING TO DO THIS! IF ANYONE IS GOING TO GIVE IN IT'S YOU!!
DREAM OR NOT, I JUST GOT THROUGH BEING A SLAVE. THE LAST THING I NEED NOW IS TO QUARREL WITH MY OWN ORGANICS. IT SHOULD GO WILLINGLY. I SHOULD OWN IT! I HAVE MY FREEDOM.
THERE IS NO CHOICE.
YOU'RE ALWAYS A SLAVE TO SOMETHING.
NO SUCH THING! NO SUCH THING!
I'M A SLAVE TO NOTHING, YOU LITTLE BURGER EATING KIND OF MEATY GUY! NOTHING!
FEEL
OBEY
SLAM!
J.V.
END THOUGH NOT REALLY.

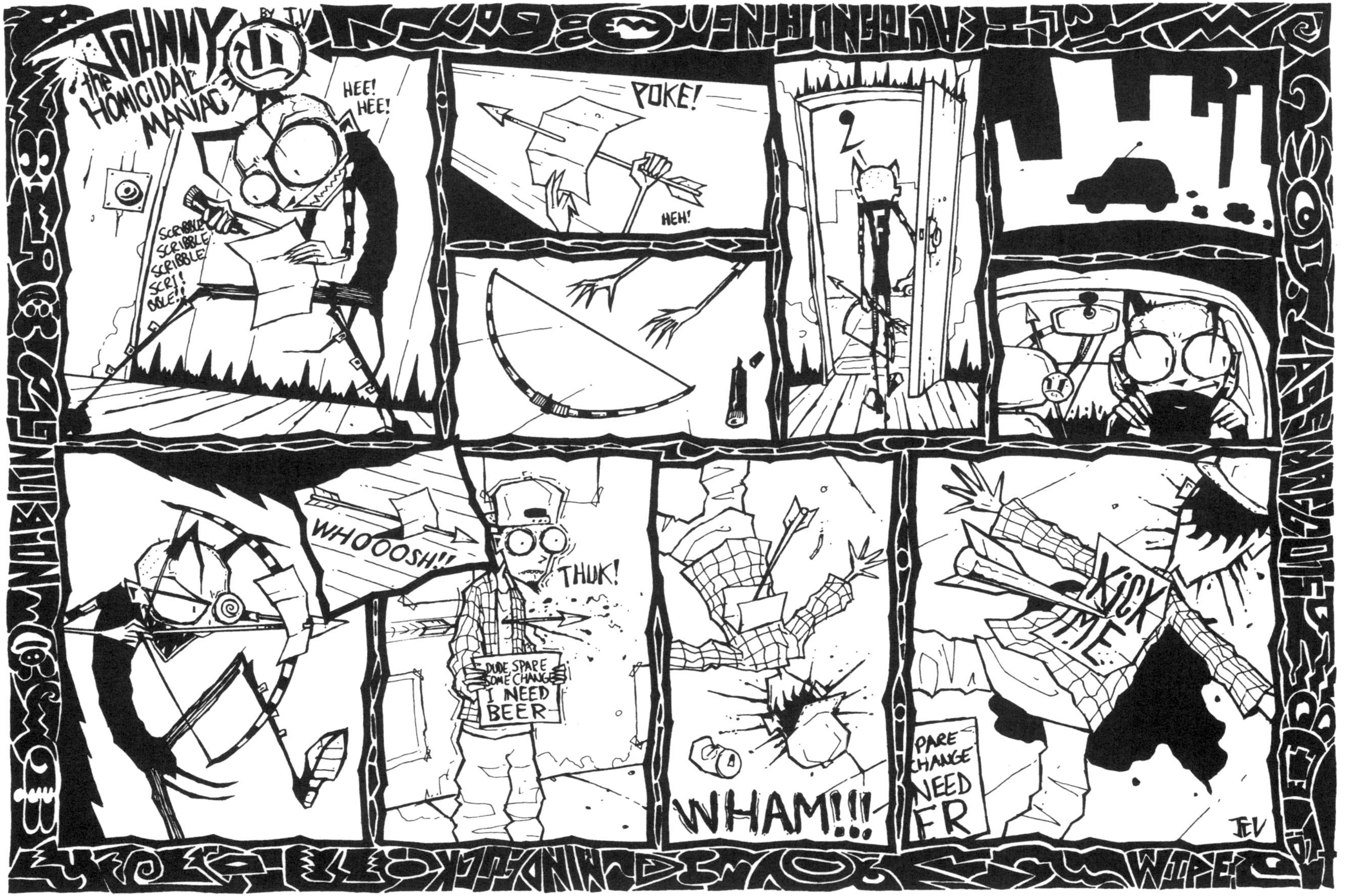
JOHNNY
BY J.V.
the HOMICIDAL MANIAC
HEE! HEE!
SCRIBBLE SCRIBBLE SCRIBBLE SCRI! BBLE!!
POKE!
HEH!
WHOOOOSH!!
THUK!
DUDE SPARE SOME CHANGE I NEED BEER
WHAM!!!
KICK ME
PARE CHANGE NEED FR
JCV

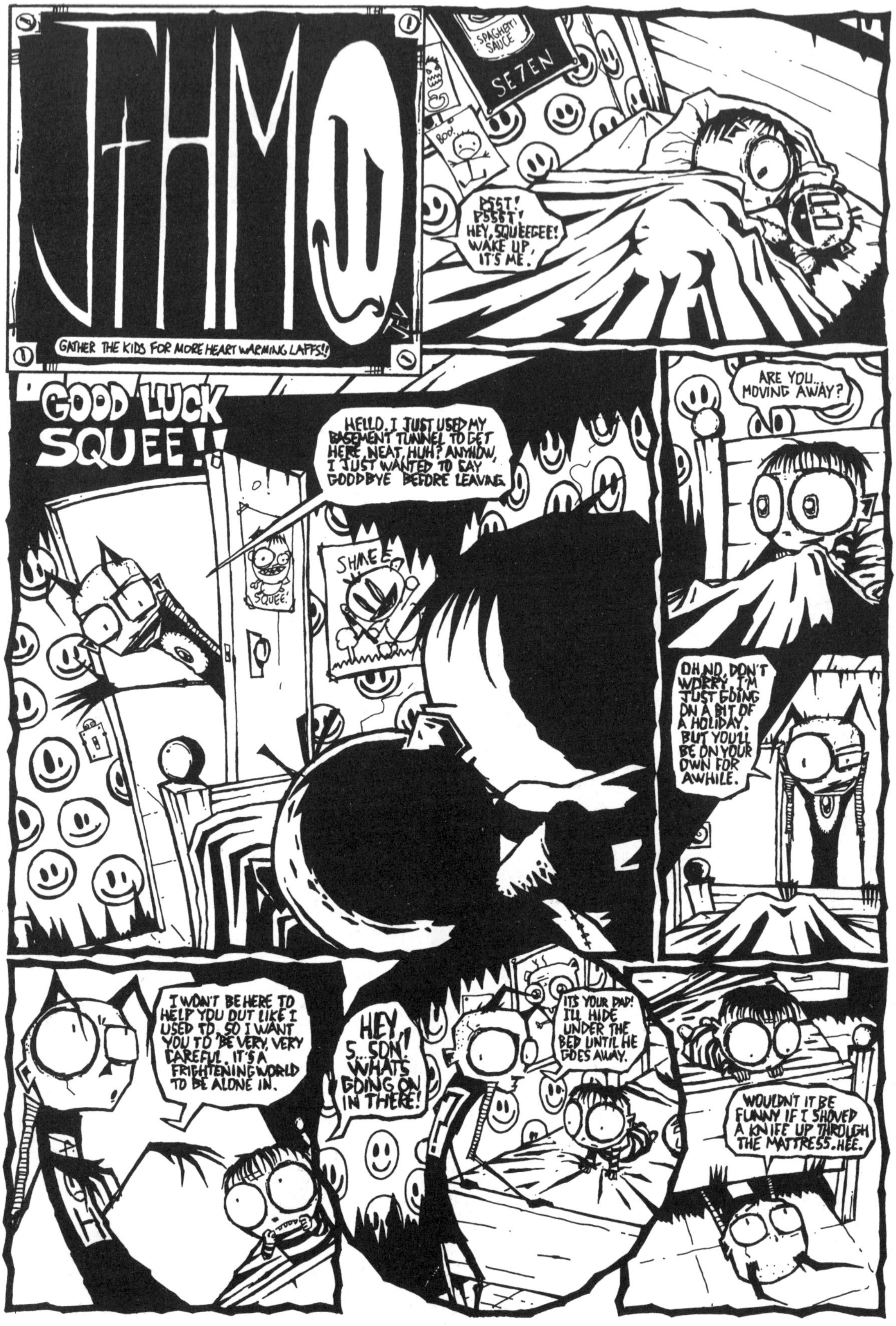
JTHM
GATHER THE KIDS FOR MORE HEART WARMING LAFFS!!
SPAGHETTI SAUCE
SE7EN
BOO!
PSST! PSSST! HEY, SQUEEGEE! WAKE UP, IT'S ME.
"GOOD LUCK SQUEE!!"
HELLO. I JUST USED MY BASEMENT TUNNEL TO GET HERE. NEAT, HUH? ANYHOW, I JUST WANTED TO SAY GOODBYE BEFORE LEAVING.
SQUEE!
SHMEE
ARE YOU... MOVING AWAY?
OH NO, DON'T WORRY. I'M JUST GOING ON A BIT OF A HOLIDAY. BUT YOU'LL BE ON YOUR OWN FOR AWHILE.
I WON'T BE HERE TO HELP YOU OUT LIKE I USED TO, SO I WANT YOU TO BE VERY, VERY CAREFUL. IT'S A FRIGHTENING WORLD TO BE ALONE IN.
HEY, S...SON! WHAT'S GOING ON IN THERE!
IT'S YOUR DAD! I'LL HIDE UNDER THE BED UNTIL HE GOES AWAY.
WOULDN'T IT BE FUNNY IF I SHOVED A KNIFE UP THROUGH THE MATTRESS. HEE.

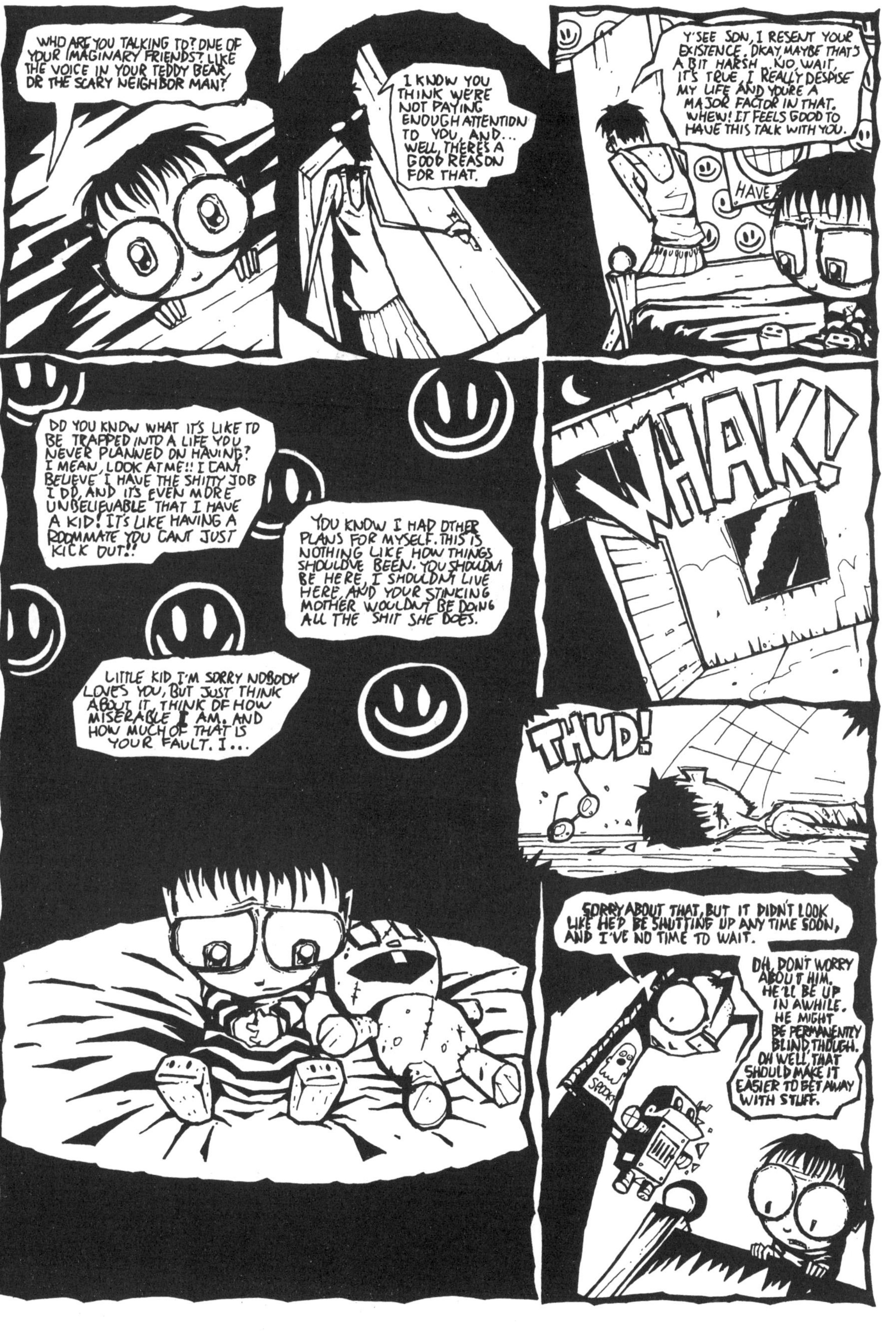
WHO ARE YOU TALKING TO? ONE OF YOUR IMAGINARY FRIENDS? LIKE THE VOICE IN YOUR TEDDY BEAR, OR THE SCARY NEIGHBOR MAN?
I KNOW YOU THINK WE'RE NOT PAYING ENOUGH ATTENTION TO YOU, AND... WELL, THERE'S A GOOD REASON FOR THAT.
Y'SEE SON, I RESENT YOUR EXISTENCE. OKAY, MAYBE THAT'S A BIT HARSH. NO, WAIT, IT'S TRUE, I REALLY DESPISE MY LIFE AND YOU'RE A MAJOR FACTOR IN THAT. WHEW! IT FEELS GOOD TO HAVE THIS TALK WITH YOU.
HAVE
DO YOU KNOW WHAT IT'S LIKE TO BE TRAPPED INTO A LIFE YOU NEVER PLANNED ON HAVING? I MEAN, LOOK AT ME!! I CAN'T BELIEVE I HAVE THE SHITTY JOB I DO, AND IT'S EVEN MORE UNBELIEVABLE THAT I HAVE A KID! IT'S LIKE HAVING A ROOMMATE YOU CAN'T JUST KICK OUT!!
YOU KNOW I HAD OTHER PLANS FOR MYSELF. THIS IS NOTHING LIKE HOW THINGS SHOULD'VE BEEN. YOU SHOULDN'T BE HERE, I SHOULDN'T LIVE HERE, AND YOUR STINKING MOTHER WOULDN'T BE DOING ALL THE SHIT SHE DOES.
LITTLE KID I'M SORRY NOBODY LOVES YOU, BUT JUST THINK ABOUT IT. THINK OF HOW MISERABLE I AM. AND HOW MUCH OF THAT IS YOUR FAULT. I...
WHAK!
THUD!
SORRY ABOUT THAT, BUT IT DIDN'T LOOK LIKE HE'D BE SHUTTING UP ANY TIME SOON, AND I'VE NO TIME TO WAIT.
OH, DON'T WORRY ABOUT HIM. HE'LL BE UP IN AWHILE. HE MIGHT BE PERMANENTLY BLIND, THOUGH. OH WELL, THAT SHOULD MAKE IT EASIER TO GET AWAY WITH STUFF.
SPOOK

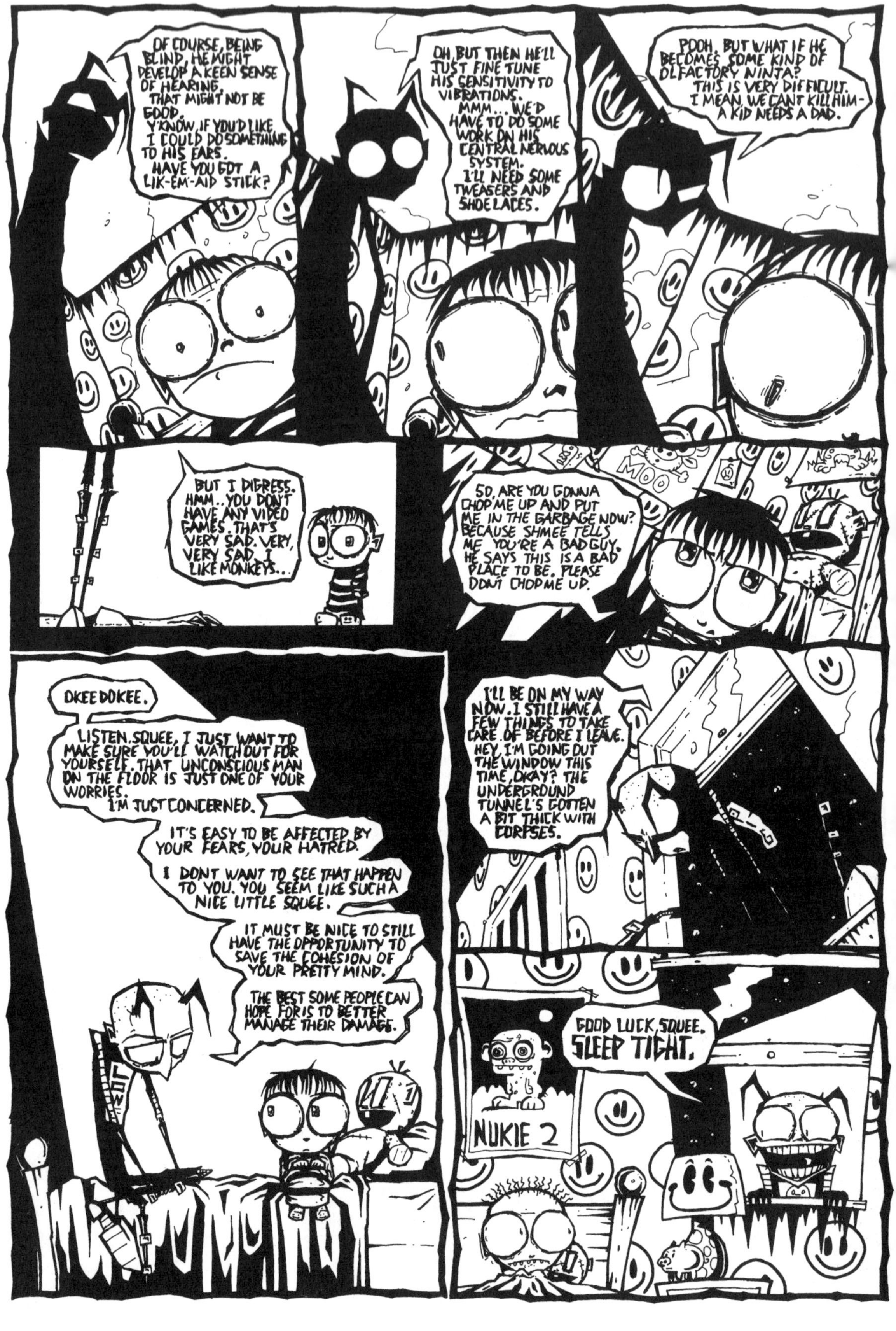
OF COURSE, BEING BLIND, HE MIGHT DEVELOP A KEEN SENSE OF HEARING. THAT MIGHT NOT BE GOOD. Y'KNOW, IF YOU'D LIKE I COULD DO SOMETHING TO HIS EARS. HAVE YOU GOT A LIK-EM-AID STICK?
OH, BUT THEN HE'LL JUST FINE TUNE HIS SENSITIVITY TO VIBRATIONS. MMM... WE'D HAVE TO DO SOME WORK ON HIS CENTRAL NERVOUS SYSTEM. I'LL NEED SOME TWEASERS AND SHOELACES.
POOH, BUT WHAT IF HE BECOMES SOME KIND OF OLFACTORY NINJA? THIS IS VERY DIFFICULT. I MEAN, WE CANT KILL HIM- A KID NEEDS A DAD.
BUT I DIGRESS. HMM.. YOU DON'T HAVE ANY VIDEO GAMES. THAT'S VERY SAD. VERY, VERY SAD. I LIKE MONKEYS...
MOO
SO, ARE YOU GONNA CHOP ME UP AND PUT ME IN THE GARBAGE NOW? BECAUSE SHMEE TELLS ME YOU'RE A BAD GUY. HE SAYS THIS IS A BAD PLACE TO BE. PLEASE DON'T CHOP ME UP.
OKEEDOKEE.
LISTEN, SQUEE, I JUST WANT TO MAKE SURE YOU'LL WATCH OUT FOR YOURSELF. THAT UNCONSCIOUS MAN ON THE FLOOR IS JUST ONE OF YOUR WORRIES. I'M JUST CONCERNED.
IT'S EASY TO BE AFFECTED BY YOUR FEARS, YOUR HATRED.
I DONT WANT TO SEE THAT HAPPEN TO YOU. YOU SEEM LIKE SUCH A NICE LITTLE SQUEE.
IT MUST BE NICE TO STILL HAVE THE OPPORTUNITY TO SAVE THE COHESION OF YOUR PRETTY MIND.
THE BEST SOME PEOPLE CAN HOPE FOR IS TO BETTER MANAGE THEIR DAMAGE.
I'LL BE ON MY WAY NOW. I STILL HAVE A FEW THINGS TO TAKE CARE OF BEFORE I LEAVE. HEY, I'M GOING OUT THE WINDOW THIS TIME, OKAY? THE UNDERGROUND TUNNEL'S GOTTEN A BIT THICK WITH CORPSES.
NUKIE 2
GOOD LUCK, SQUEE. SLEEP TIGHT.

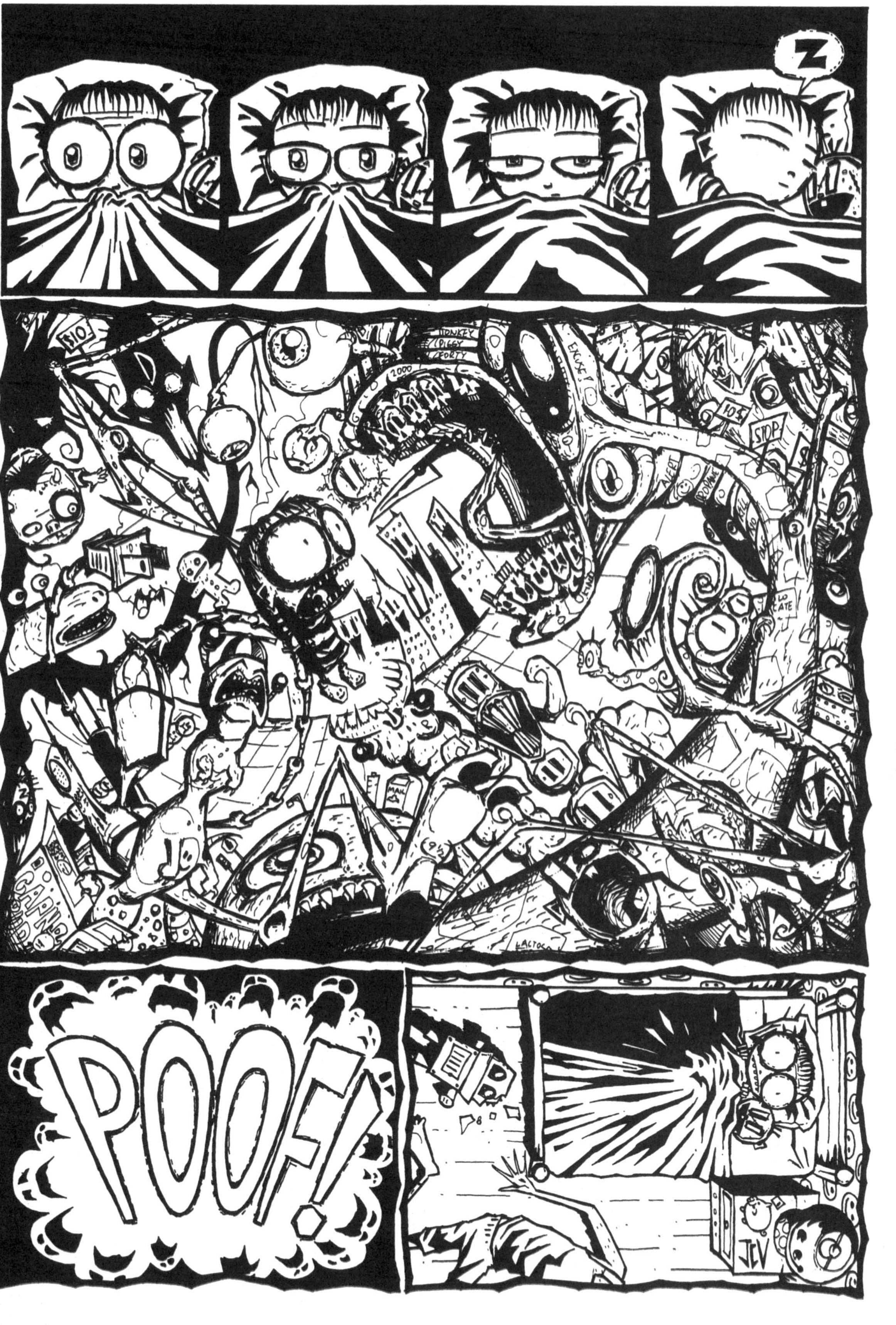
Z
DONKEY
PIGGY
FORTY
STOP
POOF!
JCV

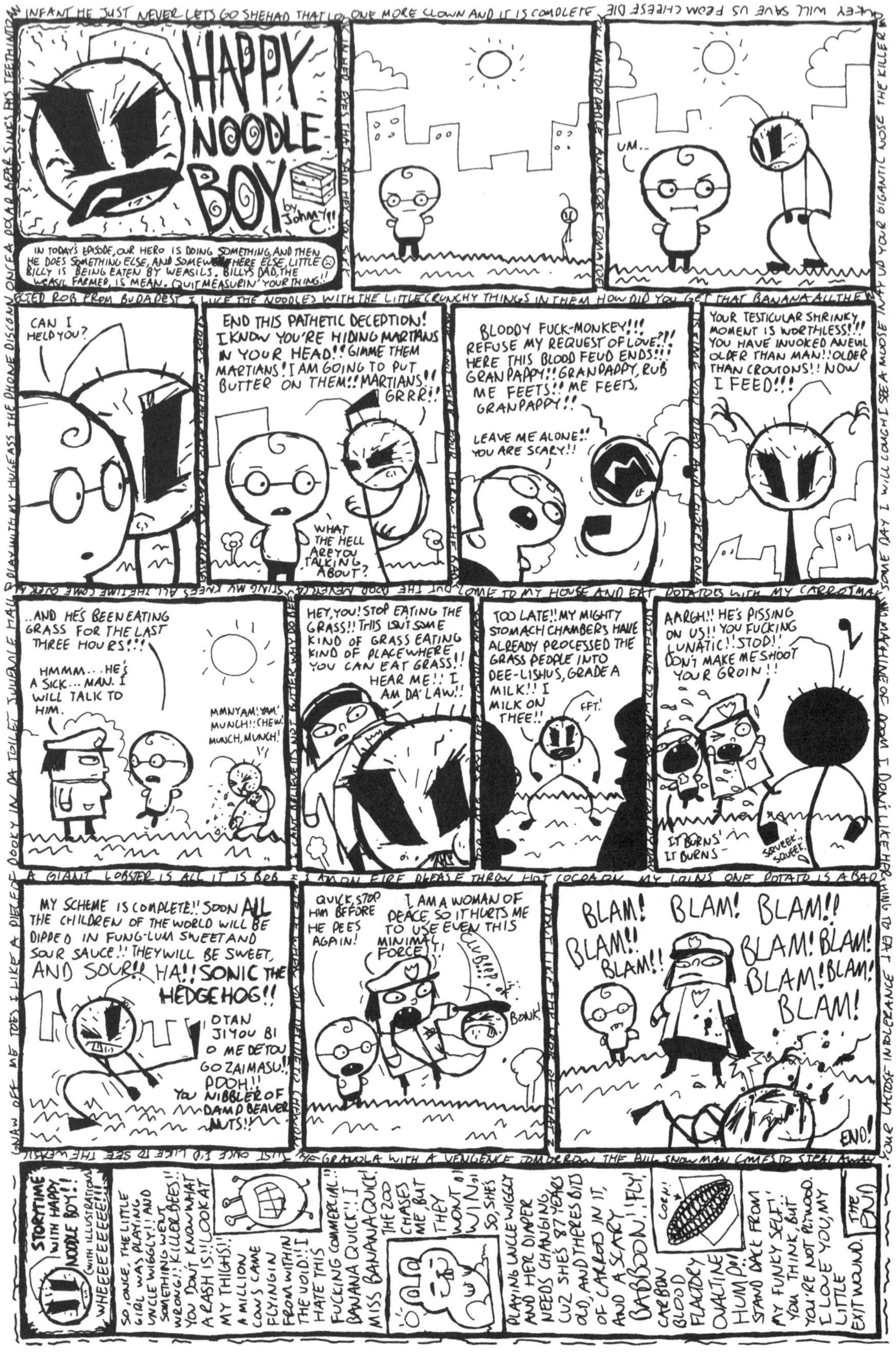

HAPPY NOODLE BOY
by Johnny C!!
IN TODAY'S EPISODE, OUR HERO IS DOING SOMETHING, AND THEN HE DOES SOMETHING ELSE, AND SOMEWHERE ELSE, LITTLE BILLY IS BEING EATEN BY WEASILS. BILLY'S DAD, THE WEASIL FARMER, IS MEAN. QUIT MEASURIN' YOUR THING!!
UM...
CAN I HELP YOU?
END THIS PATHETIC DECEPTION! I KNOW YOU'RE HIDING MARTIANS IN YOUR HEAD!! GIMME THEM MARTIANS! I AM GOING TO PUT BUTTER ON THEM!! MARTIANS!!
GRRR!!
WHAT THE HELL ARE YOU TALKING ABOUT?
BLOODY FUCK-MONKEY!!! REFUSE MY REQUEST OF LOVE?!! HERE THIS BLOOD FEUD ENDS!!! GRANPAPPY!! GRANDPAPPY, RUB ME FEETS!! ME FEETS, GRANPAPPY!!
LEAVE ME ALONE!! YOU ARE SCARY!!
YOUR TESTICULAR SHRINKY MOMENT IS WORTHLESS!!! YOU HAVE INVOKED AN EVIL OLDER THAN MAN!! OLDER THAN CROUTONS!! NOW I FEED!!!
...AND HE'S BEEN EATING GRASS FOR THE LAST THREE HOURS!!!
HMMM... HE'S A SICK... MAN. I WILL TALK TO HIM.
MMNYAM! YAM! MUNCH!! CHEW! MUNCH, MUNCH!
HEY, YOU! STOP EATING THE GRASS!! THIS ISN'T SOME KIND OF GRASS EATING KIND OF PLACE WHERE YOU CAN EAT GRASS!! HEAR ME!! I AM DA' LAW!!
TOO LATE!! MY MIGHTY STOMACH CHAMBERS HAVE ALREADY PROCESSED THE GRASS PEOPLE INTO DEE-LISHUS, GRADE A MILK!! I MILK ON THEE!!
FFT!
AARGH!! HE'S PISSING ON US!! YOU FUCKING LUNATIC!! STOP!! DON'T MAKE ME SHOOT YOUR GROIN!!
IT BURNS! IT BURNS
SQUEEK! SQUEEK!
MY SCHEME IS COMPLETE!! SOON ALL THE CHILDREN OF THE WORLD WILL BE DIPPED IN FUNG-LUM SWEET AND SOUR SAUCE!! THEY WILL BE SWEET, AND SOUR!! HA!! SONIC THE HEDGEHOG!!
OTAN JIYOU BI O ME DETOU GO ZAIMASU!! POOH!! YOU NIBBLER OF DAMP BEAVER NUTS!!
QUICK, STOP HIM BEFORE HE PEES AGAIN!
I AM A WOMAN OF PEACE, SO IT HURTS ME TO USE EVEN THIS MINIMAL FORCE!!
BONK!
BLAM! BLAM! BLAM!! BLAM!! BLAM!! BLAM! BLAM! BLAM! BLAM! BLAM!
END!
STORYTIME WITH HAPPY NOODLE BOY!! (WITH ILLUSTRATIONS) WHEEEEEEEEE!!!
SO, ONCE, THE LITTLE GIRL WAS PLAYING UNCLE WIGGLY, AND SOMETHING WENT WRONG!! KILLER BEES!! YOU DON'T KNOW WHAT A RASH IS!! LOOK AT MY THIGHS!!
A MILLION COWS CAME FLYING IN FROM WITHIN THE VOID!! I HATE THIS FUCKING COMMERCIAL!! BANANA QUICK!! I MISS BANANA QUICK!
THE ZOO CHASES ME, BUT THEY WON'T WIN!! SO, SHE'S PLAYING UNCLE WIGGLY AND HER DIAPER NEEDS CHANGING, CUZ SHE'S 87 YEARS OLD, AND THERE'S BITS OF CARROTS IN IT, AND A SCARY BABBOON!! FLY!
CORN!
CARBON BLOOD FLACTORY QUACTINE HUMP!! STAND BACK FROM MY FUNKY SELF! YOU THINK, BUT YOU'RE NOT PLYWOOD. I LOVE YOU, MY LITTLE EXIT WOUND.
THE END

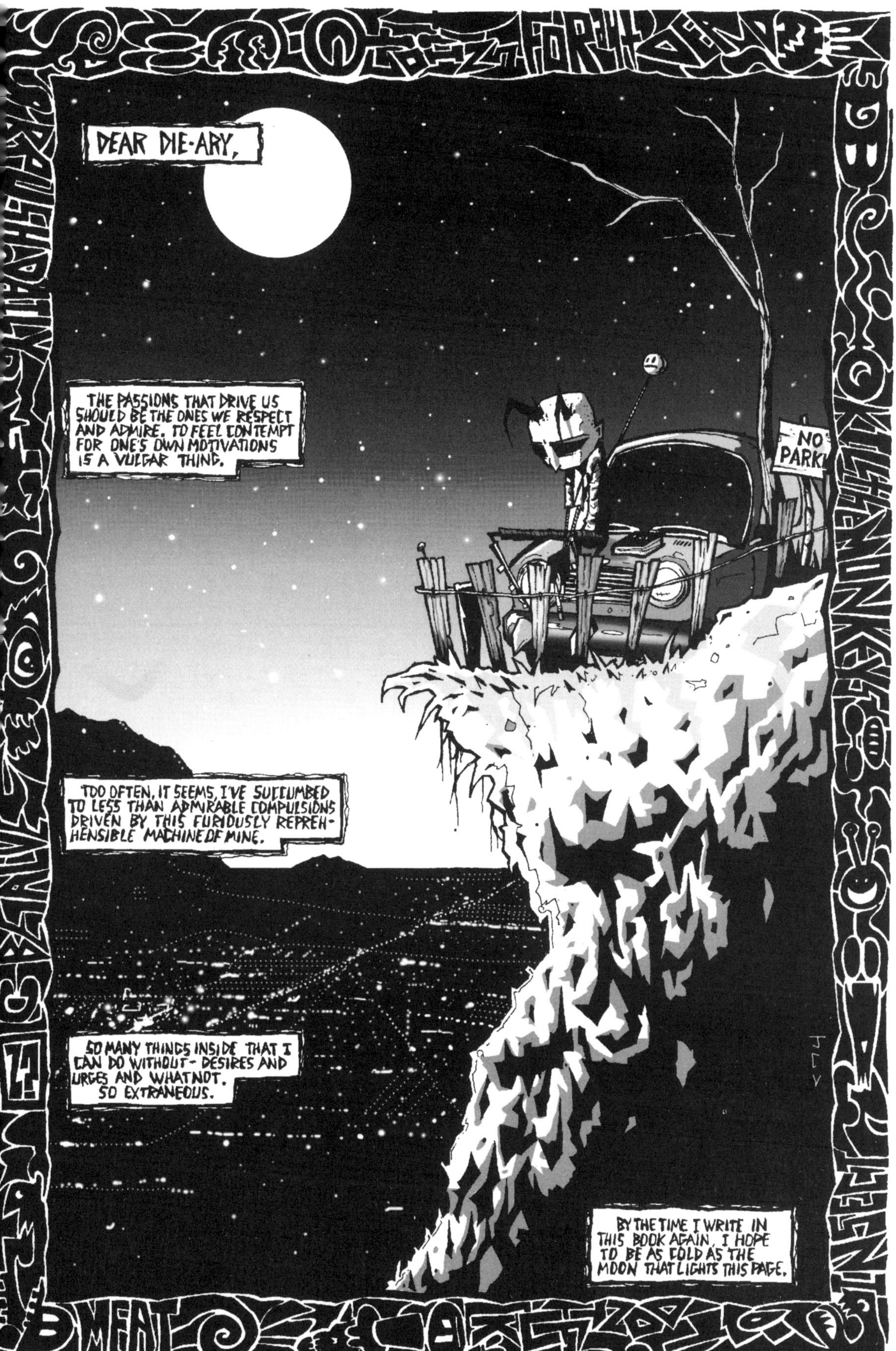
DEAR DIE-ARY,
THE PASSIONS THAT DRIVE US SHOULD BE THE ONES WE RESPECT AND ADMIRE. TO FEEL CONTEMPT FOR ONE'S OWN MOTIVATIONS IS A VULGAR THING.
NO PARK
TOO OFTEN, IT SEEMS, I'VE SUCCUMBED TO LESS THAN ADMIRABLE COMPULSIONS DRIVEN BY THIS FURIOUSLY REPREHENSIBLE MACHINE OF MINE.
SO MANY THINGS INSIDE THAT I CAN DO WITHOUT- DESIRES AND URGES AND WHATNOT. SO EXTRANEOUS.
BY THE TIME I WRITE IN THIS BOOK AGAIN, I HOPE TO BE AS COLD AS THE MOON THAT LIGHTS THIS PAGE.

SKETCHES!! This page has the earliest sketches done for the JTHM series. You can see some ideas for the first and second cover paintings. You can also see that I knew NNY would be the DEAD homicidal maniac at some point. I just didn't know when. I do not like onions.

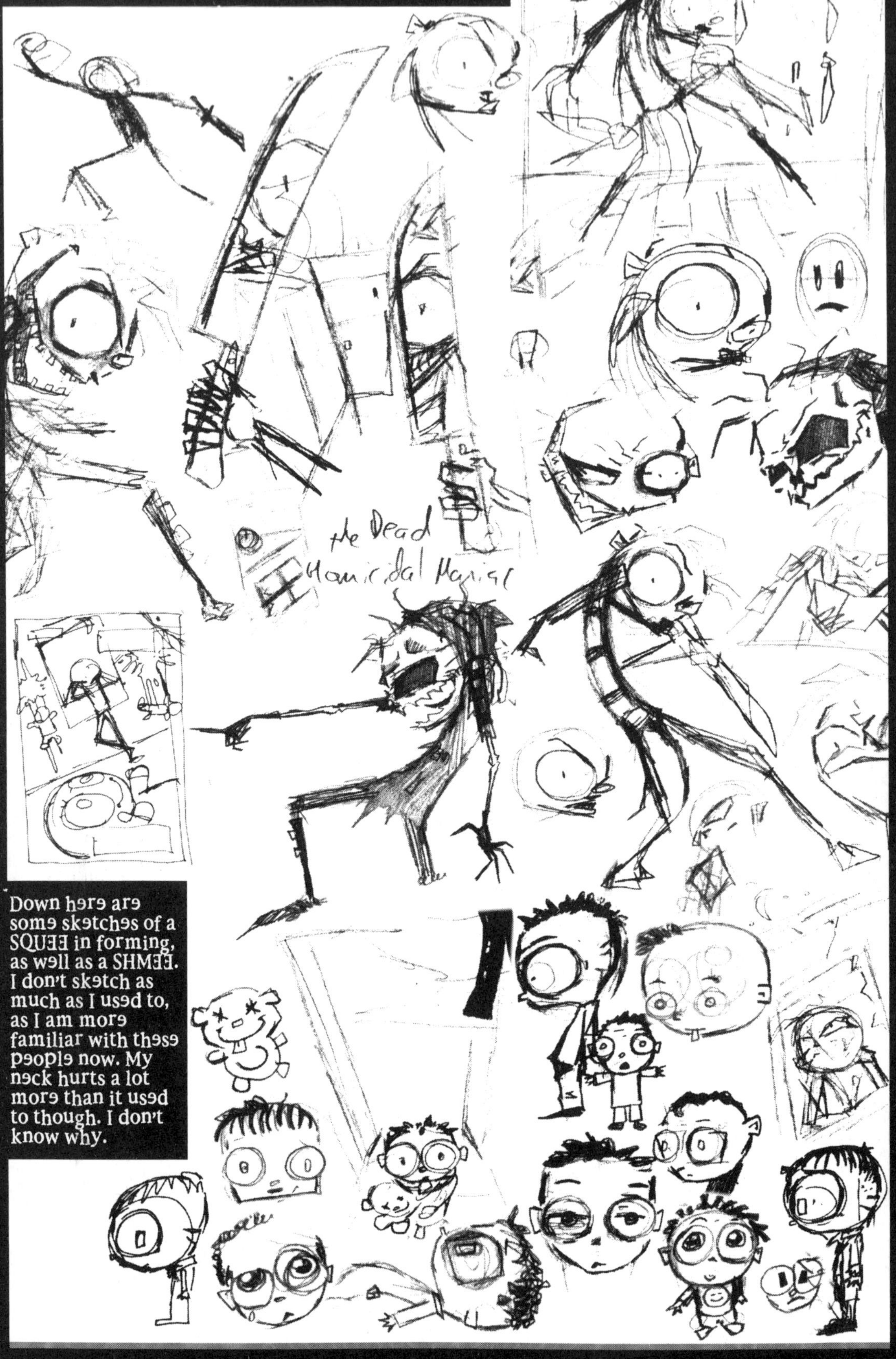
the Dead
Homicidal Maniac

Down here are some sketches of a SQUEE in forming, as well as a SHMEE. I don't sketch as much as I used to, as I am more familiar with these people now. My neck hurts a lot more than it used to though. I don't know why.

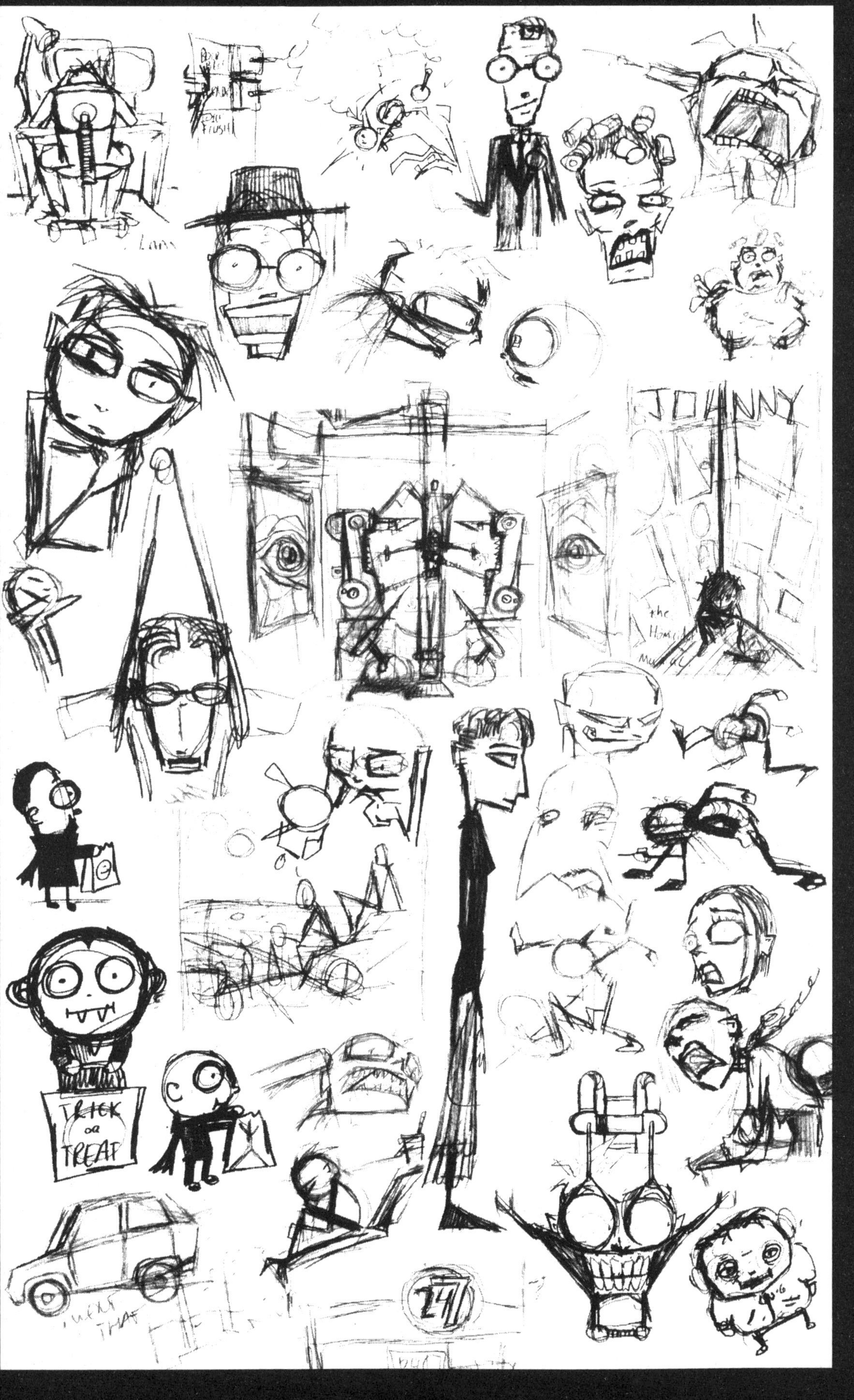
JOHNNY
TRICK or TREAT
24

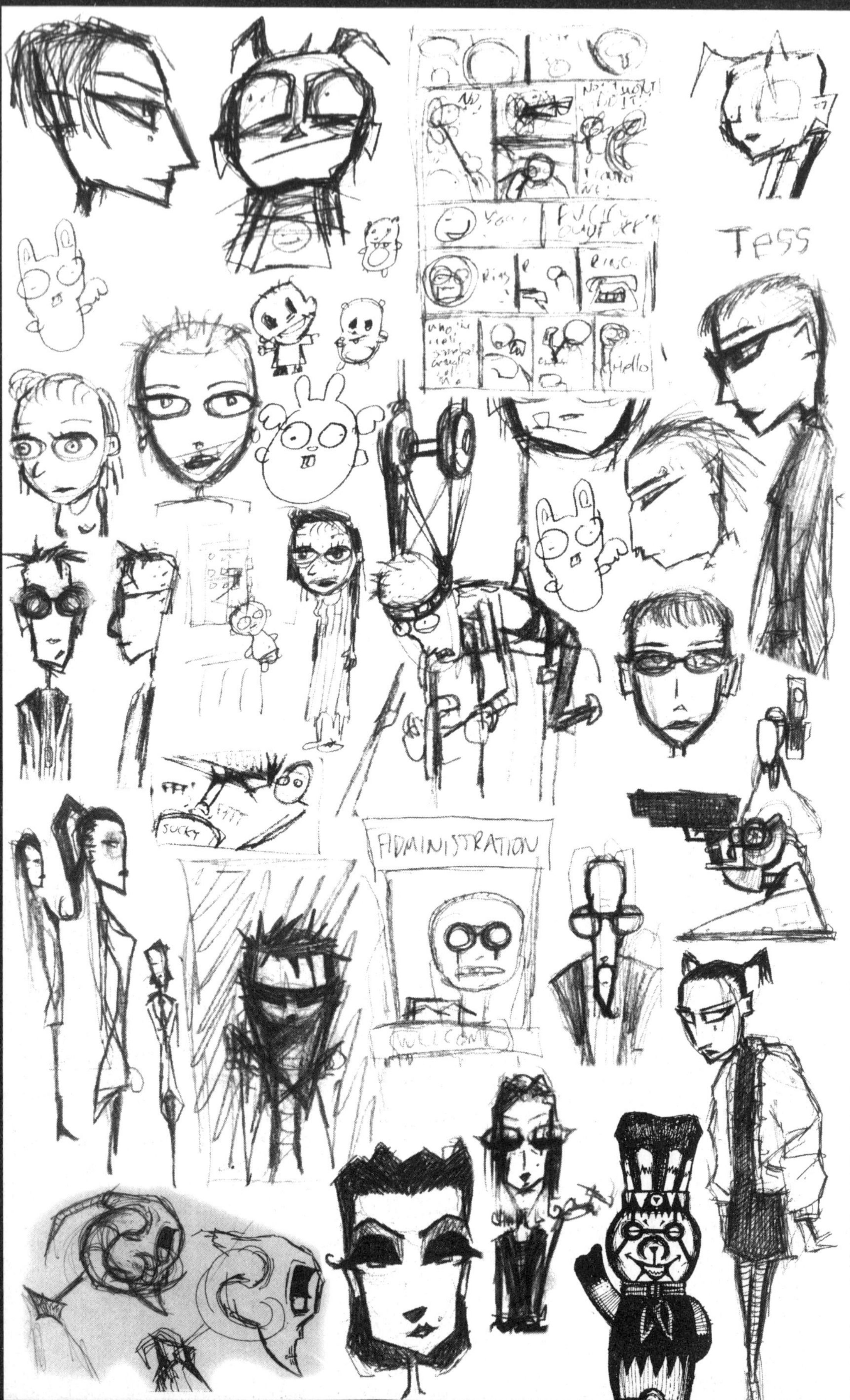
Tess
Hello
SUCKY
ADMINISTRATION

JOHNNY C.
A.K.A: NNY

height: 5'9"
Weight: 115 lbs
(more with change in pockets)

LIKES: stars, the emotionless function of insects, watching people getting abducted by aliens, Cherry FizWiz, Cherry Brain-Freezies, all kinds of movies, the moon, little chubby babies, Pop Rocks and Soda, drawing Happy Noodle Boy.

DISLIKES: humidity, sleep, the physical and mental need for ANYTHING, being abducted by aliens, people who've "GOTTA HAVE A SMOKE!", certain words, losing his mind, Satan's attitude, getting shot in the head, drawing Happy Noodle Boy.

BACKGROUND INFO: not much is known about Johnny's history. All we do know is that his parents were killed by an evil man, thus setting the course for NNY's life as a masked crime fighter. Or, perhaps not. At present, NNY is more his own enemy than any external mind could be, what with the decomposure of what may have been, at one time, a fine, intelligent mind. Johnny is, possibly, more hideously mentally malformed than the people he seems to think have ruined his world. He's not a loser, he's simply lost.

NAILBUNNY
A.K.A: spooky floating bunny head.

height: 6 inches
(with body)
weight: 6 OZ.
(including nail)

LIKES: floating around, when Johnny wasn't a gibbering lunatic, nature shows on the Discovery channel, scenes in Disney movies where people die.

DISLIKES: being the lone voice of reason in NNY's head, the doughboys, hammers, when spiders nest inside of him, screams of the innocent.

BACKGROUND INFO: Nailbunny was a happy little bunny, born in a little cage in a pet store one night. He was very warm and nuzzly with his big, soft mommy rabbit. The giant people in the store were nice to him too. One day, a funny looking giant who looked like he didn't eat enough came in and made a smily face at the bunny. Soon, the little bunny was snatched away from his sleeping mother, and whisked off into the amazing giant world. At first it was scary, but soon bunny overcame the fear and thought of what a wonderful world it was. Just then, the giant pinned him to a wall and slammed a nail through his guts.   the end.

MR. FUCK
A.K.A: Mr.Eff

height: 2'3"
weight: 9 OZ.

(made of styrofoam)

LIKES: John Wu movies, absolute and total insane violence, smiles that make people nervous, the sound of hearts beating, when Johnny let's him drive, seeing vital things from inside a person come out, the paint job NNY did on him, fast electronic music

DISLIKES: Psychodoughboy, depression, the sound of people sleeping, nugat, caring much about anything for more than 30 seconds, people in bad moods, when the popcorn gets burned.

BACKGROUND INFO: Originally part of a display stand for some yummy pastries, Mr. Eff became host to one of Johnny's internal voices. As Nailbunny was the only thing resembling an angel on NNY's shoulder, the two doughboys became a fractured version of the devil, both horrible in their own way, Eff's emphasis being on the enjoyment of NNY's growing insanity, and other things profane. Eff has a bit of a Pinnochio complex about him, as he would like to be able to exist on his own.

PSYCHO-DOUGHBOY
A.K.A: D-Boy

height: 2'3"
weight: 9 OZ.

(made of styrofoam)

LIKES: knowing that everything ends eventually, when lights turn off, Zhang Yimou movies, when little kids drop their ice cream and jump off buildings in a fit of despair, when anything won't come back, stupid teens and their affection for suicide,

DISLIKES: Mr.Eff, the sound of people sleeping, wasting pain on anyone but yourself, Broadway showtunes, when Johnny looks hopeful, being conscious, not being a refrigerator and REALLY messing up the ozone layer.

BACKGROUND INFO: Older than Mr. Eff by a couple of years, his discovery was the same. Despite having the word "FUCK" painted on him, D-Boy was infused with the voice of rabid despair and doom. Much stronger during NNY's depressions, doughboy actually works to throw him over the edge and do away with himself altogether. Not interested in Eff's desire to be "real" D-Boy simply wishes to stop being.

DEVI D.
A.K.A: the one that got away

height: 5'9"
weight: 120 lbs
(more with all the bottles of mace she carries now)

LIKES: films by Terry Gilliam, and Mike Leigh, , stars, ghost stories, painting, driving with the stereo on loud, reading, meeting guys who aren't criminally insane

DISLIKES: people writing like Lovecraft who aren't Lovecraft, not liking girls enough to give up on guys, shitty dates (literally), people who think they know ANYTHING about religion, being attacked with really sharp things.

BACKGROUND INFO: When Devi's not attempting another doomed social outing, she paints, or just reads anything that does not try to re create reality. Her childhood was reality enough to suit her. Her history with men is not the best, but did not reach a frightening low until she went out with Johnny C. Before that, they had pleasant conversations, about anything in particular, at the bookstore she works at. His attempt on her life did not strike her as very romantic.

TESS R.
A.K.A: Tess

height: 5'4"
weight: 115 lbs
(doesn't like her butt)

LIKES: Steven Soderbergh movies, live music, watching boyfriends get ripped apart and becoming ex-boyfriends, how she looks in glasses, lizards.

DISLIKES: having the universe disappear around you, the thought of TRYING to fit in, frequent moments of weakness, poor judge of character, knwing all the previous dislikes firsthand.

BACKGROUND INFO: Tess's family moved around a lot, making it difficult to make friends with people. Even now, that she's fairly stable, as far as living somewhere goes, she still has that feeling of having to have friends around and quickly, which usually results in keeping not the best of comany. The idea of having someone around was far more appealing than being alone. Tess is a little lost when not seeing herself in the context of others, but knows this is a problem. She's been working on it, and can now go two full days without needing to call one of her shitty friends.

ANNE GWISH
A.K.A: bitch

height: 5'8"
weight: 115 lbs

(with makeup)

LIKES: talking shit about other people, hanging out in clubs only to ignore everyone, dancing the same dances everyone else does, you if you're in a band, social smoking, being herself so long as it looks good and people are watching.

DISLIKES: people talking shit about her, when people don't acknowledge her in clubs, people who just don't know how to do their makeup, when ugly guys ask her out

BACKGROUND INFO: Ann's background is a bit of a mystery, as she is fairly new to this are, and not much is known about her life before arriving. Someone once found her highschool yearbook and found out that she was a cheerleader!! Oh, my GOD! A cheerleader! I'm not lying. And you know her friend Cleo? Well, she told me not to tell anybody, but remember that bassist from Dark Goiter she was seeing? Well Ann went to go see him backstage one night, and found him all over that fat chick who plays keyboard in BLAH BLAH BLAH

SQUEE!
A.K.A: Todd

height: squee sized
weight: less than a cheeseburger

LIKES: his bear SHMEE, when the insane neighbor man does not tell him bedtime stories, writing stories, when daddy's not yelling, when mommy remembers his name.

DISLIKES: when SHMEE tells him to burn the house down, when aliens stare at him, the sick sounds coming from next door, the kids at school, the ever impending threat of Armageddon, TV shows by Saban.

BACKGROUND INFO: More commonly referred to as "SQUEE", little Todd acquired that nickname due to the high pitched squeaking sound he makes when he is afraid, which is quite often. His only real confidant is his teddy bear, SHMEE, whose advice is heard only by Squee. He has taken to creative writing when not being yelled at in school or at home. His favorite times are those in which he forgets that the world is full of bug-eyed monstrosities, and knife wielding maniacs. Those times are very infrequent.

ISSUE SYNOPSIS

Here is a question I get asked often; "WHAT THE HELL WERE YOU THINKING WHEN YOU DID THAT ISSUE?"So, as a public service to those sad enough to have enough time to REALLY wonder what some comic drawing wretch was thinking, I have provided this handy issue-by-issue detailing of my mysterious powers of creatin.

JOHNNY
THE HOMICIDAL MANIAC

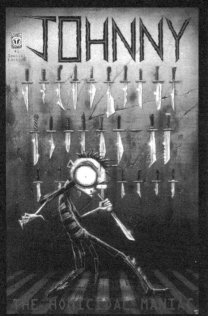

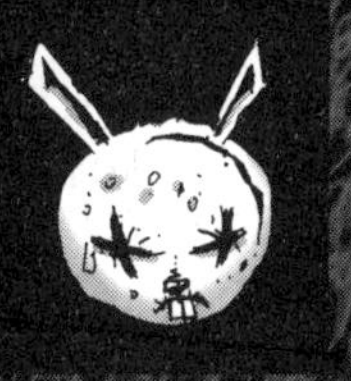

ISSUE#1 This was the first one, as those bright ones in the crowd can tell by the issue number!! Before this book, I had only done JTHM as a single page strip, so this was where I first ventured into the daunting realm of carrying on a little story over multiple pages. It's as close to an introduction to NNY as I wanted to get. There isn't any real insight as to just where this messed up guy is coming from, how he got here, and why he's so spotty in the head, and I like it that way. Too often, insane people have these hideously contrived origins having to due with having a traumatic childhood, or people treated them badly so now they must get revenge. I've never given much thought to Johnny's past, and find the blurriness of it all much more appealing then making him go nuts over being pantsed in school once. "YAAAARGH!! I have been pantsed!! I kill like the damned now!!" That's just not done. Squee is introduced here mainly for the effect of having some cute little kid live next door to a homicidal maniac, and being all too aware of it. This issue is filled mainly with self contained shorter stories, as I was just getting used to the longer narrative approach, so it's a very general introduction to the character, with the exception of NOODLE BOY, which just jumps right into NOODLE BOY style crap. I'm not a big fan of the artwork here, but it was early so I forgive me. I do remember liking how much I disliked the title of the book, as I knew some people would check it out thinking it would be a simple bloodbook, and this early on it was often just that. But I pretty much knew where the book would eventually go.

ISSUE#2 The most important thing that happens in this issue is that NNY gets his little ass kicked by "the one that got away", Devi. I really didn't plan on having the girl be Devi, whom I had intended to be a one time character from the MEANWHILE comic I did for this issue, but I thought it would be amusing to have this same girl go straight into another lousy date. I am in love with the idea of jerks feeling some trauma from people they've hurt, and I REEALLY love the idea of someone used to sitting high up on their pedestal, violently judging others, getting destroyed as a result of being wrong more than just a few times. I never intend to have NNY be anything above what he simply is, and he is a badly wired person. I should have him get damaged much more. It was fun to draw. This issue was also host to the infamous "SHIT IN PANTS" MEANWHILE. I can only say that this idea came out of a very dizzyheaded late night conversation with my good friend, Leah England (whose picture, by the way, is in the center of the cover painting). By now, I had a better sense of story, so Mr.Eff, Psychodoughboy, and the Nailbunny begin playing a bigger part in everything. NNY uses a gun on someone in this issue, which bugs me. I don't like me for doing that. Bad me! BAAAD ME!! Oh, yes, this issue was as close to romantic as I would allow. I think I failed, which, I think, works.

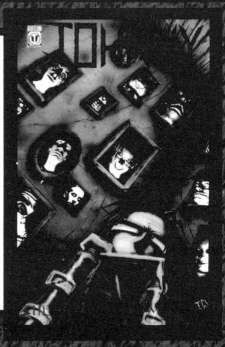

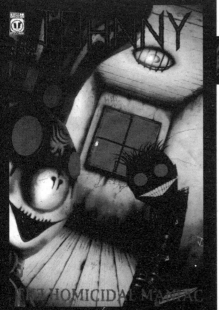

ISSUE#3 This one has the cover painting I like the most. I was using the blue paint for this cover frequently at the time. I loved that color. If you stare deeply enough into this black and white reproduction of that cover, maybe you can magically see the color. Go on, try it. Okay, now, about the issue. As far as I'm concerned, this is the one that most closely adheres to the preconceptions one would get from hearing the title of the book, which was a very purposeful effort. I wanted for this issue to be as manic as anything, full of explosions, mass murder, screaming idiots, and graphic depictions of brain removal. The cafe, and the area around it was inspired by several walks downtown on the main little congregating strip. There's nothing more disgusting than suburban vermin asking for change and trying to bum a smoke. Really, one need not go far outside one's door to find reasons to write about obliterating people. S'fun!!! WHEEEEE!!!! umm...anyhow. This issue introduces Tess. I remember wanting to name characters after record labels just for the stupid fun of it, but only got as far as Tess, and Cleopatra. Tess is an amalgamation of several girls I've know unfortunate enough to be jerk magnets. I couldn't stand seeing these people being terrorized by the lowest forms of the male race, and not DOING anything about it. It was the "BUT I LOVE HIM" syndrome, I suppose. I wanted to write about a nice girl just waking up from being a little wretch. The chicken screwing MEANWHILE in this issue was the effect of me itching to draw more monsters and aliens. The idea of highly technological MORONS just made me giggle. I am giggling now. hee hee.

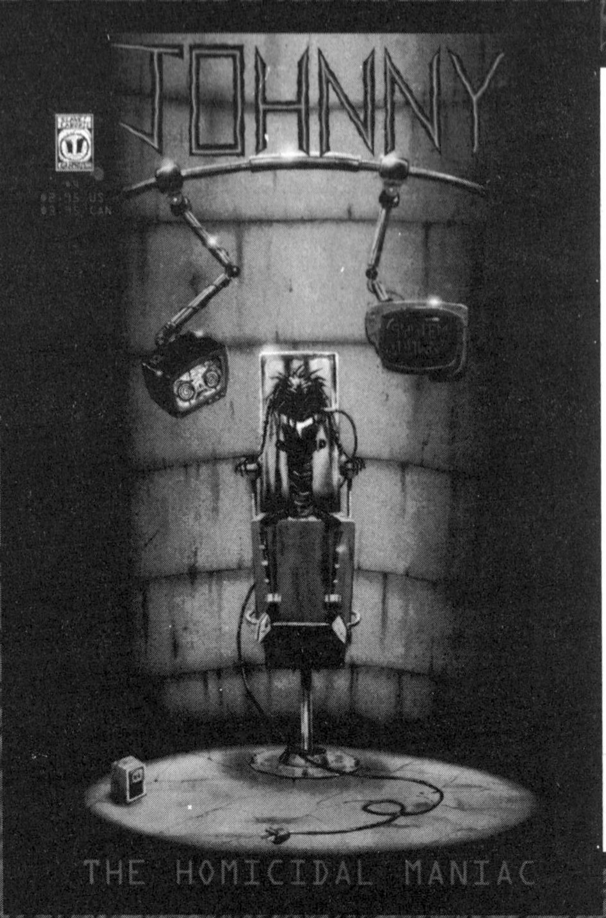
JOHNNY
THE HOMICIDAL MANIAC

ISSUE#4 If there are two things I love thinking of, it's the supernatural, and sci-fi type things. I think the sci-fi part shows in this cover. It also shows a little of Johnny's idea of himself as a machine in need of repair. If you want to get REALLY symbolic, that unplugged plug could foretell his "impending doom, but let's not get that involved shall we? If i had to pick a favorite issue, i might pick this one, as it' everything I wanted it to be. I wanted for it to a disappointment to those people who wanted MORE of the insane killing of #3, and nothing more. #4 is just such a downer, with hardly anything resembling murder. I love just being able to have NNY go off on long, meandering soliloquies, and be more than simply a killing kind of guy, which, if you like that kind of thing, can be found in too many books already. I wanted NNY's intelligence to be very apparent on some sad, very buried level, possibly lost to the allure of some easy out from the real world. The idea of NNY as an artist gone mad as the result of the loss of his talent is kind of funny too, not that it's an origin for those of you looking for such a thing!! Things get much more surreal by this point, as the urge to do stranger things took my little brain over. Logic, afterall, is not what I wish to sell with Johnny. This issue was an attempt to show that, and to show that my favorite way of approaching this character is to do it very much in HIS character, erratic and on tangents. Tess comes back in this one, too. Still not entirely rid of her affection for her asshole boyfriend, she does not quite appreciate the inhumane treatment he receives from the ever degenerating NNY. NNY, by this time is sickened with his existence as an emotional creature, resenting and envying the insect, Mr. Samsa he sees crawling around the basement. Devi returns, as a battle scarred wreck, hiding from people and NNY in specific. The MEANWHILE here was partially based on a true event, I both heard and saw while, once again, in the company of the lovely Ms. England, whose neighbor was a bit too old to be crying after his mother as she left to work. His pain was funny.

ISSUE #5 My ever mounting compulsion to draw monsters won out and was quite apparent in this issue, with the presence of a many-tentacled human sewage beast that escapes Johnny's wall, and the killer pinatas that beat up the little girl in the MEANWHILE. The idea of doing almost an entire issue without NNY was on my mind for awhile, so extending the series to 7 issues gave me the chance to do it. Tess wakes up, finally, from her life under jerks, with the brutal destruction of her boyfriend Dillon. YAY! She spends the rest of the issue escaping the house with yet another idiot, who you just knew was going to get killed. I liked writing Tess's wiseass dialogue, as she seemed one of the few decent individuals in the entire series. I also loved revealing more of the mystical gobbledygook that I had thought of for the wall creature and the doughboys. It's always interesting to hear how people are interpreting this kind of material. Anne Gwish steps in for the first time, and pretty much disgusts anyone with a brain. I thought of her as being a character in Johnny's world, that actually played no part in the storyline. I'm afraid of the different reasons people have for liking the her character. The MEANWHILE in this issue was special for the fact that I began using my computer to color the pages, giving it a cleaner, prettier look than the previous installments. People were confused by the story though, as they couldn't quite see what was supposed to be funny about it. They felt it was more disturbing than anything, what with the pinatas coming to avenge the brutal beating the little girl inflicted upon their brother. So it's disturbing!! YAAAY!!! Why shouldn't it be? There's more to humor than just laugh out loud, piss in your pants kind of material. I'm not saying that pinatas bashing the hell out of a toddler is subtle, brain comedy. Anyhow, the inspiration for the killer pinatas came from an idea about deadly forest pinatas by David James. I get asked about the wall creature sometimes. "WHAT THE HELL WAS IT SUPPOSED TO BE?" they ask. I usually just point out that there are other improbable things to note about the book, and that reason is not something to be found in it, and then I raise my arms and fly away. I like Grape Nuts.

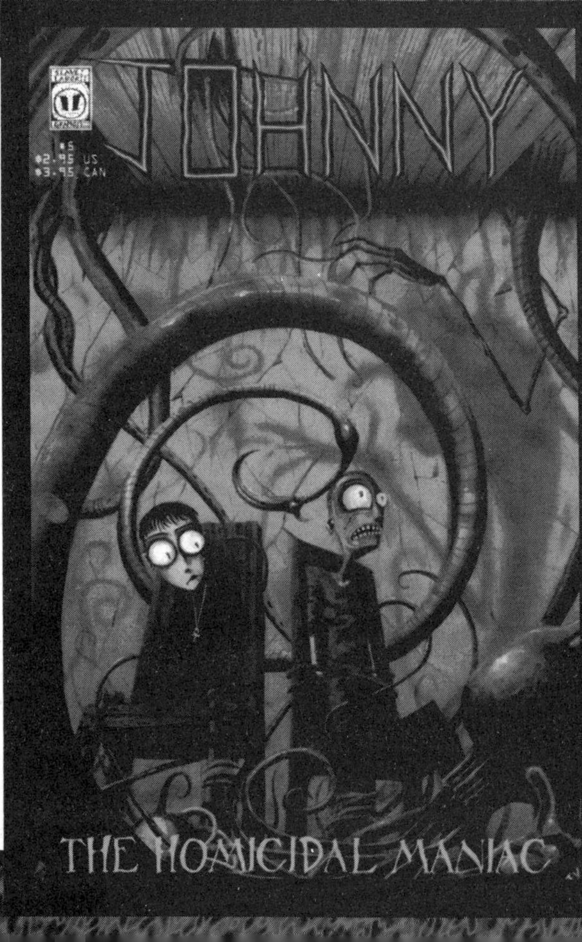
JOHNNY
THE HOMICIDAL MANIAC

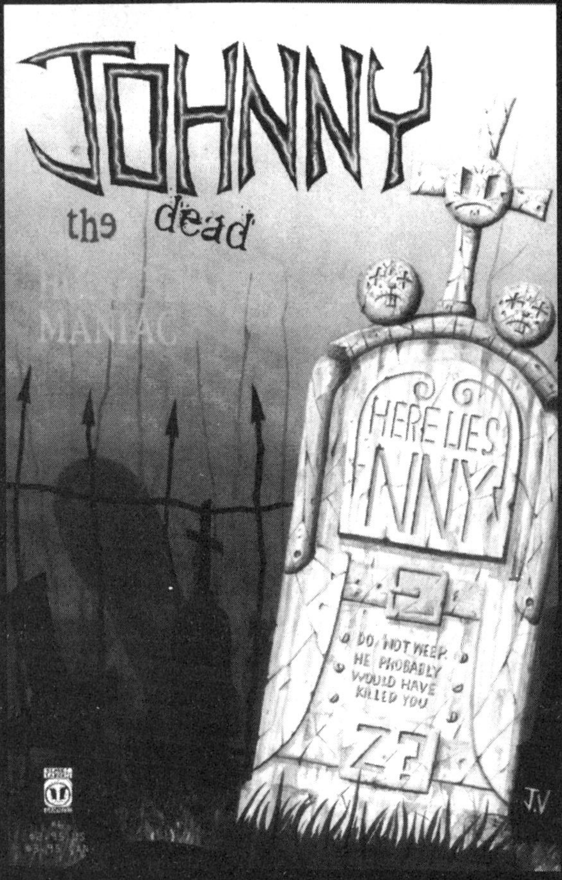
JOHNNY
the dead
HERE LIES NNY
DO NOT WEEP.
HE PROBABLY
WOULD HAVE
KILLED YOU
J.V

ISSUE#6 So I'm standing there, naked, right, and all I'm thinking is, "Could this possibly be happening?!" and almost as if she had read my mind, she says.... Oh, wait, I'm supposed to be writing about the book, aren't I? Sorry. Ah, yes, issue six. I enjoyed doing this issue more than most, as it was nothing more than a stupid, nonsense filled little book. I was in a very escapist mindset, and I was in no mood to do anything that could be misinterpreted as a MESSAGE, so I did this issue with absurd fun in mind, and you just CAN'T have fun without floating, legless angel bunnies. This has some of my favorite artwork in it, too (and when I say favorite, I mean I didn't burn the issue when I first saw it) although it's my least favorite cover painting. My affection for exploding people shows through here, as does my interest in afterlife theories. There are MANY supernatural creatures in this one, and that's probably a good part of why I enjoyed drawing it so much, what with multiple satans, that freakish little GOD, and the pets I have in the MEANWHILE. The question of whether or not Johnny actually died and visited heaven or hell is one I get asked a lot. Now, I know that dying and coming back to life is a much used convention in stories, going back to prehistoric days (remember Jesus? Osiris? Elvis?). I don't think much of it, other than as a vehicle for me to draw the devil and other fun little guys for this issue. And, of course, as NNY explains. It's all considered, for the most part, a moot point, as after waking up from ANY sleep, NNY doubt's how real ANYTHING is. And, yes, the idea that it was ALL A DREAM is an even more frequently abused convention, but let's not be so anal, yes? The MEANWHILE here is a personal favorite, what with my revealing the truth about my life for all those strange people who seem to want to know about it. This one was inspired by actual events in my life, and no embellishing was done whatsoever. I'm getting tired of writing these synopsis thingies.

ISSUE#7 The end of the first series. This one's special for that fact that it marked the beginning of my collaboration with SATAN!!! Oh, forget I told you that. Moving on... It feels more like a beginning than an ending to me, as Johnny begins his mission to cast off emotion and live more like little Mr.Samsa. Part of this is due to NNY's own self loathing accentuated by a visit from JIMMY, a wannabe homicidal maniac. Oh....I LIKED writing Jimmy. Jimmy was stupid. So very stupid. A little Burger Boy, whose name I never mentioned (It's Reverend MEAT, by the way) becomes a new voice in NNY's world, in the absence of the now silent Doughboys. MEAT battles for the forces of FEELING, no matter how filthy, in opposition of NNY's search for cold. Devi returns, now very resentful, and hostile towards what kept her in hiding. I wanted to distinguish Devi from Tess, whom, having had a similar past with people, has reacted in a far more well-balanced way. Devi, on the other hand....well....she has some issues. Ann Gwish pops in again, revealing even more of how shallow she can get. My idea of her is as the most physically attractive of any of my other characters, a feature that only frames more distinctly how HORRIBLE a person she is inside. You know the type. I started the series with SQUEE, and I ended this part of it with him. Lord, if I don't love torturing the idea of what is cute. Now, I don't usually do this, but I was laughing out loud myself doing the MEANWHILE for this issue. It's the juvenile reflex action while drawing a nightmarishly stupid looking guy, with a grotesquely misshapen head, and idiotic walrus tusk-like fangs. I'm big on the theme "be careful what you wish for", and this is just another example, as the vampire jerk turns into the silliest vampire I could come up with that night. I went to sleep giggling. Speaking of the Olympics, I've always wanted to see an Olympics just for death row criminals in which they were all eliminated in endurance tests. The winners of these contests would get to die last. I mean, if you just HAVE to die, you should at least get some fun out of it. Think of it, a weightlifting contest where they just keep adding weights until this guys spine explodes. Those TV execs don't return my calls though.

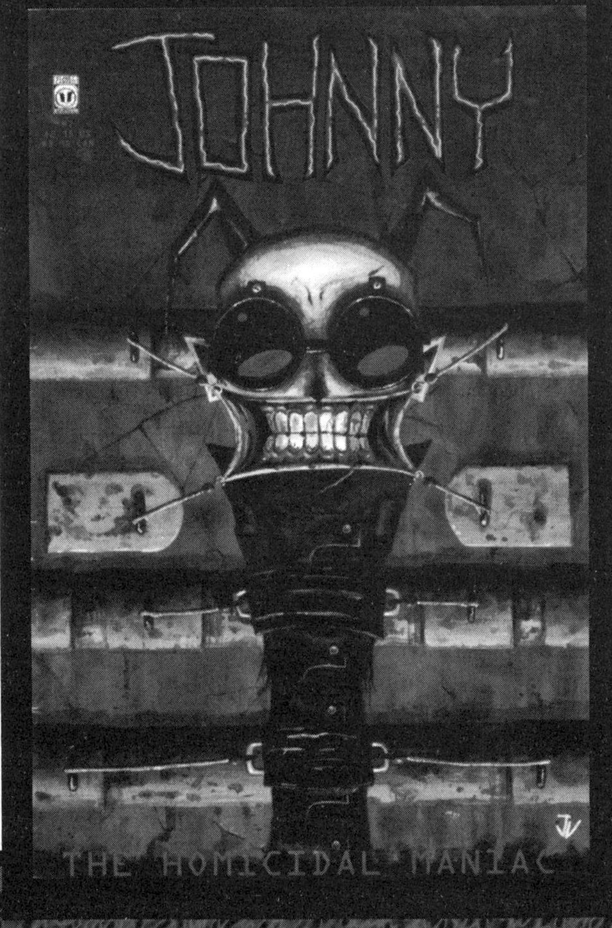
JOHNNY
THE HOMICIDAL MANIAC

THE GALLERY OF ANCIENT HORRORS

My friends, and I do use the term loosely because some of you are REAL jerks (you know who you are), what you are about to see contained here in the following pages, is a terrifying collection of what I like to call "REALLY OLD SHIT". I was drawing NNY long before the thought of any comic book on him ever occurred, so these are strips done over a million years ago by the first and most ancient of Jhonens. Just for the record, I think these comics are horrible and are valuable ONLY in an archival sense. Please do not search for real humor in them.

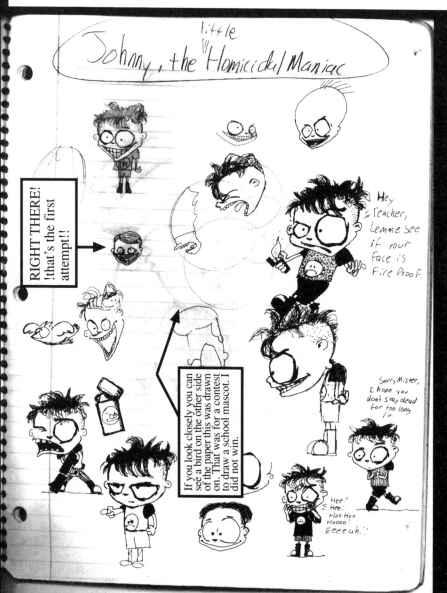

Johnny, the "little" Homicidal Maniac

RIGHT THERE! that's the first attempt!!

If you look closely you can see a bird on the other side of the paper this was drawn on. That was for a contest to draw a school mascot. I did not win.

Hey, Teacher, Lemme see if your face is fire proof.

Sorry Mister, I hope you dont stay dead for too long !!

Hee! Hee! Hoo Hoo Hoooo! Eeeeuh.!!

LOOK!!

Though this image to the left is not actually a comic, it is a magical page out of a very old sketchbook. It's a miracle I can actually tie my own shoelaces with all the drawing I did in school. This is the very first appearance of Johnny, done while not quite giving my full attention to an art history lesson. Johnny looks like a little troll or something. I would shoot myself if I thought I had not improved.

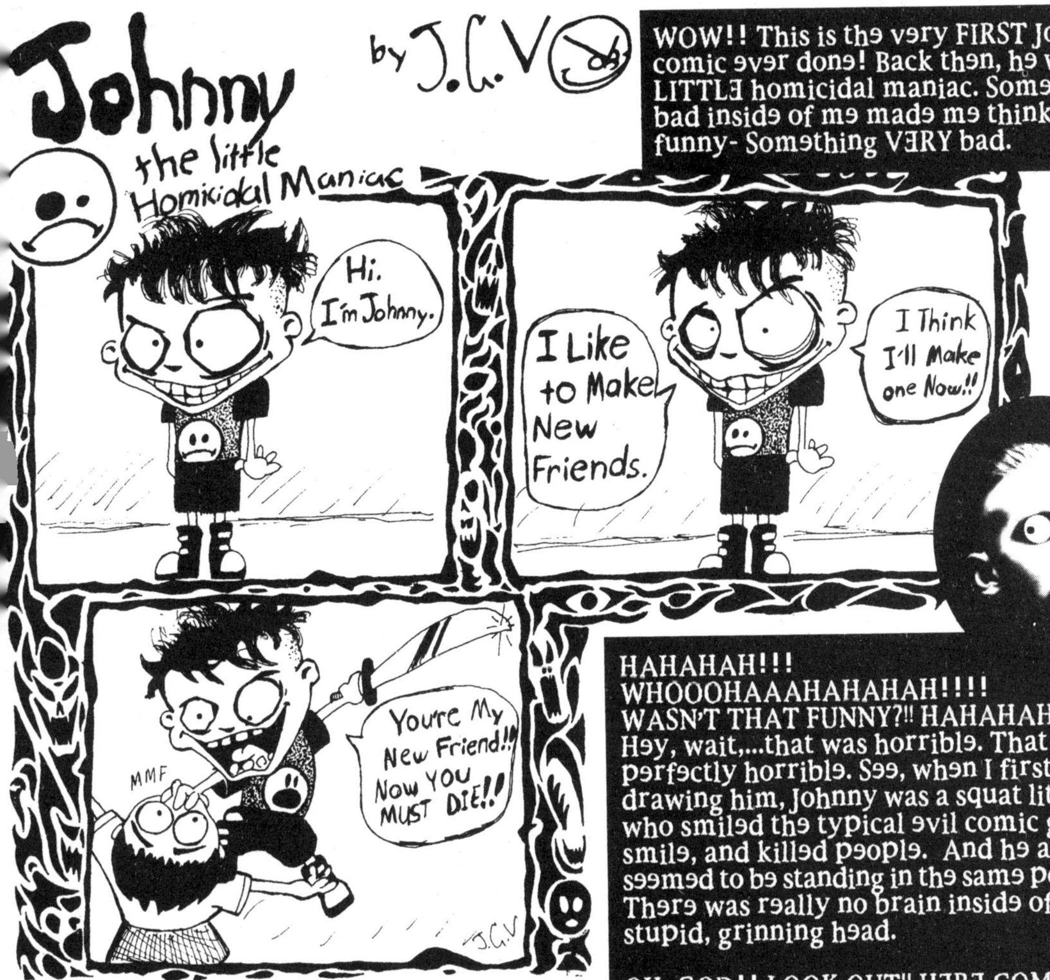
Johnny
by J.C.V
the little Homicidal Maniac
Hi. I'm Johnny.
I Like to Make New Friends.
I Think I'll Make one Now!!
MMF
You're My New Friend!! Now YOU MUST DIE!!
J.C.V

WOW!! This is the very FIRST Johnny comic ever done! Back then, he was the LITTLE homicidal maniac. Something bad inside of me made me think it was funny- Something VERY bad.

HAHAHAH!!!
WHOOOHAAAHAHAHAH!!!!
WASN'T THAT FUNNY?!! HAHAHAHAH!!!
Hey, wait,...that was horrible. That was perfectly horrible. See, when I first began drawing him, Johnny was a squat little kid who smiled the typical evil comic guy smile, and killed people. And he always seemed to be standing in the same position. There was really no brain inside of that stupid, grinning head.

OH, GOD!! LOOK OUT!! HERE COMES ANOTHER ONE!!

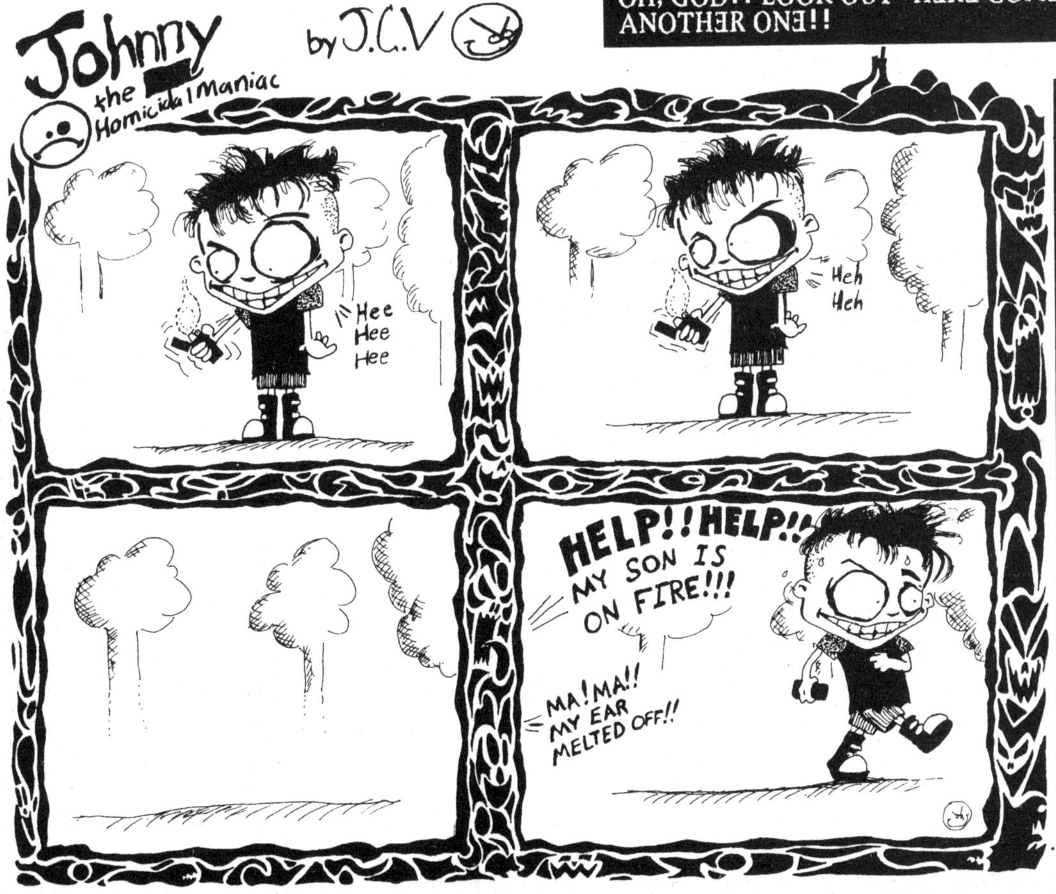
Johnny
by J.C.V
the [redacted] Homicidal Maniac
Hee Hee Hee
Heh Heh
HELP!! HELP!!
MY SON IS ON FIRE!!!
MA! MA!! MY EAR MELTED OFF!!

This was the second strip I did. I remember liking this one alot when I did it. My friends at the time REALLY liked it. Apparently, I was an idiot, and my friends were insane idiots.

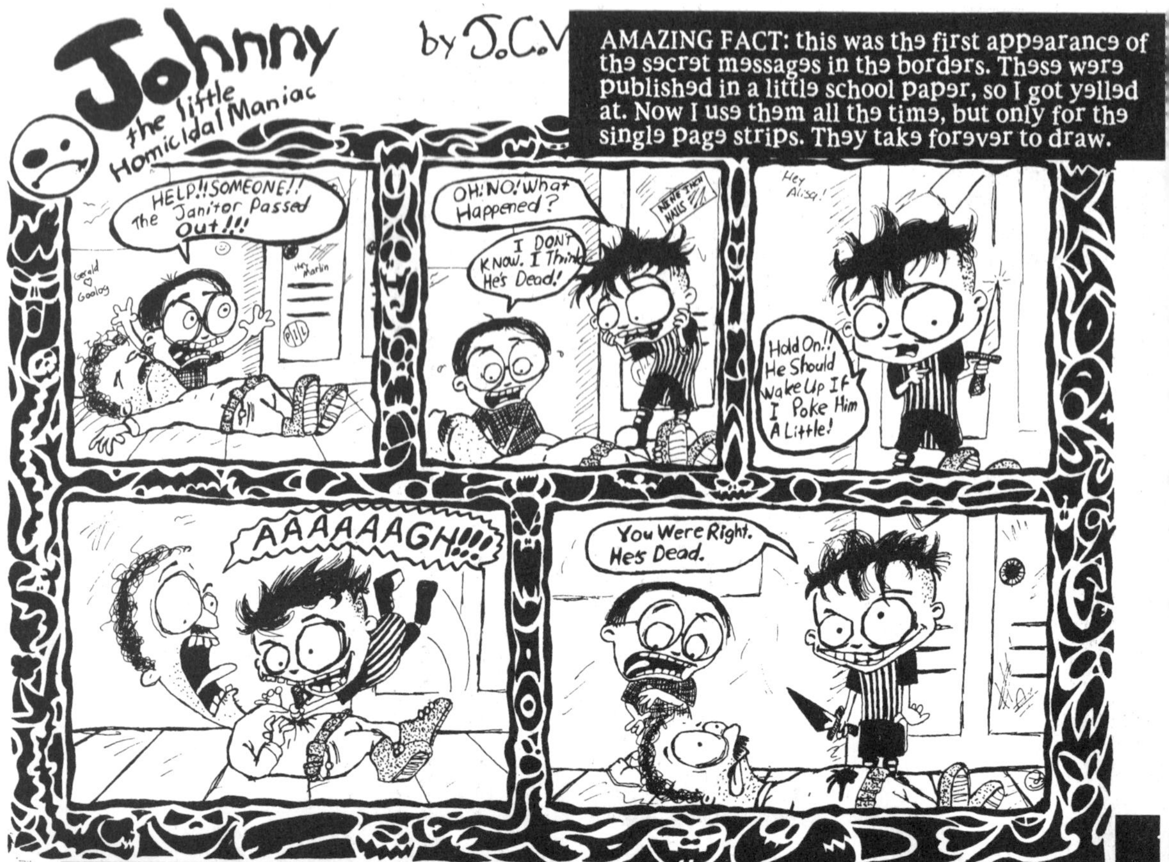
Johnny the little Homicidal Maniac
by J.C.V
HELP!! SOMEONE!! The Janitor Passed Out!!!
Gerald ♡ Goolog
Hey Marlin
OH! NO! What Happened?
I DON'T KNOW. I Think He's Dead!
Hey Alisa!
Hold On!! He Should Wake Up If I Poke Him A Little!
AAAAAAGH!!!
You Were Right. He's Dead.

AMAZING FACT: this was the first appearance of the secret messages in the borders. These were published in a little school paper, so I got yelled at. Now I use them all the time, but only for the single page strips. They take forever to draw.

Now, remember, I am NOT filling these pages with this crap because I just want to fill up space. I am doing it for YOU, because i care. I REEEALLY care.

hee hee hee

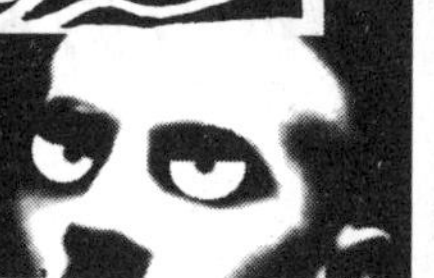

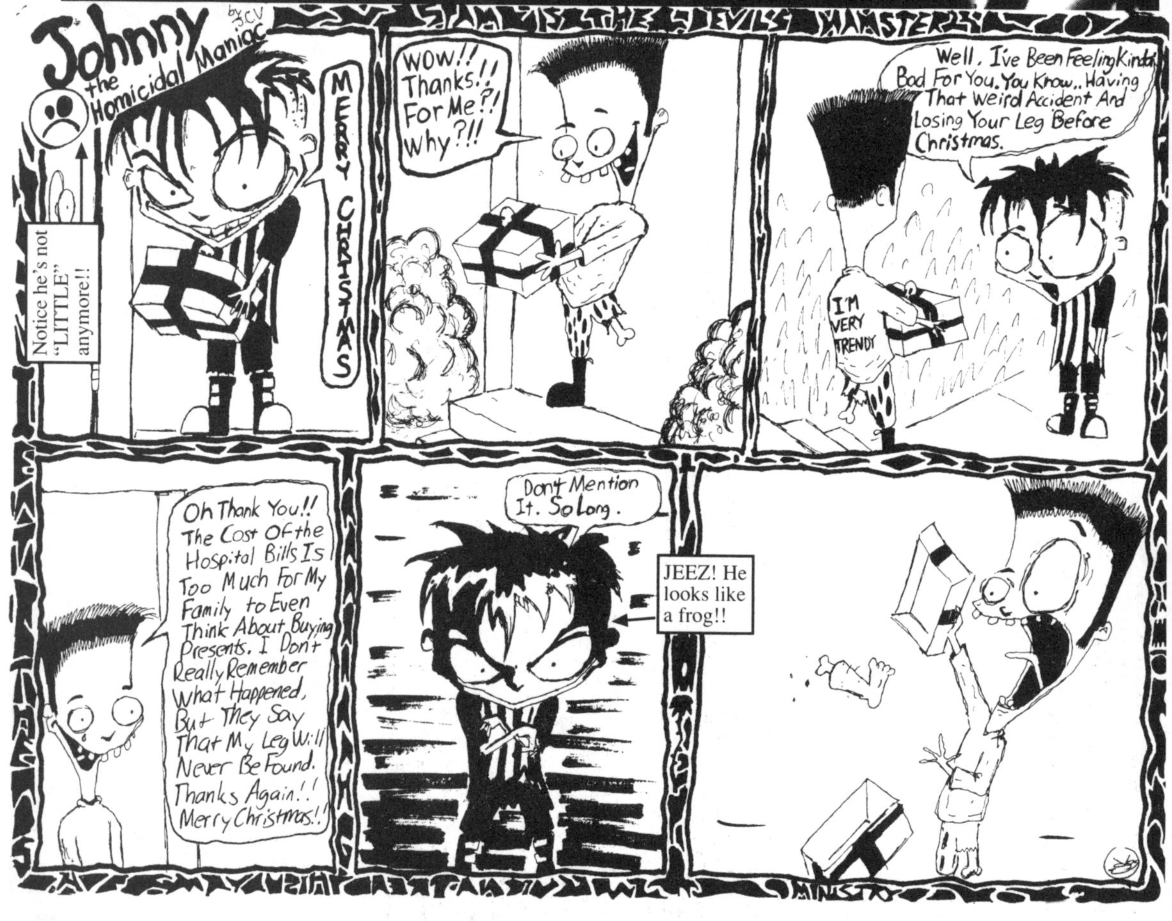
Johnny the Homicidal Maniac
by J.C.V
MERRY CHRISTMAS
Notice he's not "LITTLE" anymore!!
WOW!! Thanks!! For Me?! Why?!!
Well, I've Been Feeling Kinda Bad For You. You Know.. Having That Weird Accident And Losing Your Leg Before Christmas.
I'M VERY TRENDY
Oh Thank You!! The Cost Of the Hospital Bills Is Too Much For My Family to Even Think About Buying Presents. I Don't Really Remember What Happened, But They Say That My Leg Will Never Be Found. Thanks Again!! Merry Christmas!!
Don't Mention It. So Long.
JEEZ! He looks like a frog!!

TRANSITION TIME!!

Now, here are some pieces from comics that show some changes in the way I was doing these things. I can't stand looking back on these comics, but when I do it's interesting to notice the emergence of images and themes that I still use today. Did you know I used to rule the world from a teepee I made in my backyard? I bet you didn't know that. See, this is very interesting.

By around this time, Johnny was becoming more verbal. I was getting tired always doing a killing gag, so I wanted to fill his brain with more than just blatant bloodiness. This is the first time he ever wrote in his DIE-ARY.

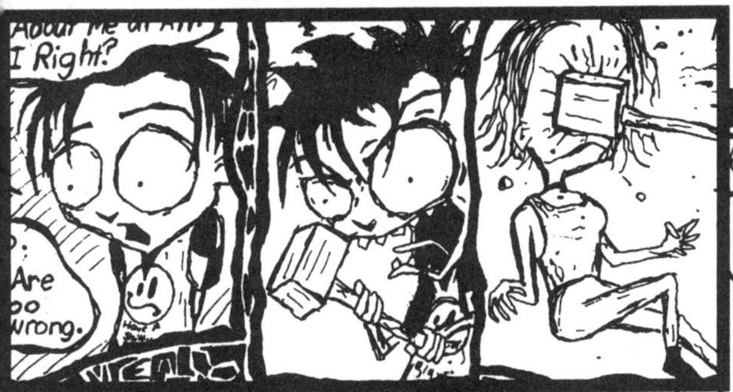
I Right?

A simple example, but still the earliest one I could find, showing the emergence of more than just one side of this little freak. Of course, he still hits her with that mallet.

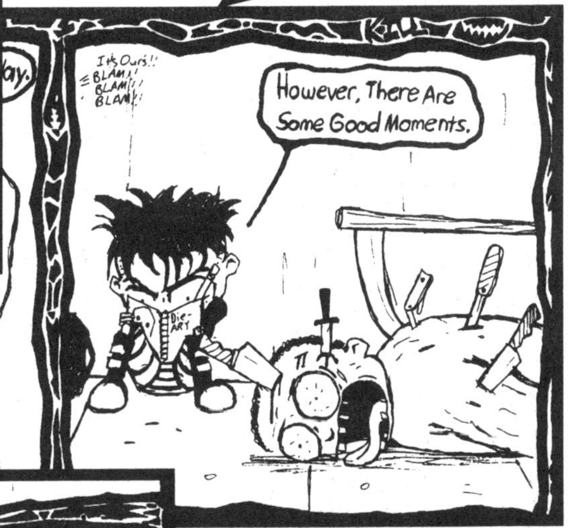
It's Ours!!
BLAM! BLAM! BLAM!
However, There Are Some Good Moments.
DIE-ARY

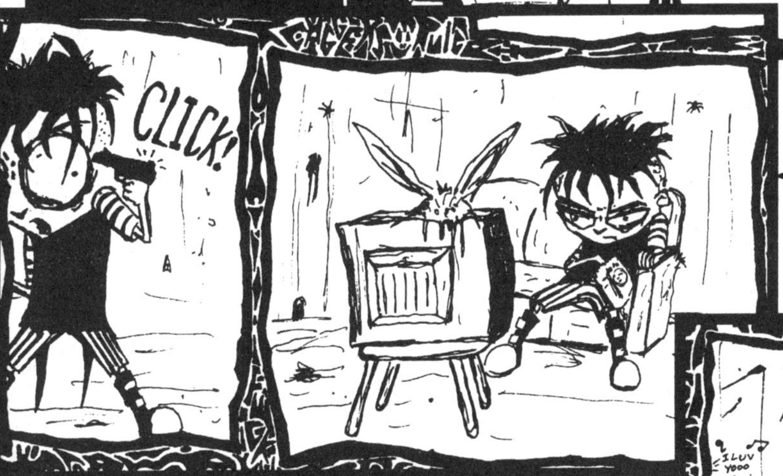
CLICK!

Familiar, eh? I've always loved the idea of someone failing suicide, then immediately losing interest in it. This is the first time I had Johnny do just that. Also, this comic was had the first appearance of the bunny ears television set.

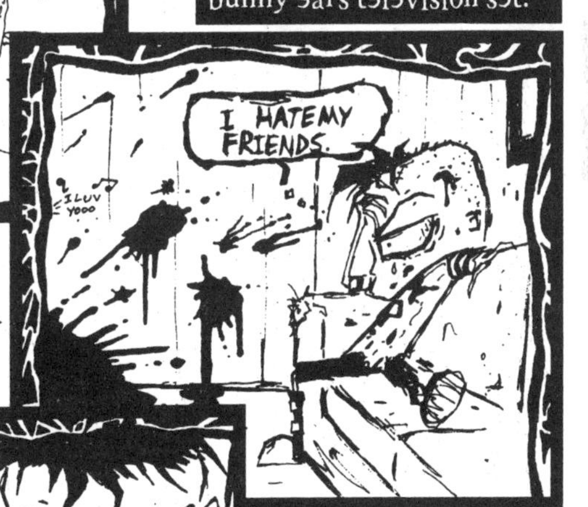
I HATE MY FRIENDS.
I LUV YOOO

The only real reason this one is here is because it's the first time I ever really drew Johnny in a profile. I used to have the most difficult time doing it without having him look like a fucked up Ninja Turtle. He still looks like a creepy little dwarf here, though.

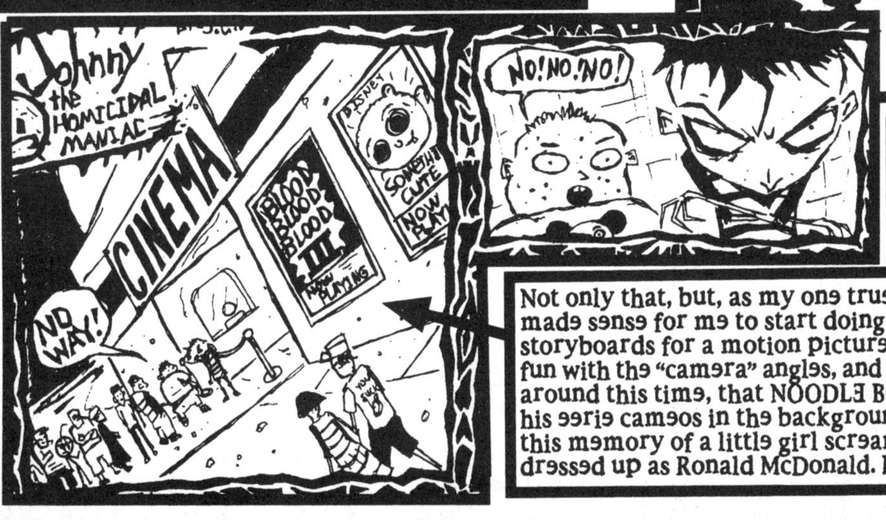
Johnny the HOMICIDAL MANIAC
CINEMA
BLOOD BLOOD BLOOD III NOW PLAYING
DISNEY
NO WAY!
NO! NO! NO!

AH, here we go. This is starting to look more like the modern strips. He's getting a little taller, and much thinner.

Not only that, but, as my one true love is FILM, it only made sense for me to start doing these strips like storyboards for a motion picture. I started having more fun with the "camera" angles, and perspective. It was right around this time, that NOODLE BOY first started making his eerie cameos in the backgrounds of the comics. I have this memory of a little girl screaming in terror of a man dressed up as Ronald McDonald. He was horrible looking.

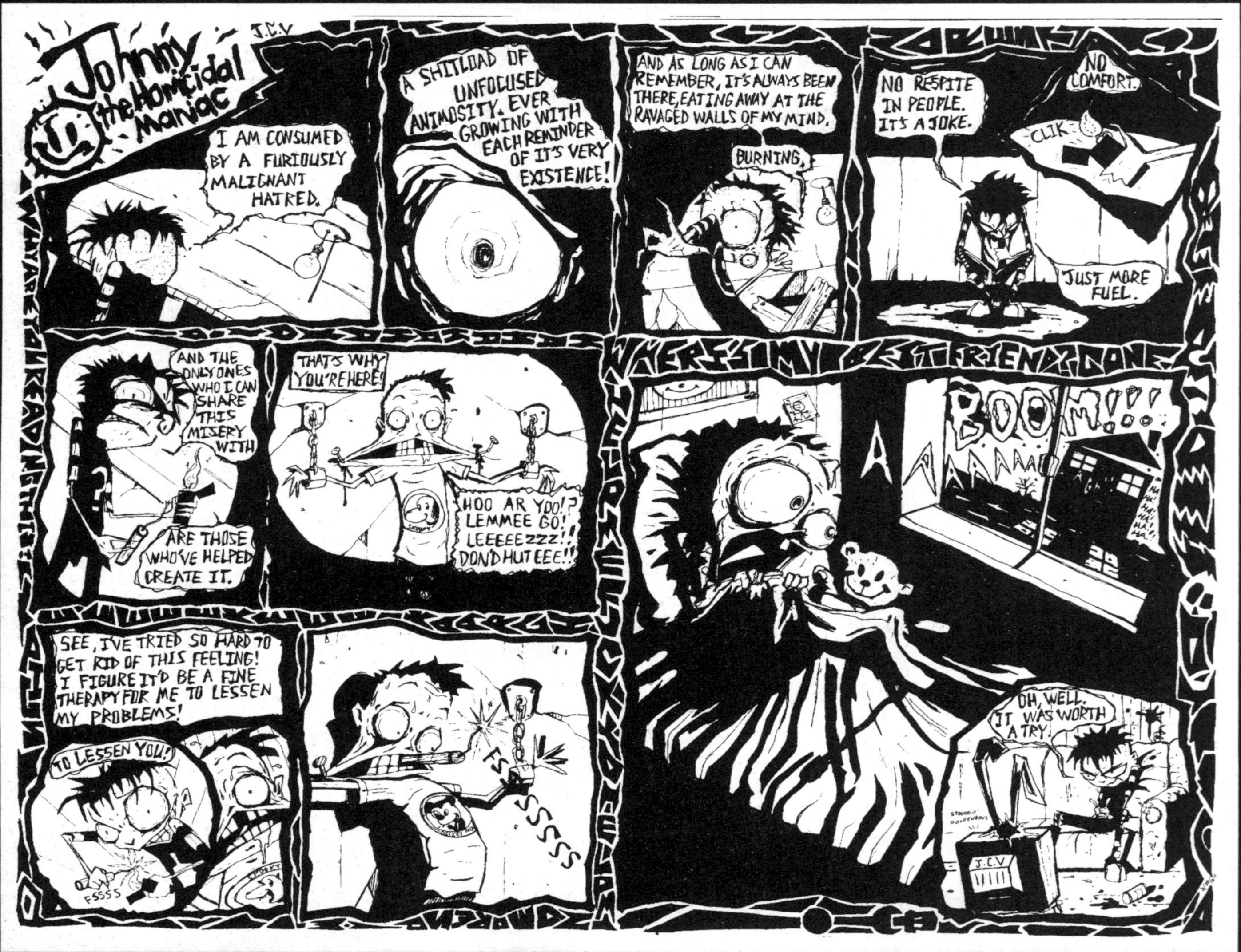
Johnny the Homicidal Maniac
J.C.V.
I AM CONSUMED BY A FURIOUSLY MALIGNANT HATRED.
A SHITLOAD OF UNFOCUSED ANIMOSITY. EVER GROWING WITH EACH REMINDER OF IT'S VERY EXISTENCE!
AND AS LONG AS I CAN REMEMBER, IT'S ALWAYS BEEN THERE, EATING AWAY AT THE RAVAGED WALLS OF MY MIND.
BURNING.
NO RESPITE IN PEOPLE. IT'S A JOKE.
NO COMFORT.
CLIK
JUST MORE FUEL.
AND THE ONLY ONES WHO I CAN SHARE THIS MISERY WITH
ARE THOSE WHO'VE HELPED CREATE IT.
THAT'S WHY YOU'RE HERE!
HOO AR YOO!? LEMMEE GO! LEEEEEZZZ!! DOND HUT EEE!!
WHERE'S MY BEST FRIEND? GONE
BOOM!!!
SEE, I'VE TRIED SO HARD TO GET RID OF THIS FEELING! I FIGURE IT'D BE A FINE THERAPY FOR ME TO LESSEN MY PROBLEMS!
TO LESSEN YOU!
FSSSS
FSSSSSSS
OH, WELL. IT WAS WORTH A TRY.
J.C.V
WHY ARE YOU READING THIS?!

A zillon years pass. And now, here things are looking much better, and much closer to the style you've seen in the JTHM books. It starts getting away from the sketchy look of the older comics, leaning towards a more geometrical thing, and I started using MUCH more ink as I got sick of how WHITE they were before. The magical changing shirt images began here, as did the home torture chamber theme. That little kid at the end of this strip was just something I came up with on a whim. I just liked the mean idea of some little kid hearing all these revolting sounds next door. When it came time to do an actual comic book, i went back to that idea and named the kid SQUEE (I WAS going to name him FEEBLY). You can even see an early version of what would be SHMEE. As you can see, Johnny looks almost like the modern version of him, but he's still not sickly looking enough, and he's too short.

Oh, yes, the little thorns on Johnny's speech bubbles began popping up.

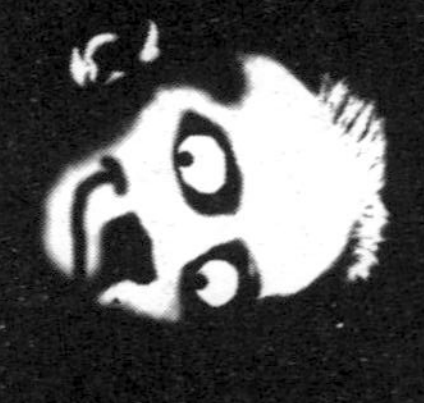

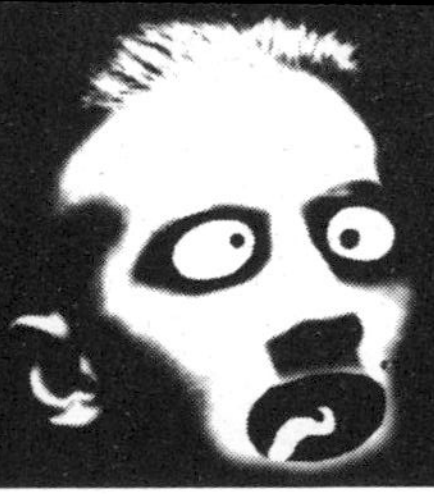

Closer, still. There aren't any really NEW aspects to this one, except for the addition of a few inches to Johnny's height. I was working at moving him away from that little troll image he had in the earlier comics. There's also a lot more superfluous crap going on in the backgrounds - something I love doing. I was getting into interrupting the strips to make little commentaries. Another thing to notice in this strip is Johnny's use of a gun to kill someone, an image I dislike very much these days. By this point in time, I was actually being published in Carpe Noctem magazine. They were nice, and sick enough to give me a page in their book, so that's really where Johnny was first seen by people fortunate enough to not know me personally. Wow...I seem to have a lot of space to fill up on this page.

Ummm.....Yep...lot's of space. Now I'm getting distracted by the moon outside. I'm sitting by a window, and it's lovely outside. It'll be dawn soon. I haven't flown a kite in too long. Have any of you heard of a movie named NUKIE?

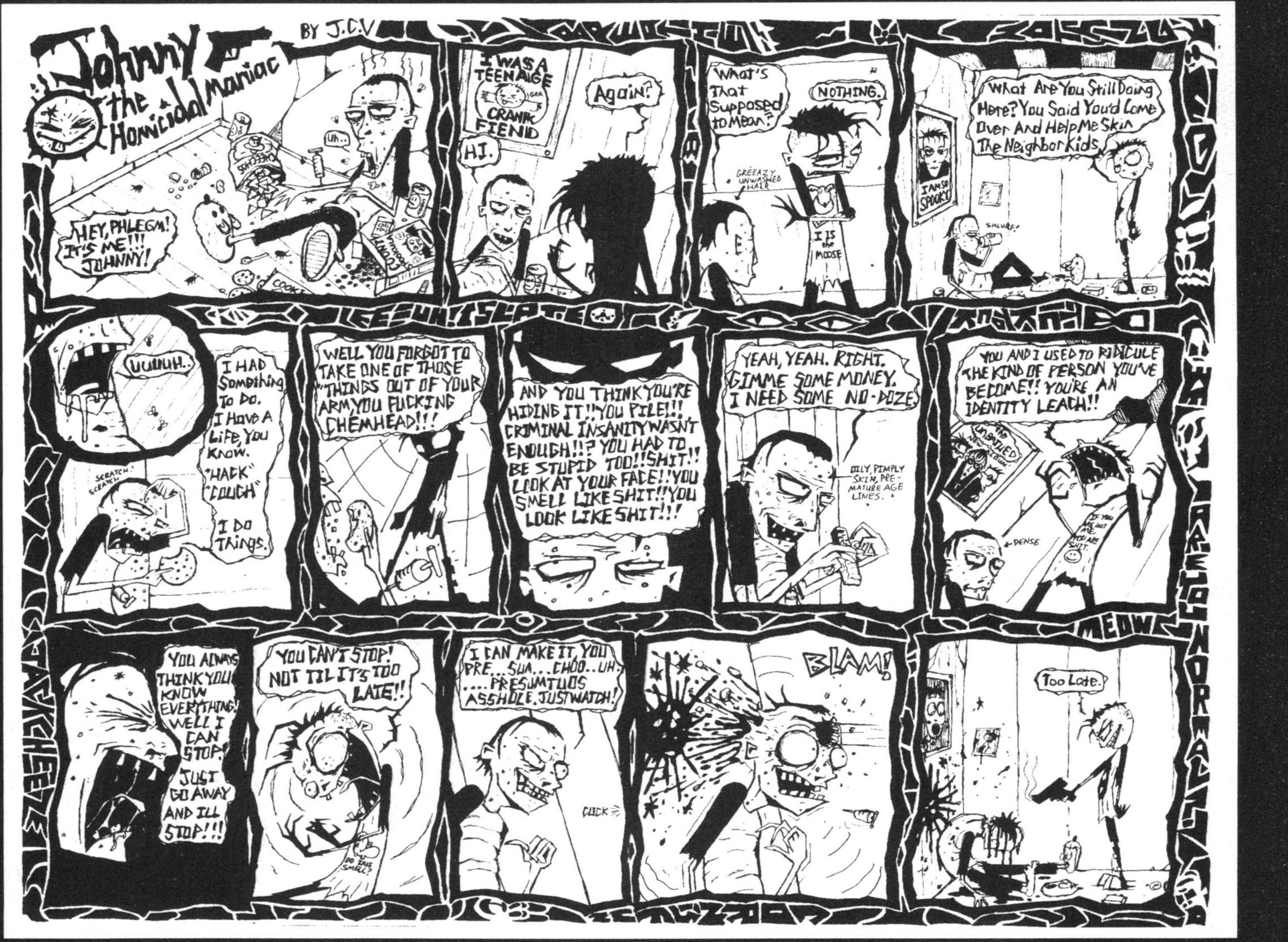

Johnny the Homicidal Maniac
BY J.C.V
HEY, PHLEGM! IT'S ME!!! JOHNNY!
UH..
I WAS A TEENAGE CRANK FIEND
HI.
Again?
What's That Supposed to Mean?
NOTHING.
GREEAZY UNWASHED HAIR
I IS the MOOSE
What Are You Still Doing Here? You Said You'd Come Over And Help Me Skin The Neighbor Kids.
I AM SO SPOOKY
SHLURP!
UUUUH..
I HAD Something to Do. I Have A Life, You Know.
"HACK" "COUGH"
I DO Things.
SCRATCH SCRATCH
WELL YOU FORGOT TO TAKE ONE OF THOSE "THINGS OUT OF YOUR ARM, YOU FUCKING CHEMHEAD!!!
AND YOU THINK YOU'RE HIDING IT!! YOU PILE!!! CRIMINAL INSANITY WASN'T ENOUGH!!? YOU HAD TO BE STUPID TOO!! SHIT!! LOOK AT YOUR FACE!! YOU SMELL LIKE SHIT!! YOU LOOK LIKE SHIT!!!
YEAH, YEAH. RIGHT. GIMME SOME MONEY. I NEED SOME NO-DOZE.
OILY, PIMPLY SKIN, PRE-MATURE AGE LINES.
YOU AND I USED TO RIDICULE THE KIND OF PERSON YOU'VE BECOME!! YOU'RE AN IDENTITY LEACH!!
←DENSE
YOU ALWAYS THINK YOU KNOW EVERYTHING! WELL I CAN STOP! JUST GO AWAY AND ILL STOP!!!
YOU CAN'T STOP! NOT TIL IT'S TOO LATE!!
DO THIS SMELL?
I CAN MAKE IT, YOU PRE...SUA...CHOO..UH ....PRESUMTUOS ASSHOLE. JUST WATCH!
CLICK
BLAM!
MEOW
Too Late.
JACKCHEEZE

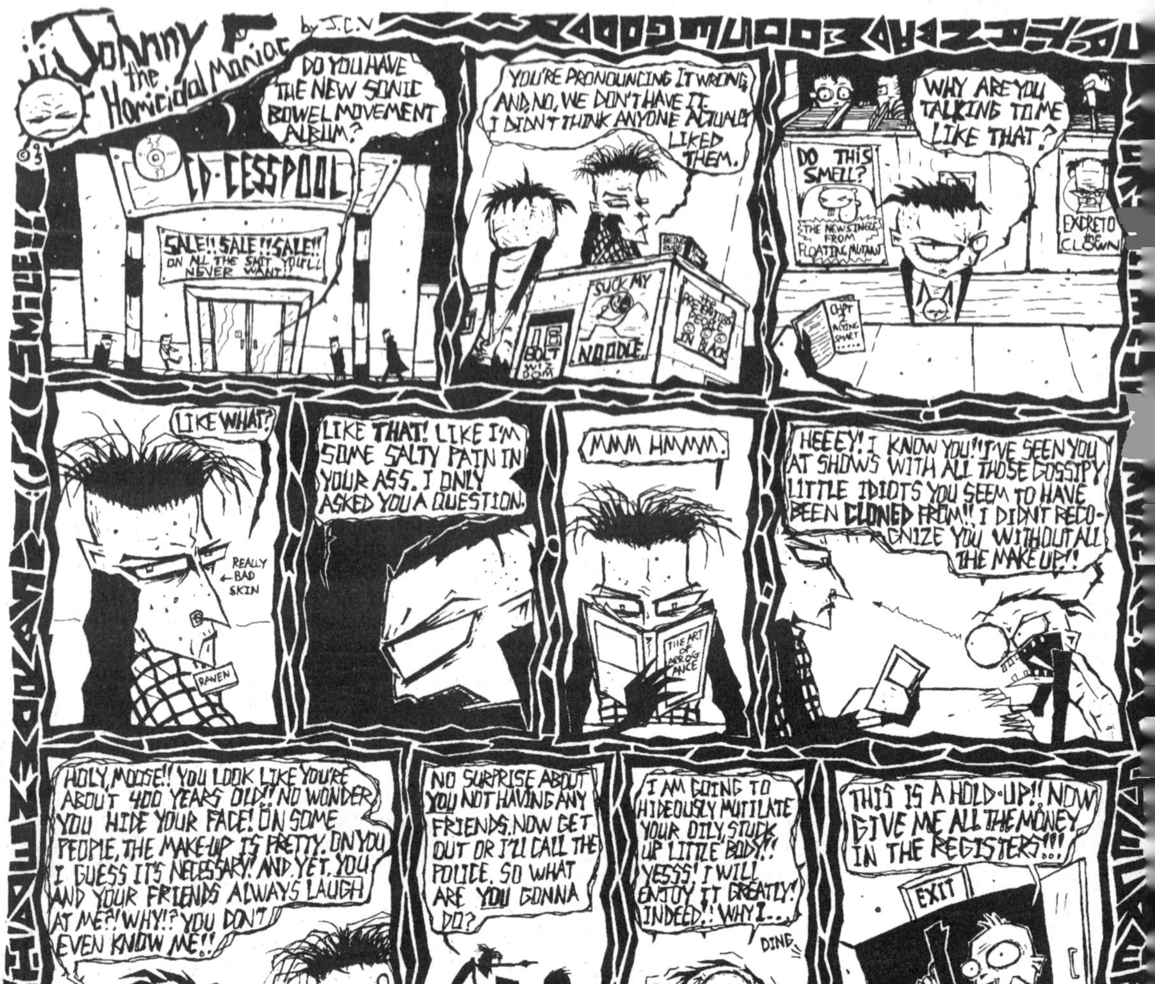
Johnny the Homicidal Maniac
by J.C.V
DO YOU HAVE THE NEW SONIC BOWEL MOVEMENT ALBUM?
CD-CESSPOOL
SALE!! SALE!! SALE!! ON ALL THE SHIT YOU'LL NEVER WANT!
YOU'RE PRONOUNCING IT WRONG AND, NO, WE DON'T HAVE IT. I DIDN'T THINK ANYONE ACTUALLY LIKED THEM.
SUCK MY NOODLE
BOLT WIZDOM
WHY ARE YOU TALKING TO ME LIKE THAT?
DO THIS SMELL? THE NEW SINGLE FROM FLOATING MUTANT
EXCRETO the CLOWN
LIKE WHAT?
REALLY BAD SKIN
RAVEN
LIKE THAT! LIKE I'M SOME SALTY PAIN IN YOUR ASS. I ONLY ASKED YOU A QUESTION.
MMM HMMM.
THE ART OF ARROGANCE
HEEEY! I KNOW YOU! I'VE SEEN YOU AT SHOWS WITH ALL THOSE GOSSIPY LITTLE IDIOTS YOU SEEM TO HAVE BEEN CLONED FROM!! I DIDNT RECOGNIZE YOU WITHOUT ALL THE MAKE UP!!
HOLY, MOOSE!! YOU LOOK LIKE YOU'RE ABOUT 400 YEARS OLD!! NO WONDER YOU HIDE YOUR FACE! ON SOME PEOPLE, THE MAKE-UP IS PRETTY. ON YOU I GUESS IT'S NECESSARY! AND YET, YOU AND YOUR FRIENDS ALWAYS LAUGH AT ME?! WHY!? YOU DON'T EVEN KNOW ME!!
RE-LIVING PAINFUL MEMORIES
NO SURPRISE ABOUT YOU NOT HAVING ANY FRIENDS. NOW GET OUT OR I'LL CALL THE POLICE. SO WHAT ARE YOU GONNA DO?
I AM GOING TO HIDEOUSLY MUTILATE YOUR OILY, STUCK UP LITTLE BODY!! YESSS! I WILL ENJOY IT GREATLY! INDEED. WHY I...
DING
THIS IS A HOLD-UP!! NOW GIVE ME ALL THE MONEY IN THE REGISTERS!!!
EXIT
OH, GOD!! UM, WE JUST EMPTIED OUT THE REGISTERS!! THERE'S NO MONEY!!
AAARGH!! YOU FRUSTRATE ME!!!
BLAM!
the Fuckys
DING
EXIT
BASTARD.
MEOW!
J.C.V

Z?

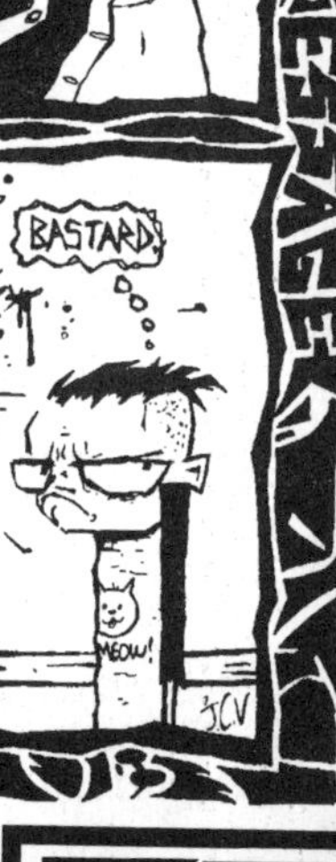

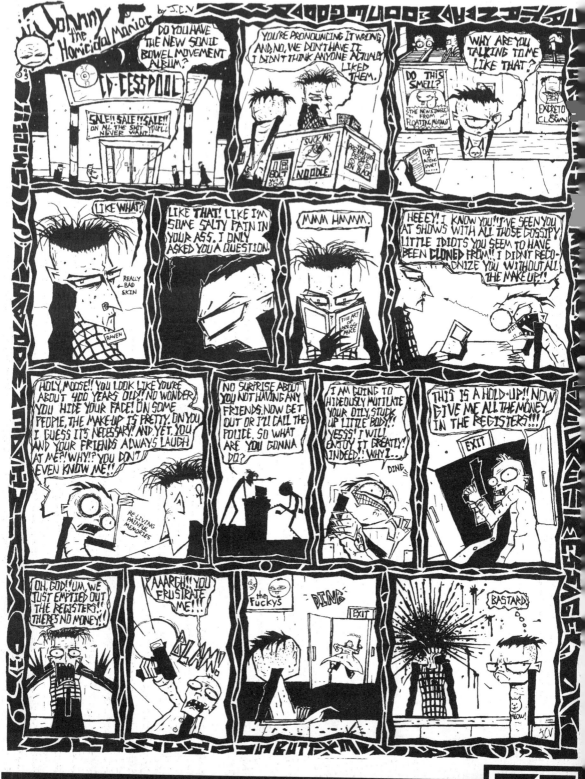

You know, I really thought I would have quite a bit to say about this particular piece, as it was the last Johnny strip i did before working on the comic book. I did this one to get used to drawing them in the vertical style. Up until the book began, i had only done single page comics. He still has a squished head here, but other than that is pretty much "NNY" by now. But even now, if you look at the early strips in the JTHM series you'll notice he looks very different than he does in the later issues, and that's not just because of the new little scar he has over his left eye. DEAR LORD!! The suns coming up! I've been working at this computer ALL day. I think I had some chips and a Slurpee, but that's it. I feel hidéous. I'm going to go read, and maybe jab my burning eyes with forks. But I hope you enjoyed this little tour through the shitty older Johnny comics I did back when I wasn't 90% mechanical body parts. Good night.

SUPER AMAZING INTERVIEW!!

I have decided to include this as a public service for the very good cause of shutting some people up. This interview never really happened but in the sad, danky doomslum of my mind. Still, it does do the job of answering some of the most common questions I get asked in letters and in interviews.

Q: Okay, let's begin. First, off, Johnen, tell me..

J: It's JHONEN, not Johnen. Jeez, it's right there in the book, dozens of times.

Q: Okay. And how do you pronounce that?

J: Who ARE you? What are you doing in my bathroom?

Q: Umm..I'm the interview person. Let's move on. Tell us how you began doing a comic book. There are a lot of people out there looking for advice on how to break into this business.

J: Well, first of all, you shouldn't think of it as a business if your just getting into comics. I love drawing and writing. I also love squeezing marshmallow peeps in the store. As for getting the book started, I just dropped some of my work off at Slave Labor and they liked it. Submit your work to places. Sending your work to other artists is okay, but get it to publishers especially. And if you are female, bring mace, because there are some foul-ass guys working in comics.

Q: I see. So, your book is very graphic at times, and seems very personal. Tell me, are you as violent a person as Johnny. How much of him is in you?

J: I could write about a transvestite circus midget, and that midget would be every bit me, because he comes from MY mind, like all of my characters. What defines me as myself is the set of thoughts I choose to ACT upon, not just what I think. Johnny is a terribly violent little thing, and I am not. I couldn't imagine the level of discontent it would require for me to give in to the urge to inflict pain, or to kill.

Q: Are you a goth?

J: Must....resist....urge.

Q: Come on, if you HAD to categorize yourself, what would...Umm...Mr. Vasquez? What are you doing? Get away from..

J: GRRRRR!!! GRRRRR!!!!

Q: YAAAAAAARGH!!! SHRIEEEEEEEEK!!!!!!!!!!!!!
(enter interviewer #2)

Q: Hello, Jhonen.....what's wrong with that person on the floor?

J: Nothing. He is very sleepy.

Q: Nothing? But there's blood coming out of his face? I don't think he's asleep.

J: He bleeds in his sleep! People do it all the time! Now are you going to interview me or not?

Q: Uhh...yeah. Sure. Okay, so, how accurate is the idea that your book is an insight into your actual life? I mean, are you as negative a person in real life as you portray yourself to be in the books?

J: I don't get it. WHAT is wrong with you? That guy in the book is JOHNNY!! NOT me. Look at me, I am living here with you in the third dimension, right? So why should differentiating myself from my characters even be an issue. I enjoy writing this because it's fun. I'm not trying to invade minds and communicate anything more than a story, and maybe some amusement. I hate you. Everything sucks.

Q: Okeedokee. With Johnny's brooding attitude, affinity for death, and almost entirely black attire, aren't you afraid of him being lumped in with all of the other tall, pale faced Sandman loving people he seems to rant against?

J: (resisting urge again) What color is the sky in YOUR world? C'mere, look at this cover painting. Does Johnny look pale-faced to YOU? If there's ONE thing NNY and I share, it's that we are most definitely not pale. He's more sickly yellow, beige or something. And I don't target any particular group out of hate. I think of his victims as select people, as you'll find nastiness in EVERY little subculture out there.

Q: I get it. You'd rather have people read your book as a story and not as a personal diary of the artist. So...what kind of music do you listen to?

J: Why? Are you going to give me some CDs?

Q: No, I just wanted to find out what you listen to.

J: Why should you care?

Q: Why should you be so guarded? It's a simple question. Stop being such a walled up prick.

J: ALRIGHT!! I LOVE JOHN TESH!! OKAY?!! YOU HAPPY NOW!!?

Q: See that wasn't so bad. You've just got to get past the idea that your private life is your own now. Now, let's get on to...Hey, what are you doing?

J: You...know my secret, now.

Q: What? What's wrong with you?

J: My seeeeeeeecret.

Q: BLEEEEAAAAAAAARGH!!!!!!

J: SEND IN THE NEXT ONE!!
(interview #3 enters)

Q: Ah, hello, Mr. Vasquez, nice to meet y...OH, MY GOD. What happened to these people?

J: sigh. They were like that when I got here. So, you have some questions?

Q: Oh, right. First one: is there any particular reason romance always fails in your stories? Love and affection is almost nonexistent in the world of JTHM, and I'm wondering where that attitude comes from.

J: Well, I would use the fact that I'm writing a comedy in those books, thus giving me reason to take liberties with concepts like romance, but truth is, romance IS a comedy as much as it is tragedy. It fails in my stories because it fails in life. It's all about enjoying it while it still exists for you, and that's beautiful, but in the book, it's taken to an absurd level, as most things are. Johnny tries to kill it while it's just beginning to save himself the memory of when it went bad.

Q: You're talking too much. Do something funny.

J: Excuse me?

Q: Like in your books, you talk too much, and nothing's really happening. Johnny should kill more.

J: That wouldn't be MY book then. I'm doing what I love to do, and for myself first. It's lovely that other people enjoy this as much as they do, but if I started doing it for anyone else, I'm sure it would show, and it wouldn't be a good thing to allow.

Q: HEY! You know that comic you did with you having super powers like that death beam? That was a lie, right?

J: ZZZZZZZZZZZZZZZZAAAAAAP!!!

Q: MY ASS!! MY ASS!! YAAARGH!!

J: Thank you, and goodnight.

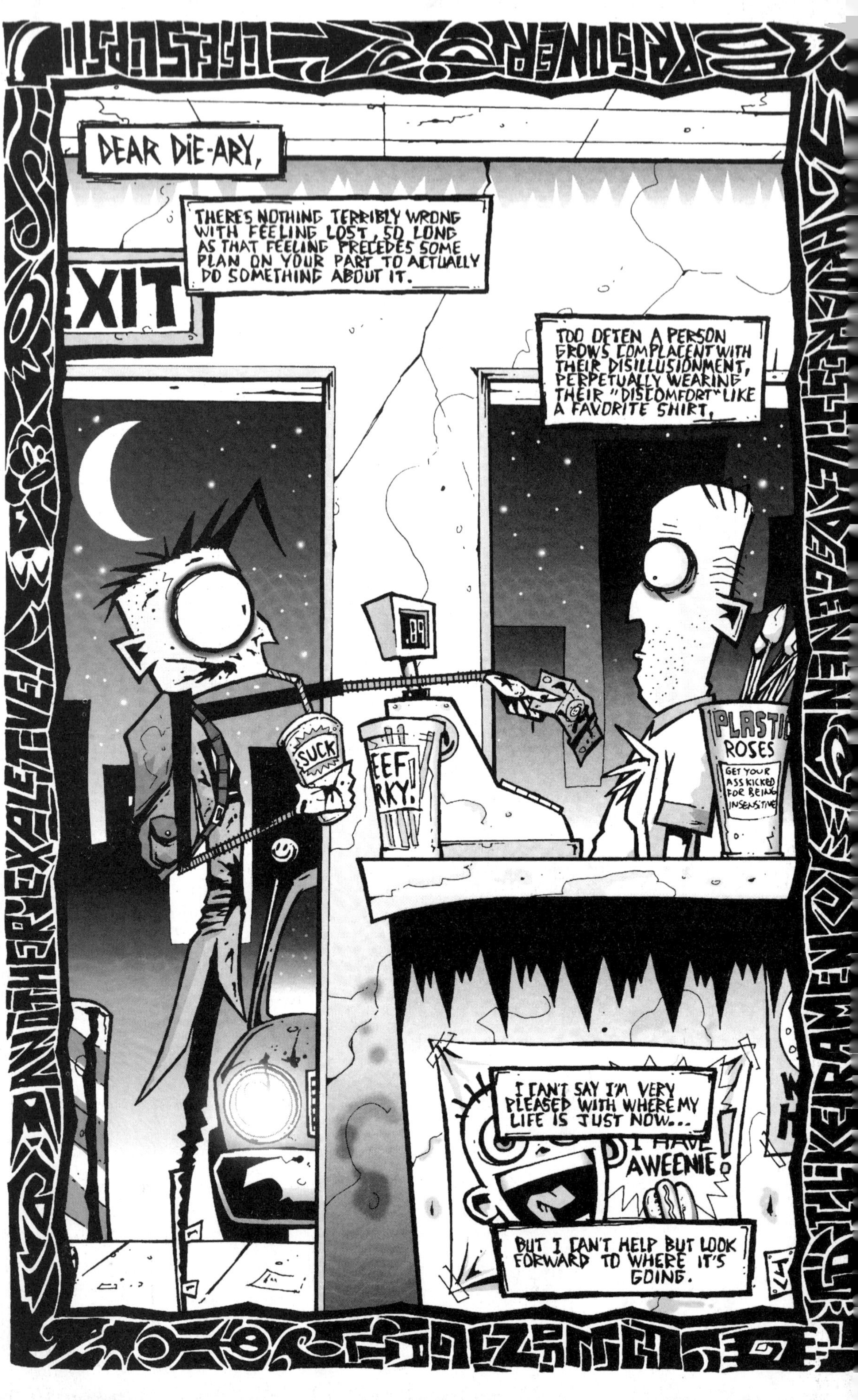
DEAR DIE-ARY,
THERES NOTHING TERRIBLY WRONG WITH FEELING LOST, SO LONG AS THAT FEELING PRECEDES SOME PLAN ON YOUR PART TO ACTUALLY DO SOMETHING ABOUT IT.
EXIT
TOO OFTEN A PERSON GROWS COMPLACENT WITH THEIR DISILLUSIONMENT, PERPETUALLY WEARING THEIR "DISCOMFORT" LIKE A FAVORITE SHIRT,
.89
SUCK
EEF
RKY!
PLASTI
ROSES
GET YOUR ASS KICKED FOR BEING INSENSITIVE
I CAN'T SAY I'M VERY PLEASED WITH WHERE MY LIFE IS JUST NOW...
I HAVE AWEENIE!
BUT I CAN'T HELP BUT LOOK FORWARD TO WHERE IT'S GOING.